DRESSED FOR THE PHOTOGRAPHER

Dressed for the Photographer

Ordinary Americans and Fashion, 1840–1900

∾

JOAN L. SEVERA

The Kent State University Press

Kent, Ohio, & London, England

© 1995 by The Kent State University Press, Kent, Ohio 44242
All rights reserved
Library of Congress Catalog Card Number 95-1155
ISBN 0-87338-512-8
Manufactured in the United States of America
03 02 01 00 99 98 97 96 95 5 4 3 2 1

LIBRARY OF CONGRESS CATALOGING-IN-PUBLICATION DATA
Severa, Joan L., 1925–
    Dressed for the photographer : ordinary Americans and fashion,
1840–1900 / Joan L. Severa.
            p. cm.
    Includes bibliographical references and index.
    ISBN 0-87338-512-8
    1. Costume—United States—History—19th century. 2. Fashion—
United States—History—19th century. 3. Portrait photography—
United States—History—19th century. I. Title.
GT610.S42 1995   95-1155
391'. 00973'09034—dc20   CIP

British Library Cataloging-in-Publication data are available.

This book is respectfully dedicated to
Dr. James Morton Smith,
who in 1976 gave me the world's pithiest advice.
Jim, I finally got my "stuff" together.

Contents

∿

Foreword

BY CLAUDIA BRUSH KIDWELL, WITH
NANCY REXFORD

OVER THE LAST thirty years, some historians have expanded the definition of historical evidence, going beyond written documents to include material culture—objects and images— including photographs. With these new types of evidence being considered, historians have developed new methodologies to deal with them. As a rule, most objects seem to be best understood when placed in a historical context. For example, we can speculate most confidently about a photographic portrait when we know its date, the identities of the sitter and the photographer, the circumstances under which it was taken, and the expectation of the audience for whom it was made. When these facts are known, portraits may reveal a great deal. However, this leaves a very large mass of anonymous photographic portraits of unknown sitters by unknown makers under unknown circumstances and at unknown times. Considering the dearth of context, can these images, which account for the vast majority of those extant, ever be made meaningful?

There is, in fact, one element in these images that can be identified; the clothing the sitter is wearing. The problem is that few historians have the depth of knowledge about clothing necessary to know what they are seeing. When people unfamiliar with the clothing really worn in the past try to interpret the dress shown in a portrait, they are likely to make mistakes, no matter how much skill they bring to other kinds of historical analysis. I have become particularly aware of this in my current research on the colonial portraits by Bostonian John Singleton Copley. Copley's portrait of Paul Revere, for example, has been misinterpreted by scholars as able as Richard L. Bushman, who discusses Revere's clothing in his 1993 book, *The Refinement of America.* The Revere portrait is unique in its period for showing the sitter in his shirt sleeves with his vest unbuttoned and no neck cloth. This is the common attire of a tradesman or laborer who needed the freedom, as Bushman describes, to "reach, lift, and swing as was necessary for the work of commoners but unnecessary and unsuitable for the gentry." Bushman is right in thinking that the choice of clothing in this portrait is very significant, but wrong in declaring that Copley "stripped [Revere] of all pretensions to gentility, at least for the purpose of the picture." For someone with a knowledge of extant garments, it is obvious that Revere is not wearing a laborer's coarse shirt but, rather, one of fine linen. Although the neck opening has no ruffles, ruffles do appear at the wrists. These sleeve ruffles are not obvious to the modern eye unacquainted with eighteenth-century dress because they are folded back inside the wrist band, allowing only a corner to escape the buttoned slit. Copley was careful to locate that bit of ruffle near the center of the portrait where it would not be missed by contemporary viewers, who would recognize its significance at once. They would have seen Revere not as a laborer or common tradesman but as an elite craftsman dressed in a fine shirt, his tools displayed on a highly polished table rather than a workbench. They would have understood that at any moment Revere could be dressed like a gentleman.

Copley, Revere, and their contemporaries brought to the production and viewing of a portrait a bundle of shared cultural assumptions. The decision to show Revere without his suitcoat was a conscious break with what they knew to be the way Englishmen were portrayed. Whose idea was it to use tools, clothing, a polished table, and the thoughtful stance to suggest Revere's complexity? What occurred during the interaction between sitter and artist that led to this particular choice of cultural clues? By understanding his clothing, we may be closer to seeing what Revere's contemporaries saw: a man who, without being at all embarrassed by his identity as a working man, wants us to know that he has risen both economically and intellectually above the common limits of a craftsman's life. As T. H. Breen speculates in his chapter, "The Meaning of 'Likeness,'" in *The Portrait in Eighteenth-Century America*, edited by Ellen G. Miles, the sitter's clothes may be the central element for portraits of provincial Americans in the mid–eighteenth century. Similarly, understanding the clothing worn in nineteenth-century American photographs opens new ways of thinking about these images.

What Joan Severa brings to the study of photographic portraiture is exactly the depth of knowledge about clothing that historians generally lack, a knowledge that provides the context in which many otherwise anonymous photographic portraits can begin to acquire meaning. In her years as costume curator at the State Historical Society of Wisconsin and as a consultant and scholar visiting many other collections, the author has seen literally thousands of extant garments and images, including fashion plates, prints, and paintings, not to speak of the photographs. Her years of research with these materials allow her to date the images in this book with a far higher degree of probability than most historians could hope to attain.

In addition, the sheer quantity of garments Severa has seen allows her to understand for any one period the range of clothing available. The Wisconsin collection of which she was curator differs from those of most museums, which tend to emphasize special-occasion clothing, for it contains a large proportion of the practical and useful clothing that necessarily make up the greater part of most people's wardrobes. As a result, she knows the difference between garments that represent the high end of fashion and garments similar in cut but made from less expensive materials and between those middling garments and others that echo only feebly a distant fashionable model. This experience, unavailable to most viewers of nineteenth-century photographs, supplies the rich context within which she approaches the portraits in this book. If Severa perceives a particular sitter's dress as "middle class," it is because she has seen and handled dresses essentially like the one in the picture and knows that this one falls clearly below the level of other dresses that are more elaborate, of richer materials, and better made. While this is not proof that the sitter was "middle class," it *is* real evidence, evidence that is especially valuable when everything else about a photographic image is unknown. What Severa calls "intuition" is really this amassed experience with clothing, the complex understanding—visual and sensory rather than verbal—on which she draws when she describes and interprets the clothing in the photographs. She is able to give in this book not only a reasonably reliable date for a great number of anonymous images, but she also provides a personal response to the images informed by a lifetime of working with extant American clothing.

As we look at these evocative images, however, it is wise to keep in mind the pitfalls in interpreting portraits in general and photographic portraits in particular. We have a natural tendency to assume that what we see in a photograph is real. Graham King argues in his 1984 book *Say "Cheese"* that this tendency was created by the heavy reliance of our modern society on relaying information through visual media. Indeed, "for the majority of us, our awareness of reality has been powerfully influenced by received photographic and related cinematic and video images." As a consequence, "we accept photographic evidence instantaneously from a very early age and become further convinced of inherent photographic truth as we proceed through life."

But photographs should not be accepted uncritically. It is possible, certainly, to arrange the truth—if not exactly lie—for the occasion of the photograph. Looking at my daughter's high school graduation picture, one might assume that she owns a low-necked black velvet formal dress. In fact, what appears to be a dress in her portraits is the photographer's black velvet drape secured behind her shoulders with a clothespin and donned over her blue jeans only for this single brief moment. My daughter has never owned or worn anything that looks remotely like what she "wears" in her school portrait. Naturally, none of us familiar with the conventions of graduation pictures and high school yearbooks is misled. We know that such draperies are commonly used to identify these photographs as formal portraits distinct from ordinary snapshots, to emphasize membership in the graduating group by showing everyone in similar clothing, to create a look of order and uniformity in the yearbook, and to prevent whatever lapses of taste the students might otherwise betray if allowed to choose their clothing.

Occasionally a photographer or sitter will arrange the image of the photograph in order to manufacture a "truth" that can be used to support a particular agenda. One of the most famous cases of this occurs in the work of the American photographer Edward S. Curtis, celebrated for his definitive twenty-volume record of Native Americans, begun in 1896 and completed in 1930. In his 1982 book, *The Vanishing Race and Other Illusions: Photographs of Indians by Edward S. Curtis,* Christopher M. Lyman shows, however, how Curtis was as much a mythmaker as a documentarian. By comparing Curtis's original negatives with the published photographs, Lyman reveals that Curtis, intent on producing dramatic photographic art, regularly bent ethnological truth. Curtis retouched and cropped prints and often supplied costumes and prop artifacts to assert the primitiveness of the American Indian when in fact they were well on the way to being Westernized. These manipulations served his goal of recording Native Americans as "Noble Savages," dignified in defeat. He eliminated the diversity of appearance that existed—ranging from quality fashions suggesting economic and social success in middle-class society to shabby "white man's" dress that might make Indians appear as individuals who had been deprived of their native way of life and left in poverty without the means to participate in the American mainstream. In fabricated "Indian dress," however, Curtis's Native Americans were of a distinct race—apart and independent, more comfortable to look at—in whom the viewer might take a certain detached interest, but for whom he need feel no personal responsibility nor view as social equals.

Even for quite ordinary portrait photographs, both photographers and sitters considered it perfectly appropriate to arrange reality for the photographic occasion, although the result was rarely so misleading as with the Curtis Indian portraits. In the early days of photography, sitters were often advised how to dress in order to photograph well, given the technical limitations of the medium (just as, during the early black-and-white era of television, people were told not to wear white shirts when appearing before the camera, even though white shirts might be their normal everyday choice). In the 1870s and 1880s photographers often provided painted backdrops to simulate an attractive setting, whether indoors or out. Backdrops painted to suggest the outdoors were supplemented with imitation rocks, stumps, grasses, garden walls, and trailing ivy. Indoor backdrops showed windows, walls, and furniture painted in perspective to suggest an elegant home. No one was deceived by these backgrounds even when the sitter wore clothing to match, as when ladies wore furs and carried muffs when photographed against a snowy backdrop. These were merely conventions of the day. One should also remember that the muffs and furs could have been provided by the photographer.

The use of such props and backdrops shows that photographers were consciously working in a portraiture tradition borrowed from painting. The pillars and draperies that set off the upper-class sitters in seventeeth- and eighteenth-century portraits, for example, became available to just about everyone in nineteenth-century American photographic studios. Photographers posed their sitters with more or less skill, showing them how to lean gracefully against chairs, cut-off pillars, trees, and fences. Often the sitter's individuality was lost in the conventionality of the pose, as also happens in many a painted portrait. The least skilled photographers failed even to achieve this stereotypical charm, and the sitters merely looked awkward. But occasionally photographers managed to transcend the conventions within which they worked and show something of the character within.

Photographers and sitters both knew how the sitter ought to appear in a portrait photograph, including how they should be dressed. Painted portraits had for centuries shown subjects dressed in fine clothing (or in another costume understood to convey status and respectability). This convention seems still to have been generally accepted in the mid–nineteenth century, and no doubt many sitters chose to appear in their very best clothing, with appropriate jewelry, accessories, and carefully styled hair. Some may even have borrowed clothing especially for the occasion. This sort of manipulation of reality is likely to be a large factor in the very early photographic era, when having a portrait taken was a rare occurrence. But these notions about how one should look in a photograph continued even as the technology developed and it became possible to take pictures quickly and in less controlled circumstances.

For most of the period covered by this book, the prevailing conventions of photographic portraiture impose a certain uniformity on the images. This tendency to look alike makes it particularly important to have the comments of an experienced guide, like Joan Severa, who can point out the significant details and distinctions. The quality of being well dressed that most sitters convey becomes even more meaningful once we have been taught to see the crooked seam, the strained fit, the wrinkled skirt that suggest that this quality may have taken some effort for the sitters to achieve. Severa not only points out the significant details in the more conventional portraits, but she also has managed to select a great many images that contain unusual elements. There are many portraits of African Americans, Asian Americans, and Native Americans. Others show clothing outside the mainstream, such as the series of portraits of women in reform dress, and some show people in what appears to be their real everyday work clothes. A few images actually flaunt the conventions (notably the back view of John French showing how his hair was parted, as well as showing his naked shoulders).

All of us in the fields of costume and material culture studies can be grateful to Joan Severa for the work she has done in this book. Her overview chapters for each decade provide a background especially valuable to readers new to the study of costume. The commentaries on the individual photographs guide us through each image helping us recognize and identify significant elements of dress. Without the ability to see what is really being worn in such pictures, we cannot hope to make the photographic portrait meaningful.

Preface

In sociological studies fashion plays the role which has been allotted to Drosophila, the fruit fly, in the science of genetics. Here at a glance we can perceive phenomena so mobile in their response to varying stimuli, so rapid in their mutation, that the deceptive force of inertia, which overlays and obscures most other manifestations of human activity, is reduced to a minimum. In obeying custom we undergo distresses which are needless and futile. We do so for the sake of something that transcends our own immediate interests. There are some who can rejoice in fashion, others may detest it, but as any photograph will show, there will be very few ready to defy its laws.

. . .

Emulation occurs where status can be challenged, where social groups become strong enough to challenge the traditional pattern of society, in fact in those places where a strong middle class emerges to compete with the aristocracy and, at a later stage, a strong proletariat emerges to compete with the middle class.

—Quentin Bell, *On Human Finery*

THE ABOVE CONDITIONS uniquely pertained to America in the early nineteenth century, much to the surprise of foreign visitors. In Europe it was different; the social hierarchy was much more strongly perceived and was also more visible in distinctions of dress. In America anyone of any birth could aspire to anything, be it wealth, fame, or political or social preeminence, and the social hierarchy was perpetually being assaulted from below.

It is necessary to set the stage for this study by saying at the outset that the perception of culture in the United States in the nineteenth century was in very large part based on appearances and that there was a powerful drive toward a "proper" façade. It was of tremendous, almost *moral,* significance during the nineteenth century that one appear cultured. Material and social culture historians such as Kenneth

Ames and Joan Jensen have studied the importance of appearances and the forces driving this ethic. Certain possessions at certain times, they report, have served as icons for the attainment of culture: the parlor organ, the impressive front hallway, wall-to-wall carpeting, and the sewing machine, for instance. It is implicit in these studies that the appearance of having attained culture must necessarily have included one's bodily presence, the manner in which one was dressed. But clothing itself as material culture has not been specifically addressed to any degree. As Kenneth Ames wrote in *The Stuff of Everyday Life,* "two of the most fundamental components of material culture [are] the way people hold their bodies and the clothing they put over these bodies.... the study of the body as artifact is underdeveloped in America" (105).

In *Dressed for the Photographer* I have addressed the problem of how ordinary Americans of this period handled the often conflicting dictates of fashion, hard work, and economy in their clothing choices. In so doing, I have used a modified material culture approach; this method of study seeks to define a culture through its artifacts, and not the reverse. The precept is that, given a thorough background in the type of artifact, information about both the creators and the users of selected artifacts can be brought out through a series of investigative steps. This is what Ames calls "informed intuition." Thus, I am able to judge the caliber of a woman's dress by the skillfulness of her alterations or the fit or the taste (not to mention the relative expense) involved in selecting her dress material, style, and trimmings by comparison with the going standards. Then, based on these observations, I can make certain judgments about her position in life.

Not least among the questions raised at the beginning of this project was whether, or how, ordinary people followed the fashions. Quentin Bell presented me with a scholarly and logical basis for my belief that fashion was indeed important and that even poorer people must have followed it, but it remained for me to discover how the system worked. One important function of this book lies in presenting the arguments that support this belief. It is not by any means a commonly held theory; many of my peers are very hesitant to accept it. There is evidence, even photographic, of out-of-date clothing in use for many years; yet, I argue, that does not mean in every case that the sitter did not own more fashionable clothes. I needed to put all my faculties into a dispassionate look at this question, the first and probably most important function of this book.

But the secondary function is equally important. Having been one of them, I sympathize with the numerous individuals who have suddenly found themselves in charge of period-clothing programs, costume collections, or theater costuming and who are ill-prepared for the nuances of the game. The usual across-the-board training in history of costume glosses over details, ignoring cut and finish, besides often skimping on the nineteenth century. Printed materials are available, but in bits and pieces, and most are poor in visuals. Visual evidence is the straight line through the eye to the brain; it confirms and locks literary evidence in place. Without it, the novice, especially, is handicapped. I hope to provide both visual and written resources for these people.

The photograph, at first in the form of the daguerreotype, made its debut in this country in 1840, so I had a wealth of indisputable visual material for the entire sixty-year period. But I soon discovered that the photograph is not often usable as a reliable primary factor in dating garments or fashion trends, because so very few retrievable photographs are documented. This meant that I would be using the photographs as final evidence and would need to develop an exceptionally strong supporting text.

What I decided to do was look for clear images, documented or not, of every known style change during the years between 1840 and 1900 and to base an intensive study on the precise dating of fashion elements, how the clothing looked in actual use, in what combinations it was worn, and just who wore it, with an emphasis on people of low or modest income. Though a far-too-ambitious plan, I am satisfied that, in the end, it has provided much new evidence toward defining a possible American norm.

Only about 20 percent of the photographs used in the book were fully documented. These I was able to space fairly evenly throughout the period, and used together with a good timetable for the introduction of stylistic details into fashion, they help in dating other photographs.

It is important to state here that this book is not intended as a history of photography, or anything approaching it. I am not conversant with photographic techniques, and except for noting the medium where known, no technical information is included. For this study, the photographic means is unimportant except in a demographic sense, as it relates to the economic and social status of the sitter, and thus to the clothing under analysis.

I will be the first to say, as well, that women's fashion information forms the basis for this study and that men's and children's styles, for which there is much less information, are for the most part peripherally identified. I justify this by repeating two well-known facts: women's fashions are more easily tracked and identified, and many group photographs showing women in datable costumes contain men and children. The same is true with older men and women in group photographs; the "fashion lag" so often discussed is highly visible in the outdated garments worn by older people, when seen in conjunction with fashionable women. I certainly added to my own knowledge of common usage through this exercise.

Fascinating as the visual evidence has been to me, I found the contemporary records almost as intriguing. I knew that I needed to look for evidence concerning not only manufacturing and transportation as they affected clothing but the social aspects as well. These included the availability of current fashion information, the desire to be fashionable, and the limitations that might be imposed by a low budget or great distance from cultural centers. For these concerns, my research assistant was asked to search personal accounts and records for hitherto unpublished letters and diaries and to pull from them references to clothing and fashion information. For an understanding of the percentage of income devoted to clothing, an important factor, I had to resort to secondary studies, where the work was all done for me. Works on demographics, social history, and material culture were my background reading.

One interesting problem with which I initially had to deal was the basic need to establish precisely what I meant by "ordinary Americans" or "middle class." I found I was not alone. Social historians have always had trouble defining middle-class populations. Clifford Edward Clark, Jr., in *The American Family Home, 1800–1960,* says that this is because Americans have not liked class distinctions; that the upper classes preferred not to be called wealthy because of the implicit suggestion of being undemocratic, and the lower classes as a whole preferred to think of themselves as middle class. This statement suggests in itself a reason for the spread of fashion across class boundaries and reinforces Bell's declination of emulation. While there were visual clues in some photographs, such as madeover dresses, outdated hats, and, in some later images, farm buildings in the background, I had to face the fact that some of my photographs would inevitably be of wealthier persons, because I could not easily tell them apart. I found that this was not at all contradictory to the conclusion I finally reached after studying all the data, which is that common clothing modes were nearly universal. But it did reinforce my determination to find as many images of known poor people as possible and then make a heroic attempt to identify which other photographs represented which level of affluence. The more background I acquired, the more clues I found in the clothing.

While my work with Nancy Rexford had given me a good basis for dating fashion elements as "not before" a certain date, it left me very much aware of the old bugaboo of the costume historian: how long an individual garment or a style might have been worn, which includes how long it might have been worn at the time of the portrait. Every smallest bit of evidence has been brought to bear on this facet of research as the period progresses, and conclusions have been very cautiously drawn throughout. It was patently evident in many of the well-documented photographs that poorer people did wear currently fashionable clothing, and personal records certainly testify to an intense interest in fashion, but I committed to long study of the photographs and evidence before drawing any conclusions.

There is one aspect of these photographs that I was not able to discuss to my satisfaction, as it had no actual bearing on the clothing analysis: the emotional impact of these faces from the past. I wanted to say that a certain sitter was extremely proud of her appearance in this costume or that another face bore the ravages of grief or that a handsome old man showed great dignity. It is my very strong attachment to the people shown in this book that has been my chief joy. And, of course, the images do speak for themselves. What they show is that it was important to these people to have their pictures taken; it was an opportunity to leave for posterity an image of themselves at their very best. A camera portrait had somewhat the same momentous significance in the early years as a painted portrait and was undertaken with the same sense of destiny. A few lines I discovered beside an early-twentieth-century woman's photograph are poignant evidence of this:

Look upon this face, and know
that I was a person, here, in this time and place,
and I was happy.

Acknowledgments

 ∾

THIS BOOK WAS made possible by a museum grant from the National Endowment for the Humanities, through the State Historical Society of Wisconsin, and a fellowship from the National Endowment for the Humanities.

To all of the people who encouraged and helped me in the making of this book I owe profound thanks. I could never name them all. They range from the clerical help at the State Historical Society of Wisconsin all the way to the directors of museums and photographic archives.

My greatest debt is to my research assistant, Merrill Horswill, without whose knowledge of research and understanding of computers this book could never have been completed. In one of those inexplicable, miraculous manifestations, Merrill appeared at my desk practically on the day I had to write the specifications to NEH for a research assistant for the initial grant. In that position, Merrill worked with me for the year of the grant, and she has remained on call throughout the ensuing years. All of the unpublished manuscripts used in the book, and many more, were found during her personal forays into archives all around the country. She recorded the retrieval information for her notes, along with much of the bibliography, on disks for our twin computers. For all this and for friendship and support, no amount of thanks can truly compensate.

My immediate support community also consists of a group of people originally brought together as consultants and advisers for the NEH grant, because it was through their direction and urging that this book was conceived out of the original grant project and I was encouraged to apply for the fellowship to complete it. They were as a group a noisy, demanding, argumentative debating society whose uncompromising standards were exceeded only by their genuine affection and concern. Those meetings I recall as among the most stimulating events of my life. I list these people in alphabetical order.

The consultants, those approved by the grant officers and paid (a pittance) for the several meetings, are Patricia Altmann, social anthropologist at UCLA; Inez Brooks-Myers, curator of costumes at the Oakland Museum; Marna King, professor of theater arts at the University of Wisconsin, Madison; and Robb Shep, publisher and costume-book specialist of Mendocino, California.

Advisers, those who of their own free will joined the sessions, include William Crowley, museum director at the State Historical Society of Wisconsin; Beverly Gordon, professor in the School of Family Resources at the University of Wisconsin, Madison; and Jean Weber, then director of historic sites for the State Historical Society of Wisconsin.

One special adviser must be mentioned individually—Nancy Rexford, indefatiguable scholar, perceptive author and editor, and friendly critic extraordinaire. Nancy, who is currently working on a set of her own encyclopedic books on the dress of American women, has been involved in my search for truth since the beginning. She was both visitor and host to me several times during the progress of this book. She opened her considerable library to me, including all of her hard-earned resource material, and worked many hours with me over the photographs in this book, and all with unflagging zest. She has done the same for many others. Nancy's zeal in reviewing this manuscript is responsible for much of its organization and clarity. I can pay no higher tribute than this: Nancy Rexford has that dedication to scholarship that drives her to perfection and makes her totally unselfish—in fact, practically manic—in the cause of truth.

My gratitude also goes out to my editor, Joanna Hildebrand, whose knowledge, attention to detail, and patience have turned this manuscript into a professional book.

I am grateful, too, to the Costume Society of America, for providing such an atmosphere of enthusiastic scholarship in the field of costume and for the friendship and support I find there. Membership in this important organization has always been my top priority, beginning with my first introduction to Claudia Kidwell, a fellow member of its board of directors. It was she who first encouraged me to continue my research into common dress, because, she said, we needed to prove to social historians that fashion has always been a driving force in America, even, or most especially, among the economically disadvantaged. "If you do not think costume is important," she said once in a memorable speech, "try going to work someday without yours!"

Last, but not least, I owe a debt of gratitude to my training ground. For then director Jim Smith's belief in me, for autonomy, for a fantastic library and an outstanding photograph collection, for the opportunity to learn my profession, and especially for staff support during the period of the NEH grant, I am grateful to the State Historical Society of Wisconsin.

CHAPTER ONE

The 1840s

Here is a piece of the first dress I ever saw, cut with what were called
"mutton-leg" sleeves. It was my sister's, and what a marvellous fine
fashion we all thought that was. Here, too, is a remnant of the first
"bishop sleeve" my mother wore; and here is a fragment of the first
gown that was ever cut for me with a bodice waist. Was there ever so
graceful beautiful pointed a fashion for ladies' waists before? Never, in
my estimation. By this fragment I remember the gown with wings on
the shoulders, in which I supposed myself to look truly angelic; and oh,
down in this corner a piece of that in which I first felt myself a woman—
that is, when I first discarded pantalettes. . . . Here is a piece of the first
dress which was ever earned by my own exertions! What a feeling of
exultation, of self-dependence, of self-reliance, was created by this
effort.

—Harriet Farley, "The Patchwork Quilt"

FROM OUR MODERN vantage point, it is impossible to appreciate fully
the impact of successful photography on the America of the 1840s or to
realize how the availability of the photographic image would subtly influence taste from that time forward. In the late fall of 1839, an autho-
rized agent arrived in New York aboard the *British Queen*, selling the
rights and equipment for the unique process developed by Louis
Daguerre. Daguerre's work was already very well known in this country,
and there were plenty of applicants. Literally within weeks, hundreds of
budding photographers in every city and town were setting up shop. It
was a sure-fire road to success. Not only was this mysterious method of
"sun-printing" on silver-washed plates a bona fide scientific miracle, it
provided the one universally irresistible product—a personal image. The
grand, well-decorated studios in the larger cities, especially, were patronized by young and old, rich and poor, even at five dollars a sitting.

Within two or three years, studios were common even in small towns,
with practitioners moving west with the earliest settlers. The western
movement actually occasioned thousands more sittings, as people left
behind pictures of themselves and carried with them treasured images of
family and friends. By the 1850s, some three million daguerreotypes were

made annually in this country (Taft 76); thus prices eventually went down. Because of the lower prices, people everywhere flocked to the smaller studios, and entrepreneurs soon brought "daguerreotypy" to local fairs. Even though only a comparative few of these fragile plates have survived, these remaining images cover a broad social base, leaving us a body of most convincing information about the material culture of their time.

In America, according to idealists, it was possible to have all things: there was adequate, if not rapid, transportation to bring goods and information to every area of settlement, there was a growing number of American goods available, along with the entrepreneurship to merchandise them, and there was a social climate that fostered the ambitions of the lowest classes to attain higher standing, meaning money and social status. An intense revival of religious and moral values in the 1840s augmented the latter, ensuring that women, at least, had a common code. Women were to dress properly and within the mode as an outward measure of "decency" and as a necessary means of gaining public respect. This ideal was constantly in the minds of the lower classes, who felt themselves judged by their conformity or lack of it. While there is always a poverty level below which conformity is not possible, the impetus given to a common standard of dress by this kind of social pressure has never been adequately assessed.

Sarah Hale, popular editor of *Godey's Lady's Book,* wrote that women of modest means should "pay attention to their costume, and, so far as is consistent with delicacy and condition in life, conform to the prevailing modes of dress" (*Godey's,* December 1844). Women, and even husbands and fathers, trusted her advice, since *Godey's* was mainly an uplifting, quasi-religious, moralistic collection of prose and educational materials for women.

American business acumen quickly developed the means to meet this national tendency toward social acceptance through dress. The latest styles for men and boys had already been made readily and cheaply available through mass production. Several major importers of French and English goods had developed early wholesale clothing manufactories in New York, Boston, and Philadelphia by the late 1830s, producing mostly men's and boys' wear, their production of women's garments being mainly limited to wraps. Shoes and boots of all varieties and for all ages were mass produced in this country in quantity by the 1840s.

At first, all of the clothing in factories was hand sewn, but many manufacturers installed the new sewing machines near the end of the forties, thereby multiplying their output (Kidwell and Christman 77). Many clothing manufacturing companies sent seasonal flyers throughout the South and West, attracting multitudes of retail buyers twice yearly for "openings" of spring and fall goods, where orders were taken and goods shipped to dealers in every city. These openings were also attended by fashion editors from the ladies' magazines, who then described the seasonal innovations for their readers, along with other fashion information. These magazines were largely responsible for the spread of women's fashion information in the 1840s. There were several of them, and they were mostly aimed at middle-class women. Personal records indicate that they were actually read and studied in the home by every social class and in all areas of the country. While *Godey's Lady's Book* was the most widely read, having a circulation of ten thousand in 1839 and forty thousand by 1849 (Entrekin 99), there were several other American magazines, and English and French ones also circulated to some extent. Even women wealthy enough to travel to Paris to purchase the latest styles subscribed to these magazines for the patterns, children's styles, and uplifting prose and poetry. Less wealthy women used the magazines more fully, as their "bible" for dressing well and maintaining a cultured outlook. The influence of these magazines was felt second hand by those women who had limited access to them; the time-honored practice of drafting patterns by copying the costumes worn by fashionable local women was followed by both professional and private seamstresses.

In the 1820s, Sarah Josepha Hale had been invited by Rev. John L. Blake to become the first editor of a ladies' magazine, called the *American Ladies Book* and to be published in Boston. In its first issue in January 1828, Mrs. Hale stated that the magazine would carry no fashion plates and would not cater to vanity but would instead feature uplifting articles for women. She claimed that fashion was dictated by "foreign courts," and, since we in the "Republic" had no courts and peers of the realm, we should not copy the courts of other nations. By the spring of 1830 this rule had already broken down, and fashion plates were included in the magazine, but only, according to the editor, in "American versions" (*American Ladies Book,* April 1830). Later, as editor in chief of *Godey's Lady's Magazine* in Philadelphia, Hale remained indifferent, at best, to fashion plates and fashion information (she was never the fashion editor). But fashion plates were an economic necessity for a ladies' magazine, and *Godey's* doubtless kept its circulation and reputation mainly through this function. The field was too competitive not to have done so. The colored fashion plates were evidently the most popular feature, and subscribers eagerly awaited them in each month's issue. The plates were copied directly, if not always immediately, from French publications. While in English publications the plates, also taken from the French, were quite current with Parisian introductions (an agent often having been sent from London to Paris for the seasonal shows), in American publications in these early years there was an occasional lag between the introduction of a fashion innovation as shown in the French and English magazines, sometimes as much as a year. Many fashion changes were thus not in general use in America for some time after a French introduction, and some were never popularly adopted.

Yet, based on examinations of personal records, it is apparent that women everywhere did follow the fashions as presented in the ladies' magazines, if only distantly. What appears to have been chiefly in effect was an understood American level of acceptance of such fashion introductions: the latest cut and silhouette, extrapolated from the exaggerated fashion plates, were followed by all as faithfully as bodily limitations allowed; but the illustrated, elaborate surface decorations and accessories were adopted more conservatively. This philosophy, moreover, easily permeated social boundaries, since the results were so uniquely visible. It is evident that upper and lower social levels alike—if we exclude the extremely wealthy and the desperately poor—knew about and observed, and at least conservatively accepted, French fashion introductions within one year or less.

Young mill girls writing for *The Lowell Offering*, a periodical written by, and for, the women working at the Lowell, Massachusetts, mills, discussed at length the fascination of pretty dress and its moral effects. Their writings indicate that girls at this economic level were aware of and purchased some quite expensive and fashionable items. Eisler quotes an unsigned article: "Is there not among us, as a class, too much of this striving for distinction in dress? Is it not the only aim and object of too many of us, to wear something a little better than others can obtain?" (186). This same unknown author also quotes from an article written by Sarah Hale "more than two years since" that illustrates quite clearly current feelings on the subject:

> O the times! O the manners! Alas! How very sadly the world has changed! The time was when the *lady* could be distinguished from the *no-lady* by her dress, as far as the eye could reach; but now, you might stand in the same room, and, judging by their outward appearance, you could not tell "which was which." Even gold watches are now no sure indication— for they have been worn by the lowest, even by "many of the factory girls." No lady need carry one now, for any other than the simple purpose of easily ascertaining the time of day, or night, if she so please! (Eisler 184)

The "factory girls," those who went to work in the weaving mills of New England, saw themselves not as "the lowest" but in quite a different light, and in fact they were praised by many observers for their studious and ladylike habits. And they did dress well. Farm girls went to work in the mills, for a fraction of what male laborers earned, doing so most specifically, according to contemporary records, in order to be able to afford good clothing for themselves and sometimes for their families back home.

> Sister Sarah I suppose you feel by this time as though you had worked long enough in the factory, & I should think the money you wrote me you had erned [*sic*] with what you had before would be as much as you would need to spend during this year, you know. . . . If you make any purchases I have only to say satisfy yourself & I assure you I shall not be dissatisfied. Study what will be profitable & becoming for us the ensuing

season if we should live to enjoy it which may it be the pleasure & will of Divine Providence that we may & be blest in fully realizing what our fond hopes now anticipate. (Dublin 50)

Working in the mills was not the only means of earning spending money; girls also worked as domestics or in shops, though for lower wages. "Mary or I want to come to Haverhill and spend the summer if you think we can get a good chance and good wages. If Mary comes she will want to do housework or nursing. Mary says if Mrs. Sweet will give her nine shillings a week she will come and live with her. If I come I should like to sew and will go out by the day or go into some family as seamstress or go into a milliners shop just which way you think I can do best"(Dublin 83). Nine shillings was at that time equal to $1.50, a good wage for a domestic who would also have received room and board.

A modestly well-educated young woman could of course teach school, and a skilled seamstress could become a dressmaker, though even those occupations would rarely net as much as might be earned by a skilled male tradesman. The average daily wage for women was significantly lower than that of men. And when measured against their paltry wages, the costs of fashionable clothing were great; yet records kept by women and girls show them to have been most interested in being in style—at any price. Nice clothing definitely accounted for a very large percentage of their expenditures.

The enormous output of printed cotton in the United States in the 1830s and 1840s, and its consequent low price, contributed to the ability of low-income families to have new clothing. The "factory cottons" sold for as little as nine pence a yard during the forties, and almost everyone could have a new cotton dress once a year at that rate. The amount of money spent on clothing by wealthier families was naturally larger than that by the poor, though not proportionately as large. It is interesting to note what both contemporary and modern writers consider to have been a minimum expenditure, even though extrapolations for various levels of income are only suggested by these figures.

Norman Ware, in *The Industrial Worker,* says that a husband and wife both hand-looming fabrics in 1843 in the state of Pennsylvania, working sixteen hours a day, could not earn over $2.50 per week between them. About male wages, Ware cites that in 1845 journeyman weavers working ten hours a day in summer and twelve in winter earned at best $6.00 per week, but the average was about $4.00. Also in 1845, hatters making twelve to fifteen hats per week could earn $8.00 to $12.00, and finishers in the hatting industry earned from $9.00 to $10.00. In the same year a mason could earn $1.75 per day, or $11.50 per week, and mason laborers about $1.00 per day, or $6.00 weekly. A bookbinder's average wage for the decade was about $8.00 to $15.00 per week, and the Upholsterers' Society reported weekly earnings of $7.00 to $9.00. An Irish railroad laborer's wages in 1845 were .65 to .70 per day, or $4.20 per six-day week, and strikes were called for a maximum raise to $5.25 per week. The average laborer's wage in the United States, in fact, was .80 per day, though the New York City average was higher at $1.00 to $1.25, for a maximum of $7.50 per week (N. Ware 63–68).

In comparison, the earnings of women in a York County, Maine, cotton mill in 1841, for instance, ranged from $1.48 per week for carding to a maximum of $2.73 for dressing, after payment of board and room, which ranged from .50 to .75 and up to $1.21 per week at different times during the decade. Salaries actually went down from the above figures by 1845 (C. Ware 238). As for the modest seamstress, who took in the sewing of shirts, for instance, her pay was from .07 to .12 per garment, and the most diligent application of her needle could not earn her a living wage, since one shirt took an average of some fourteen and a half hours.

A schoolteacher could do better, however. Elizabeth Hodgdon kept a record of her wages as a teacher in New Hampshire from 1832 through 1841, the two last entries being:

> 1840: taught school in Somersworth 7¾ months at 7 dollars per month. $54.25
> 1841: taught school in Somersworth 6 months at 9 dollars per month. $54.00.

Dublin notes that "the wage figures here probably refer only to Elizabeth's earnings above her room and board. Her overall salary was most likely $12 and $14 per month" (55).

The microfilm collection *American Women's Diaries* includes the personal records of Susan Parsons (Susan Parsons Brown Forbes) for the year 1847. Her entries show how she managed her yearly income (after room and board) as a rural teacher in New England, give some prices for women's clothing needs, and define some of her priorities:

Earnings:
Teaching School	18.00
Binding shoes	3.50
Picking blueberries	.58
Teaching in Dunfield	10.00
Total Earnings:	$31.58

Expenditures:
4½ yds flannell [*sic*]	2.70
Shawl	3.50
Dress	1.20
Stockings	.25
Cambric	.18
Muslin dress	4.75
Whalebone, gimp	.15
Graham's Magazine	1.50
Plaid dress	2.10
Total Expenditures:	$16.33

This annual figure indicates that roughly half of Susan's wages went for clothing (together with the magazine), which breaks down to .325 per week, and this is not an all-inclusive inventory of her clothing needs for the period; such things as shoes, hats, and heavier wraps are not listed.

Even Susan B. Anthony, who was raised as a Quaker, was, in her first years of financial freedom, addicted to nice clothes. In 1846, for her interview with the citizens of Canajoharie, New York, for the position of schoolteacher, she wore "a new muslin gown, plaid, in purple, white, blue, and brown, with two puffs around the skirt and on the sleeves at shoulders and wrists, white linen undersleeves and collarette, new blue prunella gaiters with patent-leather heels and tips, her cousin's watch with gold chain and pencil. Her abundant hair was dressed in four long braids, which Cousin Margaret sewed together and wound around a big shell comb" (Harper 50). For the winter of 1846, her first year of teaching, she purchased a broché shawl for $22.50, a gray fox muff for $8.00, a white ribbed-silk hat (which "makes the villagers stare") for $5.50, and a plum-colored merino dress at $2.00 per yard (Harper 50). Anthony's wages for that period are not recorded, but if they were at all comparable to those of Susan Parsons, she certainly dipped into her savings for these purchases.

Fashions for Women

Styles for women in the 1840s reflected not only a wearer's modesty but also a popular trend toward extreme bodily constriction and the inhibition of natural movement. In the very beginning of the decade, fashion illustrations began showing a rigid, bust-altering bodice shape and floor-length skirts with voluminous petticoats, which tended toward one basic silhouette: a rounded triangle that sloped down from the neck and shoulders and a severely constricted long torso with a flattened, upward-spreading bust and a full, bell-shaped skirt brushing the ground. Even given the observable variations in waist length and sleeve style, a woman's silhouette was quite similar throughout the decade, whether in working or better dress.

In 1837 the sleeve had only just collapsed from the enormous gigot of the 1830s. One popular sleeve shape going into the forties still carried much fullness but was taken in close to the upper arm in a variety of manners, either gathered or pleated. This style appears in the fashion plates through 1843, although the narrow bias sleeve predominates after 1841. Painted portraits of the early forties often feature the pleated-in sleeves, but they are rare in photographs.

A rather narrow bishop sleeve style, gathered at the wrist into a cuff but not gathered at the shoulder, was worn throughout the decade. In the fashion plates this sleeve shape is mostly reserved for sheer summer goods, though in the photographs it appears often on day dresses of printed cotton or challis. In fact, most of the wide variety of sleeve choices represented in fashion plates seem not to have been commonly worn. By far the most usual sleeve shape appearing in photographs throughout the forties is the one-piece, narrow bias sleeve, with or without sleeve caps.

"There is a good deal of variety in the sleeve; tight ones are very extensively seen, but in general they have some kind of trimming to take off from the extreme plainness" (*The Ladies' Cabinet,* December 1844).

To achieve a perfect fit in the bodice and sleeves of this period, one had to be or hire a good seamstress. There were many seamstresses operating in villages and cities everywhere, and their fees were within the reach of a fairly modest budget, judging from the records of many economical housewives. (Records of seamstresses for this period were not found.) The practice was to measure each customer carefully and to cut the bodice so that it was smoothly fitted, with no ease whatsoever, over the corseted body. By this time there were some drafting systems available to professional dressmakers that made it possible to cut a pattern from measurements, but most seamstresses probably still used the fitting method.

Several construction details are especially associated with women's dresses in the 1840s. The most easily recognizable is that nearly all frocks were back-closing, usually with hooks and eyes set very close together under a concealing placket and often with every other set opposed in order to prevent gaps. Also, an extremely fine piping was frequently used on all bodice seams, even down the sleeve. A third characteristic is the length of the skirt: women's skirts were made to touch the floor, and a "hem-saver," usually a stiff braid of wool and/or horsehair which protected the floor-length skirts from wear, was sewn at the hem after 1841. Skirts were lined either fully or merely in the lower portion, where a crisp facing from eight to eighteen inches wide was used as flatlining. The upper edge of this facing was handpicked to the skirt fabric, a technique that meant taking very small vertical stitches (only a thread or two in depth, not too closely together) across the top of the facing, which was usually on a selvage.

Bodices were very long and tight and were pointed in front through most of the decade, shortening somewhat in front, lengthening at the sides, and taking on a rounded dip at front at the end of the decade. A very short waist with a rounded point and fan bosom shows up in the photographs in everyday dress at the very end of the decade and into the fifties, but it is mainly seen on elderly women. Speculation is that this style reflected the leaving off of the fashionable long, rigid corset for comfort in middle age.

The usual form of the fashionable bodice followed the corset: very flat down the front and over the abdomen with no bust curve, the bosom being flattened upward and out toward the armpits by the stiff, busked corset that covered the hips. The fit was supposed to be smooth and wrinkle free; but in practice only a very good dressmaker could accomplish such a fit in this demanding shape. The armscye was cut high and snug and was nearly horizontal to the outside of the arm, giving an extreme slope to the shoulder. This shoulder slope was modified at the very end of the decade, the seam then rising to about the outer shoulder point. The shoulder seam connecting the bodice front and back was always dropped to the back about two inches, and, until nearly the end of the decade, there was often front fullness taken into that seam, either with gathers or pleats. This fullness converged toward the center front waist in a variety of treatments. One popular bodice front style was the fan-pleat, with all lines converging at the low waist point. A variety of modes were used to control the front fullness, from plain gathers to a kind of cartridge pleating or sometimes well-defined, graduated knife pleats. The V-shape was also sometimes accomplished with tapered bretelles that were applied over the shoulders or with braid trim. At times, the waist and ribcage section was defined by a panel edged with either braid or piping, with a point raised between the breasts and the bodice fullness taken in to this inverted V. The fashionable bodice shortened in front toward the fifties, when a softly rounded, dipped front became more common, but at this time the side front seams were correspondingly lengthened, actually producing a longer waistline. A plain, well-fitted bodice, made with long darts and featuring a rounded front waist and long side seams, is seen at the end of the decade and into the fifties. The ease of fit was derived solely from the bias cutting of both bodice and lining fronts; the apparent ease of the popular full fan-bosom is illusory, since the fitted and boned underbodice was always present.

A typical bodice treatment included padding, usually of lambswool, placed above the breast on either side, to lend a soft, triangular shape to the torso that was carried up over the shoulder to some extent. Some silk winter dresses had the bodices fully padded with thin sheets of lambswool, with thicker padding above the bosom, evidently mostly for warmth.

In spite of their apparent structural complexity, similar dresses were made at home by poorer women, if in lesser fabrics. Most women did some home sewing, many were seemingly overwhelmed with it. Women often helped one another, sometimes meeting to "cut a fit" and leaving the sewing to the wearer. Virtually all women in rural districts sewed their own dresses, as evidenced by this 1845 diary entry of Sarah Pratt, a young schoolteacher in rural Rock County, Wisconsin:

> June 23, Mon.: I have been fitting a dress for Phebe since school . . .
> June 25, Wed.: I fitted Jane a dress this noontime.
> Aug. 23, Sat.: Am sewing on a silk dress, finished today.
> Aug. 26, Tues.: I am sewing on a pair of pantaloons.

In many such references to home sewing, the phrase "bought my dress" appears with subsequent notes following—for days or weeks "worked on my dress." The terms "dress," or "wrapper" were usual when referring to the parcel of material purchased for a garment, at least for women's clothing; ready-to-wear dresses were not available at this time. A woman had her own "pattern" in the form of a dress already worn, and seasonal fashion changes could be made on that pattern when planning a new dress. While details such as waist and sleeve treatment changed, and there was always some new complexity of fitting in the bodice, the similarity of cut and the simplicity of silhouette throughout the decade made it possible to extrapolate from the fashion plates, or a new style worn by a friend, and apply the changes to the dress pattern. This abstract method was quite popular. Patterns as such are not found in 1840s ladies' magazines, though there are occasional directions and even illustrations for undergarments and trimmings: "We have a few models of caps and capes, which, to those who are in the habit of making their own dresses, will be found very useful. Taste and ingenuity, with a very small amount of cash, will enable a lady to appear always fashionably attired. . . . No excellence of mind or soul can be hoped from an idle woman" (*Godey's*, September 1845).

HEADDRESS

The dressing of the hair was a fashion element shared by all classes, as it could be accomplished without any expenditure at all. Through the medium of the plentiful ladies' books with their fashion plates, it was possible to keep up with the latest look, and a little practice before the mirror enabled a poor girl in the 1840s to have as lovely a hairdo as the richest belle, except for whatever fashionable accessories she might not be able to afford. A large decorative comb was a treasured accessory in the forties, and long jeweled spikes of various materials were used in the massed hair at the crown. These had either one or two prongs and were often made of tortoise or bone and had stones set in the heads.

A daycap of more or less sheer white cotton is associated with 1840s dress, both everyday and dressy attire. Though many caps survive, it is difficult to prove from photographs that they were generally worn, for few photographic portraits show them. The etiquette of daycap wearing evidently did not need to be spelled out for the 1840s woman, as no such explanation is found in any of the ladies' magazines. We can, however, deduce from personal accounts, and some fictional articles, that at least early in the decade the cap was worn by both young and old and that later in the decade it may have been relegated to older women. While young girls are not shown in caps in any of our images, a reference is found in the Lowell mill girls' writings that relates to the care of caps and the importance of their appearance. In a description (possibly fictional) of a typical dormitory room, the author says, "Everything was in the most perfect order. The bed was shaped, and the sheet hemmed down just so. Their lines that hung by the walls were filled 'jist.' First came starched aprons, then starched caps, then pocket handkerchiefs, folded with the marked corner out, then hose" (Eisler 101).

The bonnet was the proper head covering for a lady and hence was worn by women of all classes. Bonnet prices found in personal records ranged from about $3 to $8, though women could buy foundations and trim their own at lesser cost. Most bonnets were low and horizontal in the crown line, with a face-concealing, deep brim that had long drooping ends reaching below the chin line and a neck curtain, or "bavolet," gathered to the back. In the early part of the decade, the brim was quite deep and close to the sides of the face; toward the fifties it opened out into a more circular, somewhat shallower, shape, at the same time retreating toward the back of the head. Bonnets were made either of straw (straw braid for hats was an early factory product in New England), which was worn all year long with different trimmings, or of silk-covered buckram or of fabric gathered or drawn on hooped reeds, most often silk but sometimes plain, colored cottons, and felt or beaver bonnets were also worn for winter. Trimmings were of wide ribbons worn flat on the crown and outer brim (several ribbons of different colors in woven stripes, plaids, or flowers were sometimes used together on one hat), and later in the decade, when brims widened out, lace or ribbon rosettes, flowers, and grasses were attached around the inside of the brim, framing the face. Frilled silk net was often attached all around and just under the edge of the brim as a frame for the decorations. While placement of these underbrim decorations varied during the forties, the usual effect was asymmetrical.

Thickly padded, fleece-stuffed silk or wool hoods were also worn as windproof winter head coverings, and dressy velvet hoods were popular with the young women. Bonnet styles were avidly watched and imitated, though most women of limited means kept bonnets several years at least, changing only the trimmings to suit the season and any new fancy. When the shape evolved drastically, even working girls were able to keep in style if they chose to spend their money in such a manner, though a complete bonnet cost more than a week's wages from the mills.

As a rule, hats, as opposed to bonnets, were for boys and girls and, of course, men but not for "ladies." A wide-brimmed straw hat was permissible for women in the country or at the seashore but only up to middle age (forty). The only exceptions made to this rule were the versions of the masculine-styled silk top hats and derbies used in formal riding apparel.

Accessories

The wearing of mitts, or fingerless gloves, of knitted silk or openwork is another detail left mostly to the understanding of the women of the time. Though it does not go unmentioned in the fashion literature, there is never a clear statement that the mitt is a fashion item, or has gone out of fashion. The photographs show very young girls, some well-dressed young women, and many older ladies wearing mitts. From written references to their accustomed use with dinner and party dress, it is clear that mitts were not for everyday wear. Patterns and instructions were included in some periodicals, indicating that they were sometimes made at home, knitted or netted of silks, most popularly in black. In January 1840, for instance, Godey's assured readers that "Long and short gloves and mittens, of black filet are universally adopted. They are trimmed at the tops or round the wrists with narrow black lace." Mitts were also commercially available. Susan Parsons, then nineteen, single, and employed by the Middlesex Mill in Lowell, recorded in her diary that on July 7, 1843, she received her monthly wages of $15.70 and that on July 10 she "Went shopping, bought mits [sic] and calico dress." Fashion commentary only rarely gives us a graphic description of mitts in use: "Occasionally, for dresses of transparent materials intended to be worn within doors, the sleeves descend only half way down the lower arm, and the mitten of black filet completes the graceful costume" (*Peterson's*, August 1848). In the 1840s gloves for outdoor wear were always of dark kid and wrist length, and were worn very tight, so when seen in photographs they are stretched to a glossy smoothness and cause the hands to appear small and neat.

Necklines throughout this decade were of two general types. Very young women often wore, in warm weather or for "best," dresses with a wide, shallow, horizontal neckline that nearly reached to the shoulder points, a fashion remaining from the 1830s. Worn by many women throughout the decade was a narrower, very deep V neckline with a sheer white chemisette, a decorative, bib-shaped garment worn under the dress. The chemisette was known variously during the forties as gimp, guimpe, bertha, berthe, and spencer. Less deep V necklines were either filled with the chemisette or simply edged with a frill of white. A heart-shaped neckline was popular in the early 1840s, but the most common shape was round, varying from extremely high on the neck to a collarbone style; most necklines of this type were completed with rather small white collars. A late forties innovation was the cadet style; the dress bodice, usually in black silk, was cut in a close, round neck style and buttoned over the white chemisette only at the top and at the lower rib cage, showing a narrow ellipse of the white, frilly front.

White collars were universally worn for daytime. Collar shapes of the forties vary; early collars made for the V necks were often quite wide and deep at the back and tapered to nothing where they followed the V in front. Later collars were relatively small and were either made simply as a neat turn-down of whitework, sheer fabric, or lace, often with a shaped band for sewing inside the dress neckline, or as a frill of lace or fabric simply stitched in place or mounted on some form of underpinning. These frills could be standing or falling. Flat collars evolved during the decade as necklines opened somewhat from very small, close-fitting, rounded shapes to a shape that lay open, with straight bottom edges almost horizontally placed. One collar shape, seen very late in the decade, was named for the famous singer Jenny Lind: "For dresses high in the neck, the little straight collar called the Jennie Lind, made of edging and inserting, or narrow ruffling, is very fashionable" (*Peterson's*, June 1848).

The always-white collars and cuffs, so familiar from the photographs, were not mere fashion fripperies; rather, they were necessities that, because of their visibility, were subject to the fluctuations of fashion. Their function was, at least in part, to protect the dress from body soil. Interchangeable and washable, collars were meant to be changed daily. Neck linens were always in use, but during the period of snug, bias sleeves, the white cuffs were sometimes omitted. A bell-shaped, somewhat shortened sleeve became popular about 1843. From about that time, and throughout the rest of the decade, the long undersleeve, or engageant, was worn fastened inside the flared dress sleeves, which reached somewhat below the elbow, to cover the arm to the wrist. Undersleeves were made long enough to attach high under the flared sleeves, at about the underarm seam on the inside. The earliest of these undersleeves were fairly narrow and gathered into snug cuffs; the later ones were often made bell shaped and sometimes were of lace. At the very end of the forties and into the fifties, long, sheer, white muslin bishop sleeves, rather full and gathered into a band, were sometimes seen worn under the short, flared cap sleeves of a dress bodice. Very young women sometimes wore full bodices of sheer white linen or cotton with long sleeves with a lightweight skirt. This easy style provided a cool summer alternative to the popular snug bodices. A ribbon belt completed this costume, the pleated ribbon usually pulled down to the bodice point and pinned.

A collar-cum-wrap, the popular pelerine, was worn by women of all ages in the early 1840s, and much later by older women. It was usually an elbow-length cape modified from the wider, more elaborate capes of the 1830s. While pelerines were quite often cut of dress material to match cottons or silks, the dressier types were either of lace, net, or cotton lawn—plain or decorated with either tambour chain stitch, tape or muslin appliqué, or whitework embroidery (broderie d'Anglaise)—and were edged with either piping, a bias-cut self-frill, or lace. A pelerine was most likely unlined, though lined examples survive, especially those made of dress fabric. The cut was either straight at the hem, rounded, or pointed in back and front. The pelerine front sometimes had long tabs or points, which were worn either tied at front, lapped and pinned, or tucked under the belt. When made of white cotton, surviving examples of pelerines and collars are usually found with only white decoration, but mentions of very fine silk piping in a deep hue blending with the dress colors have been found for printed cotton pelerines.

Ribbons are another neckline treatment frequently seen in portraits. Rarely illustrated in fashion plates, no doubt because they would obscure the detail of the garment, neckline ribbons were nevertheless much discussed in the fashion literature, and the kinds of ribbons in favor even changed periodically. As seen in the photographs, the ribbons, made of plain, plaid, checked, or printed silk, are worn over all kinds of dress fabrics—monochromatic, striped, plaid, or printed cotton, silk, or wool. Often a waist ribbon, sometimes a matching one, was worn. Most ribbons seen in the photographs are between one and a half and two and a half inches wide, but some are wider.

Evidently the gold watch and pencil on the long watch cord or chain was an important symbol to the young woman of the forties. A "lady," according to the fashion literature, must have such an accessory; in turn, the working girl desired to have one as well, and many did: "Many of the factory girls wear gold watches and an imitation at least of all the ornaments which grace the daughters of our most opulent citizens" (*Godey's*, April 1842). Unfortunately, the watches do not appear in these photographs, since they were tucked neatly into the waistline pockets of skirts; only the black cords or gold chains indicate their presence. A small slide always closes the cord or chain partway. Some surviving skirts have watch pockets sewn into the side front waistbands, where the watches were kept to protect them against accidents.

Sometimes worn in matching pairs, bracelets are boldly in evidence in many photographs at this time because of their substantial width. The bands, which measured up to an inch wide, were cinched tightly to the wrist and usually bore a locket, an enameled roundel, or a cameo. Coral bas relief heads were extremely fashionable and were made either of real or the new imitation coral. In the portraits some wrist bands are dark and appear to be of ribbon or hair plaits, a common sentimentality of the time. One's own hair or the hair of a loved one was sent to a manufactory, along with a description of the goods wanted made from it, and it came back made up complete with the gold findings of choice. Directions for home manufacture of hair goods appear in some ladies' magazines of the 1840s, and some women certainly did pursue this craft, as evidenced by the many hair flowers and wreaths still seen in museums.

Not seen much in the early 1840s photographs are earrings, because at this time the ears were frequently completely covered with the hair. Earrings do appear later in the decade, when they were of moderate size, often simply a gold hoop that hung from an ear wire or a gold ball on a chain. Rings, however, were very popular. Made of gold and stones and rather narrow and delicate, they were worn on all fingers, except the thumb, sometimes all at once.

Wraps

In the shawl, as perhaps in no other detail in the 1840s, comparative wealth was immediately apparent, often differentiating the classes for the contemporary eye. Few poor women could afford one of the fine, richly patterned shawls of middle value, though there is written evidence that even working girls saved for such purchases. Only the wealthy could afford the more expensive woven and embroidered Kashmir shawls of India, but these wraps were widely imitated. The Kashmir shawl commonly worn was, by this time, not always twill-woven in India or even woven of the famous Indian goat wools; more often they were loom products of European countries or the British Isles, especially Scotland (where the term "paisley" came from), and France, and they were highly valued for their softness and fineness. Most 1840s shawls of this type were of the square style, worn simply folded on the diagonal and draped over the shoulders.

The silk broché shawl was, apparently, the second most desirable style at this time. Based on Chinese originals, these were of heavy silk crepe embroidered in satin stitch, mostly in monochrome. They were nearly all either black or white, though sage green and pastel-colored examples are found in collections and some have other colors in the embroidery. Worn folded in a triangle, the shawl was usually square (although occasionally had rounded ends) and was fringed with deep silk.

To appear graceful, women studied and practiced the art of draping and wearing the shawl. Nearly identical ensembles could present, to the contemporary eye, quite a different appearance depending on the shawl one could afford and how it was worn. A wide variety of plain and embroidered silks and wools, woven or printed paisley patterns, and even knitted shawls were available; every woman had at least one, and that being the best she could afford. It is important to remember, however, that shawls seen in portraits are not necessarily representative of the manner of actual wear, since they may have been adjusted by a photographer for effect.

A wide range of other wraps besides shawls were worn. True capes, lightweight pelerines, fitted long basque shapes (a waist-fitted form with a deep flare below the hips) of silk or lace, mantillas of lace or silk, padded silk Pardessus, sacques, and full-length cloaks—all were featured in the 1840s fashion plates and literature. Wraps had long been available readymade from the cloak maker, particularly the long, lined garments of silk or wool, and some of these had fringe or lace trim. Wraps were assigned names, such as "the Pamela," which led to confusion in the advertisements in the fashion periodicals, one name having been used arbitrarily for different shapes (making classification impossible). Wraps were not always purchased; an occasional reference is found in personal accounts to show that women made, and made over, wraps from new and used material using information gleaned from fashion plates as well as shared information.

UNDERGARMENTS

The fit of the stylish bodice during this decade depended entirely on the extreme corset. The corset shapes of the 1840s are well illustrated in the Brown-Larimore thesis (35–37). The many styles of long corsets introduced during this period had in common a tendency to flatten severely the front of the torso well down over the abdomen and to push the breasts up and out toward the shoulders. Fastening in the back, all corsets were bias-cut at front and sides for a glovelike fit and straight-cut in the back sections to allow extremely tight lacing. The variations came both in length and in bosom shaping; toward 1850, bust fullness was all but obliterated by the fashionable long, flat-fronted corsets. The stiffness, or body, of the corset of the 1840s depended on the many rows of cording run between rows of channel stitches; flexible whalebone was sewn at only a few strategic points for rigidity. The 1840s corset generally carried a long, wide, solid busk of bone, steel, or wood in a front pocket, the busk varying from about one and a half to over three inches in width. During most of the decade, the corset front was extremely long, so that the busk extended over the belly, and, for this reason, many busks were shaped with a slight convex curve below the waist. Such was the devotion to a long, smooth, triangular torso that often these corsets were shaped to fit over the many petticoats. Naturally a woman's posture was affected by this corseting, as it was impossible for the wearer to bend forward at the waist. The resultant stance is readily apparent in photographs, so much so that it serves as a dating tool. "The modern stay extends not only over the bosom but also over the abdomen and back down to the hips, besides being garnished with whalebone to say nothing of an immense wooden, metal or whale-bone busk, passing in front from the top of the stays to the bottom. . . . the gait of the English woman is generally stiff and awkward, there being no bend nor elasticity of the body on account of the form of her stays" (*The Handbook of the Toilet* 33).

One further consequence of the wearing of these rigid "stays," or corsets, especially toward the end of the decade, was a slight ridge of flesh that was visible around the upper torso. This effect was inevitable given the concentrated lift applied by the snug, high lacing. This pressure acted on the soft tissues below the waist as well in a downward thrust. While the corset was almost certainly worn for working situations without the rigid busk, and was only lightly laced for active pursuits, for dressy occasions lacing was often so tight that the inner organs were forced into crowded and unnatural positions. This concession to style caused considerable uproar in medical fields. The reduction in diameter of the lower rib cage caused by 1840s corseting varied from three to five inches for active pursuits to several more inches for formal dress. The constriction of the breasts was even more drastic. Especially when childbearing was considered, doctors spoke out bravely against this custom:

> And again it has an injurious effect upon the breast, the glandular structure of which is sometimes so injured, and the nipple so compressed, as to render suckling a very difficult matter, or altogether impracticable. . . . As in all probability she has been accustomed from her girlhood to wear corsets, it would not be wise, nor is it necessary in order to obtain the object sought, to throw them aside; but they must be altered. They must have lacings over each bosom, so that they may be loosened or otherwise at pleasure. (Bull 6)

> Women are too prone to continue to wear the same dresses they have formerly done, as long as they are able to do so, even by tightly compressing their waists. This is wrong. The waists of the dresses should be "let out" at an early period. (Tracy 30)

Holistic specialists of this period also suggested that up to ninety-seven other ills were attendant upon tight corseting, from epilepsy to ugly children. Corsets were also reputed to have a disastrous effect on a woman's uterus, but so were sex, sports, undue exercise, and heels over one inch in height (Brown-Larimore 35–37).

While corsets were always available in shops, and some special styles were even imported from England and France, instructions for making corsets in the home were included in many ladies' books of the decade. Any of the corsets were washable, though this was probably not frequently done. A corset was a relatively expensive purchase readymade, and the handmaking of a corset was a time-consuming and intricate job. Since body and shape were lost with every washing, it was practical to keep a corset as clean as possible, and the wearing of a long cotton chemise underneath the corset was universal.

In dressing, a woman in the 1840s first pulled over her head the knee-length, full chemise of cotton or linen with its wide neck (sometimes adjusted by draw cords), short sleeves, and narrow white trimming on the edges and hem. The corset was secured over the chemise (and sometimes, as noted, over the petticoats as well). The short sleeves of the chemise provided some protection against perspiration stains on the dress; the chemise was easily washed and bleached and thus could be kept fresh. Stockings were most easily put on and gartered just after the chemise and before the corset; these were above-the-knee length, knitted either by hand or machine, and for daytime usually of white cotton. Machine-knitted silk hosiery, though more expensive, was available commercially, as were the more common cotton ones. All were held in place with garters, some of which were made with elastic cords. Elastic, while it was in use by this date, deteriorated very rapidly before the vulcanization process was developed, and not much has survived intact.

Under the chemise, young girls wore long pantalettes, or drawers. When she went into long skirts at about age fourteen (at which age a girl usually completed her schooling and went out to work), a young woman for the first time could relinquish the ankle-length drawers of childhood. Harriet Farley wrote, "I first felt myself a woman—that is, when I first discarded pantalettes" (Eisler 152). Harriet did not, unfortunately, record her precise age at this momentous date, but the fact remains that pantalettes (or drawers) for women are not mentioned in the fashion literature during the forties. A girl was put into long skirts when she relinquished the pantalette underdrawers, a point, however, that is not easily determined from the literature, though apparently it varied from about age fourteen to sixteen, depending possibly on whether the girl went out to work and where. As a child she had already become accustomed to wearing generous petticoats; now she was required to wear them long and in enough layers that her legs could never be distinguished through the skirts. The number of petticoats, and the consequent fullness, varied somewhat throughout the decade and also depended on the occasion, with at least two layers required for everyday and up to six for full dress. The petticoats were, for ordinary wear, thickly gathered and layered over the corset and, for more formal wear, sometimes tucked beneath it. The majority of them were of white cotton, and many were corded for stiffness. All were very full. Especially toward the end of the decade, horsehair (crin) was used to stiffen and enlarge the edges of petticoat ruffles for evening wear, giving petticoats the nickname "crinoline," and some dressy petticoats were made entirely of horsehair. From various references, mainly in fiction, we can deduce that the more elaborate petticoats were used on top of lesser ones and that at times, when needed, the inmost petti was of wool, either white flannel or knitted or woven colored yarns. The bottom sections of cotton petticoats were occasionally stiffened with enclosed cords or quilting. For very important ensembles, such as winter wedding dresses, a hand-quilted silk petticoat, stuffed with fine lambswool, was frequently worn as the top, or "show," petticoat and was sometimes white, but examples do exist in drab, brown, or bright blue, the fashion for white in wedding dresses not having been universal at this time.

SHOES

Most shoes were still "straights" in the forties, meaning that one could alternate wearing them on left and right feet, though most of those found in collections are shaped distinctly from habitual wear on one foot. Shoes for women were without heels, except for rough outdoor wear, when heels were low and fairly broad, and the toe of the 1840s shoe was quite squared and close to two inches wide. The dressiest women's shoes somewhat resembled today's ballet slipper and frequently, but not always, had ribbons to tie around the ankle. A short, ankle-high boot, called a gaiter, with cloth uppers and squared patent-leather tips and heel sections, was extremely popular for cool-weather wear with street dress. As noted, Susan B. Anthony's footwear for her job interview in 1846 consisted of purple "prunella" (wool twill) gaiters with patent heels and tips. Such boots laced at the inner ankle. The most common style for dress was a low, slipperlike shoe with a straight squared toe, some with slit vamps that tied. Some low shoes were also made of a fabric and patent-leather combination; a variety of materials, either prunella, strawcloth, or woven linen, made up the vamp, and black patent leather was used in the toe and heel sections. Thus women's dress boots and shoes were fragile and light. Sturdier footwear, made of tougher leather, was suggested for the country because "dust penetrates the prunella, and defaces the patent leather" (*Godey's,* June 1849). For the fastidious, there were clogs, with wooden soles and canvas or leather straps, to be worn over shoes or gaiters in mud, snow, or dust.

Fashion for Men

The ideal male figure depicted in early 1840s fashion plates was slim, youthful, mostly beardless, pinched at the waist, and sometimes puffed unnaturally at the chest and had small and dainty hands and feet. Near the very end of the decade, the idealized male figure became more substantial through the body and was commonly depicted with moustache and sideburns in a more mature image. The fact that this change coincides with the rise of the industrial age and its corresponding financial boom is interesting to contemplate. Did the figure of the successful "nouveau riche" older man suddenly seem more attractive? That is certainly apparent in nineteenth-century literature, where the young heroine frequently makes "a good match" with a fatherly sort. It is also true that fashions for men from the end of the forties tended to flatter the fuller figure.

In the earlier years of the decade, men's corsets and padded vests were popular among better-dressed citizens, though among this study's subject population they were probably rare. Men did not have as much recourse to fashion literature as women did in selecting their clothing; they relied on their tailors or the latest in ready-to-wear offerings to keep them in style. Still, the fashion ideal, as always, did influence all dress, down to the poorest level.

Almost every article of men's clothing, as already noted, was universally available readymade during this decade. The mass-production of men's clothing was well established by this time, as evidenced by pages of ads in local papers. An 1846 advertisement from J. C. Booth, a New York tailoring firm, offers

DRESS, FROCK, PELTO, SACK, and OFFICE COATS, OVER-COATS and CLOAKS, PANTALOONS and VESTS, & C: in every Variety of Figure and Fashion.

Through most of the decade, retailers in all southern and western cities received catalogs from wholesale suppliers in the east and either ordered shipments by mail or traveled to select their own goods for resale. Kidwell and Christman quote extensively from 1849 catalogs from the Warshaw Collection to demonstrate this. Along with directions to their warehouses and other helpful information for their prospective out-of-town patrons, one Booth catalog listed an astonishing variety of cloth coats for men: "frock, sack, half sack, and shad," in "colors of olive, brown, blue, black, drab, and fancy." There are six additional categories of coats, pages of jackets and pants, fifty-four kinds of summer vests, and four different types of shirt. Utilitarian clothing listed, but not pictured, included drawers, overalls, frocks, heavy cotton and flannel shirts, plus waterproof "oil clothing" (61). It was in fact due to these large and successful suppliers that fashion was so rapidly dispersed to "people in Charleston, Savannah, Mobile, New Orleans, St. Louis, Cincinnati, Chicago, San Francisco, and many smaller places in between. . . . As a result, a common style, rather than a number of regional styles, spread throughout the country as the nation grew" (Kidwell and Christman 63). Readymades in the 1840s were sold in stores in every settlement in the country into which a wagon or a ship could haul goods. A Wilson Dry Goods advertisement in the *Janesville* (Wisc.) *Gazette* in 1847 claimed, "We keep up with the styles by distancing by telegraph—all the newest styles west of Lake Michigan," and a list followed of some readymade men's clothing, including linen and tweed coats from $1 to $15, pantaloons from .75 to $6, plus overalls and linen "bosom shirts."

Coats with extra-long, narrow sleeves, fitted high under the arm, mark most of this decade; and even though a slightly more relaxed sack coat appeared quite early in the forties, it too had uncomfortable-looking skinny sleeves and was, at its introduction, closely fitted and long, as were all other coat styles. The main contributions of the sack to a more leisurely appearance were its lighter weight, softer material, and lack of lining and waist seam. A sack coat was at first always unlined and was often made of linen or cotton blends in natural colors, sometimes in woven plaids or checks. As a relatively unfitted and untailored style, and therefore easy and inexpensive to make, it could obviously be rapidly and cheaply mass-produced. Sacks could be purchased readymade in every material from the cheapest "slops" of cotton, through linen and every weight of wool, including the common black of commerce. The sack was usually worn buttoned only at the topmost button and hung fashionably open below to show the vest and watch chain. The familiar waisted styles of frock coat and cutaway were still very much in evidence throughout the decade, mostly for more formal occasions or as worn by more important—or at least older—personages, but the sack was versatile enough to take over in the areas of leisure wear and daytime business wear.

The wearing of a sack coat, while it represented informal attire, did not mean that a man would go out without hat, tie, and vest. The most threadbare and wrinkled sack coat, worn by an obvious working man, is in photographs usually accompanied by all three. A man would rarely, if ever, be seen in public in his shirt sleeves during this decade, and he usually wore a vest over any shirt. Like the woman's chemise, the shirt was considered to be underwear, and even a hatless, coatless man without a necktie generally kept on his vest. Vests were of several types, all snugly fitted and most terminating at about the waist. They had either shawl collars, in which case they were mainly double-breasted, or notched collars in either single or double-breasted styles; a few were collarless and single-breasted. They were made to match suits or in cut velvets, plain wools, plain and fancy silks, and sometimes white cotton in a piqué or some other crisp weave. A daytime sack suit style in which coat, trousers, and vest were of the same fabric was advertised in the trade as "dittoes," and dressier suits in which all three pieces matched were uniformly of black wool throughout most of this decade.

The tailored, white cotton shirt had narrow set-in sleeves and sometimes a pleated linen bosom. The dress shirt collar of this period was not large and was worn stiffly starched and turned up under a tie, sometimes with a narrow turndown over the tie. Collars were often separate and buttoned to a neckband; separate starched "bosoms" and collars were advertised by many merchants.

Smocklike work shirts of woven stripes, checks, or plain colors were sold by retailers but were more often made at home. This full shirt—actually the same style of garment worn as a dress shirt in past centuries—was worn throughout the forties by working men and was generally tucked into trousers. It was usually made without a shoulder seam by folding a length of fabric and then cutting a neck hole and a front placket slit at the fold. These edges were bound and a plain straight collar added, with front fullness gathered in. Sleeves were a half-width, gathered at the shoulder and into cuffs, and there were diamond-shaped gussets under the arms to give ease.

Smocks, somewhat more bulky, but made on the same plan, were either of linen, cotton, or wool and sometimes had buttoned shoulder plackets. Considered overgarments, related to the venerable European smock, they fell to the knees. Immigrants brought the use of this traditional garment from the British Isles, Scandinavia, and Europe and continued using the smock as a practical solution to the problem of providing and maintaining a wardrobe suitable for work. A smock served equally well to replace or cover better clothing during hard work, making a smaller wardrobe more serviceable. Some smocks worn in the photographs cover full attire underneath. As may be gathered, the chief differences between the smock and the shirt proper were the oversize quality of the smock, its short front placket, and its tendency to have either a very soft spreading collar or simply a band, so that it was never worn with a necktie. Not very many American photographs show the smock for working dress, but this is probably due to the fact that a man would seldom choose to be photographed in his work clothing. Fashion literature is strangely silent about this, though it is quite likely that the "frocks" listed by Lewis and Hanford in an 1849 advertisement found in the Warshaw Collection refer to smocks.

The most popular necktie of the 1840s, judging by the photographs, was of modest width and was soft and tied in a small horizontal bow-knot, though the stock form of a thick silk scarf is sometimes seen folded and tucked into the vest fronts. Light- or dark-colored silks were used. A stock was sometimes pre-formed on a wire framework, which hooked around the neck. An accurate contemporary description of this type of tie is found in the following newspaper account of a duel carried out in the lead-mining area of southwestern Wisconsin in 1842: "Bracken had shot his enemy. The ball struck his collar, and glancing around it, entered the back of his neck, below the left ear. It made an ugly but not fatal wound. Welsh wore, as was at that time the custom in the mines, a collar or cravat, known as a 'stock,' being a wire frame covered with silk or satin, and fastened behind by a buckle. This collar saved his life" (Rodoff 338). A narrow black "string" tie was also worn, especially in the early part of the decade. While dark-colored ties predominate in most photographs, an occasional stripe is seen in the stock. Toward the end of the decade, a jaunty exaggeration of the horizontal line developed in the black necktie, which by this time appears to have been quite stiff, or thick, and about two inches wide and tied in a flat bow extending widely to one side in a crisp end. Another variant at the very end of the forties was the use of a dark or bright, patterned silk kerchief tied asymmetrically and filling most of the collar line. In all forties photographs found for this study, the white shirt collar is turned up under the tie and extends slightly above it.

Trousers changed little in the 1840s and were mostly made with a fly-front. The fly-front trouser in general use was worn low, around the natural waist. This smooth fit gave a trim appearance, which was accentuated by the extreme length of coat and the narrowness of the overall fashionable cut. Trouser fabrics seem to have been mainly woolen or part-woolen weaves, and black predominated for dress throughout the decade, with some tweed effects showing up very late. All-cotton duck or twill trousers are mentioned in contemporary accounts. No trouser crease is evident in the photographs. Most working men probably owned one better black suit, usually a sack suit with fly-front trousers and matching vest, if only for weddings, funerals, and the occasional formal photograph.

The fallfront trouser, made with a front flap that buttoned at the side-front seams and a comparatively high waist, was still available mass-produced in the 1840s, though its use seems to have been left to the working man. Fallfronts found in collections are made of common wash materials (sturdy cotton, linen, or wool and wool blends) suitable for active work and wear by men with no pretensions of higher stations. The waist size of the fallfront trouser was often adjustable with drawstrings or buckles at the back. These trousers were made in neutral colors for the most part, usually tan or brown, and sometimes had blue stripes or so-called "log cabin" checks.

While the more common kinds of clothing do sometimes appear in photographs, the main source of information is through fiction or news items, such as the following from Dodgeville's *Wisconsin Tribune* on September 29, 1848:

ESCAPED

A liberal reward will be given for the arrest and detention of three prisoners that made their escape from the jail of this county, on the evening of the 30th of August last, viz: Patrick Walsh, Henry Brown and Francis McCleary, Jr., all from LaFayette county, and described as follows:

Patrick Walsh, was about 20 years of age . . . had on when he left, a white cotton shirt, black cloth waistcoat and pants, an old cloth cap and a pair of coarse brogans.

Henry Brown, was about 19 years of age . . . had on an old black cloth cap, a pair of bedtick striped pants, and a pair of coarse boots.

Francis McCleary, Jr., is between 19 and 20 years old . . . had on a white cotton undershirt with a blue woolen one on over it, light colored cotton pants, coarse brogans and was bare headed.

Levi Sterling, Sheriff
Iowa County, Wisconsin

HEADGEAR

The number of different kinds of men's hats found in 1840s portraits is impressive. They range from stocking caps and wool peaked caps through every style of soft felt in brown, black, or cream. Some were made in tall, flat-topped shapes. Dressier styles included bowler shapes of hard black felt and very tall silk top hats (shiny black silk hats had virtually replaced real beaver felts during the 1830s) and were worn with full suits and overcoats for the most part, though one of our early photographs shows a man in shirtsleeves and an outdated beaver top hat. The hat was evidently such an accustomed part of being dressed that a man was more comfortable with than without one. When not actually worn in photographs, hats are often held, or seem to have been laid aside at the injunction of the photographer. A dent around the crown line of the hair, left by a hat recently removed, is frequently quite visible. The probable reason that photographers asked a male patron to remove his hat was to avoid having a shadow cast across the sitter's face.

Hair and Beard Styles

A change in men's hairstyles took place just at the end of the 1830s, when the softness of fringe around the face was replaced by plain, ear-length styles parted high at one side. About 1849–50 the hair was dressed to rise at the forehead in a high, deliberately oiled wave (macassar oil was the popular type) and was combed toward the face and trimmed straight up the sides, forming a vertical fringe at the temples.

A clean-shaven look was most prevalent, but a short fringe of beard from the sideburns down under the chin is sometimes seen during the decade, especially with the high-fronted hairstyle. Moustaches, which were mentioned in the fiction of the day and even appeared in some fashion plates by about 1848, were substantial, mostly horizontal with downward-twirled ends. They actually seem to have been affected mostly by the younger men and were considered very "dashing."

Men's Footwear

Throughout the decade, men's footwear most frequently consisted of short pull-on boots with substantial soles and low, broad heels and squared toes. Boots were kept blacked; other colors in footwear are not mentioned for men. Low shoes of black leather are occasionally seen in photographs, these also having rather wide, squared toes and broad, low heels or none. For day dress these shoes were slit at the vamp and fastened with ties; slip-on pumps were worn for evening.

Children's Clothing

Juvenile styles of the forties most often imitated those of the adult, though there were special garments designed to allow normal child's play. Very little children, both boys and girls, wore for everyday loose, simple frocks or smocks that were made without waist seams and were often drawn up on drawstrings at the wide neck and at the short sleeve edges. These frocks were short enough to allow the toddler to begin walking without entangling his or her legs, and they replaced the cumbersome skirts of baby dresses at about nine months of age. White cotton drawers, about midcalf length, were worn by both boys and girls. Up until age five, in fact, there was little difference between the clothing of boys and girls; both wore dresses, either the frock type or ones with set-in belts and full skirts, though little boys sometimes wore full-length dark "trowsers" under the frock. Toward the end of the decade, the waistlines of children's dresses became fitted and quite long (a little below the normal waist) and showed a slight downward curve at waist front. A favorite children's sleeve style of the forties was the cap, often formed into an overlapping point at the top of the shoulder or sometimes tied up to the shoulder point with cords.

At about age five, little boys began to wear a one-piece garment with long legs, like a coverall, with a trapdoor arrangement of buttons and buttonholes at the back for convenience. For summer, the sleeves were short and necklines wide and easy; for winter, sleeves were long and narrow. (Earlier in the century a similar type of garment was called a "skeleton suit.") When separate trousers were worn, they were of the fallfront variety and were usually buttoned to white cotton waists. The jackets most often worn with these outfits were called "roundabouts" and were close fitting and waist length and buttoned from neck to hem.

A girl's dresses became progressively longer after age five and were never above the knee even for a very young wearer; by age twelve, skirts came to midcalf. Long, narrow drawers of white cotton reaching to the ankles (usually called "pantalettes") seem to have been worn from about age five to about age thirteen or fourteen. All of the fashionable bodice styles worn by women are seen on girls from at least the age of eight, and dresses have the same overall appearance as those for ladies, except for the shortness of the full skirts and the frequent use of the cap sleeve for girls. Every women's sleeve style was represented in children's clothing, though it is true that the more elaborate of these styles were usually reserved for older girls. Quite young girls were trained to the corset with gentler cotton constructions and sometimes appear in the photographs in dresses with pointed waists, even when they are young enough that the skirts are just below the knee, and they are still wearing long drawers.

Beginning in the forties, clothing for eight or nine year olds imitated some of the styles worn by adults. Little boys' clothing, however, is much more closely related to women's styles than to men's. For instance, the fashion plates frequently show boys' dressy roundabouts with front fullness brought to the waist point, as in women's dresses. Boys began to wear miniature versions of men's clothing by about age thirteen, and the sack coat, because of its adaptable fit, was a popular choice. It was offered in either woolen suits of dittoes or as a separate jacket in any of several materials. Boys also graduated into the fly-front trouser at this time. A very tightly buttoned roundabout jacket is frequently seen with this trouser, both in fashion plates and in photographs, and its rather formal appearance, with a bow at the neck, suggests that it was a special-occasion costume. Boys' wear of every variety was to be found readymade throughout the decade in most communities.

Children's shoes of the 1840s were often of sturdy cowhide with thick soles and flat, low heels. Girls probably wore the same type for everyday, and, in situations where money was short, they may have had no others, though for dress both boys and girls wore neat, light shoes of thinner kid, which approximated those of their elders. Girls' dress styles were either the low slipper or the ankle-high boot, or gaiter, of cloth and patent leather; boys wore either the low, plain leather shoe with laces or a pull-on boot style.

There seems to have been little difference in the wide-brimmed, shallow-crowned hats worn by little boys and girls, which were of straw and tied and decorated with ribbons. Smaller hats, mere ovals of straw with ribbons, were sometimes worn by girls with dressier daytime costumes. When boys and girls reached about age twelve, their dressy hats became smaller versions of adult headgear—a trim little top hat for boys and any of the light bonnet shapes for girls.

Summary

Throughout the 1840s, clothing choices for men, women, and children were limited. Styles were fairly simple and remained quite static throughout the decade, with comparatively little change and no violent revolution. Most of the styles for women were established through the dictates of a fashion mainline originating in Paris and spread through the use of French fashion plates in English and American journals, along with French and English imports in American shops. These styles were widely, if selectively, adopted in this country. Men's styles, primarily of English origin, were established by tailors and a growing ready-to-wear industry.

Evidently American clothing habits were much like those of any country where the French and English fashion information set the standards. This is true of the middle and upper classes—on both sides of the ocean—but not of the lower classes, because of the time-honored class systems in England and Europe. What was different about America was the hope of upward mobility; the lower classes were not prohibited from becoming middle class, and the middle class could rise to the upper without restriction. The only requisite was money, and the opportunities for monetary success in the forties were plentiful. From all accounts, appearance, and thus dress, was critical to social achievement, if not business achievement, which was great incentive for a tremendous interest in being fashionable. This process inevitably resulted in a typically American phenomenon, as reported with surprise by many English visitors: most everyone on the streets, even the poor, appeared well dressed and well groomed.

The poorer women and girls were able to have stylishly cut dresses because they could use the cheap calicoes, or "factory cottons," being turned out by the millions of yards by American mills, and sew the garments themselves. And the varying grades and prices of fashionable ready-to-wear provided inexpensive alternatives for men and boys.

Differences between classes in this decade were mainly visible in the upper class's ability (and occasion) to wear "full dress" and to possess a variety of expensive clothing and accessories of the kind that promoted exclusivity. This does not enter into this study, which instead is of a median level of daytime attire—that level most clearly depicted in the daguerreotype of the 1840s—a level representing dress forms that exhibit a distinctive and recognizable American style for the 1840s.

PHOTOGRAPHS
1840

DAGUERREOTYPE, 1839–40
Courtesy of Matt Isenburg

THE UNKNOWN DAGUERREOTYPIST who took this portrait was definitely among the first in the country to use the process, and it is quite likely that this is one of his first experimental images. Many stylistic details pinpoint this dress style to 1839 or 1840. The earliest possible date would have been November 1839, when the sales representative for the daguerreian process arrived in New York Harbor aboard the *British Queen.*

Among the most telling details for the early date is the cut and fit of the bodice. It is center-seamed and has the side fronts cut on the bias and darted in long vertical darts about two and a half inches on either side of the center seam. This and the wide, shallow, horizontal neckline are 1830s characteristics. The waistline, gently elongated at front in a soft point, is a late-thirties style, popular just before the time that the extremely long, flat-fronted corset of the forties was introduced, initiating a change in bodice cut and fit.

The collar is another indication of late-thirties styling: of sheer lawn with fine whitework borders, it is broad enough to hang over the shoulders and folds down at the neck edge to form a wide V. It is reminiscent of the pelerine collars of the last decade, though smaller in scale.

The sleeves, too, have a late-1830s silhouette, with the tight upper-arm portion made very short on the arm, and the sleeve below it still keeping much of the fullness of the thirties. While similar sleeve shapes survived in fashion until 1843, the upper-arm tightness became progressively longer and the sleeve fullness progressively less until the sleeve finally evolved into the tight bias-cut style more typical of the 1840s. A number of different techniques were used to confine upper-arm fullness; these sleeves appear to have bands of puffing around the arm. The cuffs, which match the whitework collar, are inserted and turned up around the dress cuff and fastened with cuff buttons.

At a guess, this light-colored silk taffeta dress was made in one of the popular shades for the late 1830s: lemon, lime, rose, or tan.

DAGUERREOTYPE, 1840–42

Courtesy of the International Museum of Photography,
George Eastman House (68.134.5)

In spite of the obvious damage to the plate, this portrait of a man with a child is extremely valuable as a clothing study.

The image is given a date early in the decade because the man is wearing the same kinds of shirt, trousers, and hat as were worn during the 1830s. And while William S. Mount's paintings of farm laborers show somewhat similar garments as late as 1846, this particular hat shape is not seen that late; instead, the working men in his paintings wear a broad selection of caps and hats of more casual style. This hat is quite possibly still a beaver felt, though the early silk hats were made in this same exaggerated shape—very tall and widening toward the top—and silk had replaced beaver well before 1840. (The market for beaver pelts was heavily based on the hat trade in the thirties, in fact, and when silk hats took over the market the trade in beaver furs was nearly destroyed. A pelt worth $6 in 1832 brought only $1 in 1842.)

This photograph is unusual because it offers a close-up of an ordinary man's daily habit of dress. A photograph of the same man dressed for church, or a wedding, would give different information, perhaps equally valid for the time period but less interesting.

We see him not only in shirtsleeves, as might be expected in hot weather, but in a shirt type that is by this date considered a work garment; mass-produced dress shirts of the forties had narrower sleeves set into armholes and were narrower in the body. This shirt is loose and full, with front fullness applied to the band with fine gauging. The material appears to be of the substance and density of linen, possibly home woven and sewn, although such shirts had long been mass-produced and continued to be so through the sixties. It is of the common cut, a type worn for many decades with minor differences in neck treatment. Shirts and smocks made on this plan were worn from at least the seventeenth century (for dress) into the 1860s

by farmers, rivermen, miners, and other workers and were made in cotton checks and calicoes as well as wool. The wide sleeves of this shirt are rolled up to the elbow as if the man has directly come from working. He wears no collar or tie, though the shirt placket is fastened up to the band.

The light-colored vest worn over this shirt is of a dressier type. It is typically skin tight, reflecting the narrow profile of 1840s clothing, and single-breasted, fastening closely with small buttons, and has a narrow shawl collar. Transverse wrinkles attest that in full dress, under his coat, the vest has been worn frequently with all the buttons closed. The fabric appears to be pale colored and lightweight, either a dull silk or a cotton marcella, with a small woven design. A vest of such excellent fabric is often seen retired to everyday use; after a specific formal appearance, perhaps with a wedding suit, and a few years of use for "best," a good vest was likely to have had little other use for a working man, and thus it could safely be relegated to everyday wear.

The extremely high-waisted fallfront trouser is close to 1830s styles, with its wide band and shaped cut. An edge of one of the shoulder braces is visible under the vest and above the child's head.

The child wears her hair in the manner of most little girls of the 1840s and 1850s, parted in the center and cut straight across at about chin level, though here it has escaped the usual tidy behind-the-ears placement. Her short gingham frock is of the simplest style, cut in two pieces (a front and a back) and made with a wide, shallow neck drawn up on drawstrings. The short sleeves of these everyday garments are usually drawn up around the bottom, leaving a frill at the cuff. This garment type seems to have survived several decades (beginning at least by 1810) as either dress, oversmock, or pinafore apron for active children, though changing in length and sleeve style occasionally to mirror women's fashions.

DAGUERREOTYPE, 1841–46

Courtesy of the International Museum of Photography,
George Eastman House (68.97.11)

The hats are getting smaller, and a more becoming shape. The front and crown seems all of one piece, and towards the back the form gradually slants, so that the back of the crown is even lower than the bonnet. These little bonnets sit very round and comfortable to the face; they are very long at the sides; the trimming is as simple as possible or quite the contrary. Some have flowers and lace, others only a trimming of the material.

—*Godey's,* August 1840

THE DATE OF this photograph coincides with the above description of close-to-the face early bonnet styles in 1840, as well as the early bodice and sleeve cut of the fitted walking dress at lower left. Yet wraps like these, being expensive and not subject to an extreme amount of wear, were probably worn for several years by economical women in order to justify their cost and must be viewed carefully as dating tools. Bonnets, cheaper and more easily changed, are more accurate in this regard.

This daguerreotype of three women in outdoor attire is rare enough to outweigh the handicap of the blurred faces. In these costumes there is a wealth of information of a type hard to gain without the photograph.

The woman at lower right has perhaps the most interesting combination of elements. The wool plaid coat she wears has a pelerine-style shoulder cape, and its long bias sleeves appear to have leather cuffs with dark braid trim to match the trim of the cape. The coat is probably full length, as it can be seen over her knees below the frame mark. The white silk ribbons tied under her chin are the "strings" for the bonnet, which, like the other bonnets, is made of silk drawn over reed hoops (a "drawn" bonnet). The bonnet is made in a narrow, drooping shape, with her cap frills showing at either side to soften the face between the deep sides of the brim. An especially nice daycap was often worn for visiting, so when the outdoor bonnet was removed the fancy cap set off the "visiting dress," but bonnets of this period often had the same kind of frill fastened inside the brim to simulate the wearing of a cap underneath. The ombre-shaded knitted wool neck scarf is made with rounded ends and cut balls of yarn for the tassels and is fastened at front with a brooch, just as would be a neck ribbon in warmer weather. While of very similar plaid to this cloak, the pouch bag that appears to be hanging from her shoulder is not hers; rather, it belongs to the central figure and depends from her gloved hand by a twisted bi-color cord.

The other seated figure wears a wool walking dress (probably too warm for indoor wear) that fits as snugly as a party gown and fastens up the back. The cutting and layout of the stripes is most effective, with the bound bertha collar edges meeting just under the bosom. Black silk strings tie the bonnet, under which are the full lace cap frills at either side. The squared, white end beside the black capstrings is the end of the daycap string on that side. What could be a square brooch is at neck front between the ties.

The clothing of the woman standing is not clearly visible, but she can still be seen to be wearing a dark, probably black, cloak (the sleeve appears quite thick and not as snug as a dress sleeve) with apparently a long silk scarf around her neck, which hangs over the shoulder of the figure in stripes. The bonnet is drawn and appears to be of a light color and to have colored wide ribbon strings.

The neat, tight, dark leather gloves worn by all are discussed in many fashion articles during the forties.

Daguerreotype, 1842–43

Courtesy of Matt Isenburg

THIS EARLY SOUTHWORTH and Hawes portrait is of Albert Sands Southworth's sister, Nancy Southworth Hawes (1820–95), who married Josiah Johnson Hawes in 1849, some six years after this image was taken. Hawes painted the portrait that hangs behind Nancy not later than 1836, when she was sixteen. The Southworth-Hawes partnership began in 1843 when their "Artists' Daguerreotype Rooms" were opened in Boston. Nancy herself was active in this enterprise, not only serving as a greeter in the Exhibition Room, showing off the artistic work of the team, but in the studio as well, where she tinted the portraits with dry colors and added decorative touches to the frames.

While undated, this image offers many clues that place it near, and possibly even before, the time of the opening of the studio in 1843. First, it is necessary to consider the painted portrait, in which Nancy is shown wearing a fine silk dress in the very height of fashion for 1836. It has the extremely wide, dropped shoulder and the huge gigot sleeve that marked the apogee of the over-inflated sleeve shape and that just preceded the end of the style.

Not visible in this print, the bodice of the dress in the portrait would be short, and there would almost certainly have been a very wide contrasting belt of moiré silk ribbon with a large rectangular buckle. The bodice is made "habit-front," with the front opened almost to the belt over a chemisette whose broad collar lies back over the shoulders. This is a most fashionable outfit, and it indicates that Nancy had the means and the taste—even at age sixteen—to keep in style.

The juxtaposition of the painted portrait and the figure is revelatory of the early vision of daguerreian photography as art. The Southworth and Hawes rooms were in a building that housed several portrait painters, and their interrelations with portraitists were frequent, Hawes himself having come from that background. Many portraits were set up to mimic great works of art with modern sitters, and others were posed to suggest the muses or aesthetic ideals. Many portraits, painted and photographic, of women in the 1840s were manipulated to exemplify the idea of "true womanhood" featured so prominently in the literature. Women's forties fashions were considered to conform to this ideal to an exceptional degree.

The dress Nancy wears for her daguerreian portrait is extremely stylish. It features a late version of the collapsed sleeve, as indicated by the very long enclosure of the upper arm and the greatly reduced fullness of the lower sleeve. Such sleeves disappeared in their own turn in 1843, when the already-popular tight, narrow sleeve became the fashion leader. It may be confidently assumed that such a fashion-conscious woman as Nancy would have abandoned this sleeve style by 1844 at least.

The bodice of this dress is formed over the long, busked corset into stiff, boned darts in a fairly deep point at waistfront. The top three rows of silk fringe at the sleeve cap descend and taper to meet at the side fronts, and the two lower rows on the sleeves accentuate the length of the arm enclosure. The bosom fullness is released above the boned front panel and softened by the wide, shallow neckline and its fall of sheer lace-edged net. The frilled manchettes at the sleeve cuffs complete the elegant toilette.

DAGUERREOTYPE, CA. 1843

Courtesy of Historic Northampton (59.277)

Tight sleeves (though very trying to the slender arms of our American ladies) are still generally, though not universally, worn. They are now so far improved as to have always something corresponding to an epaulette near the shoulder; sometimes puffings or frills, sometimes a cap-piece, cleft and trimmed.

—*Godey's*, December 1842

THIS FASHIONABLY DRESSED young woman is Clarissa Stebbins Lathrop of Northampton, Massachusetts. Born on June 19, 1823, she was approximately twenty years of age when she sat for this portrait. Clara, as she was called, wears the close, over-the-ears hairstyle popular since 1840, done with a low-placed bun of dressed hair at the back of the crown. The dress has a waist slightly shorter in front than the extreme points of the fashion plates, but the V yoke, shaped waistband, and tight sleeves are very up-to-date.

This well-fitted dress of the striped silk fabric sometimes called "pekin," made with the fullness over the wide bosom laid into pressed tapered pleats, is not an amateur production. The trim tightness of the bias-cut sleeves and the waist section plus the flawless fan of the bosom pleats are the result of skilled workmanship. It is true that nearly every girl was taught to sew, and most could make their own clothing, but dressmakers of good quality were available in even the smallest villages. Even women who did most of their own sewing had some of their better dresses made, if they could afford to do so.

Some final touches may have been added to this costume at home; the frills at the wrists, called manchettes, and the lace-edged small collar are optional, interchangeable additions. While it was possible to spend a great deal of money, proportionately, on such trimmings if they were completely of handmade lace (machine-made lace had been available for some years), Clara has chosen a less expensive, simple, plain lawn collar with a frilled lace edging and matching frilled lace for the manchettes. The set was quite possibly made by her own hands with purchased lace.

The shawl, too, is of middle value, although it was a favored style of young women, who called it "the zebra" because of its striped patterns. (This type was popularly termed the "Boston shawl" by 1879.)

Cameos of coral, shell, or layered stone were extremely popular; the rather large example at the neck of this dress is of shell. The bracelet worn over the sleeve is of an expanding band of hairwork, with gold findings and a heart-shaped locket. No earrings are worn for daytime at this early date when the hair covered the entire ear.

A printed shawl drapes the photographer's prop table.

DAGUERREOTYPE, CA. 1843

*Courtesy of the International Museum of Photography,
George Eastman House (68.134.10)*

IT IS THE placement of the front point, the low position of the armscye, and the length of the cap sleeves on the arm that help date this undocumented photograph to 1843. The conservative, ear-covering hairstyles of the two women, with the back hair worn too low to be visible from the front, confirm this early date.

In this dual portrait, probably of two sisters, we see an unusual treatment of the bodice. Here the line of bretelles and pelerine have been more or less combined into a tabard shape. Cut on the bias and seamed at center front, the tabard piece appears to be attached to the dress front—and almost certainly the back as well—only at the waist, where it is incorporated into the waist seam. The center-front seam does not conform to the body, suggesting that it is not included in the bodice seam underneath.

These dresses are from the same bolt of goods and were probably made at home. The slight amateur quality of the construction is betrayed by the looseness of the fit, resulting partly from the cutting of the bodice side pieces on the straight rather than on the bias. (While the sidefront sections were usually cut on the bias, several examples seen in photographs show the sections as having been cut on the straight; bias cutting uses more material.) Yet even with this looseness and the looser sleeve, a crisp and attractive appearance is made by the dark stripes set into the chevroned fronts, sparked by the small snow-white collars.

These are probably cotton dresses. The making of dark wash dresses for second-best is documented throughout the nineteenth century, and in view of the difficulty of hand washing such volumes of material, it makes sense that dark-colored cottons were so often selected and that they became so popular.

YOUNG MARY FRANCES STEBBINS, a sister of Clarissa Stebbins Lathrop and also a Northampton native, is between fourteen and sixteen in this charming portrait.

Beneath her silk dress Mary Frances is wearing one of the long, rigid corsets, and her bodice conforms to its lines in a long frontal point. The V shape of the bodice is emphasized by the silk fringe edging on the fronts. Matching trim is used on the double epaulettes and the cuffs. The dress is of a woven check, probably of silk, and differs from fashionable adult attire mainly in the loose fit over the bosom and the open, rounded neckline. It is possible that Frances is still a bit too young for a full-length skirt and that this dress comes only to midcalf. The very full skirt is attached with bountiful cartridge pleating to the boned bodice and is supported by several petticoats.

Mary Frances's simple, youthful hairstyle appears to be a pair of looped braids tied low on the neck with dark ribbons. A fine gold chain encircles her neck and holds either a small watch or gold locket at bosom level. A very narrow, simple bracelet adorns one wrist, and she wears an equally simple ring on the index finger of the other hand.

The shawl is of a lightweight plaid weave, either of wool or raw silk, done in bright colors on neutral ground, a style featured in the fashion literature for everyday wear and one suggested for girls.

DAGUERREOTYPE, 1843–45

Courtesy of Joseph Covais

THE DATING OF this group portrait is best determined by the bodice style of the visible dresses and not the dressing of the hair, as the women are of the age when conservatism might have bound them to earlier hairstyles. Still, the fact that not even the youngest of them has hair puffed out at the ears holds us to no later than 1845; it cost nothing to change the hairstyle, and some of these women would certainly have followed the latest arrangement as a way of looking fashionable.

It is rare to come upon such a revealing gathering of women in a single image, one in which so much comparison of dresses, accessories, and hairstyles is possible. These middle-aged women are dressed in the kind of conservative clothing that wore well and needed little change from year to year. While there is none of the usual precision fitting or precise pleating to be noted, waist length, sleeve shape, shoulder slope, and collar styles all fit mid-1840s criteria. The general appearance of these women is an indicator of the common understanding of proper cut and style at the median level.

The similarity in hair styling is immediately obvious: all have the center part and smooth, close, downward dressing without any side fullness, and while the ears show in three cases, several still have the ears covered with braids or curls in the universal style of the first years of the decade. The one woman wearing a daycap has the strings tied under her chin in a manner old-fashioned by this date; she appears to be one of the oldest of the group. The woman next to her has pinned across the top of her head a lace lappet with flowers and/or small lace rosettes probably at both sides. This style of headdress is one used with dinner dress in the forties, and that this sitter is wearing it indicates that having a portrait taken was considered an event worthy of "dressing up." This impression is also supported by the sheerness and quality of the pelerines worn.

The dresses appear to be mostly of dark silk or lightweight wool, and those visible are nearly alike in styling: all have the narrow, long sleeve, somewhat loosened for practicality, and the fan-front bodice fullness gathered and held to the torso at center front at a low point. The variations of tone in the photograph indicate that the center two dresses may be colored, as opposed to black; popular colors at this date were brown, drab (an olive tone), deep blue, or dark green. While most of the dresses are plain, an economical choice for "best," at least one is of the popular plaid cotton or wool.

Necklines are all somewhat open with a tendency to the very shallow V, and each is finished with a whitework collar of the same small proportions, several with that typical straight front edge that lies horizontally when the collar is attached to a slightly open neckline. Whitework cuffs are equally in evidence, with the manchette, or wrist frill, used alternately. The figure at upper left wears a band collar that stands above the pelerine. The two pelerines are similarly rounded and deep, with the proper close fit over the shoulder, and appear to be of embroidered net. Their shape, with tab ends at front, is of the midforties. An earlier habit of wearing the pelerine closed with a brooch at the throat is followed by the woman standing, and the manner more typical of the midforties of closing the ends of the pelerine at the waist, where it is gathered either into a pin or under a belt, is followed by the woman sitting.

The one handbag visible is of the flat style, made on a frame, is either beaded or embroidered and has a cord or chain handle and horizontal closing. The shaped bottom probably carries a bead fringe.

The seven women together represent any gathering of ordinary women across a span of several years during the 1840s. Their clothing, considered to be in good, conservative taste and not meant to represent the latest fads in fashion (so that they would not look out of date even if they did not have a new dress for three years), reveals a conformity in dress and attitude that was important in their time.

DAGUERREOTYPE, 1843–45

*Courtesy of the State Historical Society of Wisconsin
(WHi [X3] 35783)*

THE DATE OF this image of a young, perhaps sixteen-year-old, sitter, labeled as "probably Mary Oakley, later Mary Hough," is determined primarily by the hood style, one illustrated in ladies' magazines from about 1843, and from the distinctive bodice with its relatively deep point.

Mary is wearing a dark silk dress with a fancy bodice formed by placing a shaped, boned panel at front. The panel is about five inches broad at its widest and rises to a low point under the bosom, where the fullness of the upper garment is taken in with fine gathers. The effect is enhanced by the easy V neckline with its narrow lace frill and the brooch. The dress sleeves are plain and narrow with no trimming at the cuff.

A gold chain with a slide carries the popular gold pencil accessory, which she holds in one hand. A printed shawl is draped softly just below the shoulder line.

Her black silk hood is of a youthful style seen in the fashion plates of 1843. It has a full, gathered bavolet at the back of the neck and a turned-back brim of contrasting silk velvet; other soft materials were sometimes used around the face on such hoods, including fur or feathers. Long tassels on twisted silk strings hang from the inside of the brim. An unusual feature is the eccentric hair part; nearly all women and girls parted their hair in the center in the forties.

DAGUERREOTYPE, 1844–46

Courtesy of Matt Isenburg

THOUGH NANCY SOUTHWORTH (Hawes) is possibly twenty-two years old in this portrait, she still has a youthful and buoyant appearance and still wears her hair in the same manner as she did at age sixteen. While not an ideal 1840s beauty (because of her rather generous features), Nancy has an animation and grace that suits the styles of this period perfectly. Her demeanor is at once alert and demure, subservient and capable—as "true womanhood" demanded, according to contemporary writers. Certainly no other style of the nineteenth century is so utterly feminine as this, with its sloping shoulders, graceful neck, and slender waist, all appearing above the doll-like slender rigidity of the corseted torso and the full, concealing long skirts.

This heavy silk satin dress has been made of some rich color, possibly a wine-red or a deep brown, by a good modiste. It is well fitted and beautifully styled. The long sleeves are unusual in that they have deep self-cuffs. The bosom treatment is especially noteworthy, having soft, tapered pleats perfectly formed of bias-cut satin, with the center point of the pleats neatly tacked into a diamond shape and lying flat over the smooth front. The pleated fullness is carried over the shoulders and stitched into the dropped shoulder seam where it joins the bodice back. It was usual to add some light stuffing to give the "pouter-pidgeon" look of this puffed front. The long, corset-fitted bodice point is stiffly boned and edged with piping where it meets the cartridge pleats of the skirt.

A fine, rather narrow whitework collar and manchettes are worn. For jewelry, Nancy wears what is evidently a daguerreian portrait of a man in her brooch; quite possibly it is of Josiah Hawes, to whom she was probably engaged at this date.

NORTHAMPTON NATIVE Jane Sophia Damon was born on February 22, 1816; she married Josiah White Smith on May 27, 1841, and had her first child, Isaac Damon Smith, on April 6, 1845.

Because of the suggestion of a front closure, seen as a vertical shadow, it is probable that this dress was made and worn during the period when Mrs. Smith was nursing her first child in 1845. Except for such adaptations, no fashionable dress was made to open in the front during the forties. Otherwise this dress is very proper. It is of a woven plaid and may be either of cotton, wool, or silk. Possibly it is a combination of blues and violets on a light ground, or of browns and tans, since these colors are written of in many personal records. The sleeves are narrow, though loosened from the early skin-tight shape. The skirt shows nicely the generous amount of cartridge pleating and the numbers of petticoats worn; it puffs becomingly at the sides and back. Sheer, white muslin manchettes edge the sleeves, and a small whitework collar is fastened at front by a large brooch. The light-colored shawl is probably European and printed on wool.

Jane is broad shouldered and has a long and graceful neck. Not even the low shoulder line, actually somewhat modified in this case, can disguise such "figure faults." Women with this "flaw" were admonished to taper the collar to rise high on the neck, as she has done, to create the desirable illusion of sloping shoulders.

The back hair is worn as low as possible, almost falling on the neck. The hair is done into one long braid, which is twisted and coiled up like a serpent. The front hair is . . . frequently either in smooth or furred bands, and falling at each side of the face.

—*Godey's,* January 1840

THIS PHOTOGRAPH MAY be fairly closely dated at 1845 by the long, boned bodice front, the extremely long point at waistfront, and the absence of the wide earpuffs of hair. While it is generally true that slave women who served in the home were well dressed, this sitter seems to have finer accessories than would be expected of a servant. And, from available information, it would not be incorrect to surmise that a black woman this well corseted and dressed at such an early date is probably, in fact, a free, Northern woman.

The daguerreotype, delicately printed on its silver ground by sunlight, does not often survive with its image intact. This beautiful portrait shows the effects of time and is not perfectly readable; nevertheless, it is a landmark image. Its importance lies in the fact that no differences are discernible between this woman's dress, accessories, or grooming and any of the portraits of white women of the time—especially remarkable during this period when most African Americans were still slaves.

The fabric of this fashionable dress has the dark ground and bold pattern of one of the most popular print types and could be either a cotton calico or wool challis. The color may be extrapolated from existing examples: one probable scheme is a wine-colored ground with russet, cream, and sage-green figures.

The delicate and good collar and cuffs, together with the silk plaid ribbon and the brooch and earrings, are correct for the midforties. The watch chain, which probably holds a watch and a gold pencil, is worn at front in the usual manner, with the slide pushed high at the neck.

Daguerreotype, ca. 1845

Courtesy of the State Historical Society of Wisconsin
(WHi [x3] 33417)

HERE A GROUP of fourteen nicely dressed people —possibly a church choir—most without hats, gloves, or wraps, pose at a balcony railing probably in some public building. This full-length portrait provides an excellent opportunity to compare styles of dress.

The young woman with her gloved hand on the railing is the most datable female figure: the long point and tapered scalloped bretelles of her bodice, its superb shape and fit (the bias cut of the side fronts can be seen even in this small image), are very new for 1845. The narrow, open-V bosom displays a neat white chemisette with small buttons, and the well-rounded hips and wide, neatly laid pleats of the skirt date to mid-decade. Her paisley wool shawl, however, which is draped over the railing, represents a style worn several years earlier; all-over patterned shawls, as opposed to this bordered pattern, were much more popular after 1840.

This young woman's hairstyle provides another good detail for dating; her hair is carried somewhat out at the ears in a loop, and a bun of dressed hair sits high on the crown. Two of the younger women wear their hair in a similar way, but not all of the women have followed this style. This mode of hair dressing was introduced in 1845 and lasted well into the fifties.

Obviously these people are dressed for some occasion of importance the men in their starched shirtfronts and fancy vests, the women in good silks and well-fitted woolens. For some sort of special indoor occasion, they are clothed in their "best" daytime cool-weather attire. The ladies are wearing dresses mostly of dark colors; and the men all wear black suits, white shirts, and ties. Outer clothing has been laid aside for the portrait.

The young woman in ringlets at left front wears a fine, dark, wool dress draped in the fan-bodice shape and with a deep skirt flounce. The shallow V-neckline and the sleeves are finished with the smallest of white frills, and the sleeves have a slight puff around the upper arm.

The woman nearest center front wears a dark dress with light-colored printed reserves (probably a challis) in the fan-front style with a small cream frill at the neck fastened by a brooch. The sleeves of this dress are somewhat looser than the extreme fashion. Her shining, probably oiled, hair is raised in a magnificent bun high on the crown, and the side hair is carried slightly out at the ears. After 1846 the bun diminished in size, and the side hair became more exaggerated.

At right in the second row, a young woman wears a dark silk. Its relaxed folds suggest that the portion showing is a matching pelerine worn over the dress. The whitework collar extending over the pelerine neckline is set off by a length of light-colored, two-inch, silk ribbon diagonally clipped at the ends and fastened at the neck with a large brooch. A light-colored printed woolen shawl of a fairly small square shape is turned back diagonally and draped over her elbows.

The other three women are wearing plaids, which could be either of cotton, silk, or wool, and one shows a broad, white silk ribbon pinned at the neck within the whitework collar line with the ends flaring widely. A somewhat longer checkered ribbon can be seen on the dress front of the woman at left rear.

The men's narrow black ties, black coats, trousers, and snug, colorful vests are nearly uniform, though it is impossible to tell whether the sack or frock coat are worn. Two of the men have their shirt collars turned down narrowly at the neck; the rest show the straight vertical style more commonly worn. The men's hair is mainly cut at about the ears and combed to one side, with the natural body causing a puff at either ear from the habitual wearing of a hat. The hair is worn somewhat long in most cases and is brushed to one side. All of the men are clean shaven.

DAGUERREOTYPE, 1845–47

Courtesy of the International Museum of Photography,
George Eastman House (74.193.719)

Hair in bands, brought low on the sides of the face, where it is turned
up again.

—*Godey's,* April 1, 1841

IT IS THE rather short waist with its shirred point
that helps date this conservative costume. The
very early hairstyle must be taken as a personal
idiosyncrasy in this case, one worn at least five
years earlier and deemed becoming by this unidentified middle-aged sitter. A certain "homemade" quality to both the hairdo and the dress is
inescapable.

This "spotted" ("polka dots" is a term not
found in the literature until the 1870s) dress of
cotton or silk was almost certainly made by the
woman herself. Though possibly over forty, and
thus middle-aged by her own standards, the sitter is properly corseted and erect, and her costume reflects current fashion as interpreted in
common everyday dress. The front bodice fullness is controlled with bands of shirred gathers
in a low placement at waistfront.

Her hair is done in what were called in 1840
"Victoria loops," which are brought down along
the face, back under the ears, and up to join the
low knot of hair at the nape of the neck. These
were sometimes done in thin braids.

The dress has a matching pelerine cape that is
fastened at the neck with one hook and eye and
held closed with a brooch at the bosom. The cape
is a typical early forties shape—straight across at
the hem, with straight fronts, and made quite
long—and may therefore also be considered a
conservative item, one perhaps cut from a long-
favored pattern. The dress's small whitework collar, with its horizontal lower edges, lays out over
the cape. The cape is collarless.

Of dark silk, with ivory or bone ferrule,
handle, and ring, the small folding parasol on her
lap is typical of the forties in its size and style.
Throughout the decade the parasol, mostly of
dark green or blue silk, was a treasured accessory
and was featured in many portraits.

Daguerreotype, 1846

Courtesy of Historic Northampton (59.53a)

In this handsome portrait, Northampton milliner Mrs. R. B. Dickinson is no doubt dressed in her best wares. It is said that Mrs. Dickinson's local fame was greatly enhanced when Jenny Lind shopped at her establishment during her later visits to Northampton in July of 1851 and in 1852.

In an 1858 advertisement in the *Northampton Courier,* Mrs. Dickinson says that her "Bonnet Rooms should be visited by every lady that wishes to procure a BONNET." The bonnet rooms were on the second story of a building at Main and King streets in Northampton. Thus it is her bonnet that dates this portrait. As a milliner, she had a vested interest in being seen, and photographed, in the most up-to-date bonnet styles.

Bonnets were widening somewhat around the face by 1846, to shapes like this, to make room for the asymmetrically placed trimmings inside the brim. The bonnet stands substantially away from the face, allowing room for the delicate sprays of silk flowers and grasses. It is of dark silk, possibly black, and has a fine, black net veil with embroidered edge turned back over the brim. (At this time a veil was a piece of lace, either black or cream, up to forty inches wide and half a yard long with a border on three edges and one plain long edge, which was gathered around the crown of the bonnet. Worn down over the face, the veil fell to shoulder level, but it was usually thrown back in the manner shown here.) Just visible over the collar is a small end of half-inch white ribbon, one of the "strings" that secured the bonnet, meant to be concealed beneath the more decorative ribbon bow of the cap strings. A fancy woven border along one edge of the silk ribbon is a popular feature of midforties styles. Frills of fine lace frame the face beneath the hat trimmings, which at this time are fashionably irregular in their placement and size and consist of delicate sprays of grasses, down, and small silk flowers, all worn inside the bonnet brim and hanging downward along the face.

It is also possible to date Mrs. Dickinson's cloak as an 1846 style from a fashion plate in *La Belle Assemblé* in January of that year. Of a plaid woolen, it is made like a full coat. It closes with jet ball buttons, and the long overcape is joined to it under a wide collar in such a manner as to leave it falling open down the front. The cloak shown in *La Belle Assemblé* is a three-quarter-length style with the overcloak nearly as long. The sheer triple collar that shows over the cloak collar is worn with the dress beneath and is carried outside the collar of the cloak. Larger collars were worn in winter because they could be drawn out over heavy outer wraps to make a good show.

DAGUERREOTYPE, CA. 1846

Courtesy of the Neville Public Museum (5111)

IN THIS UNIDENTIFIED photograph of a young mother and her two daughters, found in Green Bay, Wisconsin, the exceptionally readable clothing information defines a family of some means.

The style of the gathered bodice front dates this portrait. The shirred gathers in this position and the softness of the bosom pleats became the style in 1846, replacing the long, hard waist points. The hair is also now raised to show distinctly above the crown, and is slightly puffed above the ears.

The older girl, perhaps fourteen, is wearing a dress of weft-striped silk that is cut in a very womanly style. The bodice front is laid on the straight and made with fashionable fullness at center front and over the shoulder. The neckline is high, and a black velvet band encircles the neck with a barely visible small brooch at front. The long sleeves are narrow and bias cut and have enough ease to allow for slight gathers at the wrists. The snug short sleeve caps are trimmed with braid, and piping can be seen in the shoulder and armscye seams. The waistline is almost at the natural waist and is set on without a waistband. The skirt, of straight lengths of the striped silk, has as many cartridge pleats as possible in order to give it a very rounded, full shape, which is then supported with several petticoats. The horizontal weft stripes accentuate the breadth of the skirt.

Of silk, and therefore a "best" dress, this costume may be a first floor-length style for this young lady, although it may still be just of midcalf length. Her hair, which is carried behind the ears, is done in a juvenile fashion with the suggestion of a possible hanging braid at back.

The woman's dress is most likely of a woven wool plaid. The straight-cut bodice is seamed at center front, where it is pinned to a high V and finished with an inserted standing collar of lace and a lace bow with a brooch. Front fullness is taken in with shirring at the waistfront, which is seamed to straight-cut side-front panels. The narrow sleeves clearly demonstrate their bias cut; they are very closely fitted, with narrow caps set low. Her hair is styled with the back hair set with a squared tortoise comb in an arrangement high on the crown, and the front hair is puffed and fastened at the temples and terminates in short ringlets in front of the ears.

The youngest child is wearing a shallow-yoked dress of dark, checked gingham of a type often seen at this time. It has short, snug sleeves trimmed with a light braid like that on the sleeves of her sister. The bodice fullness is confined at the waistband and yoke. Her hair is cut at jaw level and is tucked behind her ears in a normal fashion, but she has an unusual off-center part.

THE BODICE FRONT of this dress is finished in a low point, a feature common in 1845, though usually modified by 1846. The very low placement of the pleats and the soft fullness above them indicate that this may be a transitional treatment adopted by the sitter; the soft puffs of hair at the ears and the placement of the back hair suggest a date close to 1846.

This frontal portrait gives an excellent look at the dark "cloth" (woolen) dresses fashionable at mid-decade and the way ribbons were used for trim, details not shown in fashion plates. The unknown young sitter wears her hair with loops widened at the earlobe and with a long braid coiled high at the crown. The drop earrings, pierced comb, whitework collar and cuffs, and ribbons are all mentioned in contemporary fashion literature as "in the best taste." Her waist and neck ribbons do not match, a detail not frequently seen in our photographs. The warp-printed silk neck ribbon appears to have been folded narrowly and carried around the neck under the collar and then pinned and puffed to fall in a wide inverted V. The waist ribbon, narrower and of moiré with light borders, is fastened to cross at the low waist point with a double-ellipse brooch edged with seed pearls.

The bodice waistfront is gauged and stroked in a pattern of fat cartridge pleats, which spreads the newly popular soft fullness to nothing at the shoulders and reaches to a moderate but fairly deep point at the waist. The slightly eased narrow sleeves of this soft wool dress are finished around the upper arm with either puffs or thick silk fringe. The small, rounded collar and matching cuffs are of fine muslin work, with either applied muslin leaves or dense embroidery, and scalloped edges.

Of course, under this neat dress—and gracefully erect posture—is the ever-present, extreme corset, which has a busk well down over the abdomen and brings the flattened bosom up and out nearly to the armpit. This style of corset is carried over into the early fifties.

Seen in this remarkably clear and readable plate are many fine details of construction and accessory. The bright sunlight of the studio shows the dress to be of a woven plaid and also rather new, since the fabric has good body. The gathers consist of from ten to twelve rows of drawn cords pulled up very tightly and stitched to the waist-front panel. The fabric flaring upward from these low front gathers is pulled in by more gathers at the shoulder seams toward the back of the shoulder. These gathers are flatter and less full than usual.

The photograph gives a rare view of the sheer whitework chemisette most popular at this time. This one, of fine lawn, is probably decorated with chainstitch and is fastened at the back of the neck. It has the narrow standing band collar often seen in chemisettes of this period. There are other distinctions in trim: the cuffs, composed of rows of sheer lace insertion with an added frill of the lace, do not match the chemisette. The narrow bias sleeves are finished at the wrists by a band of double puffs of self-fabric, and there are no cap oversleeves or other upper-sleeve trim.

A rather large gold forefinger ring and a bracelet comprised of large links set with stones are worn, but no earrings. A gold chain, held high within the dress neckline by a slide, apparently holds two objects: one is probably a gold pencil and the other a watch.

The fine cartridge pleats at the join of the skirt and bodice are plainly visible. That they are attached all around, even at the very edge of the point, indicating that the skirt fabric has been precut in a broad V before gathering; many dresses at this time had the bodice point simply lying unattached over the gathered skirt front. In this easier way, the skirt could be made of straight lengths and gathered all around into the waistband, and the bodice could then be fully attached to it only at the sides and back.

The shawl, carefully manipulated by the photographer to frame the figure, is of a fine wool with a colored center, possibly red, and a border of great distinction and clarity.

This sitter is Mrs. Charles Campbell, wife of a noted Virginia historian and a woman of at least moderate means.

Because of the bodice shape, somewhat shortened and shirred low at front, with unpressed pleats running back over the shoulders, we know this dress to be an 1846 style. Yet Mrs. Campbell wears her hair almost without the exaggerated puffs over the ears that had become so fashionable by this date, instead wearing the forelock snugged back with a comb and the side hair flat over the ears, a style that marks her as conservative.

This portrait must be dated on the basis of the somewhat shortened waistline of the dress, with its low panel of shirred gathers, and the softly pleated front—details seen about 1847.

A very elongated paisley print, a design element taken from early-nineteenth-century Indian shawls, creates the striking directional quality of the components of this cotton dress. The fullness of the straight-cut bodice is taken in with nearly a dozen rows of shirring low at waistfront and extends in soft folds over the shoulders to the dropped-back shoulder seam. The skirt is cartridge-pleated into the bodice and shows the light, full puff of the typical single thickness of calico over several starched petticoats.

A small collar of fine lace is closed by a brooch, which is pinned over pale ribbon loops that possibly match those of the cap strings. Small matching lace frills are attached inside the cuffs, extending up the opening at the inside wrist.

Of light, sheer cotton or linen lawn, the daycap as seen here is the standard for a "best" cap in the forties and is worn in the common manner for the time, with the deep, frilled brim turned back halfway and the strings of light-colored ribbon untied. Bows of the ribbon decorate the sides.

The pattern of the calico used in this dress, an attenuated version of the paisley cone design that became popular in 1830s shawls, is just a bit old-fashioned to have been used in this fan-front forties style. The sitter is not a young woman, by her own standards, and is thus at an age where fashion may have been expected to take second place to function. Consequently, she has shown economy in judgment as well as taste in the creation of this garment from good, even though old-fashioned, fabric that she had at hand.

Miss Etta Estabrook was the daughter of a prominent Northampton family, and thus she was able to afford fine clothing.

The style of her pelerine, the most visible element of the costume, is of the midforties, with its short shoulderline, attached collar, wavy edge, and long front points. The suggestion at the dress waistfront is of the shorter waistline of the last years of the decade, and a ribbon bow has been pinned to hold the ends of the pelerine together at the waist point. Much more so than earlier, this kind of prolific use of ribbons is found in the fashion literature beginning in 1847.

Etta's ringletted hairstyle is not one that was universally worn, as it was reserved mostly for younger women (though some women in their thirties did push the boundaries somewhat). Often a comb was tucked into the high chignon so that it would show from the front, as does Etta's openwork tortoise-shell example. Writers in the early forties described some mill girls as having their hair fashionably done in such ringlets, and the style is occasionally seen in photographs throughout the forties and into the fifties.

The dotted cotton dress is made in a simple style, but Etta sets herself apart by wearing this elegant sheer pelerine cape collar of finest lawn, rather an extravagance with its applied tape embroidery. The collar showing above the neck ribbon is a part of this pelerine. The addition of the fine patterned ribbons is a personal touch, seen in many such portraits, and indicates a bit more expense, since ribbons were relatively costly.

The sleeve is a slightly looser version of the long, one-piece, bias sleeve of the forties, a style common at the end of the decade. The cuffs are of three rows of narrow lace. The dress is quite possibly of Etta's own manufacture.

Daguerreotype, 1847–50

Courtesy of the State Historical Society of Wisconsin (WHi [X3] 35725)

Mrs. William Cowper Noyes, born Elizabeth Waddy, sat for this portrait in Madison, Wisconsin, when she was about forty. The Noyes family was one of relative wealth and prominence, and Mrs. Noyes is no doubt wearing this highly recognizable dress style at the height of its popularity—that is, about 1847.

The smart dark silk moiré gown, probably black, is made with narrow belled sleeves under rather long, closely fitted caps. To show off the white undersleeves with frilled manchettes, the caps and sleeves are finished with dark silk lace flounces under bands of ruching. The same trim finishes the bodice fronts and neckline.

The style of this dress features a "cadet bodice" buttoned at the throat but open in front to display the elaborate chemisette, the small collar of which is folded down over the neckline and closed with a brooch. The pointed, boned waistfront is emphasized by a two-inch, colored silk moiré ribbon pulled through a mother-of-pearl buckle and fastened firmly to the point. The skirt is attached with gauging and is extremely full over several petticoats.

This hairstyle shows fashionable loops partly covering the ears and drawn back to the newly lowered crown line. She is wearing very small, gold drop earrings.

The dresses are still made with tight backs and points behind, and to open in front, some in the cadet style, with a button confining the dress at the throat, and is then opened halfway down to the waist . . . over a chemisette of fine worked or puffed muslin.

—*Peterson's,* January 1850

The rather exuberant felt hats are nearly alike in their large size and pale buff color. The hats are soft enough to allow for personal idiosyncrasies in shaping both brim and crown and are of the large size that becomes noticeable in photographs toward the end of the decade. Even the men's beards are similar and help date this triple portrait; the jaw-framing style represents a variation that began about 1846 and extended into the fifties.

The shaped mat of the daguerreotype case also supports a late-forties date, since earlier frames were plainer.

The central figure wears a frock coat with a notched velvet collar, as usual buttoned only at the top, and sporting the very large buttons typical of the forties. The dark silk vest, which shows slightly, has small brass or gilt buttons. A wide silk tie is knotted into a flat, symmetrical bow (a detail that becomes asymmetrical about 1850). The turned-up collar points are stiffly starched and extend at the jawbone.

The seated man at left is equally well tailored, the fit of his black wool sack perfect over his square shoulders. His wide revers are of silk faille, and his vest is of dark (not necessarily black) silk jacquard. His necktie shows the rather dashing, horizontal line seen in many portraits close to 1850: loops are at one side, and ends extend sharply at the other. After 1850 the placement of the bow becomes even more asymmetric and the tie becomes wider.

The third figure's shoulders slope more, but he is equally well fitted in this velvet-collared wool broadcloth coat with both buttonholes and buttons on either side (designed to create a double-breasted effect when buttoned), a style often called the "Lord Chesterfield." His matching wool vest may indicate that he wears an entire matching suit, or "dittoes." His casually knotted silk kerchief, which has a bow with one long end, represents yet another style of late-forties neckwear. It is probably of brilliant colors, possibly red with yellow or black with red. This casual form of tie appears near the end of the decade and lasts into the fifties.

THESE THREE UNIDENTIFIED, well-dressed Northampton gentlemen are similarly attired in the narrowly fitted coats of the forties. This close fit, which gives an attenuated dark silhouette, with high armscye and narrow tubular sleeve, is the most distinguishing feature of their dress.

Belonging exclusively to the 1840s are the narrow cut and large buttons on the coat of the man standing and the collars and neckties of all three gentlemen. By the early 1850s all of these details were to change considerably. Yet a date close to 1850 is indicated by the tall hats and the broadly horizontal neckties on two of the men, as well as the soft tie on the third. It is a strong likelihood that, if these tall hats were removed, the hair would be raised in the distinctive frontal wave so prevalent in the early fifties. These appear to be men aware of the latest in sartorial details.

Daguerreotype, 1848–50

Courtesy of the Neville Public Museum (4675/3234)

IN THIS SIMPLE but important portrait we see an unidentified young girl, about ten to twelve years of age, probably from near Green Bay, Wisconsin, where the photo was found. This portrait is dated close to 1850 because of the natural waistline and wide waistband of the child's dress. These narrow sleeves, while mainly associated with earlier 1840s dresses, continued in use, alternating with narrow bishop sleeves, for both women and children well into the fifties.

This homemade dress is of inexpensive calico. From surviving cottons, a good guess at colors would be a light-brown ground with deep ombre-red to pink in the round reserves. Part of the bodice's front fullness has been dispersed to the shoulders, but most has been brought to center front of the somewhat open, bound neckline. The bodice is cut in one piece and does not have the bias sidefront pieces that cause the snug, tapered fit in similar women's styles. Surprisingly, the shoulder seam is at the top of the shoulder rather than to the back, and the top of the sleeve is thus attached with the center on that seam. Neck and shoulder seams are piped. The narrowness of the upper arm and the position of the armscye are in keeping with women's dresses.

The unusually wide waistband, nearly at the normal waistline, indicates a date very late in the decade. It has been carefully cut to frame a band of the printed ombre circles. Both skirt and bodice front are tightly cartridge-pleated to the band, and the skirt is extremely full, probably falling about midcalf, and is supported by at least one full petticoat.

Her simple hairstyle, cut below jaw length, is tucked neatly behind the ears in the fashion most often seen in photographs of little girls taken in the forties and fifties, though such a cut is rarely found in fashion plates.

THIS RARE PHOTOGRAPH, taken in the 1870s of a treasured 1840s daguerreotype, shows two slave women from Savannah, Georgia. The older woman, Judy Telfair Jackson, cooked for the Telfair family; the younger woman, Judy's granddaughter Lavinia, stayed on with the Telfairs after the Civil War as Mary Telfair's maid. Both women are extremely well, though simply, dressed, as was common for those slaves and/or servants working in the main house.

It is the rigid-bosomed, plain, short-waisted dress worn by Lavinia that sets the date for this portrait. This style of bodice, with its slightly raised shoulder seam, is seen alternately with the shorter fan-front by about 1848, most often in dressier garments of silk or wool.

The grandmother's dress appears new, if somewhat out of date; this was not unusual in the dress of any woman over fifty, let alone a servant woman, since "keeping up with fashion" was considered a vanity reserved for the young. The dress is of a dark material, possibly a good-quality black cotton, and is cut short-waisted, for comfort, with a low, dropped shoulder and narrow, long sleeves, which are slightly relaxed to allow full use of the arms for active work. The corset was either relaxed or not worn by most elderly women as they gained weight. There appear to be many petticoats under the full gathers of the skirt.

The plain white neckerchief Judy wears is an archaic holdover; not the typical 1840s pelerine, it is instead a large square of fine lawn starched, folded diagonally, and pinned at the waist in the manner of the fichu of the late eighteenth century. Her head covering, the turban wrap worn by older slave women, is apparently composed of a strip of white fabric (like fine toweling) woven with colored borders.

Lavinia, who faces the camera with greater poise, wears a plain, everyday dress. She is between fourteen and sixteen and appears to be lightly corseted, as her dress bodice is well-fitted to her straight, young form with several long, boned side-front darts, a popular style of 1849 and 1850. This style is associated with the gently down-curved waistfront, much shorter than the former waist points.

The fabric, most likely chintz (often mentioned as proper for servants or for country dress because it shed dirt), features a white "spot" on a neat, dark ground, and it is worn with a plain, starched, white collar. The spots are irregular reserved roundels, rather than plain dots, and have a pattern printed in the centers. The skirt is attached by generous cartridge pleats. The narrow sleeve, set into the raised armscye, is bias cut.

Lavinia's hair is drawn down close to the face and back up to the crown, creating the wide "wings" worn by nearly all women at this time, and she has pulled the width to a fashionable puff just above her ears.

DAGUERREOTYPE, 1848–50

*Courtesy of the National Museum of
American History (N86-14224-dag)*

WHILE THERE IS no documentation for this portrait, and no rings are in evidence, it may well be one taken to commemorate an engagement or a wedding. Certainly the sitters are dressed and groomed for a special occasion. The date is set by the plain, darted, rigidly boned, rather short, rounded dress bodice so typical of the late forties and early fifties.

Of light-colored woven plaid, the dress is most likely silk. The cut is fairly simple, featuring long, slanted, boned darts at the bodice front over the extreme, boardlike, bust-demolishing line of a straight corset. The fit is excellent, and the dress is probably the product of a good seamstress. The bodice is made rigidly to the form of the corset, with no relief other than the double vertical band of light "puffing" at center front. The black line at front is a silk watch cord; the watch is tucked into the front of the ribbon sash. The bodice front is composed of two pieces cut on the bias, as are the sleeves and sleeve caps, which are of moderate length and well trimmed with three rows of covered cording. The sleeves are cut with some ease but are the familiar one-piece bias style finished with a generous whitework manchette frill to match the semistanding collar. The lawn used in the whitework is so sheer that it is possible to see the plaid ribbon around her neck through the collar.

The young woman wears her hair in a conservative version of the temple puffs, simply looped rather high to a chignon at the back of the crown, where a tall tortoise comb is tucked into the knot of hair. The back hair is not worn as high as in most contemporary photographs, but the good comb gives the same rise to the crown. Most of the ears show in this late forties hairstyle.

Common through the decade, and particularly prevalent in the latter half, was the wearing of a short length of ribbon, about two and a half inches wide, just long enough to cross and leave about six-inch ends in front, either about the bare neck or under the collar and brought out to be fastened with a brooch at the collar neckline, so that the ends cross prettily over the dress front. Frequently, as here, a matching long piece of ribbon, folded double lengthwise, was fitted around the waist and pinned snugly down into the bodice front point. Most ribbons were of woven silk plaids, whether used on a dress of another plaid or check or with a printed one. Flowered ribbons, while seen, were more expensive and thus not as commonly worn.

The gentleman's most striking accessory is certainly his natty, striped silk vest. It has a shawl collar and small buttons, probably of pearl, and has been cut on the bias to create a lively pattern. Along with his black silk necktie (possibly one of that variety called a stock, made on a wire frame and hooked in back) and starched tucked shirtfront, the well-cut, black cutaway coat of glossy wool indicates the serious investment he has made in this occasion. His trousers, cut with a fly-front and held by suspenders over the stiffly starched shirt, are also well fitted and made of good woolen cloth, though of a different fabric than the coat. The nonmatching materials of trousers and coat are not unusual, even in such semiformal attire.

His hair is parted on one side and combed back severely from the forehead, a style that is seen from about mid-decade as a general change from the flat, side-combed hair of the earlier years and one that differs greatly from the 1850s styles.

Daguerreotype, ca. 1849

*Courtesy of the State Historical Society of Wisconsin
(WHi [X3] 35903)*

That the tired-looking mother of this husky baby is really quite young, in spite of her drawn and hollow-eyed appearance, is suggested by her ringlets. The most important feature in dating this image to the late forties is the style of her light, calico wrapper. Several late-forties details are seen in this wrapper; the shortened bell sleeve with its scalloped caps and flared whitework undersleeve and the fashionably wide whitework collar are especially telling. The neckline is nicely set off by the plaid bow and brooch at her throat.

The wrapper has a front-closing bodice, which, unbelted, may hang full and loose to the hem of the skirt in front. The back will have been cut to fit the body, and a set of ties in the waist seams were brought to the front to hold the garment to the figure in back. This garment was probably worn during her pregnancy as well as for nursing the baby and was made to conform to the idea of proper dress, as the mother would be seen by visitors to the home. It was not, however, a proper garment for visiting, except among close family members, and was not to be seen on the street.

Daguerreotype, 1849–50

Courtesy of the Museum of American Textile History (P 1406)

This is the first known photograph of a mill girl at a power loom. While power looms were in operation at the mills in the early forties, without a known date this image, because of the costume and hairstyle, must be placed later in the decade. The hair is done in wide, smooth wings that loop down and then back up to a knot behind the crown. Details of the hairdo are not clear, but the hair appears to be soft and wide at the temples, a style typical of the late forties, with rather short sidecurls at the ears.

The correspondence and memoirs of such girls frequently allude to the "mill dresses" that they made and wore for work. We know that these dresses were made of dark, often black, washable cotton, sometimes of calico or chintz, and can extrapolate that they were frequently made with short sleeves so as to keep the arms free and safe from the machinery. A sleeve of this style is often seen in the day dresses of younger girls and children. The dress has the "infant" bodice, one set on a shallow yoke and made with a high neckline; the gathered bodice and yoke are undoubtedly repeated in back. The yoke appears to have been cut with some ease, as it shows stress folds from the action of the shoulders. The garment is a full dress, not merely an over-apron, as witnessed by the fact that the bottom of a lighter-print calico apron hem may be seen over the skirt front beneath the loom. The skirt is floor length and no doubt worn over at least one petticoat for the sake of modesty and conformity.

Every record indicates that the girls did not wear these work dresses except at their jobs and that they dressed well enough in their free time that they often had the same appearance as daughters of well-to-do families.

Daguerreotype, 1849–50

Courtesy of the State Historical Society of Wisconsin
(WHi [X3] 32369)

THIS YOUNG MOTHER, Betsey H. Smith, wife of an army officer stationed in Madison, Wisconsin, sits for her portrait with her daughter, Laura, and son, George.

Their hairstyles indicate a date close to 1850. The feminine style at this time calls for heavy side wings of hair looped to a point rather low on the crown at the back and widened over the ears, with the crown hair again placed somewhat lower so as not to show from the front. The fashion for males was to create the narrow, high, central wave at front with macassar hair oil.

Another dating element is the shape and length of the rigid, boned bodices of both dresses, which are joined to the skirt not much below natural waist level and have the gently rounded front waist point.

The mother's light-colored plaid dress is either of cotton or wool. The cut shows clearly the common form of the tight corset, which has forced a slight, visible roll of flesh around its high top. The narrow sleeves are trimmed at the top with a double row of bias bands, and the skirt is attached with cartridge pleats. The fine and expensive woven floral ribbons are especially wide and look attractive with the plain, small whitework collar and sleeve frills. The collar sits very high on the neck, quite differently from earlier forties shapes.

Laura, who is between fourteen and sixteen, also wears the plain, dart-fronted style of the late forties in a dark, hard-finished wool. The good, sheer lace frills at the linen cuffs and throat, with the neck ribbon and brooch, are quite grown-up touches. The brooch may be of the popular branch coral.

Other than the small turn-down collar over the high-buttoned jacket and the suggestion of a black silk tie, young George's attire can scarcely be seen. The jacket is most likely the short, close-fitting roundabout. The soft tie is neither like a man's necktie—which by this date was usually more crisp—nor like ribbons worn by women and girls; rather, it is distinctly a boy's style of neckwear at the turning point of the decade.

WHILE THE ROUNDABOUT jacket was worn by boys throughout the forties, this portrait is given a late date because of the oiled, stiffly waved hairstyle characteristic of the turn of the decade.

This young lad of twelve or thirteen wears his roundabout, a tight-fitting, just-below-waist-length jacket, buttoned to the neck in the 1840s style. Not at this date related to men's attire, the roundabout style relates more to men's fashions from the early years of the century. The shoulder line and extremely long, narrow sleeves, however, reflect current men's fashion. These sleeves are cut so narrowly that they require a vent at the wrist, which just shows its single button on the hand holding the daguerreotype case. The starched, white shirt cuff shows properly beneath the sleeve. The crisply starched turn-down collar is more like a woman's than like the stiff, rising shape of men's collars at this date. The drooping silk necktie—not like the flat ribbons of women's types nor the crisp horizontal affairs of men's— is a typical boys' style.

The coat is probably not black, as at this date a soft brown, or drab, a blue, or even a red would have been more common. Similar flat gilt or brass buttons were popular during the forties on women's jackets and men's vests; these have stone centers. White trousers such as these, of either linen or cotton duck, were fashionable after the midforties with these jackets. The trouser front, covered by the jacket, may have been either fly- or fallfront.

DAGUERREOTYPE, 1849–51

Courtesy of the National Museum of American History (86.115.99)

THE DATE FOR this portrait is determined by several details, among them probably most clearly the hair, with its wide puff level at the ears, a detail associated with end-of-decade styles. The plain darted and boned bodice is another indication of the late date, as are both the gently flared sleeve with its narrow, cuffed undersleeve and the slightly raised shoulder line.

This dress is probably either of cotton or of wool challis. Small-print patterns of this type were popular all through the forties and into the fifties, many descriptions mentioning "coralene," "twig," "vine," and "leaf" patterns. The bodice of this dress is darted and impeccably fitted and is cut into a moderately deep waistfront of the rounded form used with such bodices. From the slightly raised dropped shoulder, the plain, gently flared sleeves are cut rather short, with a whitework frill over a self-ruffle, and are worn over narrow, closed, white muslin undersleeves. The wide, crisp, printed ribbon is worn in an unusual standing band, with a white frill at the upper edge, and is pinned in pleats to cross at the throat. The corset does not display the extreme crunch at the top so frequently seen near the fifties and may still be a more relaxed, youthful style, as the sitter is probably not out of her teens.

The girl's hair is oiled and brushed into a horizontal bend at the ears, where it is then folded sharply back up into a crown twist. The wide band at the forehead point is carried back to the crown knot and held tightly by a looped tortoise comb.

DAGUERREOTYPE, 1849–50

Courtesy of the California State Library (neg. 21.197)

THIS IS REPUTEDLY the first daguerreotype taken by J. E. D. Baldwin, "an early day photographer" in Sacramento, according to the California Historical Society. It is recorded as having taken three minutes, twenty-nine seconds of exposure. The subjects are *(left to right):* Mary Baldwin, the photographer's sister; Mary Davis Baldwin, his mother; and an unnamed aunt.

All three of these ladies' dresses have the shorter waistlines of the late forties, and the one at left shows the shallow, rounded curve and boned front that especially marks it as close to 1850. The youngest, and most attractive, of the women, the aunt at right, wears a hairstyle current for 1849–50, with the curve pulled out almost horizontally at the ear and the ears showing slightly.

The two younger women chose to wear their best dinner dresses, rather than daytime outfits, something rarely seen in photographs at this early date.

The lace mitts are interesting; Mary's have no finger apertures at all and are simply tubes of fine, black net ending at about the knuckles, while the aunt's are more elaborately worked and separately fingered. Both wear the gold watch chain, though not around the neck, as usual in day dress, but at the waist; the aunt has spectacles hanging from hers.

The younger Mary's dark (probably black) silk is closely fitted with darts and a center seam and is trimmed at front with rows of black braid converging at the shallow, rounded waist point. The bosom is flattened upward by the corset in true late-forties fashion. The short sleeves flare very slightly and are probably finished with narrow tucks. The skirt is attached with cartridge pleats all around. While somewhat indistinct, her collar arrangement seems to be a small whitework collar fastened at front by a white ribbon bow held by a brooch. Her hair is done in short curls from temple to jawline, with the back hair raised in a twist.

The young aunt's dress was probably made two or more years before this portrait was taken, since it still has the waist point and fan bosom. It is a dark silk taffeta gown with the fan shape brought together just above the waist point with shirring and then tacked into unpressed pleats to release their fullness at the bustline. The wide, low décolletage (called *à la Grècque*) is inexpertly accomplished, as are the short sleeves with their chantilly lace frills. With her bare shoulders, the use of the plaid neck ribbon appears awkward. But as neck ribbons are mentioned but not illustrated in use in contemporary fashion information, it is possible that this was a common way to wear them. While not elegantly fitted and sewn, this gown has obviously been made from a fairly recent fashion reference with as much care as limited skill would provide. She holds a light-colored fan, probably of silk, in her lap.

Mrs. Mary Baldwin wears the close daycap with strings traditional for older women, with the brim turned back, and small wire-rimmed spectacles. Her untied ribbon strings and collar and neck ribbon are displayed quite fashionably. The dress is made with ease, short-waisted over a shorter and easier corset, and has the typical small whitework collar and cuffs of the decade. Her sleeves, with their large caps, are very loose and comfortable. The short waist and loose sleeves are typically seen on elderly women in photographs of the late forties and early fifties, even in their best silk dresses.

Daguerreotype, ca. 1849

Courtesy of the International Museum of Photography,
George Eastman House (69.202.214)

THIS VERY YOUNG lady, with her hair done in long lovelocks and plaited puffs, poses here in a good, silk pekin dress. The bodice, cut with no center seam and with two diverging sets of boned darts from the rounded waist point, and the rather short waist point itself are the chief dating tools. The very high neck and the oddly plaited horizontal extensions of the hair over the ears are other indications of a late-forties date.

The usual corset is worn, although it does little to her already slim torso other than narrow the rib cage slightly. The extremely tight fit of this style, especially at the armscye, is demonstrated by the stress folds under the arm.

The flared and dagged short sleeve caps are set low and are worn over flared, fine muslin undersleeves with an allover pattern of chain-stitch sprigs. The undersleeves are tied above the elbow, probably by narrow ribbons, to puff just under the caps. The coarse silk, knitted mitts are probably readymade. She wears a coral-bead bracelet of several strands on her lower arm.

The neckline is high and close. The neat, small whitework collar, made on a standing band, is finished off with a fold of black velvet ribbon not passed around the neck but pinned at the front by a large oval brooch backed by a rosette of narrow black ribbon.

Daguerreotype, ca. 1849

Courtesy of the Atlanta History Center (4017)

There is at present great diversity in the form of sleeves, and several different forms are all equally fashionable; whether full or tight, short or long. Sleeves quite tight to the arms are most generally adopted with silk, satin, and other massive materials.

—*Peterson's*, August 1848

This arresting portrait is a hand-tinted daguerreotype of Cornelia Banner Everhart, a young Atlanta woman.

It should be noted again here, where it is so visible, that the shortened, rounded bodice front of the late forties is accompanied by a *lengthening* of the underarm seam, giving a longer-waisted effect rather than shorter. This darted, perfectly fitted bodice, with its gently rounded waist point, is the most obvious dating tool for the end of the decade, but further corroboration is found in the fashion literature, where descriptions of more and more elaborate sleeve styles abound. Hair and jewelry styles also support the late date.

This simple but elegant afternoon dress appears to be of fine wool challis. Unfortunately, while the face in this portrait is tinted, the dress is not, making it impossible to determine the colors of the dress and ribbons. Everything about this costume indicates wealth: the expensive fabric, the precision of cut and finish, and the quality of the accessories.

The narrow sleeve had been variously widened at the wrist throughout the decade, and this is an example of the richness of detail often accomplished. The wrist opening is finished in piped points that fasten to a tight, dark velvet cuff with small buttons, the interstices being filled with the sheer white undersleeves. A fine and costly lace collar tops a silk ribbon tie with embroidered ends; a jeweled brooch clasps both collar and tie.

The well-fitted, darted bodice is laid flawlessly over the corset. The close fit carries over the bosom and through the shoulders and sleeves; obviously this dress is the product of an experienced dressmaker. The round buttons so neatly picked out by the light are probably of gilt, an extremely popular fashion. Front buttons almost certainly do not indicate a front closure; rather, they are merely a decorative trim for an otherwise plain front. A gold watch chain is pinned low at one side, and the watch disappears into a small pocket in the waistline.

Cornelia, who must have been widely admired for her looks, and probably for her wealth, is one of those "ideal" models of a fashion period, one who is emulated and copied. Her hairstyle is perfectly up to date; the tops of her ears are covered in a smooth, shining "ravenswing," and a coronet twist adorns the crown.

In a very painterly fashion, the light for this portrait has been directed to define the features, the richness of the materials, and the grace of the corseted figure. The photographer has the eye of an artist and an appreciation of his subject. The commanding presence of the sitter is due in part to these circumstances and in part to her unusually direct pose and self-confident mien.

Dear father it is important that you should know what kind of clothes are necessary for the children to bring with them. You will please tell Rachel that they do not want white dresses, but if they have one made let them bring it. Dark calicoes, gingham bombasets or Circuesion are such as is required, black or dark colored stockings, dark handkerchiefs or Capes made of the dresses something dark for undercoats[,] dark calicoes for bonnets, for the uniform we have dark dresses, white aprons, capes and bonnets trimmed with blue riband this is the dresses we wear to church, I would be pleased if the girls would bring linen for aprons. . . . Let the girls get good strong shoes . . .

—Maria M. Lawe to John Lawe, April 26, 1839

This unusual portrait of Rachel Lawe Grignon (1808–76), the daughter of Judge John Lawe of Green Bay and his Chippewa wife, Therese, was donated to the State Historical Society of Wisconsin in 1859 by Rachel herself, but, unfortunately, it is without written documentation. The excerpt from a letter written to Mr. Lawe by Maria, a younger sister, indicates Rachel's status as the oldest sister who remained at home while siblings went away to school.

In this rare image, this half-Chippewa woman is wearing a Native American blanket and jewelry over a (probably) silk dress in the ordinary line of fashion. According to the information available on Rachel and her family, this is not her normal attire; rather it is her way of recognizing her Chippewa heritage in a formal portrait. Records indicate that in her daily life Rachel wore the same kinds of clothing as any other woman in town. Her straight, glossy black hair is apparently not changed from her ordinary style for the portrait and appears similar in style to that of any woman of the period.

The Native American items Rachel wears in this formal portrait had belonged to her mother and, even then, had probably been reserved for ceremonial occasions. The necklace is made of many strands of black jet and other strands of fine beads, including one strand for a cross. A large silver trade brooch is fastened at about waist level, and several smaller ones are worn above the waist, in the manner her mother would have placed them for display. The enormous Native American cluster earrings are composed of silver cones, with the cone ends filled with domed pieces of silver, strung on a wire hoop.

The blanket, while it is worn in this photograph much in the manner of a shawl, was ordinarily wrapped very differently by Native American women, who instead covered the entire upper body with it, concealing the hands and arms. This is a trade blanket of plain red, blue, or green wool trimmed with colorful bands of silk-ribbon appliqué. The ribbon work on the blanket is typical of that of Woodland Indian women, who cut broad silk ribbons or silk cloth into intricate shapes and applied them in colorful wide borders to their blankets. This blanket was no doubt made by Rachel's mother, who probably wore it into the 1830s.

Rachel would never have worn these items as parts of her own dress. Records indicate that the family lived as a white family, with "traditional" church, social, and educational affiliations. Rachel married Pierre Bernard Grignon in 1840, when she was thirty-two, and bore him several children. Pierre, partly French, was born of a Menomonee mother, and his paternal great-grandfather was Charles de Langlade, who was half Ottawa. The Lawe family carried on a trading business with Native American and white people in Green Bay for many years.

It is certainly true that many Native Americans in Wisconsin during this period lived very differently from the Lawe family, more separate from whites and closer to the old life-styles, though with modifications in clothing and tools. The dress of those people was, for everyday, a mixed bag of accepted white styles and traditional ethnic items such as blankets. Even in such situations, there are many records of people going out to work in white communities and dressing exactly like their white employers and friends.

Rachel was the oldest of eight children born to the Scotsman John Lawe, who was originally a fur trader in Canada, and Therese. In 1836, only three months after the birth of a little girl, Amanda, Therese died, leaving the family of six girls and two boys, ranging in age from eight to twenty-eight, to the father and the oldest daughters to raise. As the oldest, Rachel assumed the bulk of this burden, becoming her father's mainstay in his business of trading furs. Her education was sufficient that she could read and write, and she kept the books for the firm. This was important, since her father was absent on business much of the time. The oldest son, George, had been to Canada to be educated, but from all accounts he never relieved Rachel of this job. While never really affluent, thanks to Rachel's skill, intelligence, and effort, the family did well enough during those early years.

In 1836, the year of Therese's death, the two middle sisters, Maria and Mary, were sent to St. Mary's Catholic Seminary in Somerset, Ohio. In 1839, three years later, the two youngest sisters, Jane and Appolonia, were also sent to the school. All four girls won honors and awards at school. Many letters from the two older girls are still extant, some in English and some in French. These letters are typical of those of any modestly well-to-do young ladies of the period, dealing with school and family matters, and partly with clothing, as evidenced in the above quote.

DAGUERREOTYPE, 1849–51

Courtesy of the International Museum of Photography,
George Eastman House (68.134.1)

THIS DOUBLE PORTRAIT is a rarity among daguerreotypes, where the lengthy sittings often forced stiff, unnatural poses. This casual familiarity also reflects a departure from the expected manners and customs of the times. Clearly this is no ordinary studio portrait, even though there is a scenic painted backdrop. The relaxed, intimate pose and somewhat defiant appearance of the sitters indicate that these two are more than friends and that they are probably friends of the photographer as well. The couple's slight disarray, however, allows a good look at clothing under normal stress.

Dating is easy given the clothing details. The woman's corset line, with its rigid constriction of the rib cage, is particularly visible under the very long, tapered darts of the fitted bodice. The plain, darted front, the extremely tight armscye, and the high, close neckline reflect the fashion of the very late forties. (The appearance of bunching at the neck front is caused by the torsion of the upper body.)

Her dress is probably of a lightweight wool (often used in summer for its qualities of heat dispersal) of a plain color, which at this time may have been a dull red, brown, blue, or green. The short, bias cap sleeve flares slightly over fine, sheer undersleeves in a summer style. The skirt is gathered or pleated at the somewhat shortened, rounded waistfront. The neckline is finished with a fine lace collar on a standing band, which is held in place with a stone brooch. Her gold ball earrings hang from fine chains.

The woman's hair is in a state of casual disrepair, having relaxed into natural waves and curls and become slightly unfastened from the back arrangement, though it shows plainly that it was worn in a wide, soft fold over the ears.

The young man wears his hair in the exaggerated frontal wave of precisely the middle of the century. His starched collar, still with the standing points of the forties, tops a black single-breasted vest that he has buttoned to the top. The light-colored silk necktie, woven in a small spotted pattern, is long and soft and loosely formed into a bow.

His sack coat is of linen and has fine, distinct wrinkles at the elbow that show the very narrow sleeve and high armscye typical of the forties. The extra-large buttonhole—which indicates the presence of the rather large button of the 1840s—on the jacket fold has been stressed and stretched by having been the only one closed in wear. The very narrow lapel is also typical of forties coat styles.

The straight collar called the Jennie Lind, made of edging and inserting, or narrow ruffles, is very fashionable.

—*Peterson's,* October 1848

This unidentified mother and child represent a family without great means, one possibly from the Midwest, as the print was found in Illinois.

Her cotton housedress is a silent testimonial to the irresistible demands of fashion. Probably only able to afford cotton, this young mother nevertheless has cut her goods to the best of her ability in a transitional style so that she will not appear too avant garde to her neighbors but will still be seen to be aware of the new styles. Since the corset shape has not changed by this date, she has been able to use an older dress as a guide for cutting the bodice to fit. Thus, without great expenditure she has a new dress that gives her poise and confidence after probably two years of wearing maternity and nursing adaptations.

The transitional nature of the cut is evidenced by the front fullness, which is taken in toward the center-front waist in the manner of fan-front dresses of mid-decade but disappears to leave a plain upper bosom like that formed by the new, darted bodices. The midriff pleats are not well executed and leave the bodice oddly pleated below the bust and without enough fullness. Likewise, the bishop sleeves, which are made very full and gathered at the top in a very new manner, are awkward additions to this type of bodice.

It is apparent in other ways that the sitter has not had an adequate pattern from which to cut this dress; for example, the lengthwise orientation of the calico print reveals some crudeness in cutting as well as a shortage of material.

She is, however, wearing a handsome Jenny Lind collar, a rather expensive accessory, even if made at home, because of the cost of lace; here it is set off by an elliptical brooch. Her hairstyle, a conservative late-forties shape, with the side wings of hair drawn up to leave most of the ear exposed and the crown hair not showing over the top of the head, does set off her gold hoop earrings nicely. The hand under the child's arm shows a very sheer mitt of black net, with simple hems rolled at the base of the fingers.

The sturdy child is a boy, perhaps a year and a half old, and he wears long cotton drawers under his full-skirted dress. The short skirt is attached at the natural waistline with cartridge pleats, giving him maximum fullness for walking, running, and crawling about with his toys. Cotton trousers, probably not white, show beneath the skirt. The short sleeves are also made for action, having been tied up to the shoulder seam with cords that can be let down for washing and ironing. Necklines on such dresses are wide and shallow, easy to pull on and unrestricting. This, like most children's garments, buttons down the back. The child's hair has been cut short; the custom of leaving little boys' hair long is a later one.

Daguerreotype, 1849–52
Courtesy of the Bancroft Library

THIS IMAGE OF Mrs. Sheldon Nichols is supposedly the first photograph taken by her photographer son Sheldon when he set up his studio in San Francisco.

Mrs. Nichols's portrait may be fairly closely dated by the short waist and modest cut of her cotton dress. This type of everyday dress, seen both in everyday cottons and dressier silks, is so abundant in museum collections and so frequently seen in late-forties/early fifties images that it must be recognized as a common everyday style. It is not in line with the fashion plates of the late-forties period; it instead continues the fan-front bodice style of the midforties, combining it with the very low-placed, rounded frontal area of shirring of the later forties, but at a much shorter waistline than fashionable. This style was typically worn by elderly women, doubtless those who have gained weight and require more ease in dress. Since the favored corset was long, rigid, and tight at this time, this indicates that looser corsets were probably available for those who chose not to be in fashion. However, such corsets are not easy to trace, few having survived, and were possibly made at home.

The bodice fullness is carried very broadly over the shoulders, where it hangs a bit over the low shoulder line, and is taken into the lowered shoulder seam at back with slight gathers. The waistline is definitely set atop a rounded stomach. Skirt fullness for this type of functional dress was usually reduced from the fashionable, though there were certainly always several petticoats worn. Similarly, most skirts of this nature were made a few inches shorter than the norm for ease in getting around.

In sum, this dress style appears to have been a fashion adaptation followed by older or working women during the latter half of the 1840s, when the rigid, narrow corset was particularly impossible for them to wear. This easy work-dress style remained in use for at least the first half of the fifties. The shortness of this bodice style and the fullness of the gathers create a soft contour that conceals bodily changes due to aging and puts minimum stress on the wearer.

The daycap worn for this portrait is of high quality, judging by its sheerness of fabric and delicate lace trim. It is crisply starched and pressed, with the double frills at the cheeks and a single frill edging the strings and the neck curtain. In the fashionable style, it is made to be set well back on the head, with its full, puffed crown over the knot of hair. It is not worn, however, in the manner that a younger woman would have worn it for dress, with the capstrings hanging untied and the brim folded back. Only older women tied the strings snugly under the chin.

CHAPTER TWO

The 1850s

> . . . when . . . a Bloomer was left stranded on the still shores of our
> quiet little town of Westbridge, our dismay and agitation can be but
> faintly described. . . . We frown on short sleeves; but when those short
> skirts were seen waving on our streets, when they even floated up the
> broad aisle on the Sabbath, it would be hard to say whether indigna-
> tion or horror were the predominant feeling. . . . [She wore] a sort of
> sack or paletôt of black cloth, belted around her waist and falling a
> little below the knee, and loose trowsers of the same material gathered
> into a band around the ankle, leaving exposed a small foot encased in
> a thick-soled, but neatly fitting gaitor boot. A linen collar tied around
> the throat by a broad black ribbon, and a straw bonnet and veil,
> completed the costume.
>
> —*Godey's,* May 1854

STYLES OF THE 1850s differed considerably from those of the previous decade. Except for the overlap of common older clothing styles at
first, there was soon a distinct "fifties" look that marks the period.
Photographs reveal it as an exuberant style, one with wider skirts, more
surface decoration, and flowing sleeves for women and overlarge,
bold shapes and more patterns for men. The ebullience evident in
clothing by mid-decade seemingly followed a trend toward prosper-
ity. Due to "the flourishing condition of the country, the probable
conclusion of the European war, and the consequent abundance of
money, there was the largest assemblage of fashionable visitors . . . at
the establishments of our leading milliners and dressmakers"
(*Leslie's,* April 1856).

The Crimean War was not expected to cause much disturbance in
the flow of goods to the United States in 1856, but in fact the following
year was marked by the "panic of '57." The war at that time seriously
affected trade with Europe, and there were shortages of goods, lost
jobs, and many bankruptcies in America. Judging solely from references in the ladies' books, however, one could believe that the disruption of trade was only evidenced in the shortage of furs; the flow of
information from Paris and London was seemingly uninterrupted,

and the fashion articles paid little attention to shortages of any other kind.

In photography, the daguerreotype still predominated in the very early years of the decade, and even though both the ambrotype and the ferrotype (tintype) were in use by 1853, these new methods did not become common immediately. It is apparent that during the entire decade practitioners of all three techniques survived together. The heyday of the daguerreotype was, in fact, from 1850 to 1855. It was the relative cheapness of the new modes that gradually forced many of the daguerreian studios either to change or go out of business, though a number survived into the 1860s. Some of the daguerrian studios responded by becoming more "artsy" and exclusive, and some by being more available and cheaper. Throughout the decade there were also itinerant daguerreotypists traveling the countryside in wagons producing small images for as little as twenty-five cents (Taft 8). But in February 1852 *Godey's* was still singing the praises of Philadelphia's most famous daguerreotype studio, owned by Marcus Aurelius Root:

> Daguerreotypy ranks among the chief wonders of our wondrous age, and yet the improvement made in it by Root's indefatigable labors is hardly less marvelous than its first discovery. . . . His "crayon" or "vignette" Daguerreotypes, which he alone produces in our city, are lauded by artists to the skies. He offers to vend the right of making these exquisite pictures, and will also give instructions in the entire art of sunpainting. He has apparatus for taking the largest pictures producible in this country, and keeps for sale Daguerreotype instruments of every size. The public are invited to visit his rooms, 140 Chestnut Street, and inspect his pictures.

The ambrotype image is found today in the fewest numbers, the tintype in the largest. Because of the competition, prices of all were fairly modest, so there are thousands of these three kinds of images surviving from the 1850s, and a large percentage of them are of working-class people.

The American public was by this time treated to an unprecedented quantity of both fashion goods and information, and for less money than ever before. The growing stability of the national economy during most of the fifties prompted the increased sale of goods and the spread of new styles. For men, this is particularly true; the mass production methods begun in the last decade ensured that men's and boys' clothing was fashionable, plentiful, and cheap. Shortly after midcentury Horace Greeley wrote, "No distinction in clothing between gentlemen and otherwise can be seen in the United States, as was true of Europe. Every sober mechanic has his one or two suits of broadcloth, and, so far as mere clothes go, can make as good a display when he chooses, as what are called the upper classes" (Kidwell and Christman 53). The rise of the readymade clothing industry is the most active factor in this phenomenon. The sewing machine became available for commercial use toward the end of the forties, and as goods were thereafter more cheaply and plentifully produced, prices for garments came within the reach of more purchasers. "Oliver F. Winchester. . . . In 1854, his firm, Winchester & Davis, was said to produce an average of 100 dozen shirts daily, of all different varieties, white and colored and cotton and linen . . . Hudson and Reed of Boston, which made an exclusive business of boys' clothing, advertised in 1853 that it 'made more than a HUNDRED sizes'" (Kidwell and Christman 55).

Together with their own plethora of goods, women had many times more kinds of fashion information printed in the ladies' magazines during this decade than before; subscribers' constant requests for more guidance had evidently made this necessary. The magazines had a broad national circulation, reaching wherever there was settlement and making their influence felt. For example, as evidenced in a "Chit-Chat With Lady Readers Upon Dress-Making," *Godey's* was published to meet the needs of a national market: "we do not forget that, while our magazine lies upon city centre-tables, by far its warmest welcome is in the far-off homes of the North, West, and South, where our countrywomen are, in a measure, dependent upon their own resources of fancy and invention" (*Godey's,* September 1851). Personal records verify this statement. In March 1855, Henrietta Calmes Wight of Galena, Illinois, recorded in her diary that for two months, off and on, she had been sewing everything from undershirts and "shimmies" to salmon-colored and purple silk dresses. On March 8 she wrote, "Sewed some in the morning and in the afternoon read in Peterson's Magazine," and on April 29 she wore some of the garments she had made: "This morning we were all dressed in our white basques and colored skirts. Donned my blue berage [*sic*] skirt."

"As the plainest ladies of our acquaintance have no objection to knowing how fashionable people are dressed" (*Godey's,* June 1856), each monthly issue of the several good ladies' magazines contained exhaustive reports of what "novelties" were to be seen in the shops in New York and Philadelphia or were being imported by one of the many ships: ". . . that importation by the Persia—guiperes [*sic*], rich enough to be worn by Eugenie herself; chantillas [*sic*], next in grace and value; appliqué, compositions of silk and lace, and delicate Swiss embroideries" (*Godey's,* May 1856). And many personal records of the 1850s make it clear that distance from Eastern sources did not mean ignorance of fashion. In 1853, Marie Brinker, who lived on Fond du Lac Road, near Port Washington, Wisconsin, wrote in her diary, "We received our first invitation to spend Sunday afternoon. We dressed up in our best Parisian clothes. I can still see the hats my mother, my Aunt Anna, Mrs. L'Esprit and Louise wore. They were bonnets and had white lace ruching with sprays of flowers underneath and were tied with bows under the chin. . . . Marie and I had on light blue merino dresses and white leghorn hats with light blue ribbons tied around the crown" (13). Such well-dressed ladies were patterns in themselves for isolated country women, as illustrated by the account of an

Englishwoman, Lucy Isabella Bird, of her visit to Canada and the United States in 1854. While the incident described takes place in Shediac, New Brunswick, it serves as an example of the eagerness with which women in the outposts viewed fashionable clothing: "I speedily found that being from the 'old country' gave me a status in the eyes of the colonial ladies. I was requested to take off my cloak to display the pattern of my dress, and the performance of a very inefficient country modiste passed off as the latest Paris fashion. My bonnet and cloak were subject to like scrutiny, and the pattern of the dress was taken, after which I was allowed to resume my seat" (66).

Many women, even some of those who had the means and knowledge to do otherwise, did dress unfashionably, however, at least during times of extended activity, such as when traveling west in a covered wagon. According to personal records, old clothing was worn and skirts were shortened during the overland journey to California, and shoes were often given up for Indian moccasins or even bare feet. Substitutes for some women included even the despised "bloomer," which had been stifled nearly at its introduction in this country in 1851 as a serious alternative to fashionable dress—"The 'Rome courier' says, 'We have been much gratified that Mr. Godey has given no encouragement to the bloomer folly.' We were right. Even those who paraded our streets at night have given it up. The thing is dead" (*Godey's,* January 1852). "Those who paraded our streets at night" refers to the torchlight demonstrations by dress reformers in support of the bloomer costume.

"The shorts," as some women first named the costume, at first consisted of a short-skirted, loose sacque belted over ankle-length "Turkish trousers" of the same material. The bodice and sleeves of the sacque later followed normal stylish lines, depending on the occasion. This relatively comfortable costume was made easier to wear by the relaxing, or leaving off, of the tight stays important to fashionable dress, but it did require a full complement of shortened petticoats. The "bloomer" is first recorded in this country during the winter of 1851, when Libby Smith Miller arrived in Seneca Falls, New York, to visit her cousin, Elizabeth Cady Stanton, wearing such a costume, which she claimed she had invented for traveling. (A similar "Turkish" costume had been in use on the European Continent as exercise dress for several decades.) Mrs. Stanton, eight months pregnant, happily adopted an unsashed version for the rest of her pregnancy and became an enthusiastic supporter of the reform dress, which she called "the Turkish costume." The notion spread to her housekeeper and many of her friends. Amelia Bloomer, who published a reform paper called *The Lily,* wore the costume for a time; she printed a sketch of the costume in her paper in June 1852 and later, because of extreme interest, printed a pattern for it. Inevitably, the popular name was soon changed to "the Bloomer." Mrs. Stanton, a strong feminist, incorporated the idea of freedom of dress—represented by this easy-to-wear costume—into her philosophy and worked to inform women that they need not be enslaved by masculine ideas of proper clothing for women. The downfall of the costume seems to have been its unbecomingness, as well as the tendency of the short skirt to lift higher than decency dictated, either in wind or in active wear. Whatever the cause, Mrs. Miller only wore it herself for seven years, Mrs. Bloomer for eight, and Mrs. Stanton and her friend Susan B. Anthony also capitulated somewhere along the line. Only about a hundred women of note are known to have worn the costume, and most of those gave it up in the fifties because they deemed it injurious to their higher cause of women's rights because of its controversial nature. It was too distracting. Adaptations of the bloomer costume, with the dress portion following contemporary styles, persisted through the 1860s as alternative dress under the auspices of the National Dress Reform Association but then mostly died out.

When moving into unsettled territory during the fifties and sixties, some women evidently felt that propriety might best be served by this form of dress, which was suited to a more active, frontier lifestyle. A month after her arrival at her new home in Kansas in the midfifties, Miriam Davis Colt wrote in her diary that she was "wearing the bloomer dresses now; find they are well suited to a wild life like mine. Can bound over the prairies like an antelope, and am not in so much danger of setting my clothes on fire while cooking" (Helvenston 135). The bloomer dress is mentioned throughout the decade in the private journals of women doing active farm work in isolated settlements, but it appears that later in the decade, after the first fervor had worn off, the costume was worn strictly for such activities as required mobility, such as farm work, gardening, travel, or exercise. And even then the women who wore bloomers did not often do so in public, having another more acceptable wardrobe for dressier occasions. Harriet Carr, who went to Kansas in 1858, wrote, "people are generally . . . not half so heathenish as many imagine . . . people expect taste and tidiness in dress, at least in ladies, just as much as in the East" (Helvenston 167).

Even those women who did not wear bloomer costumes were likely behind in fashion when first settling the frontier. All records imply strongly, however, that proper and up-to-date modes of dress were known and respected and were followed as soon as conditions made it possible, even though it was sometimes a year or two in newly settled territory before this could happen.

As for slavishly following the 1850s vagrancies of full fashion, there is evidence of widespread resistance in many areas, and many plainer alternatives were developed. Most adaptations were simply one-piece, economical cottons cut with the shoulder and waist seams in the newer mode and with the full round skirts, but with the ruffles and trim omitted. The expense and frivolity of unnecessary decoration were considered by women's writers to be harmful to a woman's character if pursued to extremes; near the end of the decade *Harper's Magazine* stated bluntly that

. . .

dress is not now chosen for its becomingness, but for its display. . . . woman has become subordinate to dress. . . . It is too unfortunately true that our lives in the present day offer but few objects of competition to woman, and at the same time woman is as ambitious as a man. She has all the desire to conquer worlds, but no worlds to conquer. After being educated as well, if not better than most men, she enters the world and finds nothing to strive for but the attention of gentlemen, pre-eminence in dress and style, and the dangerous distinction of being much talked about . . . and all of these efforts are degrading. (February 1858)

Godey's also felt that its mission was to educate the whole woman and claimed to play down the importance of keeping up with fashion. At the same time, however, the magazines were constantly re-creating the vehicle by which fashion was spread—printing the latest in fashion plates. The fashion editor, and Sarah Hale herself, walked on treacherous ground at times in attempting to explain this dichotomy.

Early in 1853, for instance, Godey's reprinted several articles written in England by a Mrs. Merrifield entitled "Dress—as a Fine Art" in which she expressed the typical view of the class-oriented Englishwoman: ". . . the middle and poorer classes will always follow, as much as possible, the fashion of those above them" (March 1853). And she later discussed the elements of midcentury dressing:

That it is an art to set off your person to the greatest advantage must be generally admitted . . . the rules of society require that, to a certain extent, we should adopt those forms of dress which are in common use. . . . Fashion in dress is usually dictated by caprice or folly. It is never, we believe, based upon the study of the figure.

The immediate objects of dress are two-fold—namely, decency and warmth; . . . it should also be adapted to the station in society, and to the age of the individual. . . . The best dressers are generally those who follow the fashions at a great distance. . . . From the ladies of wealth, the fashions descend through all the ranks of society, until they at last die a natural death among the cast-off clothes of the housemaid. . . . We are content to adopt the greatest absurdities in dress when they are brought from Paris, or recommended by a French name.
(Godey's, April 1853)

A year later Godey's fashion editor wrote a cautionary article.

. . . economy in dress, an essential object of many persons, . . . our first recommendation is to have but a few dresses at a time, and those extremely good; if we have but few dresses, we wear them, and wear them out while they are in fashion, but if we have many dresses at once, some of them become quite old-fashioned before we have done with them. . . . It is not economical to have the dresses made in the extremity of fashion, because such soon become remarkable; but the fashions should be followed at such a distance that the wearer may not attract the epithet of old-fashioned. (April 1854)

The fashion articles were full of advice: "We endeavor in nearly every case to select the plainest garments for our illustrations, and wish it distinctly understood that, when we give an elaborate style, it is for the novelty, and not with the expectation of having it copied. . . . our protest has been so constant against extravagance . . . yet the evil is so constantly on the increase in our cities, and is extending so rapidly to remote towns and villages . . ." (March 1856). And, in seeming contradiction to the above,

> We are constantly asked if Americans are not a year behind the Parisian styles. This is no longer the case. Our principle importers, have their partner or their resident agent abroad; and now, that steam has shortened the transit from continent to continent to a ten days' jaunt, there is no reason why our fashionable ladies should be more than two weeks at furthest behind the belles of Longchamps. It is merely a question of time, as our southern or western subscribers must depend upon the speed of the different transit companies by which their mantles from Brodies' or Levy's, their bonnets from Genin's, Miss Wharton's, or Malherbe's, are forwarded. Even here, the present business system has made reforms. The more enterprising dealers from a distance throng the wholesale rooms of city firms, while our ladies are yet in furs and velvets, thus bringing retail openings north and south to the same date. (August 1856)

Home Sewing

During this decade most American families—at least the women and children—wore some homemade clothing made either by the homemaker herself or with the help of a hired seamstress. Isaac M. Singer received the first patent for his home sewing machine in 1851, and because of it the possibility of making clothing rapidly in the home was first envisioned. While at first not many women had a sewing machine, by the end of the decade it was a fixture in many households. The sewing of women's garments was more of a necessity than that for men and boys, as there were few readymades for women in this decade, except for wraps and some elaborate undergarments available by import. A woman either sewed, hired a dressmaker or seamstress, or sent measurements and requests to a city dressmaker. Aids for keeping up with the latest styles at home were abundant. Besides the fashion plates and information in every ladies' magazine, there were actual patterns available in the fifties for the home sewer and the dressmaker. There were pattern diagrams in *Godey's* by 1853 and a full-size pattern in February 1854. In February 1855 the cost of a sleeve pattern from *Godey's* was .31, and a full dress pattern, printed in facsimile, cost $1.37½, a very high price in comparison to offerings by other firms: *Demorest's Quarterly Mirror of Fashion*, for one, offered full-size plain tissue patterns by this time for less money. Patterns were available for purchase in shops as well. None of these patterns came in sizes, however; a pattern was intended as a cutting guide only, the draft to be fitted individually. Since the cut of the bodice—the part of the dress that was fitted—did not vary greatly during the fifties, a guide was sufficient.

Shopping services also furthered the spread of fashion. Offered by *Godey's* fashion department for the first time in July 1852, such a service ensured that women far from the importation and manufacturing points could have the newest innovations in patterns and even accessories purchased for them and shipped to their homes. The fashion editor (or, more likely, people hired for this service) shopped personally at Philadelphia stores to fill orders. A small percentage of the purchase price was the charge for this service. In July 1856, *Godey's* announced, "Our Fashion Editor continues to furnish patterns of any of the dress articles in 'the book.'" A full page and a third of this issue lists notices of filled orders, a breakdown of which includes: twenty-seven patterns, two embroidery patterns, four gold pens, two packages of hair dye, twenty-eight pearl card-cases, and twenty-one pieces of hair jewelry.

Late in the decade, *Demorest's* elicited a mention in *Godey's:* "We must notice the great extent to which the business of supplying patterns of garments has been carried by Madame Demorest. There are over seventy branches of the principal establishment at 375 Broadway, scattered all through the country. The patterns are manufactured by machinery. . . . Demorest's has now a dressmaking department . . . also introduced a new spring skirt" (December 1859). And *Godey's* admonished its readers how important it was to learn to make one's own clothing:

> some of our most fashionable ladies make their own dresses, and bonnets, too, if inclination prompt. . . . A dressmaker's charge is seventy-five cents a day and, including mantillas and capes, no family can well dispense with less than a week's service for every season. . . . Besides, who knows but, in the very natural course of events, you may consent to share the fortune of some noble-minded adventurer in the new country California or Minesota [*sic*]; or, if your lover happens to be in the army, Fort Leavenworth or the Mexican frontier . . . and then what becomes of the helpless? (September 1851)

Judging from diaries and journals, homemakers often sewed even for men and boys in order to save money, in spite of the availability of readymades. In a diary she maintained for many years, Mrs. Mariella Leggett of Cleveland tells of the extensive sewing she did for her husband, Lewis, and their four children and for her mother-in-law. Not only did Mrs. Leggett sew all the children's garments, she made her husband's shirts and shirtees (shirtfronts that could be worn under vests without shirts), collars, and nightshirts, and she even did the spinning and dying of her own wool for stockings. She belonged to a large "sewing circle" of about forty-five ladies and made quilts. She did not own a sewing machine in this decade. In several entries from 1854 and 1855, she wrote of having her own dresses "cut and fitted" by a local seamstress, a task she evidently thought beyond her talents, though she often wrote of making at least the skirts for these dresses and of "finishing my dress."

The development and patent licensing of pattern drafting systems to facilitate the cutting of stylish and well-fitted garments began long before this decade and evolved as women's clothing became more complex in the 1850s. Professional dressmakers often used such systems in the fifties, and they became increasingly available to the knowledgeable home sewer. Armed with the fashion information, a sewing machine, the new array of inexpensive, American-made fabrics, and possibly even a pattern drafting system, the average woman was able to keep herself and her family looking respectable no matter where she lived. Most managed fairly well even without the newer aids, but the work did take longer and was more difficult.

Ready-to-wear production was revolutionized by the sewing machine, even though much work was still "let out" to home seamstresses for finishing. According to Kidwell and Christman, the time-saving of the new machines was estimated for professional sewing shops as follows: to make a pair of summer pants for a man by hand took two hours and fifty minutes, thirty-eight minutes by machine; a hand-sewn shirt required fourteen hours and twenty-six minutes by hand, one hour and sixteen minutes by machine; a frock coat took sixteen hours and thirty-five minutes by hand, two hours and thirty-eight minutes by machine. The machine sewing of cloaks and mantillas in the 1850s reduced the cost of making them by 80 percent and occasioned a consequent drop in prices (77–78). Ladies' wraps were in constant production in American shops in styles to rival those from Paris and, because of the new machines, also available at lower prices.

While male tailors exclusively made men's and women's suits and coats, women sewed the millions of shirts, collars, cuffs, and shirtfronts sold in men's furnishing shops, usually taking the work home in packets of cut pieces and buttons (one packet for each garment or piece) and doing the work by hand, since the sewing machine was too expensive for these poorer women. The plight of these home workers was made worse when machine-sewing shops appeared near the end of the decade. Women did staff such shops, as well as the rooms above the fancy dress and cloak shops, but for the most part the home sewer was put out of work.

According to accounts, comparative prices for clothing were still, in 1851, disproportionate to modest wages:

... what many will consider a very moderate winter outfit:

Furs	$60
Velvet Cloak	$40
Bonnet	$12
Walking-dress	$25
Veil	$5
Total	$147

... bad work for Mr. Jones, a clerk in an insurance office on fourteen hundred a year. (*Godey's,* March 1851)

Mr. Jones's fourteen hundred is far above the wages of a common laborer at the beginning of the decade, but then a laborer's wife would not have even considered buying such an expensive outfit. The estimated weekly living expenses of an urban working-class family of five in 1851 were published in the *New York Daily Tribune* on May 27:

Barrel of flour, $5.00, will last eight weeks	$0.62½
Sugar, 4 lbs., at 8 cents a pound	.32
Butter, 2 lbs. at 31½ cents a pound	.6 [*sic*]
Milk, two cents per day	.14
Butcher's meat, 2 lbs. beef per day at 10c per lb.	1.40
Potatoes, ½ bushel,	.50
Coffee & Tea	.25
Candle light	.14
Fuel, 3 tons of coal per annum, $15, charcoal, chips, matches, etc., $5.00 per annum	.40
Salt, pepper, vinegar, starch, soap, soda, yeast, cheese, eggs	.40
Furniture & utensils, wear & tear	.25
Rent	3.00
Bed clothes	.20
Clothing	2.00
Newspapers	.12
Total expenses:	$10.37

(The $2.00 estimated weekly expenditure for clothing for this family of five breaks down to .40 per week per person, or $20.80 per person per annum.) Editor Horace Greeley added, "I ask: have I made the working-man's comforts too high? Where is the money to pay for amusements, for ice-creams, his puddings, his trips on Sunday up or down the river in order to get some fresh air, to pay the doctor or apothecary, to pay for pew rent in the church, to purchase books, musical instruments?" (N. Ware 80). Mr. Greeley's concern, in light of the wages quoted above, seems valid. Not every wage earner earned $10 per week at the beginning of the fifties, and many city families lived well below the modest level he suggests as minimal.

And the wife of such a worker would not have conceived of such a lavish clothing budget as that thought "necessary" by the society woman. She would instead have made herself an inexpensive wool or calico dress in a modest but fashionable style (at a total cost of from one to three dollars, plus her time) and would wear a warm blanket shawl rather than a cloak. Her bonnet might grow somewhat out of date, but it could be reasonably updated at little expense by changing the decorations to suit the latest taste. An expensive lace veil for the bonnet would have been out of the question, as would the furs; yet the general appearance of a poorer woman who made an attempt at dressing respectably would be very like that of her wealthier sisters; the corset had the same form, there was the same bulk of petticoats and the same cut of dress, and hair and bonnet shapes could easily have been quite comparable.

Fashions for Women

The most common day dress of the very first years of the 1850s, judging from the photographs, was quite different from the dresses seen in the fashion plates. They were mostly in the style of those worn in the last two or three years of the forties; but rather than being long-waisted, these dresses had very short underarm seams, along with the current shallow rounded dip at waistfront, and they were made with the fan bosom quite soft and full. This is a style that would not fit over the long, rigid corset at all, and so we can extrapolate that it was made for women who could not wear such a corset: pregnant and nursing women certainly could not, nor could elderly women, especially if they had become slightly plump, and even some young women seem to have worn shorter, easier corsets for everyday. Since the long, busked corset had already had a long reign by this date, it is no surprise that these dresses appear in photographs of older women taken as early as the midforties and continue to be seen at least until 1853. Alternative, working-type corsets must have been available, or else such corsets were hand sewn from a familiar old pattern. The long-fronted, bust-flattening corset of the late forties persisted in fashionable dress until 1853.

The sleeve on these early work dresses is always narrow, sometimes cut on the bias and sometimes straight, though not tight, and it frequently shows a little fullness at the wrist, where it may be gathered into a cuff. The dress is seen mainly in everyday cottons, but, as witnessed in many photographs, the style was definitely used for silk dresses by the elderly. Cotton dresses of this pattern surviving in museum collections are often very worn and much mended and frequently have been shortened several inches from the floor length of fashionable dress.

By the midfifties, presumably due to the appearance of the more wearable corset form in 1853, the above survival style of dress was replaced everywhere by the plain, one-piece day dress with bishop sleeves. These dresses were moderately long-waisted, generally opening at the front bodice, and were made with or without a waistband. In most cases, the bodices were plain, with two long darts at either side; but work dresses were often made without the darts, the fullness controlled instead with gathers at the waist, centered front and back, and sometimes into straight yokes. Woven ginghams in checks or plaids were more common than prints for such housedresses. Women of all classes wore dresses of this type for everyday. Only near the end of the decade were hoops worn under such dresses, and then probably only when a gingham dress was new and worn for a while for daytime "best." Even after hoops were in general use, around 1856, for work many women did not wear them.

The more fashionable fifties styles had a distinctive, recognizable silhouette. Skirt fullness was ubiquitous, and skirts were well supported to make them stand as full as possible. Waistlines were mostly round (without points, or with very short rounded dips) and fairly close to the natural waistline, that is, with long underarm seams.

Sleeves were generally wide at the wrists. The open, bell-shaped sleeve, coming to midforearm, was well established before 1850 and continued to be popular for warm weather and/or for dressy occasions, but not for everyday dress. In 1857 it was at its widest. The "close" sleeve, one resembling the one-piece, bias-cut tight shape of the early 1840s, but more loosely fitted, was still used in winter silks, for walking dresses, because of its greater protection and, in the fashion plates, it was sometimes featured under a matching bell oversleeve. Variations in sleeve styles developed as fashion decreed a more elaborate approach: upper-arm caps or pleats and lower-arm puffs, slashings, or ruffles to set off the white undersleeves, which themselves became more elaborate. In July 1858, *Godey's* featured a new style of bishop sleeve, one heavily gathered at the top of the arm into a closely fitted sleeve cap, called an epaulet, and into a deep-pointed cuff. In November of that year, a similarly enormous bishop sleeve was pictured without the epaulet, gathered instead under the shoulder edge of wide bretelles, and with a rather narrow cuff. These loose, full sleeves were not frequently featured in fashion plates after this date, but they can still be seen in photographs of everyday dress taken many years into the sixties.

Soon after 1850 an abundance of surface decoration became popular, especially on the bodice. Wide shoulder bretelles added width and accented the narrow waist—"Bretelles, whether in braes or berthes, are still worn, as they add such becoming width to the shoulders" (*Godey's,* February 1858)—and ruffles, flounces, lace, and fringe trimming embellished most styles of dresses. Even colors and fabrics became more flamboyant: "Is it to show their entire contempt for the principles of design that our manufacturers introduced last year not only horizontal stripes of conspicuous colors, but checks and plaids of immense size . . . the prevalence of the fashion at the present time is another evidence of the triumph of fashion over good taste" (*Godey's,* April 1854).

Lightweight, printed wool barège or challis were used for dressier summer wear and silk usually for winter. A thin material mentioned for the first time for cool summer dress in *Godey's* in June 1855 is "pineapple tissue, imported by the India stores of Boston and New York. . . stripes, plaids, and checks, on a white ground." Fashion decreed that these thin materials should be made with unlined full skirts, large sleeves gathered at the wrist, and "infant's waists," which were "made high in the neck, with a yoke, corded with silk, and gathered full into a straight belt. No point whatever . . . the waist cannot be too long from the arm to the belt; but the length is not increased at the bodice" (*Godey's,* May 1850). It is this bodice form, in plainer styles, that is seen in children's cotton dresses, women's white bodices, and frequently in women's working dresses from the late 1840s and throughout the 1850s.

Particularly associated with the fifties is the basque waist. This hip-length jacket form, tightly fitted over the bust and at the waist, with a crisp flare over the hips, was made with an open, flaring sleeve and was mainly a spring and summer style. Basques were most often found ensuite with their own skirts, made of plaid or striped silk, though white cotton basques were worn with colored skirts for summer. White undersleeves, some very large and either closed at the wrist or flaring, were worn with the wide sleeves.

The fifties dress skirt was generous, with the fullness distributed evenly all around the waist in gathers or knife pleats. "Skirts are made quite full, long behind, but short enough in front to show the slipper or boot. Some prefer the skirt stiffened in the hem, by tacking a narrow braid of straw on the inside; this is a Parisien mode of showing the ample folds of the skirt, and is quite becoming to tall figures" (*Godey's,* October 1850). The flounced skirt, so often seen in 1850s fashion plates, was intended for the best and most delicate materials and for women with more money to spend: "A handsome flounced dress is always more expensive than one with a plain skirt, and ladies of ample fortune are apt to give a preference to what only a limited number can afford to wear" (*Godey's,* April 1855). Many lightweight, semisheer fabrics were woven "à disposition," or with printed borders intended for these flounces, into at least 1857. The width of the skirt was accented in other ways as well; for example, "For plain dresses, skirts with stripes across are in great vogue" (*Godey's,* October 1856). Skirts were almost never fully lined, as it was advantageous to the full, puffy style to keep them light in weight, though unflounced skirts still had the bottom facing of stiffened fabric familiar from the forties. Gored dresses, a very different style, with their vertical seaming from the shoulder to the hem, were first introduced in 1859 (*Godey's,* December 1859); at this early stage, the style was not called "princess." Vertical seams were made practical when the sewing machine was proven to produce much stronger seams than was possible by hand.

The Zouave jacket, styled after the military coats of an elite corps of French cavalry, is first mentioned in *Godey's* in August 1859:

...that gallant corps having made a wider name for themselves in the late campaign [in the Crimean War] ... made of cloth and velvet in sack pattern, close at the throat, and falling away in loose rounded lines over the hips ... close vest beneath, with a double point at the waist, and buttoned close to the chin. Sleeves round and flowing. It is trimmed with military-looking braid, set on in Greek patterns ... it is an excellent way of using up skirts of dresses whose bodies alone have suffered by wear.

UNDERGARMENTS

The chief innovation of the 1850s in women's dress was the "crinoline," or hoop skirt. Tracing the adoption of this garment in America is not simple. The enlargement of skirts began with the petticoat, but while Parisian women wore stiffened petticoats from at least 1853, and even earlier French fashion plates show the bouffant styles requiring such support, American ladies' magazines did not announce at any time "we will now wear hoops." American women current with the Paris fashions undoubtedly wore crinoline in this country early on, but its acceptance for general wear was anything but immediate, as it was considered too extreme. The growth of the size and stiffness of the petticoat was gradual; the first step was probably just to wear fuller petticoats, with perhaps an arrangement of stiffened ruffles to fit around the waist and extend out all around under the top of the skirt. Petticoats were made with more yardage and ruffles, and more of them were worn at once. Beginning about 1850, straw braids were sometimes sewn at the hems of both dresses and petticoats, and, concurrently, heavy quilted or corded underpetticoats were used to give fullness. Later the upper petticoat was made of many yards of starched cambric with several flounces: "The embroidered petticoat is replaced by the flounced petticoat; in the hem is placed a straw plait two inches in width, which is indispensable to prevent the skirt, so full at the top with the modern hoop, from falling in around the ankles" (*Godey's*, October 1855). Other materials, mainly horsehair (crinoline), were used to stiffen the petticoat hems, and sometimes entire petticoats were made of horsehair. In August 1855 *Godey's* remarked that "Skirts are made very full. Fashion exacts an immense use of crinoline. . . . Underskirts are arranged so as to meet the exactions of the modern hoop." *Graham's* also discussed "cage crinolines," which were "not confined to the extreme fashionables—not even to the city—but they enter the village church, and make their way in through the farmhouse door. The plainest ladies, with but the slightest pretension to fashion, have given up their prejudices against them and adopted them" (August 1856).

It is reasonable to suppose that, in order to reach such common acceptance, the hoop must have been worn in this country for at least a couple of years by 1855. Evidence is scant for earlier years, but by about 1857 there were many advertisements for "spring skirts," or petticoats with steel hoops. For example, "Douglas & Sherwoods Patent Adjustable Bustle and Skirt" was illustrated in *Godey's* in January 1858 as a very short arrangement of hoops that fastened at the waist and extended out all around the body in order to support the basque bodice flounce and the top of the skirt; a full lower skirt of cambric, having steel springs, was detachable; the two pieces buttoned together all around and laced at front. Similar things were available about this time in drygoods stores for about $2.00.

The shape engendered by the 1850s hoop—equal fullness all around the figure—was certainly important in merchandising women's garments. *Godey's* suggested that, as seen in one shop at least, the shawl could be draped over a dressmaker's figure with a full crinoline to give the most fashionable effect:

> [At] Mr. Brodies' establishment . . . there are always in attendance from six to eight well-bred, well-dressed young ladies, whose business it is not only to show the mantle but to try it, that the purchaser may see its general effect, either on her own shoulders, or those of the revolving combination of wire, pasteboard, crinoline, and pink cambric flounces, known as a lay figure, or "shape." The attendants adhere to black as a color in their own dress, and silk is usually the material; crinoline and flounces to discretion . . . (September 1857)

Insight into just how early the hoop was accepted in other areas and circumstances can be found in personal diaries. One diary entry made on the California Trail on June 19, 1857, is particularly pointed: "There is a bride & groom in the Inmann party. The bride wears hoops. We have read of hoops being worn, but they had not reached Kansas before we left so these are the first we've seen and would not recommend them for this mode of travelling. The wearer has less personal privacy than the Pawnee Indian in his blanket. In asides the bride is called 'Miss Hoopy'" (Myers 111). The hoop skirt was heralded by doctors and others as a health benefit, in that it removed the great, oppressive weight of the many heavy petticoats that rested on the lower abdomen. Suddenly a woman was able to go to a light, open underskirt with one petticoat over it and still maintain the fashionable silhouette.

The corset, as mentioned earlier, changed in shape in the early fifties, from the long boardlike construction that obliterated the bosom (and caused such a furor among doctors) to a shorter, more flaring form that allowed the bosom to fill out and spread and relieved pressure from the lower trunk. This change did not become general until at least 1853, when it was described in *Godey's* December magazine: "The waists are worn of moderate length, sloping out at the bottom and giving the chest full play. Nothing is more decidedly unfashionable than a waist reduced to a straight line and drawn in across the breast. Stiff whalebones give it this appearance." And in January 1855 *Godey's* reported that "Corsets are cut much shorter, no longer compressing the hip." By this time dress waistlines had risen to the natural waist and skirt fullness was released directly at the waistline, so the longer corsets were not required.

Under the shorter corset, the chemise, often nicknamed the "shimmie" by women sewing them at home, was still worn to about knee length. A chemise was most often of white cambric but sometimes, for best dress, was of linen. The neckline of the current style of chemise was wide and open, usually finished with a more or less plain band and an edging of whitework. The cap sleeves extended on the shoulders to about the armscye, which was fairly low on the arm. Sleeve edges were finished to match necklines. A wardrobe of chemises was required, as one needed to keep them washed and fresh in order to protect the corset from body oils. By mid-decade the amount of whitework embroidery and lace trim on the chemise was keeping pace with the style of the petticoat, which became much more elaborate before the end of the decade. "There are new styles of bodies, which serve at the same time as chemisettes and under-bodies; the fronts are of Valenciennes insertions and English embroideries" (*Godey's,* October 1855). A more fitted version of the chemise, about hip length, was introduced about mid-decade, though its use was probably not very general.

As in the 1840s, in the first years of the decade pantalettes were discarded upon reaching womanhood, or about age fourteen or fifteen, when most girls left school and some went to work. When the large hoop was generally accepted, however, it again occasioned the use of underdrawers, both for warmth and for decency. Drawers became, from the midfifties, an important part of the "set" of underclothing made or ordered for the hope chest and were a part of every woman's wardrobe.

ACCESSORIES

Collars in the 1850s were of whitework, lace, and sometimes even of crochet or tatting. The most typical shape was much wider than formerly, reflecting the decade's new, more open neckline. In April 1850 *Peterson's* was already announcing that "Collars are to be larger than heretofore." Collars of approximately three and a half inches wide, or even wider, were commonly seen, and these were worn differently than were the small collars of the forties, lying out flat on the shoulders and often not meeting at all at the throat. But a large collar cannot be the determining factor in dating an 1850s photograph, for, as *Godey's* reminded readers, "although large collars are the fashion, it must not be supposed that small ones are altogether laid aside. They are still worn with cloth and merino dresses, and for the street, as large ones do not set well over cloaks and mantillas. Plain linen collars and undersleeves are still worn for the street, and travelling, and for the morning" (January 1854). The large, flat collar was not the only form in fashion. Introduced late in the forties, the Jenny Lind style, a standing band with lace edging and frills, was still popular. The standing band was also made with small collars attached and was particularly popular on the chemisette.

Neck ribbons retained their popularity into the fifties as well, worn with or without a brooch at the knot. "Neck ribbons are a distinguishing peculiarity of this season. They are worn of very bright colors, usually embroidered, and tied close to the throat. The square flat knot, usually called the 'sailor's tie' is most fashionable. Three-quarters of a yard only is needed for this; otherwise, the ends would be too long" (*Godey's,* January 1852). Ribbon bows even served as multipurpose decorations at one point, "for the hair, for the waist, brettelles, bracelets for dresses, even for lingerie" (*Godey's,* February 1856).

The chemisette, well on its way to popularity before this date, is discussed in *Godey's* in April 1850: "The various titles of 'chemisette,' 'spencer,' and 'underhandkerchief,' are applied to this very pretty article of feminine attire, which was never more worn than at the present day." With a sleeveless fancy front and a plain back of good white cotton and a collar attached, the chemisette reached to the waist, where it fastened under the dress with ties. This neat arrangement allowed increasingly lower-cut bodice fronts in the 1850s, in various styles, appearing like a white shirtwaist beneath them. All of the varying collar styles were used on the chemisette form.

Undersleeves were increasingly used during the 1850s because of the popular open sleeves of dresses, which were worn somewhat short on the arm. Falling, open sleeves were at this time considered to be patterned after those of Chinese dress: *Peterson's,* in December 1850, advised that "For demi-toilette, undersleeves of lace are worn, open at the ends, so as to hang in the Chinese style." The undersleeve, or "engageante," is identified more with the 1850s than with any other decade. Mostly closed by a cuff at the wrist, undersleeves became very large and full and were at times elaborately embroidered and cut out and/or edged in frilled whitework or lace (Valenciennes lace was highly popular). Some undersleeves were gathered into several puffs on the lower arm. All were either tacked in place inside the sleeve with needle and thread or held by elastic bands above the elbow. *Peterson's* December 1850 told readers that "Thin under-sleeves are gradually disappearing in outdoor dress as the chilly weather advances. For walking-dress many ladies now wear close undersleeves of the same material as the dress." Undergarments and undersleeves were commonly made at home, and in March 1854 *Godey's* announced that "Madame Demorest has patterns for everything for a lady's under wardrobe, in sets or singly . . . can be sent by mail."

Some guidance is found in the magazines for the wearing of jewelry as well:

> Ear rings have pendants no longer. The last style is a little flat button, about the size of a half dime, ornamented with precious stones. (*Godey's,* January 1852)

. . .

Ear-rings of the drop form, which have been so long out of fashion, are now beginning to reappear. (*Godey's,* September 1856)

Now that dresses are cut away from the throat more than for many years past, necklaces are once more in vogue. Hair necklaces are once more in vogue. Hair necklaces are made in transparent globules or beads . . . a narrow black ribbon band which always enhances the purity of a white throat and neck. . . . Hair bracelets of every description are still worn. (*Godey's,* December 1855)

A popular fad of midcentury was to use some of one's own long hair to have a watch chain made for a male friend or husband or to send away one's own or a friend's hair to have sentimental jewelry made. This gave rise to an entire industry, which later even provided the hair. The following notice in *Godey's* in July 1856 indicates the variety of forms of hair jewelry available in the fifties, and their prices:

Hair ornaments—Ladies wishing hair made into bracelets, pins . . . necklaces, or ear-rings, can be accommodated by our Fashion Editor:

Breast-pins————from $4 to $12
Ear-rings————from $4.50 to $10
Bracelets————from $3 to $15
Rings————from $1.50 to $3
Necklaces————from $6 to $15
Fob-chains————from $6 to $12

The one accessory most indispensable to ladies when walking or riding was the parasol, which early in the decade was of small size and distinctive form. According to *Godey's,* "the most tasteful are without fringe or embroidery and with a joint in the handle for the convenience of packing. White or cream-colored parasols are unfit, except for an open carriage. Dark green or blue will be found the most serviceable colors, and plain mother of pearl mountings are in the best taste" (June 1850).

HEADGEAR

The daycap is so rarely seen in the photograph of the fifties that it must be considered not to have been in fashion, at least for streetwear. Patterns for and drawings of caps appear in the ladies' magazines as proper for homewear, with similar but differently decorated styles suggested for invalids and elderly ladies or as breakfast or dinner caps at home. In a very few portraits older women wear caps, sometimes still of the close 1840s shape. The ones shown in the fashion sketches were quite different: long, rather wide lappets were made to fall sheer at either side of the face, often edged with frilled Valenciennes lace, and hanging free. The cap and lappets, in fine lawn, were usually exquisitely embroidered in whitework. A puffed crown enclosed the hair, and a short curtain shielded the neck. It is assumed that such elaborate caps were "at home" wear for older women or invalids.

The bonnet, still the only proper headgear for ladies, at least in town, was wide and roundly open in the fifties, curving under the chin and falling back quite far on the head by 1853. After this date the shape was moderated somewhat, though the underbrim was still plentifully decorated:

[Bonnets are] not now suspended at the back of the hair, as they frequently were a little while ago.... Groups of wheat ears, poppies, and grass are placed at each side ... a great deal of blonde [a type of fine lace] is worn ... the two sides should by no means correspond. If a flower is placed in the blonde on one side, a knot of velvet ribbon will be seen on the other; and one will be placed on the temple, while the other is low down on the cheek. Roses and black velvet are the most common. (*Godey's,* January 1854)

In the fashion plates of 1854, however, bonnet shapes still were shown to be set back and very shallow with exaggerated "chin hooks" to frame the frills of blonde lace around the face. In August 1856, *Godey's* fashion editor expressed disgust with the bonnet fashions, claiming that she saw "a woman ... as far out of her bonnet as a snail can come out of her shell" and going on to say that such a careless attitude about covering the head could only lead to "tic-doloreux, earache, headache ..." In the January 1855 *Godey's* "Chit-Chat Upon New York and Philadelphia Fashions" described an enduring winter bonnet fashion from the last decade: "The beaver bonnetts [*sic*] ... are still worn more or less, and are particularly suited for country wear or travelling ... for what is called 'a second bonnet' though they are too heavy for full visiting or carriage dress. The favorite colors are deep brown and fawn; the usual trimming rosettes, bands, and capes of velvet or satin, approaching the same shade."

In the spring of 1856, a round, nearly flat straw hat, called the "Pamela," is shown in *Godey's* as "a new style of bonnets" but with little accompanying commentary. It is pictured as a wide-brimmed, shallow-crowned hat shape with about a two-inch frill of blonde lace hanging from the brim all around, a feather laid horizontally to one side, and wide ribbon strings. Two years later the subject of these hats comes up again, and the fashion editor deems it worthy of comment: "We are frequently asked ... whether the round hats ... are 'really fashionable'.... they are known under the general name of the Pamela. ... It will never be generally adopted in our large cities by anyone out of the schoolroom, though suitable at all times and in all places to children and [at an unnamed resort] ... they were worn by every lady from the Princess down" (*Godey's,* April 1858).

Footwear

Except in small details, women's shoes differed little in the first few years of the decade from those of the last. Gaiters were still popular, "worn with or without the patent leather tips, as suits the wearer. They should always be the same color, or in harmony with the usual walking-dress. Nothing is more decidedly ungenteel than a dark silk and light gaiters" (*Godey's,* October 1851). And a marvelous improvement in gaiters came about in the early fifties: "lacing may not be, for some, as convenient as when they are simply confined by elastic gores, as rapidly gaining in popularity as they are new in style, and comfortable" (*Godey's,* October 1854).

A slight heel was typical of most shoes of the decade. An attempt was made in 1853 to introduce a one-inch heel for the gaiter, eliciting a reaction from Mrs. Merrifield in her March "Dress—As a Fine Art" column in *Godey's:* "what shall we say to the high heel which was once so popular, and which threatens again to come into fashion? It is to be hoped . . . that this pernicious custom will not make progress." Obviously, inch-high heels had been introduced before this date, so heel height is not a good dating tool. By 1855 both gaiters and shoes had small heels, some wide and some slightly tapered.

Women's shoes of this period were made on an extremely straight, narrow last with rather narrow, squared toes—not at all in the shape of a normal foot. Mrs. Merrifield wrote, "We object in toto to the shape of the shoe, which bears little resemblance to that of the foot. We have heard a person say that they could never see any beauty in a foot. No wonder, when they saw none but those that were deformed by corns and 'bunions'" (*Godey's,* September 1853).

WRAPS

More ink was used in 1850s fashion reports in describing the numerous popular kinds of wraps than for any other single purpose, and the shawl seems to have predominated. In a very long discussion of wraps at the beginning of the decade, there is evidence that shawls were available in an immense variety from India, France, England, Scotland, and many other countries:

> And now for shawls, cloaks, and mantillas, of which there is an endless host to choose from. Cashmere and India shawls will, of course, always be worn by those who can afford the enormous prices; though their imitations are so excellent as scarcely to be detected. For ourselves, we prefer the Parisian shawls, the fabric being softer, and the patterns, bouquets, and wreaths of flowers much more graceful than the ever-lasting palm. But then they have not the prestige of the real India.
>
> . . . Blanket, or tartan shawls are quite as much in favor as ever. . . . A woolen shawl of this description is indispensable to the toilette of every lady; . . . The two favorite styles are the large, broad, bright-colored tartans, worn when they first came in more than twenty years ago, as purple, black, green, and white, blue and orange, green and crimson, etc. Another style all in one color, except a narrow border

has a crimson centre, with a little white to relieve it; stone color, with a bar of orange, blue with the same, green with a stripe of crimson, etc. etc. (*Godey's*, November 1850)

A fashion point is made in another, later *Godey's* article, entitled "Nice Questions in Dress": "If a lady sports a shawl at all, and none but very falling shoulders should venture, we should recommend it to be always falling off or putting on, which produces pretty action, or she should wear it up one shoulder and down the other, or in some way drawn irregularly, so as to break the uniformity" (November 1852). And the magazine also provided good direction in choosing correct shawl types: "The square berage [*sic*] shawls are in great variety. Those of plain white are well adapted to the toilet of a middle-aged matron, and combine cheapness with utility, coming at three dollars.... These have fringe . . . gossamer berages [*sic*] . . . . These range as high as twenty dollars" (June 1852).

The sheer kinds of shawls, including the wool gossamers and barèges, were for summer and competed with mantillas of lace and sheer muslin lined with colored silk for favor. Mantillas were favored over shawls for "very young ladies." In the November 1853 "Chit-Chat Upon Philadelphia and New York Fashions" *Godey's* imparted vital information concerning wraps for the season:

> In this intermediate month between mantillas and cloaks, shawls are worn perhaps more than any other outside wrapping. . . . The prices range the present season from $4 to $8 for the cashmeres, and $6 to $12, or $14, for long plaids, best qualities. Next in expense among the standards are the brochés, of new and delicate styles and shades, costing from $10 to $20. . . . the Indian, or real cashmeres, are of course to be found, but we know very few of our readers care to invest eighty or several hundred dollars in a single article of dress.

Fashions in cloaks and sacques during this decade were distinctive from earlier styles mainly in the sleeves, where the open style predominated, as it did in dresses. The skirts of fitted wraps were also much more flared, and the half-long unfitted wraps were fuller in order to fit over the hoop shape. Full-length wraps were not shown, no doubt because of the difficulty of fitting them over the hoop. The same number of exotic names were given to the various wrap styles as in the past decade, with the same imprecision.

Fashions for Men

The narrow sleeves and trousers of the past decade were worn well into the fifties; the wider, looser fashions were introduced mostly in 1854. Later in the decade, it appears from photographs that the older-style clothing was relegated to work dress, though such conservative styles were still offered for sale. Men seem to have been willing to sit for the photographer at times in a "come-as-you-are" condition, often appearing to have stopped in direct from the day's work, and are thus seen in more well-worn, wrinkled, and older-looking clothing than are women. A looser, more generous cut was available in coats before 1854, in sacks, frocks, and every other style. The sleeves in particular became broader and were attached to a higher armscye than in the forties. Lapels were also much wider, and there was less rise in the collar at the back of the neck.

Vests tended to be double breasted in the fifties and often had notched collars, though shawl collars are evident in photographs as well. Most vest fronts fell well over the waistbands of the trousers. Elaborately woven, patterned silks, sometimes in glowing colors, were used for dress vests, but most daytime vests were still of black wool and matched the coats. For summer, white or tan cotton vests were worn; some were single breasted in the interest of coolness. Checked vests were a peculiarity of the late fifties and were frequently worn with checked trousers, the checks not always matching in scale; and sometimes the vest collar had a check of still another size.

While narrower styles are shown in early-fifties plates, typically trousers were made with rather wide tubular legs and no creases and were long enough to "break" over the toes. All trousers were made with the fly-front. Plaids, checks, and lighter-colored trousers were popular with the "natty" dressers by mid-decade, though black is still predominant in the photographs. Wool was used year-round, and cotton or linen was worn for summer; many combination weaves of wool-cotton, cotton-linen, and wool-cotton-linen were found in summer suits, work pants, and vests.

Ordinary shirts for daytime wear with suits were mostly white, but they were also advertised in stripes, checks, small prints, and colors. Shirts were made either with collars or with buttonholed bands for attaching separate white collars, and starched collars and cuffs were manufactured to wear with them. In this decade, men's shirt collars, which were of moderate size and did not rise high on the neck, were turned down over the necktie. Dress shirts were made with pleated, stiffly starched bib fronts, and separate fancy shirtfronts of this type could be purchased.

The loose shirt, made on the lines of the smock in either wool or cotton, was still universal for workers. Some had simple slash-and-placket necklines, and others had plain bands, though some are illustrated with attached soft collars. This kind of loose shirt, worn tucked in, sometimes under a vest, was not intended to be worn over other clothing like a smock.

As before, the smock, a longer garment made in much the same manner, though usually of heavier material, was worn by some working men over ordinary daytime clothing for protection as well as warmth. Smocks seen in photographs are often long enough to cover the knees, and it is sometimes possible to determine that shirts and neckties are worn underneath. Nineteenth-century New England farmers wore white cotton or unbleached linen smocks even into the late eighties, according to an 1880s newspaper story that mentioned an old farmer who still wore one, although he was thought to be the last. The examples found in the photographs are of plain wool or tweed and appear to have been made at home.

Neckwear

The necktie fashion most seen in early-fifties photographs is a daytime style: a two-inch-wide silk tie of rather stiff appearance horizontally tied in a flat half-bow with the ends extending boldly to one side. Many appear to be black, but some are checked. This kind of tie was possibly achieved by folding a silk square in from two corners diagonally to form a thick scarf. After about 1857 this style becamed narrower and more horizontal in shape. Softer silk tie styles are also seen in photographs, as are narrow black ties.

Headgear

Hats were in more variety than ever in the fifties, with a very tall, straight-sided, soft, cream-colored felt particularly popular in the early years of the decade. The "wide-awake"—a black hat with a broad, stiff, horizontal brim and a tall, malleable crown—was extremely popular throughout the decade and is seen especially in photographs from the Western states. Young men and boys wore sea caps, apparently of dark wool with leather bills, with casual attire, and cloth caps similar to railroad caps became popular for everyday about this time. Soft felt hats of every shape were popular among working men. Businessmen often wore the stiff felt bowler hat, which was fairly deep in the crown, though the top hat was more usual and was still *de rigeur* for dress.

Hairstyles

Judging from the photographs, most men were clean shaven in the early fifties, but by the end of the decade many full beards are seen. Mid-decade, a fringe around the cheeks and jawline, with sometimes a devilish little beard just under the lower lip, seems to have been popular with well-dressed young men. A distinctive hairstyle is seen on young men and boys in photographs taken in the early fifties; the hair, well oiled with macassar oil, is worn quite long on top so that it may be sectioned and combed into a high wave at the center of the forehead. We have one exceptional photograph that shows how this was done. The height of the top-knot wave subsided after mid-decade, and the hair was more simply parted at one side and waved back from the face. Throughout the decade the back hair was about collar length. Side hair covered the ears by about 1857.

Children's Styles

Babies were extremely well dressed in the 1850s. Their garments had become more elaborate in style, and they were usually much longer. The skirts were often nearly half covered with whitework embroidery in some fancy layettes. Though not the norm, it was possible to pay an exorbitant amount for a layette of handmade and embroidered things: "Genin's Bazaar . . . one order 'for a western city' totalled $843 for a new baby s layette, cradle, and basket . . . the amount employed many hands . . . for weeks, that past hard winter, when it was the duty of those who could do so honestly to spend, not spare" (*Godey's,* February 1858).

From birth to about six to nine months, boys and girls were still dressed alike in long dresses, about a yard in length usually, though fancy christening gowns are shown in the magazines at nearly twice that length. At six to nine months children were put into short dresses so that they could move more freely and learn to walk. Both boys and girls wore "trowsers" of cotton beneath the short dresses from about age three; the boys' trousers were sometimes of dark cotton or checked gingham, but the girls' were generally white.

In a September 1850 article, *Godey's* told mothers that it was healthful to put little children in dresses "with a very short skirt. Dresses, and small sacque[s] of woolen plaids, dark green or blue, are most suitable for street dress for the little fellows." The magazine also praised these sacques as children's wear:

> All mothers have reason to bless the invention, or rather the revival, of sacques—for the prettiest, and at the same time most comfortable and convenient summer dress . . . for boys from two years old to five, is a loose sacque, girt, by a belt, over white linen jean drawers or 'pantaloons'. . . . We prefer the sack buttoning on the shoulder, with short sleeves, and rather full in the skirt, reaching above the knee. . . . The drawers are short, coming a little below the knee, and not very wide. (February 1854)

The sacque could be belted, but its shape was always full from the shoulder with no waistline seam and closed in the back, like a dress. A similar-looking style to the sacque, at least from a frontal view, was the pinafore, which was also worn by both boys and girls. "Pinafores are, of course, indispensable . . . they are made very much in sacque fashion at present . . . many belt the pinafores over the drawers and waist . . . without anything else beneath, in warm weather" (*Godey's,* February 1854). The pinafore differed from the sacque chiefly in that it was open, or at least partly open, down the back, fastening only at the neck. Both garments had a variety of sleeve styles, from cap to midarm to full length. Girls' aprons were also called "pinafores": "Little girls have crossbarred muslin, fine birdseye and Marseilles aprons of many different patterns . . . for winter, a plain waist, with a short, full skirt set on with a cord or belt of insertion, is the warmest and most serviceable. The shoulders have a slope from one to three inches long . . . and the sleeves, if long, are moderately wide, and finished by a hem and edge, or gathered into a band" (*Godey's,* December 1856).

The fabrics used for little children were printed with tiny patterns in many colors: "There is the usual variety of small patterns for children, with dots, stars, triangles, &c, on a plain ground, in pink, brown, blue, &c." (*Godey's,* May 1858). Fabrics remaining in collections show tiny toys printed on dark grounds. Tops, hoops, toy boats, balls, bats, and hobby horses, for example, seem boyish in intent; small prints in softer colors, featuring tiny stars, comets, shuttlecocks, and so on, are probably more feminine.

Both girls and boys wore wide-brimmed straw hats from a very young age, the girls' tied with wide ribbons and the boys' held with narrower plain tapes or ribbons. After about age six, boys no longer wore this style but instead went into the many kinds of caps that had been popular for many years, with the addition of a new type, the pilot's cap, which was very deep crowned and crisp and had a leather band and bill. Boys and girls alike wore straw sailor hats, a moderately wide-brimmed style with a ribbon band tied to leave long ends in back.

By 1858 the flat straw hat was popular "for little girls from eight to twelve and fourteen. . . . the Pamela flats, or to designate them by their new title, 'Equestrienne,' will be most universal" (*Godey's,* June 1858). The bonnet was a style reserved for women, and only after about age sixteen would a young girl assume such a grown-up style—that is, after she began to wear full-length dresses and had assumed the corset and hairstyles of fashion.

At about age ten to fourteen, boys began wearing long trousers and tunics or jackets. "Costume for a boy of 12: pale buff trousers of light summer cloth, tunic of plaid poplin, a deep purple shade, 'Wide Awake' hat. . . . Many prefer the cloth roundabout closed to the throat, once more in fashion, for lads from 10 to 14. They are usually in blue, green, or brown, with brass buttons" (*Godey's,* July 1855). Both the tunic and the roundabout echoed feminine garments in cut. As in the last decade, boys until about age twelve or thirteen wore upper garments more in the style of women's dress than men's; after the age of fourteen, their clothing became much more "manly," often small replicas of adult suits and hats.

Many of the little girls' cotton dresses in the photographs have fullness either gathered directly into a wide, shallow neckline or a high yoke and have very short flared sleeves, sometimes pulled up at the center with a cord tied in a bow on the shoulder. These dresses appear to be of cotton, mostly in gingham checks, and most have set-in waistbands. An alternate style, more dressy and of silk, had a longish fitted waist with a slight rounded dip at waistfront and a shallow, plain neckline that bares the shoulders. The sleeves of these dressy styles were either short and fitted with frilled edges, flared and fringed, or short and puffed into a band. The fabric used for these dressy styles seems to have been either plaid or plain, dark-colored silk.

Girls from about eight to twelve years wore shortened modifications of women's dress styles, most often with short sleeves, though the long, narrow bias sleeve was still used in winter dresses. Dressy costumes were of plaid or striped silk in patterns like those for older women. Most waistlines were at the normal waist, even longer in the early years of the decade, and many had set-in waistbands. Their skirts were supported by the same fullness of starched petticoats and crinolines as women's, though shorter. White collars were not usually worn by girls until their dresses became full length, at about age fourteen.

Many references are found to the wearing of pantalettes: "Cambric pantalettes are worn rather narrow, and never to come below the top of the boot. In most cases, there is quite a space between the gaiter and the edge of the pantalette" (*Godey's,* July 1855). It goes without saying that the leg was covered fully with a stocking, still in this decade most frequently white, though horizontally striped colored hose were popular for children, at least for everyday.

Summary

An American norm in dress continued through the 1850s. People in all portions of the country as reflected in the photographs dressed similarly and well, even allowing for the slow acceptance of the hoop at all levels. It was increasingly true in the fifties that Americans of all but the most impoverished classes were notable for their uniform ability to dress within the norm and to make a good appearance.

The greatest difference between the costume of the past decade and the fifties was in women's styles. The blossoming of huge skirt supports, widened sleeves, and flowing wraps was rapid and continued through to the end of the decade. The hoop fashion was taken up by working-class women much more rapidly than some would have liked, especially the well-to-do trend setters and some moral reformers, who would have preferred to consider such an expensive and elaborate style the prerogative of the rich. It is safe to assume, nevertheless, that the style was well established for dress by 1856. Women's fashions, while at their height much more ornate in the fifties, were easily approximated in simple interpretations and inexpensive fabrics, which accounted for the similarity in general appearance of everyday dress for women of all classes.

Men's clothing can also be dated to the fifties by silhouette alone: large hats and jaunty, one-sided, horizontally extending neckties, and, after 1854, oversized coats and trousers. Bold patterns in coats, jackets, and even trousers were popular in casual dress for both men and boys. By mid-decade, men of all classes wore similar styles. Even though individual tastes and circumstances meant widely differing choices of fabric and color, it is apparent that American men had a uniform appearance at the median level. The key to this lies in the mass production and wide availability of relatively stable styles for men and boys.

PHOTOGRAPHS
1850

❧

6-21-50:   A new Gingham dress at Hawks store 2 shillings a yard.

9-4-50:   Finished little tot's buff dress her first calico.

9-12-50:   I got me a silk apron.

7-27-50:   Cosna called here PM. Made my Bertha Cape.

10-5-50:   My Birthday, 20 years old.

10-10-50:   Mother and I have been quilting me a black skirt [underskirt].

10-16-50:   I weigh 115 lbs. I lost my green veil.

10-17-50:   Bought Sis [her baby daughter] a plaid shawl.

10-18-50:   Mother John and myself had our daguerreotypes taken. Tried to get little Sis but she could
             not sit so long.

—Frances French, Diary

FRANCES ANN "FANNIE" TREFETHAN of North-ampton, Massachusetts, married John Wotton French on July 9, 1849. From a middle-class fam-ily, Fannie was brought up to do her own sew-ing, though she never learned to cook until after her marriage. From January 1850 through De-cember 1852 she recorded in her diary warm, personal observations about her family, child-rearing, and daily activities, especially about making clothes for herself and her daughter.

Because of all we know about its maker and wearer, this garment may be considered repre-sentative of the tastes of a typical woman of the time—a woman whose husband had a moderate income but who sometimes had to do without luxuries and even some necessities to make ends meet.

Fannie's "spotted" dress and matching pelerine cape are almost certainly of her own manufac-ture, as she seems from the records to have made all of her own and her daughter's clothing at this time. On July 29, 1850, in fact, she records work-ing on a "bertha cape," which may be the one worn for this sitting, although this is more usu-ally called a "pelerine." The fabric of this costume has the appearance of a soft wool with woven spots. The pelerine is worn closed at front and is slightly ill fitting where it is shaped over the up-per arms. Bright, striped ribbon ruching trims the pelerine front and edges and also the hems of the short oversleeves. This kind of high contrast in fabric and trim is frequently recommended in fashion magazines during this period, even for day dress.

Trimmings are so frequently missing by the time garments are eventually given to museums that clothes sometimes look very plain and per-haps do not give a true perspective on popular taste. Fanny's copious correspondence enlight-ens us on the subject, however. In a letter to her husband in 1851, she mentioned a "red dress, with orange ribbons" that she wore to a ball.

Fannie's pelerine is in the popular shape of the late forties and early fifties; it fits over the shoulders and is worn closed, the long ends meet-ing at a point below the waist in front. The white collar worn over the pelerine neckline is a Jenny Lind style; it is made of rows of lace edging and insertion set on a band and appears to cross sim-ply in front under the awkwardly pinned cameo. The collar is quite possibly attached to a chemisette, in which case the dress under the pelerine will have a deep neckline to show it off. The modified sleeves are still visibly bias cut, and close at the wrist with a soft band of self-ruch-ing. This sleeve was still shown in early-fifties fashion plates, and the style persisted in working and walking dress for many years.

The hinged and decorated sticks on Fanny's lap make up the folded shaft of one of those small, dainty parasols that could be tilted to screen the face from sunlight. It could have been dark green or blue or made of a changeable taffeta of either of these colors with black. These parasols were featured in fashion commentary throughout the forties and well into the fifties.

Daguerreotype, Spring 1850

Courtesy of the State Historical Society of Wisconsin
(WHi [X3] 43176)

We have seen skirts [infants'] of a yard and a half to two yards in depth . . . but, if we be permitted to suggest, one yard is quite a sufficient length for everyday wear.

—*Godey's*, April 1852

ELIZABETH EVERETT BUTLER (1818–77) and her son, John H. Butler, who was born October 1, 1849, pose on a spring day, most likely in Whitestone, New York, where husband and father John J. Butler was a Free Baptist theologian and teacher from 1842 to 1854.

Elizabeth's short-waisted fan bodice, with its fullness softened into broad gathers and extended over the shoulders, is found in many early-fifties portraits as everyday dress, particularly for women not able to wear the still extremely rigid, long, restricting corsets. This style, worn over a shorter corset, certainly provided more ease and comfort to pregnant women and nursing mothers.

She wears her hair in a generous coronet of braids far back on her head, over the center part, with a comb tucked behind the crown portion. The folded side hair, which covers only the top portion of the ears, is a distinctive feature of the late forties and early fifties.

The baby, from six to seven months of age, is still in a long dress with a wide baby neckline and short sleeves. He wears the close, round cap typical of the forties. Formed around a roundel of handmade lace or whitework, the cap is fashioned close to the head with a small turnback brim and ribbon ties. The plain, light, woolen shawl in which she carries him is essentially no different from those worn by women as wraps. Folded double across the width, leaving both fringed edges together, the shawl covers the baby's dress so that we are unable to tell its length.

DAGUERREOTYPE, 1850–52

Courtesy of the State Historical Society of Wisconsin
(WHi [X3] 35720)

AT AGE SIXTEEN, William B. Noyes of Madison, Wisconsin, dressed in gentleman's attire, complete with silk top hat, and self-consciously posed for this, his first adult, portrait. Both the standing shirt collar, with its geometric, folded-down points, and the high placement of the rather narrow sleeve help to date it early in the decade.

Most noticeable, after the formal hat, are the unmatched checks of his coat and vest, a most fashionable combination; while both of fine checks, approximately the same size, they are of different colors. The soft quality of shading in the wool coat indicates a range of perhaps tan and brown in the checks, with either a brown or black velvet upper collar; the vest may well be black or very dark brown and white. He wears a dressy, frilled shirtfront, over which the broad silk necktie sports the requisite long, horizontal end at one side.

Some [dresses] are again made with revers
like a gentleman's vest, and others with a
perfectly tight, high corsage.
—*Peterson's,* January 1850

MRS. J. R. BRYAN, from somewhere near Richmond, Virginia, sat for this portrait in mourning
dress. Even though the style of the costume is earlier, having been shown in 1846 fashion plates, the
extreme extensions of the loops of hair above the
ears is an early fifties style.

The dress and its pelerine-style cape are of
black wool. Beneath the small cape, the bodice
front shows a simulated vest front, which would
have been attached into the side seams of the bodice with the fronts buttoned over it. Based on the
fashion information for this style, the vest front
almost certainly has lapels. On both sides of the
front button placket are narrow vertical pleats,
which create some fullness just below the bust.
The separate cape is very plain and finished with
a broad self-flounce just slightly gathered under
a double heading of cording.

The dress itself is not a "mourning dress"; it is
merely one style of dress fashionable in its day
and not too out of date in the early fifties. Instead, mourning is indicated in the sheer, black
lace collar. For ordinary dress, only white collars
and cuffs were worn; black collars were reserved
for "first mourning," usually the first year of wid-
owhood. Her bright brooch, however, if she were
to have observed the strictest dictates, means that
the first year of mourning has passed. Since the
dress style is slightly out of date, this portrait gives
the impression of a woman without the resources
to have many changes of costume.

Ambrotype, 1850–52

Courtesy of the Charleston Museum (MK 11)

All jackets for lads are rounded in front, to display the shirt bosom; frills of fluted muslin, or very small square linen cambric collars for the throat, with a necktie of black mantua ribbon, tied in a square or sailor's knot.

—*Godey's,* June 1850

A new style of undersleeves, for dinner, dress, or demi-toilette has just been introduced. These sleeves are open at the ends, like the sleeves of the dress. They may be made of tulle or net, and are trimmed with a double or triple row of rich lace.

—*Peterson's,* June 1850

THIS RELATIVELY well-to-do Charleston family poses for a group portrait dressed in very fashionable day dress. The date is best determined by the woman's dress, especially the flared undersleeves and the large collar that lies flat and does not meet at the front. The extreme extension of the hair loops at the ears is another good indication of the early date.

The dress, of a sheer, dark fabric with striped borders, probably barège, is cut "a disposition" (in flounces made from the border print). The fashionably flared white undersleeves show through the sheer, dark sleeve fabric. The bodice is cut, or turned back, in a very low V to expose the chemisette, which is closed at the throat by a large brooch in the horizontal oval shape very new in the early fifties. The watch is apparently suspended by a wide black ribbon that hangs to one side.

The hair, done in oiled folds, is fastened low on the crown; dark ribbons hang at the back. Her earrings, of the most recent style, are small—"about half a dime"—and are probably set with precious or semiprecious stones.

The oldest boy's military-effect jacket, frilled shirt, huge belt buckle, and linen pants reflect the latest fashion for boys of his age, ten or so. The necktie lies in the asymmetrical horizontal loop of the early fifties, and his hair is combed up into the popular stiff wave. His jacket sleeves are "slashed" over his white shirt and finished with a ladder of braid; the shirt itself has a frill down one side of the front placket.

The younger child, also a boy, wears a white frilled shirt and jacket over a dark tartan-plaid kilt, with a miniature version of the black belt and fancy buckle of the big brother. His hair shows evidence of having been combed to one side and back in imitation of the big brother's hairstyle; a little girl's hair would have been parted in the center, combed down, and cut at ear level.

The gentleman sports a new-style white shirt with a generous turndown collar and starched front, with the full silk bow tie nearly symmetrical. His vest and trousers are black, and his sack coat is of a lighter color, possibly drab, and apparently of linen. The trim Vandyke beard and clipped mustache are somewhat unusual, and the hair does not show the exaggerated top wave so much a fad at this time. The entire effect is of a most conservative gentleman.

THIS PORTRAIT, LABELED "Joseph Sharp of Sharp's Flats," appears to have been taken just before Mr. Sharp went to work in the California gold fields, most likely in a makeshift photographer's booth at a location where miners purchased provisions, possibly near Sacramento or San Francisco. Sharp's Flats does not appear in Goude's *California Gold Camps*. All of his gear is new, as he has just been outfitted, and the gun and his rakish pose are distinctly meant to indicate, however comically, that Mr. Sharp is prepared to defend his territory. The fact that "Sharp's Flats" was named for him probably means that he was about to become an employer of miners, one who mostly managed the operations while Chinese and/or other workers did the rough work. The purpose of this portrait was probably to show family and friends at home that Mr. Sharp was off for the gold fields well equipped and ready.

Besides having the bracket dates for early activity during the gold rush, the way Sharp has tied his necktie helps date this portrait: almost precisely in the year 1850, it seems that every man pulled out one end of the horizontally tied necktie to extend sharply. The resultant asymmetrical tie is seen in nearly all photographs of men in the early fifties.

While humorously posed, this portrait reveals some interesting things about men's everyday clothing at midcentury, things that do not show up in the plentiful fashion plates. The newness of the clothing and equipment is an indication that the photo was taken soon after Mr. Sharp's arrival in California, when he had just purchased his equipment and before he had gone out to do any actual mining. He is clean shaven, and his white shirt and necktie—garments not meant as working dress—are pristine. Even the loose woolen overshirt, so common to the gold fields, is spanking new to match the shiny pick and gold pan.

The outer shirt is of most interest, since no fashion illustrations and few photographs show such a garment in use. Different from the placket-front closures on most dress and work shirts of the fifties, this shirt-style jacket opens completely down the front. Though such shirts were available in contemporary catalogs, it is difficult to differentiate shirt types in clothing advertisements, where, moreover, there is never information included about how these shirts were to be worn.

This unlined, readymade shirt was evidently meant to be worn like a jacket but tucked in at the waist. Mr. Sharp wears it buttoned at the lower front, open at the neck to show his starched shirtfront and tie. A bit of white cuff is visible on one wrist. The cut is definitely oversized, with deep armholes and dropped shoulders, and it has a turndown shirt collar on a band.

In keeping with early fifties style, the fly-front trousers are fairly trim in cut. Unfortunately they are skewed by both his sitting position and the pistol stuck into the leather belt, so the button placket cannot be seen clearly.

The hat is a black wideawake, a style with a broad, stiff brim and a deep crown that could be manipulated at top to suit the wearer. He wears it well back on his head, showing the oiled front of the hair.

Daguerreotype, 1850–53

Courtesy of Matt Isenburg

JAMES PRESLEY BALL, a prominent black daguerreotypist, took this image of a comely young woman and her children at his studio in Cincinnati. Ball's first small studio in that city failed for lack of patronage in 1845; but after many hardships he finally opened a successful studio there in 1849. By 1851 he had established Ball's Daguerreian Gallery of the West, said to have been the finest studio in the city. Located in a three-story building in a prestigious section of town, the gallery had four photography rooms and a grand antechamber, all richly decorated. Ball became one of Cincinnati's most respected businessmen, and his clients included P. T. Barnum, Jenny Lind, and many other famous visitors to the city. He and his descendants remained in the profession well into the 1870s.

This young mother is modestly, but very well, dressed in black alpaca, a material frequently used for common day dress and one also considered "appropriate" for women working in dress or sewing shops or as governesses, nurses, or ladies' maids. The style is correct for the first years of the 1850s, as it is still based on the long, busked corset of the past decade. It was not until 1853 that the shorter, more curvaceous corset came into use, causing a change in the cut of dress bodices. The frontal fullness of this bodice lies in long, unpressed pleats simply taken into the neckline at top and tapered slightly toward center down the long, flat front. The skirt is gathered very full and supported only with petticoats, as the hoop world not be introduced until about 1853.

The older boy wears the gingham-checked long sleeved frock worn by all children, with the addition of a nice frilled white collar, over wide-legged, rather short dark trousers and sturdy boots. His hair is done in a topknot with wide hair at the ears, a clear indication of an early-fifties style. The younger boy wears a dress, as he is probably only about a year old. Of a sturdy cotton or wool, it is short sleeved and has frontal bodice pleats extending down to a long waistline, a cut similar to his mother's dress and another indication of the early-fifties date. White stockings, like his brother's, and shiny black boots complete his costume. His hair is parted at the side, as though a topknot had been attempted. (A little girl's hair would have had a center part.)

DAGUERREOTYPE, 1850–53

Courtesy of the International Museum of Photography,
George Eastman House (69.201.20)

IN A PROPER corset and faultless, white linens, this unknown black woman sits for her portrait (probably somewhere in New England). While this woman may have been a house slave somewhere in the South, it is more probable that she is a Northern black woman and thus free, though possibly still a servant.

The dating of this photograph is based on the hairstyle, which is later than the dress style. The dress is not well fitted, apparently having been altered and taken in through the body; it was probably made in 1849 for a larger woman and then handed down to the sitter. The reconstruction of such a body-fitted garment presents problems that even a good dressmaker might find difficult without taking the bodice completely apart. This bodice, however, has been left whole with simply the midsection, front and back, taken in, leaving the fronts off center at the bottom of the bodice. The off-center band of puffing down the front is itself uneven, and the bodice darts lie at odd angles to it. The shoulders and upper bodice were not altered and do not lie smoothly over the top of the body.

This dress, a very good one, is constructed of a finely woven wool, as if for Northern winters. The style of sleeve, with its flared epaulettes and the short, widened bell, is typical of the end of the forties. Under the sleeves, which are finished with puffed matching silk bands, may be seen very full, flared, sheer muslin undersleeves, trimmed with a double row of lace. Sheer white silk ribbons are tied in bows at the wrists and fastened with matching brooches. A fine white-work collar is closed at the neckline with a squared brooch. Her watch, hanging from a cord watch string with a small slide, disappears into its pocket in the skirt.

The triple gauging of the skirt top, visible here, is contoured at front to follow the long-waisted, but softened, dip of the boned bodice. Most skirts are fastened to the bodice with the gauging concealed beneath the overhang; an unusual depth of gauging is seen here.

The dress's construction and quality is still evident and points to the original wearer's sense of style. Yet this garment has more importance as a hand-me-down; it emphasizes not only "making do" but also the universal interest in fashion. It therefore serves as an excellent example of working-class dress.

This portrait was taken in Charleston, South Carolina, early in the decade, when the asymmetrical necktie and this distinctive hairstyle were most popular. Coat, trousers, shirt, and tie are almost certainly readymades. Charleston retailers dealt directly with Philadelphia and New York manufacturers at least twice yearly, thus keeping current with the latest styles in men's and boys' clothing.

This boy is quite formally dressed in his double-breasted, dark (probably blue) wool roundabout with its velvet collar and covered buttons. His long-sleeved shirt extends from the coat sleeves the correct distance; his collar is crisp and well turned; and his large horizontal bow tie, with its pin-checks matching those of the fly-front trousers, finish his up-to-the-minute appearance.

DAGUERREOTYPE, 1850–55

Courtesy of the California State Library (neg. 6996)

THIS OUTDOOR DAGUERREOTYPE shows Ford's Hotel and Bar in Placer County, California, a focus of much gold rush activity. The photo is dated early in the fifties by the narrow cut of the sack coats and trousers.

These men, like common men in any town in the country, are almost certainly wearing ready-made clothing. The gentleman on the far side of the seat wears a linen sack over his black vest; linen sacks were advertised as the cheapest alternative in men's coats in the fifties and were the logical choice for hot weather. The man standing is also wearing a sack coat, probably of linen as well, but with a matching vest.

According to photographic evidence, normal everyday clothing for men of all stations included white shirts, neckties, vests, pull-on boots, and hats, whether or not the sack or frock coat was worn. Differences in economic status are shown at the turn of this decade mainly in the quality of materials and accessories and in details of grooming.

The man in front wears what was called a "Spanish hat," a light-colored felt hat with a relatively short, flat crown and a wide, stiff brim; definitely a California addition. The other man's plug hat, also of felt, is dished-in and softened in the crown, a shape seen in numerous other photographs. Both men are wearing pull-on short boots under their trousers.

Tintype, 1850–55

Courtesy of the National Museum of American History (C68.12.1)

These two sisters are wearing a common style of everyday summer dress for the early part of the decade. The dresses may be dated to the fifties by the waist-length set-in belts.

The dresses are of a fine gingham check and are cut with full bodices and skirts taken into inset waistbands, at the natural waist, with fine gathers. The neck style is shallow and curved, simply folded over and pleated to a facing. The narrow elbow-length sleeves are set into the piped armscye plain and, in a manner often seen on much earlier baby dresses, are pulled up at the hem with an interior tape. One or two growth tucks on the skirt are usual; these also help to make skirts stand out more prettily.

The girls' hair, somewhat longer than usual, is meant to be worn behind the ears.

Daguerreotype, 1850–59

Courtesy of the National Museum of American History (C75.17.108 D)

Pinafores are, of course, indispensable, whether of birdseye or brown linen. They are made very much in sacque fashion at present, the sleeves being long or short, as the health of the child or the season demands.

—*Godey's*, February 1854

THIS YOUNG CHILD, about two to three years of age, is not identifiable by gender. Below-knee-length cotton or linen "trowsers" with a dark hem binding, worn under a checked, long-sleeved gingham pinafore, cut to flare comfortably under the arms, was common dress for both sexes. This sacquelike garment was open down the back but closed at the neck with buttons or ties. It was worn sometimes over dresses or shirts or alone over trousers that were "slightly full on the hip, opening on each side, trousers fashion, and gathered into a waistband, in turn buttoned on a plain low-necked waist, like the lining of a frock body" (*Godey's*, February 1854).

The garments shown are of everyday type. The dressier alternative for boys called for white linen trousers, a little below the knee, with either a plain hem or a ruffle and a belted version of the sacque-shaped top that was seamed down the back. Little girls wore dresses for best, with simple white pantalettes.

BELLE ALLYN WATSON, about three years old, sits patiently for the photographer in Northampton, Massachusetts. Her "best" dress is made of a light wool, probably of a weave called delaine, and the long, plain waist of the early-fifties style—the only dating point for this portrait—is trimmed with narrow, dark braid. The frock has the horizontal, shoulder-baring neckline and short epaulette sleeves that remained popular for little children for many years. The skirt is thickly pleated into the waist seam so that it is extremely full. The whitework petticoat frill that shows at one side is heavily starched and much more voluminous than it appears.

Belle's chubby legs are encased in white knit stockings, rolled down just below the knees and held by garters, and her gaiters, which fasten with buttons at the outside, are of cloth with leather soles. The pantalettes, which barely show, are knee length and gathered into a band, a new style in the fifties.

This well-dressed little girl wears a string of coral beads and a pair of fine black lace mitts with fingers to the knuckle.

The cloth used by the photographer to drape the prop table is probably printed with colored designs.

DAGUERREOTYPE, 1850–55

Courtesy of Historic Northampton (59.323)

THIS UNIDENTIFIED SITTER is, according to Historic Northampton, almost certainly a resident of Northampton, Massachusetts, or its environs. This is a very important portrait, since it is one of very few surviving images of a man in a work smock. We date this photograph by the man's short side hair and his narrow trouser legs, both typical of the early part of the decade.

The most striking element in this portrait is, of course, the woolen smock, so unfamiliar to American clothing collections. It is visible here in its full length and presents a clear view of many of its construction details. The construction method used in this case is somewhat different from the usual shirt-style smock with its separate sleeves: to make it, a wide length of wool was cut on the fold, in one piece, in a width measured from wrist to wrist with the arms out straight. Sleeves were formed by cutting the piece in a modified T-shape, leaving wide sleeves tapering to the wrists and a straight lower body. A bound slash at the front and a band collar finish the neck, which is fastened with two metal buttons. The sleeves are neatly darted into the band cuffs, which also button. Triangular gussets, placed to reduce strain, show at the side vent and at the top of the shoulder, and diamond-shaped gussets are no doubt used at the underarms for strength, as they are in a smock-shirt made on the same plan. A starched white shirt collar, the edge of a spotted stock, and the back collar of a black coat show above the band collar of the smock, indicating that a smock was a pullover-all garment worn for warmth as well as to protect better clothing.

The smock is not well documented in this country, but it is occasionally found in casual references in contemporary American fiction, especially the "farmer's smock," which, when it is described, seems mostly to have been of homespun. English horse handlers and coachmen are said to have worn the smock.

This gentleman's fancy plush "muffin" hat has a knotted braid band and three small buttons up the front. To find the muffin hat in a photograph is something of a triumph, for while it is spoken of as a favored style of coachmen in England for some years, it is not prominent in fashion information in this country.

The trousers, either of wool or cotton, are still, as mentioned, narrow in the legs in the 1840s style and are of the light-tan color so often worn with black coats and vests.

THE SIGELKOWS, a substantial German farming family from Pomerania, had this group portrait taken on the eve of their departure for Wisconsin in 1851. Given that they certainly wore these clothes after their arrival in Wisconsin and that so many German immigrants did emigrate to the America in the fifties, the Sigelkows as they are seen here are representative of a significant portion of the U.S. population at this time. When the family sat for this photograph (probably a daguerreotype), the brother at upper right was already in America taking care of the homesite in an area east of Madison that they later settled. His image was "burned in" about 1860, and the photograph remade in tintype.

This important photograph demonstrates that similar modifications and treatments of dress and hairstyle were common everywhere the current fashions were known. Such modifications must therefore be interpreted as common-sense applications made by average people in order to adapt extreme styles to daily use. The hairstyles of the women are certainly indistinguishable from those seen in American images: all have the hair looped to show only the tips of the ears and padded to curve out at ear level, and the crown hair, when it shows, is not high. In contrast with a poorer class of peasant immigrants, wearing older or more traditional clothing, the Sigelkow family, of considerable means, would not have been paid special notice for its style of dress upon arrival in this country.

The women all are wearing good, dark dresses for the portrait, rather than the calicoes probably worn for everyday. Their dresses differ only slightly from one another, reflecting the same similarities noted in American photographs.

In the dress at left front, the long narrow sleeves have the slight ease of cut of the late forties, with a fan-front taken into a small, finely pleated V over the round belted waist. This is a version of the short-waisted adaptation often seen in American plates. Her corset does not appear to be the boardlike contraption of the forties but rather a more relaxed type. The neckline is the shallow V, and both neck and sleeves are finished with narrow lace frills. A black velvet ribbon is worn with a brooch around the throat with what appears to be another chain below.

The woman next to her wears a nearly identical dress without a belt, still short waisted but with a slight dip at waistfront, and a gold watch chain.

The young woman at far right wears a more youthful style reminiscent of the late forties, well made and beautifully fitted over the old-style corset with an extreme front point to accentuate the line. The narrow short sleeves extend about halfway to the elbow. The smooth, well-shaped wide neck exposes her shoulders, and she wears a slender necklace.

Both younger girls in the back row exhibit variants of the fan-bodice style that are not readable to any degree but that have the eased, round, early-fifties neckline with lace frill.

The matriarch wears a white cap— indistinguishable from those seen in American portraits—without cap strings. The figured ribbon around her neck is familiar from many American portraits.

The youngest man wears an old-fashioned, conservative suit and necktie of a close-fitting style; the tie is plain and softly drooping at front, not worn in the crisp exaggerated fashion of American dandies but more in the late-forties style. His hair is also plainly combed, without the contrived high frontal wave.

The children's clothing styles are like those seen in photographs of American children, with the possible difference of more variety and economy in the use of odds and ends of mismatched calicoes. The youngest, probably a boy, wears striped ankle-length trousers, a dark gingham checked dress with elbow-length sleeves, and a calico pinafore apron. The girl at center wears a calico dress of the same fabric as the little boy's pinafore, with elbow-length sleeves finished with a self-ruffle, a sleeve finish not seen in any of the American portraits examined but otherwise typical, even in its length. The two children's aprons and dresses are quite possibly made from the older women's discarded dresses.

The young lad at right wears a garment corresponding closely with the loose tunic, or sacque, described so frequently in the ladies' books as worn with either leather or silk elastic belts. Buttons down the shoulders and at side front are a detail noted in American fashion illustrations for boys' tunics. The long trousers are of a dark cotton woven plaid.

AMBROTYPE, CA. 1852

Courtesy of Historic Northampton (59.57)

THIS WELL-GROOMED child of about four is Mary Jane Field of Northampton, Massachusetts. The date of introduction of the ambrotype, 1852, helps date this photograph, but the long, straight bodice of her dress, with the round waistline set below the natural waist, is a recognizable style popular from close to the turn of the decade, one that shortened by mid-decade. Children's styles changed more slowly than adult styles and are difficult to date precisely without outside comparisons, such as a fashionably dressed adult in the same photograph.

Mary Jane's dress is of dark woolen material, possibly red or deep-blue, and is simply constructed. Evident here is the extreme width of the shallow neckline used for children throughout the forties and fifties, especially for dressy occasions, which left the shoulders exposed. The short sleeves are very slightly flared on the upper arm and are trimmed with lighter-colored braid. The plain bodice is finished at the bottom with a row of topstitching about an inch above the seam, where the skirt is thickly cartridge pleated. The skirt has an unusually deep growth-tuck, which also serves the purpose of accentuating the skirt's fullness. A full petticoat, possibly stiffened with cording around the bottom, holds the skirt out nicely. The midcalf length is typical for her age and reveals the narrow, rather long starched cotton or linen drawers of the "trowser" shape. These are simply trimmed with three narrow tucks and a narrow lace edging. The boldly striped stockings of childhood are worn with black shoes, which unfortunately are not fully visible.

Ringlet curls were an alternative hairstyle for little girls at this time, the usual fashion being the blunt below-ear cut.

DAGUERREOTYPE, JULY 11, 1852

*Courtesy of Historic Northampton
(1980.19.8 and 1980.19.7.b)*

. . . am now about ready to put on her short clothes. Now mother I want to
know if you do not think I am a prudent woman. Instead of getting new
dresses for her to creep in and spoil, as she would very soon, I have made
her two dresses out of that blue delaine that you tried to get some like . . .
and they look real pretty. I have plated [*sic*] the waist and trimmed the little
short sleeves with folds and made the skirts very full . . . she was so pleased
to get down on to her feet, she danced and screamed and made all sorts of
noises that ever was heard.

    —Frances Trefethan French to Mary Jane Trefethan Abbott, March 9, 1851

same fabric, but the black coat worn over them has a different, darker appearance. Vest and coat show the many fine horizontal creases of the closely fitted style carried over from the forties. The striped silk stock is possibly of that type made on a wire frame and hooked at the back of the neck, though it may have been a square carefully folded into shape, wrapped from front to back and to the front again, and tied in a small knot.

The distinctive curl and dent of the soft, cream felt hat, with its tall, wide, flat-topped crown, are indicative of a man very conscious of his dapper appearance. These hats were purchased in a straighter, stiffer form and then molded to the taste of the wearer.

Mr. French's hair, worn in a frame around his cheeks and jaw, and with the small dab of beard under the lower lip, are in a classic style of the early fifties. The manner of shaping the hairstyle can be seen in the accompanying photograph, a highly unusual view taken of the back of Mr. French's head: the oiled hair is parted on a diagonal from crown to nape, and both sides and top are combed forward. The hair at the forehead is then combed up and over the forward-brushed top to form a high puff. His bare shoulders and back make a humorous statement, testifying to some camaraderie and friendship between the sitter and the photographer, and probably some spoofing about John French's fashionable locks.

Little Frankie, just over two years old, is dressed in a cotton dress with a set-in waistband, surely made by her mother, as indicated by the quote. The dress, formed with fullness in the bodice and puffed sleeves taken in with soft gathers, has a grow-tuck around the bottom. The wide neckline displays a string of corals, a traditional baptismal gift for a little girl, usually from a godparent. Her hair is cut short, parted in the center, and tucked behind her ears in the common style. Plain, below-knee-length white drawers can just be seen, as well as a bit of white stocking.

John Wotton French took his daughter, little Frankie, to have this double portrait made for his sister, Martha, to carry west to Ohio. The event and the date is recorded in the diary of his wife, Frances.

Mr. French wears the high, starched collar points still frequently seen at this time, standing wide and just under the jawbone. His single-breasted vest, which shows the shirtfront, has the narrow shawl collar of the late forties and early fifties. The vest and trousers appear to be of the

DAGUERREOTYPE, 1852

Courtesy of the California State Library (911)

In bonnets . . . the wide open front, allowing of extremely full under-trimmings, still continues fashionable.

—*Peterson's,* June 1850

THIS OUTDOOR DAGUERREOTYPE is labeled "In Auburn Ravine, 1852." Three gold-miners, two of whom look like brothers, and a woman are seen here at their sluice. The woman may well have been wife or sister to the miners; and according to the histories of the minefields, she probably lived in an adjoining town while the men worked the digs. Auburn Ravine is in Placer County, near Sacramento.

The woman's costume is the most datable. The dress shows the form of the corset worn under it, the rigid early-fifties style, and it is made with the darted front and slight waist dip of the early fifties. The matching notched bertha collar and the sleeve cuffs are trimmed with what appear to be puffs of mourning crape; the dress was probably packed away after a funeral and only just taken out to be worn for the portrait (the creases in the skirt suggest that it had recently been unpacked from a trunk). The dress is a good, recent cut with some ease in the narrow sleeves and a properly full skirt attached with cartridge pleats, which clearly shows the support of the mandatory petticoats. A gold watch chain hangs at the bodice front.

Her bonnet is nearly up to date, of light-colored drawn silk and with a quite wide and open brim with lace frills at the sides of the face and under the brim and a lace veil thrown over the top. Broad silk ribbon strings are tied in a bow with the loops pulled forward under the chin and the ends spread over the bosom. Both bonnet and dress are in excellent taste and perfectly acceptable for 1852, though they are possibly as much as two years old.

The message is clearly that the photograph was a planned event, as no one would suggest that this was everyday attire for a woman in the gold fields. Still, it does prove that such clothing was thought of as proper and ladylike and was brought along to the frontier. Paradoxically, at this time a woman might well have had wash dresses cut in a more current fashion, while still wearing an older good silk dress as "best."

The two older men, who have a distinct family resemblance, are similarly but not identically dressed. The one at the sluice wears (probably) red long-johns under a light-colored readymade shirt with a small collar and rolled-up sleeves. His suspenders, or braces, hold up his woolen pants, and a pair of ragged overall trousers are fastened to buttons on the lower waistband of the pants. The other man wears his shirt and undershirt sleeves rolled up together, and his pants may be Levi's. Both men wear rubber, or rubber-covered, waders that curve up over the knees. Their flat-crowned, wide hats are, like many in the gold fields, light colored for reflecting the California sun. They appear to be of felt.

The younger man, also in a well-worn soft felt hat and waders, wears a dark woolen or cotton flannel shirt, probably either black or red, and a pair of jeans typical of the Levi Strauss pants sold to outfit miners, in that there is an outer pouch pocket (attached but made quite full) on the right side of the fly. These pockets, when seen in wear, always appear to be well weighted and to hang slightly open; without a written reference, it is perhaps guesswork to say that the gold "poke" was carried in these easily protected pockets, and it is more likely that a large kerchief was stuffed in and kept handy for mopping the brow.

Daguerreotype, 1852

Courtesy of the California State Library (913)

This lone black man at a sluice "In Auburn Ravine in 1852" may work for a boss or may possibly have his own claim, though there is nothing in his attire here to indicate either. His faded and worn overalls, flannel shirt, boots, and felt hat are like those of a thousand other miners, except that his pants are bibbed and the braces have been crossed in front to hold the bib close to the chest when shoveling. The narrow shoulder straps are fastened to buttons on the bib corners by elastic cords. The side pocket vents in the overalls are positioned to allow access to trouser pockets underneath, and the pouch pocket on the right front of the pants shows the typical bulge.

Worn leather boots such as these did not give the excellent protection that the waterproofed waders did, but they may have been an economic necessity.

ON THE REVERSE of this portrait, Rosellah M. Smith Donnell Bowman recorded the year, 1852, and that it marked her eighteenth birthday.

Rosellah wears her hair in many very long curls beginning at ear level, and the folds behind the curls indicate that there is also a knot low on the crown. Such a style is not seen in little girls, and only rarely in older women, and seems mostly limited to young ladies from about sixteen to perhaps twenty.

The dress she is wearing is of a brilliant wool challis print. Vivid, rich colors in many shades were used in these prints, creating a lively appearance. The bodice of this example is closely fitted with two boned darts at either side of the plain front over the straight, early corset shape and is gently rounded at a point just below the natural waistline in front. The extremely full skirt is cartridge pleated over a full complement of petticoats. A Jenny Lind collar is surrounded by a wide, pale silk ribbon, fastened with the usual brooch to fan out smartly to either side.

The sleeves are midforearm in length, a style generally worn with white undersleeves but here worn with fine netted silk mitts reaching to the cuff. The fashion of omitting the undersleeves is a summer alternative, mentioned in the late 1840s and probably followed for some years, which bears out the assumption that the fabric of the dress is wool challis, a material often chosen for its coolness in hot weather. Long mitts were worn to dress the lower arms when leaving off the undersleeves.

TINTYPE, 1852–55

*Courtesy of the National Museum of
American History (59.229)*

IN THIS EASY pose we see two young men in working attire. Their hair, worn short above the ears, as well as the one broadly asymmetrical necktie date this photograph in the first half of the decade.

The man on the left wears his shirt collar open and his shirtsleeves rolled up over his red long-johns and has a kerchief knotted around his neck. His striped braces button conspicuously to his trouser band, where a heavy gold watch chain can be seen. He wears a wide-brimmed straw sailor hat.

The other gentleman, while also in his shirt-sleeves, wears a fully buttoned double-breasted, shawl-collared vest, a long-sleeved shirt of printed stripes, a horizontally tied silk necktie, and one of the deep-crowned cloth caps favored for working dress.

IN SPITE OF the lack of fashionable details, this unidentified portrait is datable to the first half of the decade by the narrowness and lack of upper-arm fullness in the bishop sleeve and by the high, almost horizontal loops of hair.

It is obvious that this young woman, possibly still of school age, is wearing an inexpensive cotton calico dress. The unstructured fullness of the dress front indicates that it is an everyday garment and probably homemade. The front is closed with white buttons and worked buttonholes, and one button seems to be missing. The waist treatment is nearly obscured by the slightly loose bodice and the soft folds of the full skirt, but a narrow belt, possibly of chain links, cinches in the natural waistline.

She is wearing very small hoop earrings, and a large, horizontally oval brooch, a favorite of the 1850s, is fastened to a small whitework collar made in points all around. What appears to be a dark hair ribbon hangs from the crown hair in back.

LITTLE FRANCES "FRANKIE" French, born May 6, 1850, is about three years old in this portrait. She wears a dark calico dress printed in one of the intricate puzzlelike patterns so predominant in the 1840s and 1850s, no doubt another of the many little dresses made by her mother. Its long body has a shallow squared neck and very full short puffed sleeves, both trimmed with dainty braid. The colors of these prints frequently include reds and browns, and it is easy to picture the child in those colors. A strand of branch-coral beads shows at the neck.

The drawers are long, tubular, and fairly wide, coming to the shoe top, and are finished with a narrow ruffle of whitework. The high black shoes are barely visible in the shadows.

There are frequent references in the French diaries and letters to the fact that this child was extremely strong willed. When she was one year old her mother wrote, "I have been trying to govern little Frank's disposition but she almost got the upper hands of me." About three months later she wrote, "Sis has had one of her spunky days. Her father has had to whip her and have been obliged to do the same." It is most evident, however, that the parents' lives revolved around their only child and that she was cared for and even indulged.

Sarah Greene Martin, daughter of Morgan L. and Elizabeth Martin, was born in Green Bay, Wisconsin, in 1851. While Morgan Martin was a relatively well-to-do and important citizen and lawyer in Green Bay, Mrs. Martin's personal records reveal struggles with sometimes limited means and describe her many attempts to economize.

The details of Sarah's dress are obscured by the wide, fine tulle scarf that ties her straw hat: it is either attached under the brim on both sides or pulled through slots near the crown. The underbrim of the hat is finished with fine net ruching tacked in place. This photograph helps identify surviving hats of this type as meant for toddlers and very little girls rather than for women, as they might appear.

The cotton dress that shows beneath the scarf is typical of many seen in this decade, with its full skirt gathered to a waistband and grow-tucks near the hem. There do not seem to be long pantalettes, as the chubby, stockinged leg shows to above the knee. It is likely that Sarah wears the knee-length style, which closed with a buttoned band.

DAGUERREOTYPE, 1853–55

*Courtesy of the International Museum of Photography,
George Eastman House (74.193.202)*

THE DAGUERREIAN STUDIO of Southworth and Hawes in Boston, where this image was taken, was noted in the 1840s and 1850s for its artistic experiments with the quality of light in natural settings and for its delicate and unstudied portraits of children.

The chief dating tool in this photograph is the shape of the girl's underdrawers, no longer in the "trowser" shape of the forties but gathered into a band that is buttoned around the calf some inches below the knee. While the tubular pantalette was still worn through the fifties, this cuffed style was not worn before this decade. Its use may have been mostly for very little girls.

The sleeves of the dress are set higher on the arm than earlier and flare at the elbow, a style not seen in forties photographs of children, though popular in ladies' dresses from the midforties. The open sleeve is worn over closed sheer muslin undersleeves trimmed with narrow lace, not much different from those worn by women.

Other indications of an early fifties cut are the yoke and extreme front fullness of the "infant" bodice of the dress; while smocks and aprons had been gathered to yokes at times during the forties, the yokes were much more shallow and the gathers less full.

The bodice fastens in back with buttons and is joined to the full skirt with an inset waistband at the natural waistline. The bias-cut waistband shows slightly above the puppy's head. The small frill of white at the high neck matches the cuff frill. The stockings are plain white; the shoe is black.

Her ear-length straight hair is center parted and is almost too short to stay behind the ears.

. . . for the last few years . . . corsages have been very much made to fasten in front; and the jacket corsage is both a pleasant and an easy mode of dress; but until lately you could scarcely find a dressmaker willing to make ladies' dresses to open in front: and even still it is very difficult to get stays made in that way . . . all low-priced stays (especially those made for the poorer classes, to whom any saving of time should be desirable) are made to lace behind.

—*Godey's,* March 1853

The Patent Adjustable Bustle . . . made either separate or attached to the skirt . . . the whole garment may be compressed into a small bonnet-box, it instantly expands on being released from pressure.

—*Harper's,* December 1857

Nothing looks worse than to see the basque lie light over the skirts.

—*Godey's,* September 1857

THIS PHOTOGRAPH OF Clara Stebbins Lathrop of Northampton can be dated by the curved, shortened corset shape introduced in 1853. Also visible is the kind of bustle and hoop support described above. Her crisply shaped, short-sleeved basque bodice is well supported by the small hip bustle, a contrivance often worn simply with several stiffened petticoats, with or without a hoop. Douglas and Sherwood's "New Matinee Skirt" is advertised in the 1857 *Godey's* (265) as a full-length skirt with springs with the "Adjustable Bustle" at top. Clara could be wearing either type of support.

The dress is of silk and is a summer style. With its short flared sleeves, it is of a dressy fashion and intended for special occasions. The darted and pieced construction is flawlessly fitted over the newer-style corset, which is much more curvaceous and lenient in the bust than formerly. For the student of construction, it is possible in this view to see the extent to which the shoulder seam has been dropped to the back, enhancing the sloped-shoulder look so much in favor. It is safe to say that a skilled seamstress is responsible for this costume.

The trim and accessories indicate some expense. The fluted organdie collar is an especially rare discovery. Its flutes have been "goffered" (shaped over a hot iron with rods), and the collar is longer in back. The sleeve is formed of a narrow band of bias fabric carefully matched to the plaids of the bodice at the piped shoulder seam, to which the ribbon flounce adds just the right length. The dark ribbons with their white garland-trimmed edges are only slightly gathered at the sleeve and basque and are made into flat bows down the front.

Clara is wearing a matched set of jewelry, either of jet or coral, consisting of a large brooch and a fashionable pair of identical bracelets with large central medallions.

Daguerreotype, 1854–56

Courtesy of the Bancroft Library (1905.16242)

THIS PORTRAIT, POSSIBLY taken as a wedding picture, is of Captain and Mrs. Edgar Wakeman. Captain Wakeman was master of the ship *Adelaide,* which took many miners south around the Horn to California during the Gold Rush. It is most likely that he and his young wife had this portrait made in California. In order to properly date this photograph, it is only necessary to note the presence of a hoop and some kind of bustle support under the back of the basque bodice, standard features for "best" dress by mid-decade.

A middle-aged gentleman, Captain Wakeman wears a frock coat of glossy black wool, showing a wide black bowtie of heavy silk under his up-turned white collar. A top hat would have been appropriate with such a costume.

Young Mrs. Wakeman has chosen one of the eccentric sleeve styles offered about mid-decade and a very short basque bodice for her dark woolen dress. The shape of the torso is that of the up-to-date shorter, more curvaceous corset, which released the body below the waist and opened more widely at the bust. The basque stands out sharply over the top of the skirt, thanks to the undersupport.

She has wrapped her gold watch chain once around her neck, leaving the length to hang down the front, with the watch tucked into a waistband pocket. Her hair is done in a particularly youthful manner, smoothly over the ears with ringlets falling behind the ears from a position low at either side of the crown and a plait of hair circling the crown.

Parisian journals of fashion continue to assure us that basques have gone out of fashion, but American ladies continue to wear them.

—*Godey's,* January 1855

DAGUERREOTYPE, 1855–57

Courtesy of the State Historical Society of Wisconsin
(WHi [X3] 35653)

THE DATING OF this portrait is best determined by the woman's hairstyle, a late-fifties adaptation that required a hair net and released the side hair from the former smooth "wings."

The young woman wears a dark, probably black, silk dress so new that the creases are still apparent in the skirt front. It is of the habit-front style popular since the late forties, a style designed to display the chemisette and show off a pretty neck. The sheer effect at the throat appears to be from a white net scarf worn over a chemisette with a plain V neckline; the brooch at the breast holds the arrangement in place. The bodice shows a pair of evenly spaced boned darts at either side of the front closure, and it is no doubt shallowly rounded at front waist in late fifties style. The dress is worn over the newer corset, which gives more ease to the bust.

The long, belled sleeves with their short, pointed epaulet caps are closely fitted at the top of the arm, trimmed with rows of either tucks or covered cord, and worn over open, frilled cambric undersleeves. The skirt is gauged into the waist seam.

The young woman's hair is pulled well back from the face and rounded out in a longer, softer style, approaching the styles of the sixties. The style is further softened by very short ringlets in front of the ears.

She is wearing delicate drop earrings, a black velvet neckband with a stone setting, and a little finger ring, and a dark, silk, fringed shawl is draped over one arm.

The gentleman is conservatively dressed, wearing a stiff standing collar reminiscent of the past decade, though still shown in fashion plates at this time, with a broad necktie and flat bow. His rather loose black sack coat has a black velvet upper collar, and the vest is cut low with revers. The trousers seem to match the coat and vest. While clean-shaven, he wears modest "muttonchops."

Misses Emma and Libby Marvin, young sisters from Northampton, Massachusetts, hold hands as they sit for this portrait in their very best dresses.

A mid-decade date is suggested by the slight shortwaistedness of the girls' dresses (before 1854 waistlines for children were slightly lower than the natural waistline). On the other hand, the pressed fan pleats of these bodices are not typical, at least for everyday dress, this late in the fifties. But "best" dresses often carried over some detail of a quaint or old-fashioned nature for the mere sake of being picturesque. These pleats terminate immediately at the neckline and are held by a facing. At the waistband, the pleats narrow somewhat toward center-front and are top-stitched in a manner reminiscent of ladies' bodices of the late forties.

The fabric of these matching dresses appears to be lightweight and may be a barège, a semi-sheer open-weave material made with silk warp and wool weft with woven patterns and sometimes an overprint. The skirts are extremely full and are probably worn over several petticoats. The sleeves are of narrow bands set low around the upper arm and are finished with flared cuffs trimmed with triple chevrons of black velvet ribbon.

The girls' straight hair has been oiled and severely brushed back at the temples to fall behind the ears. Their coral necklaces are decorated with gold charms.

Harriet Eliza Dart posed for this unusual portrait at about age sixteen at Hesler's Metropolitan Gallery in Chicago, the establishment of Alexander Hesler. A handwritten notation on the back of the case reads: "A birthday present for my dear Albert—Taken at Chicago, May 14th, 1856—Presented Aug. 23rd. 1856—Buffalo." Harriet was probably already engaged to "dear" Albert Plumb by this date, as they were wed on October 25, 1858.

For purposes of exhibiting costume and hair in full detail, the mirror is an excellent photo prop. It is especially valuable here as it provides a rare double view of an elaborate hairstyle of the mid-1850s, showing the construction behind the popular style: center-parted long hair is oiled and brought smoothly down over the ears, crossed at the nape of the neck, and brought up to wrap smoothly around a coil of braids low on the back of the head.

Harriet's costume is straight out of the fashion plates of 1856. The basque-style bodice had become the universal favorite for every stylish woman by the mid-1850s, and the most fashionable of them featured the broadly striped silk taffeta material with wide cut-velvet ribbon for accent trimming. Her "engageantes," or undersleeves, are also up-to-the-minute, with their dagged whitework edging, as is her wide whitework collar. Only the somewhat relaxed corseting and the very modest width of the hoop point to the fact that Harriet is indeed very young. An older woman would have worn more extreme versions. At this time the corset was full in the bust and very restrictive over the rib cage, and the hoop was approaching its widest reach. By 1857 the hoop was at its largest and was full enough to support and obliterate the hanging folds of the skirt, shown so clearly here.

... a bordering to be disposed on the waist in some way, frequently in bretelle fashion, or "shoulder capes" as they were called in our school-girl days, from four to six inches wide on the shoulder, and narrowing to a point at the back and front of a slightly rounded waist.

—*Godey's,* October 1855

THE SITTER HERE is Mary Doty Fitzgerald, daughter of Wisconsin Territorial Governor James Duane Doty and wife of lawyer and developer John Glen Fitzgerald of Oshkosh, Wisconsin.

Mary's silk dress, with its vivid geometric arrangement of stripes, is the height of fashion. This costume represents a large outlay of cash, since it was probably of imported, possibly French, silk. Havila Babcock, who kept a dry goods store in Neenah, Wisconsin, and regularly traveled east to order his merchandise, was a friend of the Doty family and often took their orders to market with him, bringing back for Mary and her mother the silks that were then made up by local dressmakers.

Colors found in museum collections suggest either a blue and brown combination or a green and gold for this woven silk stripe. The very broad stripe is used effectively in this directional placement, with wide bretelles meeting in a V at the round waist, the stripe placed so as to emphasize the shoulder breadth and the rather long silk fringe to accent the point. Very wide "pagoda" sleeves are topped with an unusual puff and edged in the silk-thread fringe. The fine, embroidered white lawn undersleeves are full and flared, although they appear to be less broad than the sleeves.

The fashionable open neckline is finished with a wide collar that lies out to the shoulders with fronts that do not meet. While there are small buttons in the yoke of the bodice, they are possibly merely decorative, as there does not appear to be a front opening. The skirt shows cartridge pleats all around, which are butted and sewn directly to a waist seam finished with a cord. The full skirts of all such fine dresses were at this date supported by a hoop skirt and petticoats.

The hair of this stylish and graceful sitter is in the latest style, brushed downward and widened fully to cover most of the ears. A woman must be a skilled hairdresser in order to fasten the heavy side hair sufficiently, and it is possible that extra hairpieces were surreptitiously tucked inside. A light hair ribbon, very much a part of fashionable dress, hangs in wide ends at back beneath a bow or arrangement of puffs.

DAGUERREOTYPE, 1856–58

*Courtesy of the State Historical Society of Wisconsin
(WHi [X3] 35785)*

GEORGE WALTER OAKLEY of Madison, Wisconsin, posed for this portrait at about age five.

A late-decade date is suggested by the cut of the tunic, which is made with a set-in belt and much decorative detail. Usually a plain garment, the tunic often followed changing women's styles in the late fifties; these elaborate open sleeves echo women's sleeve styles after 1856. Hip-length bodices worn by boys were generally termed tunics and differentiated by style; those that were without set-in belts or waistline seams were called sacques or loose tunics.

Little George is very neatly dressed in his dark plaid and white frills, yet the clothing is comfortable and loose. The entire garment, with the exception of the inset belt, has been cut on the bias ("on the cross," in contemporary terms) for ease. The short wide sleeves, front, and belt have been trimmed with ribbon rosettes around small pearl buttons, and the short sleeves are edged with ribbon ruching over white shirtsleeves, giving little George's costume a somewhat feminine flavor, as was usual in boys' clothes. The whitework neck frill and undersleeves belong to a white cambric shirt worn buttoned to the trouser band. The sleeves of the shirt appear to be gathered to a band above the elbow as well as at the wrist.

George is probably wearing long trousers of plain dark material that blends with his tunic (browns and purples were favored for boys), but shorter trousers are also mentioned in the literature.

Daguerreotype, 1855–56

*Courtesy of the National Museum of
American History (87-3815)*

Trowsers . . . are also worn by little boys from three to five years old,
with a very short skirt.

Godey's, September 1850

THE ONLY BASIS for not giving this plate a date earlier in the decade is the width of the trouser legs, a detail in children's trousers and pantalettes that followed the widening men's styles in the last half of the fifties.

This unidentified little boy is wearing the most frequently described costume of the fifties for his age and sex. The top is a loose sacque shape with a back seam, with a placket at the back of the neck that either buttons or ties, and with no waist seam. If a sacque-shaped pinafore, the back would have been open full length and fastened at the neck and perhaps waist with strings. The two garments looked the same from the front and were worn interchangeably over an undershirt that buttoned to the waistband of the trousers, which had buttonholes in the waistband for undershirts and shirts. Pinafores are mentioned as having been worn alone over the undershirt if they were then belted at the waist but were usually worn over a shirt. Checked gingham is the fabric choice most often mentioned for everyday sacques.

The construction of either garment in the fifties is the same: the front is cut in one piece, flared out from the underarms, and the back is in two pieces to coincide with the front, with the center back on the straight. Sleeves were set-in, either long or short, and the neck was bound. Both garments were made hip length.

The trousers worn by little boys were still usually made with a short fall, which buttoned at the waistband with one or two buttons at center and at either side of the fall and which had the aforementioned buttonholes for shirts. The material was usually dark linen or, for winter, linen-wool combinations.

These were play clothes, and boys had tunics to wear for best, which were often belted over white or tan linen trousers.

INSIDE THE CASE of this image James S. McKenzie (1839–62) wrote, "Miss Mary E. Smith from her cousin Jamie McKenzie, presented April, 1856 at Edgartown." Not only is this portrait well documented, but it also shows the common dress of New England seamen at the time.

In its fall 1987 issue, the *Old Dartmouth Historical Society Bulletin* tells the short story of this young sailor's life. Jamie was born in the family home on the crest of Johnny Cake Hill in New Bedford, Massachusetts, while his father, Captain Daniel McKenzie, was half a world away pursuing whales off New Zealand on the ship *Samuel Robertson*. Captain McKenzie commanded eight whalers between 1818 and 1846 before coming ashore to become the weigher and gauger of the New Bedford Customs House. In 1848 he became the first narrator of Russell and Purrington's "Panorama of a Whaling Voyage." Two of his sons took to the sea at an early age, Jamie at fifteen and Daniel, Jr., at sixteen, and both were lost at sea, Jamie in 1862 at age twenty-three when he was swept overboard in a gale.

Jamie is seventeen in this picture, fresh from a twenty-seven-month voyage to the North Pacific on the whaleship *Reindeer*. He is wearing sailor's garb, which, while not precisely a uniform, probably typifies the clothing worn off-duty by young men of the whaling ships: white canvas trousers, made with a fly-front closing and slash pockets at the hips, and a dark navy blue woolen blouse with large white braid stars on the collar points, made in the typical loose style with a front placket terminating in a loose pleat and closed with metal buttons. The wide shoulders drop low on the arm, and the sleeves, made straight and somewhat loose, are gathered into band cuffs. A black silk sailor's kerchief with a white anchor emblem is tied at the neckline. His pants are held up with a black leather belt, and his sheath knife is handy. The "sailor hat" Jamie wears is the model for similar hats, always called "sailors" for little boys in the early years and, later, and up to the present day, for similar women's styles. Of white stiff straw, a sailor hat is flat crowned and fairly wide brimmed and has dark ribbon around the crown that falls in two long ends to one side. This example also has a dark cloth-bound brim edge.

DAGUERREOTYPE, 1856–58

Courtesy of the International Museum of Photography,
George Eastman House (68:94:3)

THE LATE-FIFTIES hairstyle is the best dating tool for this photograph. In fact, the older sister's style —with the looser, dropped sides that allow some curls to form around the face—shows the evolution from the earlier wings.

A pair of young sisters, the oldest probably about thirteen, these girls pose together here to display two youthful styles of dress. The younger girl wears a pinafore-like, cap-sleeved style simply gathered at the wide neck and at the natural waistline. It is of a dark-colored calico, printed with small darker spots. The sleeves are edged in braid. The short, puffed undersleeves appear to be taken up on drawstrings at the cuffs, as the twisted loop of a cord bow hangs at the inside of one sleeve. Her mitts seem out of place, as though borrowed for the occasion, and on one hand she wears two rings over the netted fingers.

The older sister wears a resist-spotted dress, of either calico or challis, that has been cut in the fan-front style. The bodice, which is worn over an old-fashioned rigid corset, is gathered into a narrow band of shirring at the waistfront but appears to be in pleats or darts above the point. The peculiar band of smaller dots at yoke level may be a band of ribbon trim. The sleeves are open and rather short on the forearm, and the undersleeves are flared to suit. A Jenny Lind–style collar is set at the round neck. A grown-up black silk shawl covers her upper arms and dress front, giving the impression that it was assumed for the portrait.

Both girls wear slender gold watch chains, and the youngest has a gold pencil in its case hanging from the chain. A charm, or watch fob, hangs over the edge of the small watch pocket in the skirt. At the younger sister's neckline, where the small slide holds the chain, a gold cross is pinned. The long fan on the lap of the older sister is of a type extremely old-fashioned by this date, having been popular about 1835.

DAGUERREOTYPE, 1856–58

Courtesy of the Kings County Museum

HIGHLY UNUSUAL COSTUME details are noted in this photograph. The couple are Aaron Tyner and Docia Cabe Tyner. Docia Cabe, who was born on February 1, 1828, had come to California in 1854 from Arkansas with the Tyner family. She was an orphan girl, a neighbor, and a friend of the Tyner daughters, Aaron's sisters. Aaron, who had been out to the gold fields in 1849, had returned ill from scurvy and took the trip west with the family. In a series of articles written in 1906, Aaron said, "In 1855 Docia Cabe and I got married and lived together 45 years and a half in peace, love and happiness."

The dating of this handsome double portrait, taken in Fresno, California, must hinge on Docia's Pamela hat, which is described as "a new style of bonnets" in *Godey's* in the spring of 1856. A later reference to this style hat in *Godey's* indicates that in 1858 it was thought inappropriate for wear except at a resort or by children. It is interesting to speculate whether Docia wears it here at a resort or whether it may have been accepted more broadly out in California. The hat is of dark-colored straw and is trimmed around the brim with ostrich tips. It is fastened by plaid ribbon strings that attach under the brim, with a loop at one side and a fringed end at the other. Another indication of a late-fifties date is the exceptionally broad whitework collar.

Docia's costume is an informal walking ensemble, either of black or some other dark-colored silk. The bodice front seems to be made plain, probably darted, and is finished with a band of black velvet ribbon. The fit of the bodice points to the wearing of the old-fashioned straight-fronted corset, as the fit over the bust and at the armholes is not perfect. The bodice waistline will probably have been rather deep, to follow the corset line, though no longer as pointed as earlier bodices. While it is not clearly evident in the photograph, the skirt of this dress is very full, and its folds appear to fall over a hoop skirt that puffs out gracefully. The dress collar, of fine embroidered lawn, is extremely wide and very fashionable for the midfifties. It is worn rather high on the neck and closes in front.

There are no white undersleeves—a very remarkable circumstance, as the sleeves are open and flared and somewhat short on the arm. One bare arm rests on Aaron's shoulder, displaying wrist ribbons of black silk; these ribbons are wide, about two and a half inches, and are tied at each wrist in bows or puffs, a popular fad; sometimes twin brooches were fastened at the knots.

She wears a fringed silk shawl folded diagonally so that the upper section falls above the lower and the fringe of both edges shows. It falls slightly back from the shoulders and is pulled smartly to the center front of the waist point, where it may be pinned, leaving the fringe prettily spread on the skirt. She carries a light-colored carriage parasol.

Aaron's attire is more remarkable in that it shows the "Californio style" affected by many Californians at this date, usually for riding horseback. This is most pronounced in the knee-high "botas," which he wears not in the style of Mexicans and true Californios, with the scalloped wing section on the outside of the leg and aimed forward to flap in the wind of walking, but wrapped to fold backwards with the wing on the inside of the leg. They are bound below the knee with a dark band. The riding crop he holds reinforces the statement that he is wearing riding clothes.

Another "Californio" feature of his riding dress is the flat-crowned "Spanish" hat with its barbiquijo, or chinstrap, of wide black silk ribbons (sometimes of buckskin), the prescribed two fingers wide, fastened under his chin.

Tintype, 1856–58

Courtesy of the National Museum of American History (C75.8.1)

THE SLEEVE TREATMENT of the little girl's dress reveals the most about the date of this unidentified portrait. The open bell shape, somewhat short on the arm, appeared in children's dresses about mid-decade, and here it is topped with deep double puffs, an effect not introduced until 1856.

The charm of this yoked frock is mainly due to the pretty neckline, so familiar from children's portraits and a popular style for little girls for nearly thirty years. When this neckline was made with a yoke, as here, a very shallow one was used, thus allowing the bodice gathers to extend across the body well above armscye level. The fabric of the dress is a woven plaid in deep tones, probably either black and red, gray and purple, or brown and blue. The material is most likely a woven cotton gingham plaid, although it may be a wool challis.

Her double strand of coral beads was certainly a birth gift from a godmother or godfather.

Many young girls were photographed with their dolls. Details of the doll's dress are not discernible, except that the sleeves appear full. The skirt, which may well be supported with a doll-sized hoop, is worn short on the wooden legs, indicating that this is a "girl," not a "lady," doll.

THIS EXCELLENT DAGUERREIAN image was taken by J. Gurney of New York City. The subject, Mary Louise Baker Lidgerwood Brown, daughter of Charles Minton Baker, is photographed in mourning dress. The photograph is dated mainly by the coronet braid wrapped around the entire crown rather than coiled into a bun or knot. The sleeves are not as full as the fashion of the day, but that is consistent with the generally modest cut of mourning dress. Since many portraits of women show all-black clothing, even to collars and undersleeves, as seen here, it is apparent that a photograph was often taken during the first year of mourning, for at no other time would such accessories be black. At the time of this portrait the sitter, still a young woman, is probably in mourning for her first husband, Mr. Lidgerwood.

This black silk costume, with its undersleeves and collar of black crepe, is an excellent example of proper attire for the first year of mourning. (Second mourning, after the first year, would have allowed white.) The bodice of this dress shows black crepe trimming at a low yoke line, at the long sleeve cap, at the cuff, and at the edge of the flared oversleeve. The costume is of two pieces, the basque bodice having a plain short skirt parting at the front over a gathered skirt. The front-fastening basque is closed at the throat by a large jet brooch.

She wears no earrings or watch; nothing interrupts the stark simplicity of the black. The rings worn on the middle finger of the hand appear to be a wedding and an engagement ring.

DAGUERREOTYPE, 1856–59

Courtesy of the Worcester Historical Society
(1932.188.12)

The peignoir, or robe du chambre, which is better known by its old household title of "wrapper," has, of late years, been quite as fashionable for the young and gay as for the middle-aged and invalid . . . the open robe is usually cut wide on the back (though fitting well on the shoulders) and drawn in slightly with shirrs and a silk lacing inside, the front plain, and the skirt open to the feet. This allows for the display of the rich needle-work now used upon cambric skirts. It is no longer necessary to have the embroidery continued all around. The front breadth is tucked or worked above the knee, and often to the waist . . . "en tablier" . . . . Where the morning-robe is always worn, and always open, this is a very sensible fashion.

—*Godey's,* January 1859

MRS. TIMOTHY BIGGELOW of Boston opted to sit in her wrapper for a record portrait after the death of her baby daughter. In perhaps no other kind of photograph would we be likely to see a photograph of a woman in this intimate garment. Enough posthumous portraits were made that we know they were important to the families of the deceased, important enough to have the photographer visit the home so that the mother might be allowed to retain the dress of an invalid.

Mrs. Biggelow's hair has been dressed in a conservative version of the wings to cover the ears to their tips, a common style in the late fifties. Eardrops, either of hairwork or gold filigree, hang under her glossy hair.

The softly rounded shoulders, low armscye, and spreading sleeves show the line of fashion; the extremely large bishop sleeves of this wrapper are cut plain at the tops but flare enormously and are gathered to narrow cuffs. The wrapper front is cut into a shallow V neckline and overlapped slightly, showing the fine black lace edging on neck and front. A doubled watch chain shows in the open neckline and over the bosom, where the watch is tucked.

This wrapper was more likely a wool challis than a cotton calico; in either case the figures are sure to have been done in several colors on the cream reserves so as to show well on the dark ground. When found in collections such wrappers often have straight full fronts, which can be belted to fit any size, and backs cut with a waistline, so that the pleated and gathered fullness of the skirt can be nicely distributed and brought to the back. Silk-cord tie belts are sometimes found with them. The fronts of a wrapper skirt, as noted in the quote, were meant to hang open to display the fancy embroidered petticoat, or "skirt," underneath.

The angle and light do not make for a clear view of the detail of the baby's long white skirts, but the dress does seem to have a shallow yoke with some whitework and short sleeves. The dress is well over a yard in length, extending out of the photoframe.

Daguerreotype, 1856–60

Courtesy of the State Historical Society of Wisconsin (WHi [X3] 315898)

This pair of very young "sports" are identified as George Baxter and his brother. The late-decade date is determined by the shape of the neckties, neither of which shows the asymmetrical shape of the early fifties. The broad turn-down collar was also not widely used until after the middle of the decade. There is a suggestion of looseness in the coatsleeves as well, which puts the date after 1854.

Both young men are well and nattily dressed for their age and express the comic appearance of "sportiness" mainly through attitude and the cigars and with the rakish tilt (perhaps a little more than necessary) of their hats.

The brother on the left wears a double-breasted vest with a shawl collar that has a finer check than the vest proper. The vest is worn with black trousers and a white shirt with the new broad turn-down collar, underscored by the wide black silk tie. His sack coat is fashionably loose and probably of wool, of some deep shade. The white Panama hat has a smartly curled brim and a broad, black ribbon band.

George, the elder, and probably the inspiration for this pose, has a fledgling beard. His sack coat of white linen is smartly tailored with loose sleeves and notched lapels buttonholed to the top of the lower notch. A matching white vest is worn over a white shirt with the newly relaxed, large turn-down collar, and the loosely tied necktie of silk checks has fringed ends. Checked trousers nearly match the tie. A natural straw hat with a bound brim and black band complete the "look."

CHARLES J. SMITH of Northampton, Massachusetts, had this portrait taken in the spring of 1857, when he was around twenty years of age at most.

Charles wears a dress shirt with a small turndown collar and a stiffly starched front, closed by studs, under his collarless plain vest. The vest clearly shows a buttonhole and button at the top and a front that is open almost to the waist, without buttons or buttonholes.

The necktie is horizontal, only slightly one-sided, and somewhat narrower than early fifties ties, and has fringed ends. The black coat is indistinguishable as to style but has the bulk of the typical oversized garment of the period. His hair is blunt-cut at earlobe level and parted on one side.

DAGUERREOTYPE, 1857–59

Courtesy of Historic Northampton (59.370)

Boys over three years of age usually exchange frocks for loose sacks, buttoning on the shoulder, with a fullness under the arm, cut crosswise of the material, which has an excellent effect, particularly in plaids. With this, a belt, either of patent-leather or silk elastic, three or four inches wide, and fastened by a pretty clasp.

—*Godey's,* December 1856

Checques and plaids, brown and white, black and white, brown and black, etc., are much worn.

—*Godey's,* June 1858

EDDIE SEYMOUR OF Northampton, Massachusetts, appears to be about eight years old in this serious portrait and to have what is perhaps a diploma in his hand. The cut and pattern of the sacque are enough to place the date of this photograph late in the decade.

Eddie wears the short, flared sacque so frequently discussed as correct for boys under the age of ten. Its bold diagonal checks are emphasized by the front closure, where the lines are brought to meet in a deep V. The jacket has been left unbuttoned above the waist to show the white shirt in a manner reminiscent of a woman's bodice over a chemisette. The short open sleeves also reflect women's popular styles rather than men's and show off the long-sleeved white shirt sleeves to advantage. The collar of the starched shirt, too, is shaped more in line with women's styles, setting well away from the face and not meeting at the throat. A wide checked ribbon necktie is done in a loose square knot, and a glossy patent leather belt cinches the waist. Under his sacque, Eddie wears long trousers with no crease.

No checks are worn by ladies, being entirely given up to the nether integuments of the sterner sex, where they flourish in all their breadth and depth of coloring.

—*Godey's,* November 1850

THIS PHOTOGRAPH OF two young men was taken by the San Francisco photographer H. Olsen. It is datable by several details, notably the extreme length and loose fit of the coats and the oversized cut of the trousers. This oversized sleeve may be seen in fashion plates by 1854, especially in the sack coat. The moderately back-brushed, ear-length hairstyle shown is by this time universal; the extreme high front hair wave had subsided as a fad by 1855.

There is a certain spontaneity in this photograph not wholly attributable to the exuberantly unmatched checks being worn. There is a comradely, happy-go-lucky sense that, dressed up more than usual and freshly shaved and barbered, the two just happened to pass a photographer's studio and made a spur-of-the-moment decision to record the day for posterity.

The men, possibly brothers, are dressed in the flashy oversize coats and trousers currently popular with the "sporty" set. The exaggerated style of these outfits was initially introduced into fashion for very young men wishing to wear "racy" styles and soon appeared in mass produced versions for the cheaper trade. These garments represent the latter phase, as they are readymades.

The popular vests that accompany such coats are fitted and of the double-breasted variety, with notched collars, and fall below the trouser waistband. The trousers have generous leg widths, a style that began about 1854 and progressed gradually to the maximum size shown here before 1860.

The man at the left wears somewhat newer-looking garments than his companion, and the extra width of leg and sleeve are obvious. These suits may have been truly eye-catching; mismatched checks in vests and trousers are sometimes advertised in bright contrasting colors, though brown and tan seem to have been much more common.

Tintype, 1857–61

Courtesy of the National Museum of American History (C73.7.3)

This photograph is placed near the 1860s mostly by the ear-covering blunt haircut, which is seen in photographs dated from 1857. The small, dome-crowned hat, with its rolled brim, was popular at this time and became even more so into the sixties.

In a woolen smock of rather crude home manufacture, with his round felt hat and work gloves, this cheerful young man may be a recent immigrant. The smock of woven woolen check has been made up of one loom width with attached sleeves, the seams at the shoulders serving as buttoned openings that enable him to pull the garment on over his clothing. The extra fullness required to allow him to wear the smock over other clothing has been simply taken up with a box pleat at the front neckline, and one probably at the back as well. The sleeve fullness is casually pleated into the arm opening and into band cuffs. The length of this garment is well over the knee.

A plain, rather dark, soft collar band can just be seen underneath, though it is crumpled enough not to be clearly either a shirt collar or the neckband of red underwear.

AMBROTYPE, 1857–65

Courtesy of Joseph Covais

THE WIDE BRACKET date for this unidentified photograph is necessary. Since work shirts like this one were worn before and after these dates, the young man's blunt, ear-length haircut is all that limits it to the later date.

It is extremely unusual to find a photograph of a man without either a vest or coat, dressed in only a shirt, though a man might readily choose to sit for his portrait in his work shirt. The shirt, of a dark gingham or flannel plaid, is made with a band collar and a deep placket. The sleeves are set low and are slightly gathered into the seam. Shirts cut by this pattern were available ready-made in plain cotton, cotton flannel, or wool flannel, mostly in woven plaids, from the fifties through the seventies. The shirt hangs slightly over the waistline, and it is impossible to tell whether the opening is full length or whether a belt is worn, though it was usual to wear one when not wearing suspenders.

DAGUERREOTYPE, CA. 1858

Courtesy of the State Historical Society of Wisconsin
(WHi [X3] 35810)

There has never been a season when furs were so universally worn. The reduction in price, consequent upon the late crisis, and the auction sales of the holidays, have done much to bring this about . . . a full suit of furs is a cape, or victorine, with cuffs, and muff. . . Muffs are worn still very small. . . Cuffs rather deep.

—*Godey's,* February 1858

THIS UNKNOWN SITTER poses in a new set of furs and her best wrap and gloves. The portrait is nicely dated by the above quote and by the late-fifties adaptation of the padded wings hairstyle that returned to favor about 1857.

The handsome set of dark sable furs adorning this winter wrap consists of a Victorine cape of sable with long ends down the front and a pair of matching cuffs. The full-sleeved woolen wrap under the furs is closed at the neck with a silk tassel and is worn as usual under the dress's wide cambric collar. The brooch is at the neck closing of the dress and is worn to show above the tassel.

Her wrap is one of the fitted style, sometimes called a basquine, with an attached full skirt falling about two-thirds of the way to the hem of the dress, which is worn over a very broad hoop arrangement.

DAGUERREOTYPE, CA. 1858

Courtesy of the International Museum of Photography,
George Eastman House (74.193.194)

THIS NATURAL PORTRAIT is of Alice Hawes, daughter of Nancy Southworth Hawes, at age eight. It is another of the exceptional efforts of Southworth and Hawes, who kept up their business of making exemplary daguerreotype portraits for many years after the introduction of the ambrotype and tintype. The desire of this team of photographers seems to have been more directed at excellence than at merely providing portraits to customers. Many of their remaining images are of friends and family, work for which there was no pay besides their own pleasure and satisfaction.

Alice's dress—a yoked, woven plaid silk made with much ease and fullness—is an everyday style of the early fifties and corresponds to work dresses worn by women during the entire decade, except for the short sleeve. The rather deep yoke is straight cut, as are the bodice pieces; the yoke and full bodice extend around the back.

The sleeve is narrow and close, reaching just to the bend of the elbow and set into a somewhat higher armscye than formerly. A bias-cut upper arm band forms a heading for a sleeve-cap ruffle edged with fine silk fringe, a popular type of trim in the fifties. The bodice and sleeve ruffle are laid in thickly gathered small cartridge pleats, and the bodice and skirt are similarly taken into the inset waistband. The skirt would have been below the knee and was probably worn over two or three petticoats and, at Alice's age, narrow, nearly ankle-length white pantalettes. The large collar is in scale with those worn by women in the 1850s.

Alice's hair is worn in a fashion that became popular for women at the end of the decade; allowed to grow, it has been done in a thin twist or plait over the crown of the head.

DAGUERREOTYPE, CA. 1858

Courtesy of Historic Northampton (59.59)

THE BEST DATING tool for this photograph of a young, perhaps sixteen-year-old, girl is the collar, which was at its largest in about 1858.

Over her smoothly styled dark hair she wears a smart bonnet fitted so far back on the head that its outlines are obscured by the tulle frill inside the brim. Only the stiffened lace at the hem of the short bavolet is showing, and the white ribbon falls from one side of the crown. The same type of silk ribbon forms the bonnet strings, which are tied in a crisp horizontal bow directly under the chin.

The dress and wrap are too indistinct for comments on details; but with this kind of bonnet and scarf, the sitter would probably have worn one of the basquine or other fitted wraps, over which her large whitework collar would be displayed. At one side, around the neck, can be seen the distinctive narrow border pattern of the long, narrow, printed cashmere neck scarf that falls at front under her hand.

Daguerreotype, 1858–60

*Courtesy of the International Museum of Photography,
George Eastman House (69:201:58)*

THE DATING OF this double portrait is done mostly by the late hairstyles, as the clothing is anything but high fashion. Still, the broad collars and the one full sleeve are post-1858, and the skirts do appear to be supported by hoops.

These sisters wear matching dark-printed skirts, probably of wool challis, and nearly matching black silk taffeta basques. The basques have yokes and, consequently, fullness over the bosom, a definite departure from the usual basque shape. It seems that the style is an adaptation of the "infant" bodice. These garments are evidently meant to be worn as a bridge between children's and adult styles.

Both girls have heavy hair, which is done in the latest fashion. A band of black velvet crosses the crown and is probably fastened under the hair at the back of the neck, where it may assist in securing the back hair. Hair nets hold the weight of the hair in place.

The bodice of the girl at left has the more usual basque sleeve, which is widened from the upper arm restriction into a wide bell. The flared undersleeve worn with it is rather too narrow for fashion. The other girl's sleeve, differently treated at the shoulder as well, is of the bishop style, gathered into a plain cuff, and may have been thought more proper for a younger sister. Both basques seem to have very full skirts, falling quite long on the hip, and both also have the open necks and extremely wide whitework collars popular in the late fifties.

These are not overly fashionable young ladies, and their garments suggest willing hands at home. Still, it is fair to say that their appearance may have been standard for young girls in a working-class family, and they are perhaps dressed in their only silk garments.

THE MOST COMMON type of clothing for ordinary people in the late fifties is shown in this photograph of an unidentified Illinois family. The best dating tool is the shape of the woman's extra-large bishop sleeve, with its upper-arm fullness set under bretelles, a style first mentioned in the literature in 1858.

The mother, who probably made much of the clothing for herself and the children, has created for herself a good cotton frock from a fashionable pattern and wears it with the extremely wide collar popular throughout the fifties. The collar has a wide netted edge, probably done by her own hand. She has done an excellent job in cutting the dress, matching the plaids of the bretelles and the bodice front to perfection. It is quite possible that she had the help of a good seamstress in the cutting and fitting. The dress is certainly worn over a full hoop skirt and petticoats, as the hoop had been fully accepted in this country by 1855 for dress.

Her hair is done in a rather pinched version of the broad style of the late fifties, covering most of the ears but still with a coiled bun at the back rather than the coronet of braids.

The baby wears a short-sleeved dress with its full front gathered directly into the neckline under a small collar with a lace edge to match that of the sleeves. The next youngest child, probably a girl, judging by the haircut, wears a spotted dark chintz dress with the low neckline favored for children and widely flared short sleeves that show the line of tan left on the wrists by the long-sleeved everyday dress or pinafore. The white petticoat and stockings are those reserved for best, as are the lightweight black kid shoes with their open fronts.

The older brother wears a bias-cut dark gingham plaid shirt with a white collar, and a broad, light-colored neck bow of silk ribbon. His fly-front trousers are fastened over the shirt.

Father wears a black sack coat and matching vest, and his white shirt has the old-fashioned standing collar with folded points under his horizontal bow tie. The lighter trousers are probably tan.

AUGUST AND SALOME RINGLING, the parents of the famous Ringling brothers of Baraboo, Wisconsin, had this photograph taken in Missouri, where they were living at the time.

Both sitters have hairstyles that are appropriate for the late date, but it is Mrs. Ringling's dress that gives the best clues. The sleeves of this silk dress have been remade, or made from new fabric, in a very late-fifties style and do not go with the darted bodice front over its old-fashioned rigid corset. Also, while the lady wears one of the expensive wide whitework collars currently in favor, the neckline of this older dress is cut too high and in too early a style for this collar shape.

The appearance of this dress reveals that she, in fact, like most women of modest means, was not able to buy many clothes but that her interest in fashion led her to remake garments to the best of her ability so that they had a newer appearance. The dress skirt is laid with flat knife pleats at the waistline, rather than the earlier cartridge pleats, and the skirt may have been turned, cleaned, and remade by the wearer in the newer manner. It almost certainly falls over a full hoop.

Mrs. Ringling's hair is probably held by a net. An oversized watch hangs from a fine gold chain at the bodice front, and she holds a fine lace handkerchief. She wears slender gold drops in her ears.

August wears a wonderful, glossy, shawl-collared, double-breasted black satin vest, which sets off his white shirtfront and broad bow tie, and a velvet-collared black coat. His thick hair, cut at ear level, waves to one side at top. There appears to be a black ribbon fastened at the top vest button at one side and drawn around the neck and worn as a watch chain.

AN UNIDENTIFIED MILWAUKEE woman posed for this full-length carte de visite. This new kind of photo print, available from the late fifties, was made on a small, stiff paper form like a visiting card. Since the process and materials made the carte de visite relatively inexpensive, it was often purchased in multiples and given to friends. Many of them survive.

This form alone dates the photograph, but it is easy to tell the date of the dress from the sleeve shape as well; by 1859, the bell of the sleeve had become very wide and somewhat short, and it was fitted close at the upper arm. In this case, the sleeve has been newly made and applied to an older dress. The awkward shape of the sleeves is caused as much by inexpert cut as by the heavy upper arms; the sleeve has been copied from an illustration or example of the closed-top bell that had recently become fashionable, but the armscye is not right.

There is other evidence that this is a made-over dress; the skirt is still attached with cartridge pleats, whereas the current fashion was for knife pleats. Also, the corset is still one of those from the early fifties, which flattened and pushed up the bosom in an unnatural line.

The hairstyle is somewhat transitional, as well, with the twisted coronet around the head and the ears covered in the late-fifties style but not hanging as low on the neck as it would have done after 1860.

While black was considered most proper for a middle-aged woman, other dark plain colors could be worn, especially brown and deep blue; this dress may be any of these colors. The sleeve edges are finished with a wide, dark velvet ribbon, a popular choice for trimming dresses from about 1858 through the early 1860s. When not black, the ribbon, which was either of plain or cut velvet, was dark, in a color to blend with the colors of the dress fabric.

The watch on its gold chain is half visible where it tucks into its small pocket in the skirt. A small, fine collar of heavy lace, another indication of the approaching sixties style, is closed by the requisite brooch, and slender drop earrings accent the neat hairdo.

In this self-portrait of Peter Britt, taken in his own studio in San Francisco, the beard alone indicates a date close to 1860 (a full beard and moustache were the style for a few years just prior to the Civil War). The rather flat, ear-length hairstyle corroborates the date.

Mr. Britt's very long frock coat of black wool with braid finish has the larger proportions of the late fifties and early sixties. The armscye, greatly eased from the earlier cut, is more vertical than formerly and appears just at the outer shoulder edge. The lapels are notched and are bound, as are the two slash pockets and the entire outer edge of the coat, with a shiny braid.

The striped trousers are without creases and are tubular and fairly loose, not "breaking" much over the instep, a style introduced in 1854. His highly polished black kid shoes are new and have a slightly squared toe, high plain vamp, and flat heel. The neck scarf is fastened around an upturned soft shirt collar. This entire costume exhibits a conservative, well-groomed approach, well calculated to inspire trust in his clientele of fashionable San Franciscans.

Daguerreotype, 1859–61

Courtesy of the Worcester Historical Museum (R6.1)

Children's dress . . . Young ladies of twelve and thirteen do not disdain in cities to show beneath the demi-long skirt, white muslin pantalettes, or trowsers, as our London correspondent invariably calls them. They are worn quite broad, and edged with scollops of needlework, with sometimes a sprig of embroidery in each. Again, they are quite plain, and finished by three rows of lace slightly full.

—*Godey's*, July 1850

Young Laura M. Chamberlain chooses to be photographed here with her two pet Guinea hens.

This gingham dress has several notable fashion details that help in dating it close to 1860. While the dress has been made with the severely dropped armscye and the narrow bias long sleeve familiar from the 1840s, this sleeve is finished at the shoulder with very full double puffs, a sleeve detail not seen in women's fashion plates until the mid-to-late fifties. The waistband, at the natural waistline, has been raised somewhat from the early-fifties length. The presence of the small white collar is also an indication of a date close to 1860.

The "infant's waist" bodice style is still typical of children's dresses into the sixties. It is here seen quite possibly in a woolen material, as the high neck and close sleeves indicate a winter dress.

The length of Laura's skirt is not visible in the print, but the proper length for her age is well below the knee, and white drawers then almost certainly extended to just above the ankle. While petticoats could conceivably extend the skirt to this fullness, some stiffer arrangement of crinoline or hoops is quite likely at this point in time.

At eleven or twelve Laura is nearly at the upper limit of age for the simple childlike haircut and would within a year or two adopt a more mature fashion.

Daguerreotype, 1859–61

Courtesy of the State Historical Society of Wisconsin
(WHi [X3] 32371)

IN THIS APPEALING portrait Martha Bottomley is dressed in her work dress with spanking-fresh linens. While this "infant" style bodice is mentioned over a very long period, the dress can be more closely dated by its sleeves. Full sleeves with this epaulette cap are not shown until the 1858 and 1859 fashion plates; and while thereafter they drop out of style, they do not drop out of use for several years in everyday dress.

Martha has the appearance of a servant or governess; although we have no documentation as to her position in the world, a neat dress of one dark color, spotted with white, was considered to be just right for a house servant—perfectly simple, easy to keep clean, and giving a properly unostentatious appearance correct for her station. The color of this example could have been green, wine, blue, or brown, and the finish has a glaze like chintz, which was considered durable, workaday garb, very proper for household help.

The starched, white linen band collar is common for ordinary day dress and, like the tight sleeve cap, is a very late 1850s introduction that carried over into the sixties. Her daycap is also well starched and attractive, although old-fashioned. It is worn with the brim turned half back and the strings untied in a manner fashionable in the forties. Her hair is neatly but unfashionably done, worn tight to the head and just short of the ears and in a snug knot at the back of the crown. Both the hairstyle and cap represent the conservative choice of a woman of middle years and do not necessarily indicate a subservient position in life, though they are proper for such a position.

Daguerreotype, 1859–64
Courtesy of Joseph Covais

A PLAIN WORKING woman, possibly one of the many who earned a modest living doing housework or washing clothes, is photographed here in her everyday attire. The neat whitework collar is not far removed from those worn with better dress and serves the same purpose of protecting the dress neck from body soil and, by being interchangeable, always presenting a fresh aspect. It is of good whitework and in the new smaller size. This bit of neatness, and her very old-fashioned white cap, suggest that the woman is a servant, or possibly a laundress. The cap is neatly tied with narrow ribbons.

Her calico dress bodice, cut with three parallel darts at either side in a style introduced in about the midfifties for silk dresses, closes in front with white buttons and worked buttonholes and is fitted over an old-fashioned, flat-fronted corset. The late date of this portrait is easily determined by the darted bodice front and front closure and the shape of the large bishop sleeves, with their arm-hugging caps.

This dress, which appears to consist of an unmatched top and skirt, is probably really made in one piece and entirely of the small-figured cotton; the dark print is most likely an apron made from an old dress, a custom well documented in personal records.

1859–65

*Courtesy of the National Museum of
American History (C68.12.8)*

THE LOOSE TROUSER leg, wide sleeve, and long coat are evidence of the late date of this photograph.

The sack suit was by no means the only style worn at midcentury, though the proportion of sacks over other types, as shown in photographs, is overwhelming. This young gentleman wears what is apparently a long frock coat, although the terminology is problematical, since there is no waist seam. The coat is styled with the wide lapels and generous sleeves of the late fifties and a long, squared-front skirt cut in full length, flared pieces. This style is more or less derived from the easy-to-wear sack coat. A deep vent was used at center back to allow for a full stride in this rather narrow fashion. The coat is single-breasted and of black wool broadcloth.

The waist-length vest, of a lighter-colored wool, is worn just covering the waistband of the trousers. It is edged with braid and closes with fairly close-set buttons to a high neckline. The gentleman has unbuttoned the top two or three buttons and turned back the plain fronts. A stiff turn-down white shirt collar sets off the plain knot of the long dark necktie. A watch chain, fastened to a high buttonhole, leads to the watch in a side pocket of the vest.

His shoes are pull-on, ankle-high dress boots, sometimes called "booties," and much in need of blacking. Their squarish toes are quite rounded off, and the heels are low and flat.

CHAPTER THREE

The 1860s

How came the Art of Dress to be considered a silly, trifling matter, when the Bible so clearly reveals its high import?

· · ·

Are the mothers of men who rule the world found among the loose-robed women, or among the women who dress in closer-fitting apparel?

· · ·

Is there not the greatest improvement of the human race where the fashions of dress are most subject to change?

· · ·

Can a people who go naked or only half covered be Christian, or ever become Christianized unless they clothe themselves?

· · ·

Are not those nations most morally refined in civilization and Christianity where the costumes of men and women differ most essentially?

—Sarah Josepha Hale, *Godey's,* April 1865

*F*ASHION DURING THE early 1860s might have been expected to stand still, or at least be disregarded, in the face of national crisis. This was true in the South, and for many families in all parts of the country whose members were away fighting, or who were killed or injured in the War between the States. Yet with the arbiters of American style still far away in France and England, the material that reached American fashion writers, and on which they reported in the ladies' magazines, shows no change whatsoever during the war years. And evidence supports the fact that American people, at least those in the North and West who were accustomed to being in fashion and who could afford it, followed the vagaries of style almost in a normal manner. Fashions, as presented in the monthly magazines, continued to change, and, as always, the less affluent used economical measures in order to appear fashionable. Through much ingenuity, perhaps in the adding of new sleeves, resetting a skirt, or totally remaking older garments, even a poor woman could keep up with fashion trends. Therefore, there were style features in common American clothing that were recognizably 1860s and that were different from what had come before. It is worth noting that none of the 1860s style features in common acceptance seems to have had anything to do with cutting back on the amount of material used in a garment.

The Effects of War

In the first half of the decade, the stress of civil war quite naturally caused shortages, which of course meant high prices and in some areas actual deprivation. Costs were elevated because of the disruption of supply lines by Union blockades. Shortages affected the entire country. With the lack of Southern cotton, the New England textile mills faced severe cutbacks and mill shutdowns throughout the war, and the cotton trade never really recovered after the war. There was, as well, an interruption of the importation of foreign textiles in the early sixties due to a temporary halt in American shipping. The combined effect was a nationwide shortage of dress goods of all kinds. In the South, where people were short of money and cut off from most imports as well as from the textile products of the North, the shortage was devastating and was not remedied, as it was in the North, by the resumption of importation. The consequent lack of adequate clothing, warm blankets, and even bandages for the troops, not to mention civilian shortages, had perhaps as great an effect on the outcome of the war as any other single factor. Along with foodstuffs and transportation equipment, Northern officers destroyed or confiscated textile materials found in Rebel camps and captured homes.

Southern women, according to many accounts, used up every piece of textile to be found, tearing up their silk dresses to make flags and banners, making mittens and socks from unraveled wool blankets and garments, and soldiers' hats and shirts from old blankets or clothing. Shoes were made from animal skins, old felt hats, bits of canvas, or old blanket scraps. Women revived out-of-date home crafts and learned again to spin, weave, and knit, and fashion was forgotten in the wearing of makeshift homespun dresses and wraps made from old cloaks and blankets. Even mattresses were ripped apart and unstuffed, the cotton filling spun and woven into rough cloth. The lower grades of cotton, which could be grown and harvested by the few people left on the plantations, were spun into low-quality yarns and woven into inferior cloth. With even this poor cloth at such a premium of labor, ladies' skirts and children's dresses in the South were usually made of short yardage. Ryestraw and palmetto were fashioned into homemade hats and jewelry. It is said that some Southern women who still possessed hoops covered them with homespun fabric and wore them alone, having used up their petticoats for bandages or baby clothes. Many women wrote in their reminiscences in later years that there was almost a style in wearing plain, skimpy homespun dresses, since they were worn by everyone. The universality of this condition in the South, however, and the character of the clothing substitutes will always be hard to study because of the lack of existing photographs.

There were few luxuries to be had in the Southern states, and their prices were exorbitant. In September 1863 Julia Bond, a plantation woman of Abbeville, Louisiana, wrote in her diary, "Went to store today—they ask $40 for ten yards of calico, $50 for ladies boots, $5 for white cotton muslin, $25 for gaiters, $40 for dozen stockings, $50 for dozen handkerchiefs, very plain. Can't afford anything!"

Besides all the efforts to keep their own wardrobes serviceable, women banded together to sew caps, make shirts, and knit socks for the Rebel troops, then risked their lives to smuggle the items to camp. In her diary, which she kept from June 3, 1861, to February 18, 1863, Betty Herndon Maury wrote eloquently of, among other things, making clothing for the "Marylanders," a new unit going to the front under the leadership of a friend, Mr. Hill.

June 3, 1861: I have found an old black satin cloak that I have been looking for, to make a puffing around the bottom of my three year old brown silk, to make it long enough. It is the only thick dress I have with me. All my handsomest clothes were left in the trunk in Alexandria.

Have been hard at work on the clothes for Mr. Hill. Six pairs of pantaloons, six jackets, and eight shirts and havelocks all to be done in three days . . . everyone that I asked took a part . . . it will all be done by tomorrow.

Sunday, June 16, 1861: It is owing to the Richmond Dispatch and the Examiner that things are known at the North—They publish a great many things in their papers that ought not to be known north of the Potomac, and injure the cause a good deal. The other day the Dispatch told of a woman who had brought [a total of] fifty thousand caps under her hoops to the soldiers at Harper's Ferry. Of course she can not do it again now.

Susan S. Arpad notes in her book *Sam Curd's Diary* that of sixty notations of specific work done by Mrs. Samantha Curd during the war years, thirty are of sewing, including the making and remaking of clothing for herself and other women and for soldiers and the sewing of quilts and pillowcases. Sam's husband, Thomas Curd, owned Curd and Brothers General Store in Fulton, Missouri, and the family was therefore relatively well-to-do, which underscores the fact that no family in the South was immune from the necessity of "making do" during these hard times.

In exerpts from the diary of Carrie Barry, who was ten years of age in 1864, can be found the essence of what it was like for a child to exist in the besieged South, in Atlanta, during the war:

1864
8/3:   Today is my birthday and I do wish I could have a party
8/4:   Mama put me on some stockings this morning and I will try to finish them before school commences.
8/5:   I knit all the morning. Shells were thick and fast.
10/21: Mama finished Papa's coat today.
11/2:   Papa has made my shoes and they are very nice.

The Barry family did not leave Atlanta in the general exodus, and in fact a Union sergeant boarded with them for a while. Several young women undertook to teach small classes at times in Atlanta, but they all left before the war ended. Carrie's playmates, aunts and uncles, and beloved teachers and preachers also left the beleaguered city, and she was finally reduced to visiting only "Auntie," who may have been an old colored woman left alone. Carrie's notations about clothing concerns and everyday affairs are all the more poignant for being interspersed with details of visits to see what the shells had done to living rooms and windows in the city, vivid accounts of having had a shell land in their own garden, and fascinating first-hand descriptions of the burning, wrecking, and pillaging that finally took place.

In the North, at the New York City Sanitary Fair in 1864, the Women's Patriotic Association for Diminishing the Use of Imported Luxuries pledged that they would for three years, or for the duration of the war, use "no imported goods if American could be substituted." This ban included "dress goods of velvets, silks, grenadines, India crape and organdie, India lace and broché shawls; fur, wrought laces and embroidery; hair ornaments, fans, artificial flowers & feathers, & carpets." Many wealthy social leaders and hundreds of others signed this pledge.

The Sanitary Commission was organized to address the concerns of clothing, bedding, and bandages for the front and used Sanitary Fairs as fund- and consciousness-raising events.

Another indefatigable diarist, Mariella Leggett of Cleveland, continued her almost daily notations, begun in 1849, during the war years. Her husband and her fourteen-year-old son, Wells, were outfitted by her to go to war:

1861

1/1: Mr. L. has volunteered his services to his country . . . I do not know how we can get along w/o him.

1/7: Finished the night shirt and made a pocket and a long band on a strip for Mortimer.

1/9: I have been busy at the machine—made a strap and pockets for Maj. Car—to use in his tent in camp.

1/10: Mr. L. came home—received his orders to be ready to march in 6 hours.

1/11: All in suspense to know whether 78th is one going to leave to-day. Went down street for flannel for Well's shirts and commenced imm. getting him ready to go with his father. Mrs. Lamson is here on the machine for herself.

1/14: Got material for Wells to make a night shirt to use in the Army.

1/16: Sewing every moment.

1/17: Mrs. Hartman is here working on a calico dress for me. I've helped her on it.

1/18: Sewed on dress skirt and pillowcase.

1862

2/3: If I had not a machine I should feel that I had quite a job on my hands to make 6 shirts for him, but I shall soon have them done.

For economic reasons, in some cases due to the war, many women worked outside the home in the sixties, frequently in clothing factories. Lois Banner says that women working in hoopskirt factories could earn from $4 to $5 per week (21). Virginia Penny, writing in 1863, discusses a range of women's salaries: about $8 per week for typesetting, $6 to $12 weekly for forewomen in ladies' underwear factories, and $3 per week for beginners to $12 as forewomen in fashionable milliners' and dress shops (302–17). From personal records we deduce that many women used their sewing machines and took in sewing. In fact, especially after the war there was a surplus of women who took in sewing, which caused a reduction in earnings per week. Jensen and Davidson report that wages for sewing after 1861 were at that time reduced almost to the level earned in the 1830s, while living costs had approximately doubled (25).

The women's magazines, until this time such universal vehicles of fashion, were essentially a Union feature during the war and continued to be published regularly throughout, mostly in Philadelphia. The illustrations, still taken from the French, show little or no change in presentation from the originals, and the styles seem as elaborate and varied as ever, the use of fabrics as generous, and the trimmings as rich and expensive. In the midst of the war, women read that "some of the choicest silks . . . such robes cost two hundred and fifty dollars. Dress patterns of such value are never made two alike . . . there is another style which is less expensive. . . . These robes are only one hundred and fifty dollars each. Of course, only the very rich can afford such silks" (*Peterson's*, January 1863). There is virtually nothing in the text of *Godey's* or *Peterson's* during these war years to indicate the national situation. The only hint of difficulty comes in oblique references.

The season is unusually late in opening, owing to the financial embarrassments of midwinter, the time when most of our large importing houses are beginning to receive their goods. Large orders for expensive novelties were countermanded, others were delayed, and we are now seeing the effects of these things. (*Godey's,* March 1861)

It is not to be expected that the same variety will pervade the world of fashion the present season, when there is so little encouragement for the production of novelties . . . a more seasonable subject Brodie's light summer wraps, never more stylish and graceful than now, despite the pressure which has crushed other less well-established houses. (*Godey's,* July 1861)

The war has left, and will leave large numbers of women and children dependent on their own exertions. In the manufacture of thread of all kinds, there is an opening for feminine industry. (*Godey's,* September 1865)

McKey & Bros.:
King Cotton has fallen and so have our prices for the next 30 days—

dark dress prints   .10 a yd.
Smith & Bostwich:
Fine blue cloth for military suits, fatigue suits & overcoats.
(*Janesville Morning Gazette,* March 10, 1862)

Emigration

There was another large area of subsistence economy during the sixties based not so much on the exigencies of the war but on the isolation of the western frontier. Pioneer families all through the West went
through an arduous period during settlement when it was necessary
to make do with old clothing and substitute poor makeshifts for several years before circumstances again allowed small luxuries.
Helvenston reports that Sarah Everett wrote to her father in September 1863 from her new homestead in Kansas: "As for clothes I candidly
think we shall go awful shabby, and in doing so will form no invidi-
ous contrast to those around us" (150).

Women often made themselves plain working dresses of whatever
cheap or homespun material was available. Yet, as we can deduce from
existing photographs, even in such utilitarian, plain dresses, the bodice was made in the 1860s style: fitted through the back, cut with the
fashionable dropped shoulder line and coat sleeves, and darted in front.
There was no lack of interest in, or even knowledge of, fashion on the
frontier; many personal notes attest the opposite. A woman's con-
tacts with home, friends, and family were often accompanied by ex-
changes of fashion information, as though the familiar, pleasurable
thought of new clothes were an antidote for hard work and loneli-
ness. Prevailing attitudes about femininity were no less effective here
than in the East. Jenny June, in her "Talks on Women's Topics," said,
"It is a woman's duty to be as attractive as possible" (71).

The Sewing Machine and Other Aids

The now widely used sewing machine must be factored into an understanding of dress in the 1860s. In the late fifties the *New York Tribune* announced confidently that

> The needle will soon be consigned to oblivion, like the wheel, and the
> loom, and the knitting-needle. The working woman will now work
> fewer hours, and receive greater remuneration. People will have more
> work done, will dress better, change oftener, and altogether grow bet-
> ter looking, as well as nicer looking. The more work can be done, the
> cheaper it can be done by means of machines—the greater will be the
> demand. Men and women will disdain the soupçon of a nice worn
> garment, and gradually we shall become a nation without spot or blem-
> ish. (Kidwell and Christman 79)

Further developments in pattern systems also provided an ordinary seamstress, no matter how isolated, with additional means to
create more complex clothing.

The pressures created by changing fashions, more fitted styles, rising middle-class markets, and the financial needs of untrained women provoked the creation of dressmakers' drafting systems in the 19th century. The availability of a workable sewing machine when added to the interacting combination of these social pressures, provided an impetus that significantly increased the momentum of this creative activity as the century progressed. Technology filled a dramatic role as a necessary component of social change. (Kidwell 20)

Powell & Kohler produced a proportional system for drafting patterns in the late sixties that was supposed to give good fit for any size. It was based on the premise that the human torso is typically formed in increments of measurement, with the bust proportionately larger than the waist and so on. The bust measure was therefore used as the base for a proportional system for women. This method, adjusted by some direct measurements, formed the basis of the Powell & Kohler pattern system, which was designed to "enable all to keep up with, or rather in advance of, the most popular styles, at a much less expense than by taking costly magazines, which after all do not teach you how to cut, but leave you to work out the problem for yourselves or to go to a professional cutter at an annual cost of perhaps twice the price of our 'system' " (Kidwell and Christman 20). Powell & Kohler were only one of several firms producing sets of tools and instructions for making patterns.

Women whose measurements fell within the norm could use such systems fairly well, and those with more difficult measurements could adjust. But another flaw was inherent in the plan: each time a system was drafted, it was for a current cut, and any change in fashion demanded a whole new system be drawn up. To minimize this fault, Powell & Kohler published annual supplementary editions.

Even with the available pattern systems and the ubiquitous and helpful sewing machine, it was still necessary in the sixties to be—or to have the services of—a good seamstress. The perfection of fit required for a better dress was critical. Professional dressmakers, much more than the modest homemaker or even the average seamstress, kept up with the latest pattern systems and became expert in the art of fitting. The difference between a dressmaker and a seamstress was considered to lie mainly in this ability to achieve a smooth, perfect fit in a garment. Personal records of many women still tell of having bodices fitted and made by a skilled dressmaker, while they themselves made up the skirts at home.

New Year's Eve, 1864: I intended to wear my blue cashmere dress, the skirt I had made at home, but the waist was still at the dressmaker's. When I got there, I found that it was not finished—all the hooks and eyes had to be sewn on. The dressmaker was a very poor woman who lived in 2 rooms in an old house w. 3 children. While she was sewing she told me the story of her poverty. When I counted out the money for making the waist I lacked one penny, which she hoped I could bring as soon as possible. When I got home, father decided the blue dress was out of the question for I did not have time to sew the waist and skirt together. I put on my next best dress a brown worsted with red braid. (Brinker 95)

The personal records of some women of quite adequate means indicate that sewing was frequently a creative outlet. Cornelia Augusta Tallman, the then unmarried daughter of a well-to-do family in Janesville, Wisconsin, filled her diary with fashion and sewing notes, seemingly spending all her leisure hours on her personal wardrobe, which must have been substantial. There was no lack of money for materials and trimmings, and she often records using the services of a dressmaker for fitting and cutting assistance. The records include several notations of having ordered expensive materials from New York and of shopping in Chicago. Among the plentiful accounts of sewing projects, Miss Tallman records:

> March 24, 1860: Went with Ma and William to hear Lola Montez lecture on fashion. Interesting & quite a fascinating woman.
> October 9, 1860: Found Mme. Demorest Fashion Book when we returned from Milton.
> October 20, 1860: Went in search of red trimming for Zouave jacket.
> November 12, 1860: Sent to Mrs. Hydes for any corsets.
> November 21, 1860: Went to Mrs. Hyde to cut sleeve for cloak.
> November 23, 1860: Lining my cloak.
> November 24, 1860: Finished frilling cloak.
> December 3, 1860: Went to Mrs. Hydes—she fitted my solferino merino.

Knowledge of newer styles was easily come by, as always, even where circumstances made the adherence to them questionable. In a Kansas *Prairie Farmer* article in February 1867, a women's columnist wrote sympathetically for her readership of farm women:

> I am well aware that you can find the fashions in your magazines, but hardly think you will find them always exactly suited to yourselves. I have often wondered why the fashion books do not give us more common modes suitable for those in common circumstances. Not that I would be willing to forego my "Godey's" and "Peterson's" on that account—no indeed, money couldn't tempt me—but then I really can't afford to follow their fashion plates, pretty as they may be. Can you? (Helvenston 161)

And the magazines, made aware by correspondents of this issue, responded occasionally with the familiar rationale: "Expense is frequently the objection made to many of the styles that we give, but our subscribers should bear in mind that the same ideas may be carried out to suit modest purses, and at the same time be very attractive. An old garment may be remodelled by one of our plates, and be made quite fashionable" (*Godey's,* April 1866).

In practice, this was demonstrably true. Even the calico dresses seen in photographs of women in isolated circumstances were made in the newest cut and style. Thoughts of fashion were certainly far from dead, in spite of the war. Nancy Dymond, an Ohio native, visited New York City in the fall of 1863 and wrote:

> I have purchased my winter bonnet—it is green velvet with plumes to match with pink face trimming. The bonnets are not so large as they were last winter. I shall be sorry if the large bonnets go out of style for I think they were so pretty. I have another alpaca but it's black—all the ladies have the black alpaca fever it being contagious and living in the same climate—I caught the fever. I have trimmed with a magenta edge. I have a very pretty sleeve pattern, closed at the hand . . .

It is undeniable that nuances of fashion already in use in urban areas were not equally well translated throughout rural America. Marie Mathilde Brinker, who lived in the strict German settlement of Germantown in southeastern Wisconsin, wrote in her privately published reminiscences, *Backwards from Ninety,* of a visit to Chicago: "I had thought myself quite well dressed when I left home. My new cotton dress, my white home-knit stockings, and shoes the country shoemaker had made, a brown silk shawl mother had brought from Paris, over her shoulders, and best of all my blue bonnet. When I saw a group of girls my age all dressed in white with hoopskirts and straw brimmed hats called 'flats' I felt I would like to hide myself" (Brinker 95).

An excellent idea of the range of dress types worn by a college-age Kansas farm girl of mid-decade is found in Lydia Murphy Toothaker's reminiscences of her preparations to go from her Kansas farm home to Baker University in 1865.

> I was quite proud of that wardrobe resting in a horsehair trunk in the back [of] the spring wagon along with many kinds of provisions. As mother and father and I drove over the miles of prairie, I enumerated the list: The proverbial black silk dress with eight widths in the skirt and the waist 18 inches, with the length 2 inches from the floor. This was for Sunday. There was a delaine dress for Wed. night prayer meetings, 2 handsome gingham dresses, with berthes, for school, a calico dress for home, and a number of aprons. The calico cost .35 a yard. We only put five widths in the skirt. There was a hat and two poke bonnets. One of these had a gray silk curtain to match my gray poplin dress. This dress had fifteen ruffles on the skirt. My mother considered it was worldly but admitted it was "right pretty." The crowning glory was my "cloud." It was a beautiful soft scarf. This piece of vanity I had bought from money I had earned knitting blue wool socks which I sold at Leavenworth for one dollar a pair . . . there were two pairs of wristlets to keep me warm . . . warm mittens with stripes running around them, and I do not remember how many wool stockings I had but there were plenty. (Helvenston, 111–12)

Lydia and her mother had made this wardrobe themselves and, in spite of their relative isolation on the Kansas plains, had access to current patterns purchased either through one of the fashion magazines or from a catalog of patterns. Both Madame Demorest and Ebenezer Butterick were offering patterns in quantity by this time. There is no reason to believe that any city girl would have brought a more up-to-date wardrobe to school that year.

Fashions for Women

Never had there been more plentiful advice for women who wished to follow the fashions than there was in the 1860s:

> Skirts are worn as ample and full as ever, and are generally gored to throw them out at the bottom. (*Godey's,* October 1861)

> Dress skirts are now rarely seen perfectly plain. They are generally much ornamented, but in excellent taste. Soutache or braiding seems to be the order of the day. (*Godey's,* January 1863)

> Skirts are faced with grass cloth, or enamelled leather, which is now to be had in light colors. (*Godey's,* August 1863)

> Jockey waists with square ends in front, Pompadour waists, and sleeves a la condé (that is, quite small, and made with an elbow), are the most desirable styles for all kinds of goods. (*Godey's,* August 1863)

While all-around fullness persisted in dress skirts well into the sixties in common usage, with the fullness most often handled in soft pleats, the form of the most fashionable skirts altered by mid-decade, becoming flat at the skirt front, narrower across the front, and beginning to extend backward to fit over the new oval hoops. More dresses had short trains, which pulled the extra material to the back in walking. In about 1864 a gored skirt cut was introduced, which consisted of an A-shaped center-front gore and a generous gore at either side with a straight length pleated at the back. This cut resulted in a narrower overall frontal breadth, with fullness extending to the back. No pleats marred the smooth front, and wide pleats in the side gores turned toward the back, where the extra material was controlled with either deep box pleats or cartridge pleating and flowed down and back over the longer hoop and petticoats. This new shape was reflected even in calico day dresses by at least 1866.

Another innovation of the early sixties was noted in *Godey's* in August 1865: "The custom of looping dresses has now become universal." A variety of methods were used to pull up the outer skirts at intervals, mostly involving cords on the inside of the skirt. In May of 1864, *Godey's* carried a description and a drawing of "The Pompadour Port-Jupe": an arrangement of eight cords hung from a belt worn over the hoop and petticoats; the cords were attached at the bottom end to points near the inside hem of the dress skirt and by loops spaced up the skirt to the waist. The free ends, four on either side, were drawn through the eyelets to the outside of the waistband where they were held together by knots. When the skirt was drawn up, the two clusters of cords were pulled out and tied together in a bow at the waist. This custom, ostensibly originating in the need to keep walking-dress skirts from touching the street, developed into a fashion fad, with the underskirt keeping pace with design embellishments: "As the dress for the street is generally looped up, it is necessary that the jupon [underskirt] be prettily ornamented. Buff, nankeen, gray, and violet are some of the favorite colors, and jean and reps favorite materials, both it is said washing well. With us the black and white striped petticoats, with a brilliant bordering, are very fashionable for travelling and ordinary wear" (*Godey's,* September 1863).

Another recognizable element of sixties dresses was short-waistedness. This characteristic, though more exaggerated in the last half of the decade, is typical of the entire period, most particularly in the popular one-piece frock, which was frequently made with the "Empire style" waistline at the level of the bottom of the rib cage: "The short waists and scant skirts, adopted by many, are suggestive of the days of Josephine" (*Godey's,* April 1867).

The sewing machine, with its capability for producing extra-strong vertical seams, made possible the style of full-length shaped gores from shoulder to hem (not then known as the "princess" style but often called "the Gabrielle") that is much discussed in the fashion literature, having been introduced in the late fifties. All shaping in this style of garment was accomplished in the cut and the vertical seams, occasionally with added darts. There was no waistline seam. The precision of fitting required in full vertical seaming, even with the sewing machine, was likely only really well done by professional dressmakers, and thus the style may not have been as general as suggested: "The style of dress known as the 'Gabrielle' will still be popular this fall for street or house dresses, for the mixed woolen stuffs especially. It is more generally known as 'the gored dress'" (*Godey's,* October 1861); "Gored dresses continue to be paramount in public favor" (*Godey's,* June 1862). A sheet of Butterick patterns for 1869 shows two examples of such dresses, one "gored from the shoulder" and one "gored to the Arm Scye" (Kidwell and Steele 84).

The cut of the bodice back was in the sixties most often three-piece, without a center seam, but with the center back section curving in and down to a narrow shape, less than two inches wide at the waist, and the two curved sidepieces, often cut on the bias for a glovelike fit, curving into the armscye well below the shoulder seam in back. Alternatively, a simple one-piece back was used. The shoulders were extremely long and sloping again, with the armscye borne almost horizontally around the upper arm at about armpit height. Bodices all fastened down the front, most by now with buttons, and most fronts were fitted with two darts at either side. A new trick in finishing the neckline was developed when the small collars became popular: "Dresses are made very high in the throat, and in order to make the collar set well a small straight band is sewed round the neck of the dress" (*Godey's,* October 1863). Alternative bodice forms for work and everyday cottons were developed: one type was cut as usual but with no front darts, the fullness gathered into a waistband at front; another type was gathered to a shallow yoke and also into a waistband. Some of these cottons had the yoke and gathers taken across the back as well.

Colors and patterns for ordinary wear in the sixties were many and mixed. Tans, browns, and "cuir," or leather, colors were made up in plain or stripes for walking dresses, and Tattersall checks were popular, especially in browns and tans, both dark on light and the reverse. Brilliant colors, while popular in the sixties for fashionable silk dresses, were not seen in the mixed woolens or in wash dresses for ordinary wear. Black alpaca dresses were for a time a staple in every wardrobe, from rich to poor, young to old.

Plain-colored dresses were increasingly bordered with either soutache braid, usually black, couched on in border designs, or with printed or stamped borders imitating them. In August 1865 *Godey's* pictured a "Zouave robe" in "Cuir-colored percale, with a stamped design representing braiding in black." The favored designs in cotton prints were of small spots, florets, or other motifs scattered on a rather dark ground, the designs frequently of one color only, such as peach on maroon, brown on tan, or the reverse. A madder rose pink with small sprigs of flowers in white and darker madder is frequently seen. "The prevailing taste seems to be for small figures, which harmonize charmingly, and are very elegant" (*Godey's,* January 1864).

A very wide, bell-shaped flared sleeve that ended at the lower midarm was shown in fashion plates for the first three years of the sixties, generally worn over a white undersleeve and always for summer. This sleeve, though longer, was quite similar to those of the past decade. Sleeves of this type often had a snug band around the upper arm or a tight, pointed cap, and a dress made with this style sleeve is sometimes only distinguishable from late fifties examples by the late (short) cut of the bodice or the presence of the enormous, balloon-like, lace-trimmed undersleeve of the early sixties. An extremely large bishop sleeve, pleated into the armscye and gathered thickly into the cuff, is shown in fashion plates beginning in 1857 and sporadically through 1862. It apparently reached its apogee in 1861, when a "Crinoline for Sleeves" is described in *Leslie's* March issue. A drawing of this crinoline shows an open, oval balloon shape of covered wire, with bands for the upper arm and wrist, and covered curved wires joined by horizontal tapes to hold the sleeve out from the arm. The large bishop sleeve of the early sixties is most frequently seen in photographs as a drooping shape, and it persisted far into the decade for working dress, though it is rarely shown in the later fashion plates. The popular "Pamela" sleeve was a bishop style done in light fabric and tied at several points on the arm to form a series of puffs. None of these sleeve styles appear as frequently in sixties photographs as the more common two-piece "gentleman's coatsleeve" shape, a two-piece style with the narrower piece running down under the arm and having a slight forward curve in the cut (like a bent elbow). This shape was popularly made quite tight for some styles (condé) and loosely tubular for others and was sometimes enlarged greatly on the lower arm, beginning at the elbow, forming almost a scoop shape, with the cuff enlarged enough to show the bottom of the undersleeve. One interesting reference in the fashion literature indicates that certain styles were seasonal: "Sleeves, of course, loose; the tight sleeve will not be resumed until fall" (*Godey's,* June 1861).

The skirt-and-waist outfit became a fashion alternative in the sixties. The new fuller shirtwaists, or "waists," as they were called, were popular with young ladies and were worn simply with plain or checked skirts. The most frequently mentioned style of waist was the "Garibaldi," a full-sleeved, bloused type sometimes made in red or black lightweight wool, but more often in white cotton, with the full front gathered or pleated into the neckline. Military in effect, it was named for the great Italian patriot and freedom fighter Guiseppe Garibaldi, whose troops wore red shirts of this shape.

Even though such skirt-and-waist attire was for casual daytime wear, the hoop was a necessary underpinning for the full, jaunty look. Several petticoats were worn over the hoop to conceal the wires. The skirts worn over the hoops were usually simply gathered or pleated evenly all around in a youthful fashion, even after the slimmer gored skirt became more popular. Skirts worn with waists did not have trains.

ACCESSORIES

Partly because of the skirt-and-waist fad, but also because of the growing fashion for one-piece dresses, belts became particularly necessary and popular accessories: "The latest style of belt is quite wide, and shaped to the figure. These are worn with colossal buckles of mother-of-pearl, enamel, steel, jet, or gilt. Some have the initials, interlaced with bars and scrolls" (*Godey's,* October 1864). One such popular accessory for shaping the skirt and waist was the Swiss belt, the "ceinture Suissesse," which was very wide and usually of black velvet and had points both rising upward between the breasts and pointing downward at waist front. Some of these belts were boned and solid; some were laced at front. They all fastened at the back.

White collars were still worn with everyday dress in the sixties, though they became uniformly smaller. A taste for small collars made of heavy-textured lace is notable. White linen or cotton collars with points were often embroidered in the corners, sometimes in colors, with the favorite motif being the butterfly. The narrow neck band found on many dresses formed an excellent foundation for collars of lace or embroidery and for the plain linen band collars, which stood from about three-quarters of an inch to about one and a quarter inches in depth, that were frequently worn with day dresses of calico and with lightweight woolens. Lace was still the benchmark of quality:

"Lace goods . . . are valued no less as a test of social position than as the most becoming addition possible to an elegant costume" (*Peterson's,* August 1863). Most collars were still closed at the throat with a brooch, some of which became quite large by the end of the decade when there was a fad for rather bulky bog oak and jet jewelry. Neck ribbons were not as popular as in the fifties, and when worn they were very narrow, reflecting the reduced size of men's neckties. The stated popularity of fine muslin neckwear, much discussed in fashion columns, is not supported by the photographs examined for this study, but surviving examples of these ties are to be found in museum collections:

> The present furor is for muslin bows and scarfs. . . . The scarfs being more difficult to arrange, and not fitting the neck as neatly as a collar, the bows are generally preferred. We see large bows and small bows, wide bows and narrow bows, long bows and short bows, bows plain and bows highly ornamented. (*Godey's,* February 1863)

> Muslin cravats are still worn round the throat; they are made narrower than formerly, and are embroidered at both ends. Some have a narrow Valenciennes edging around them; they are tied exactly as a gentleman's cravat, with the ends standing out on a line with the bow, and not hanging down as formerly. (*Peterson's,* June 1863)

> Muslin half-handkerchiefs now come in for the neck, scalloped round with white or colors, having an embroidered bunch in the point at the back. (*Godey's,* March 1864)

Jewelry in the 1860s took on a fringed effect, earrings and brooches sometimes having several pendants. Styles tended to the exotic:

> In jewelry, the prevailing taste is for the peculiar, though the Roman, Greek, and Egyptian are greatly in favor. . . . Initial and crested jewelry is still very fashionable. (*Godey's,* January 1864)

> Just now the necesary accompaniment of all half-dress toilettes seems to be the large black beads, which have for some time been worn in England. These are worn in either a single long row, hanging low down in front, or in a double row, one of which is terminated by a black cross. (*Peterson's,* January 1863)

> Velvet necklaces are among the pretty novelties. They are a yard and a quarter long, and half an inch wide, and are ornamented with pendants, which surround the throat, the velvet being tied in a bow behind. (*Godey's,* July 1863)

> Cameos and coral all the rage. (*Peterson's,* August 1863)

> Tortoise shell is being worked in much more elaborate designs than formerly. The bow combs are very tasteful, and we see whole sets consisting of combs, dress and sleeve-buttons, pins, earrings, and buckles to match, made of shell, onyx, marquisite, and enamel. (*Godey's,* February 1863)

Still an important accessory, the typical parasol of the sixties was long and of one piece, rather than the folded carriage shape, and fancy handles were in vogue. While plain black, and other dark colors, were used by many, the high fashion parasol was now quite elaborate.

> The display of parasols this season is very good. The most elegant being of moiré trimmed with marabout feathers, or lace, or else lively shades of mauve, pink, or green taffetas, with Brussels or point appliqué covering. More simple styles are dotted with pearl, jet, or steel beads, or have a fanciful bordering formed of beads. Others are of a light or white silk, lined with colors, and chain-stitched in the color of the lining.... The handles ... richly carved out of coral or pearl. (*Godey's,* June 1863)

> In parasols there is much variety. Most of them have metal frames and handles; carved sticks are not much fancied, as they generally leave the impression of the carving on the glove ... the handsomest we have seen ... was worth $75. (*Godey's,* August 1864)

Gloves also changed at this time, with a gauntlet style becoming popular: "The fashionable style of glove, except for evening wear, is the gant de Swede, stitched with colors and made to cover the wrist" (*Godey's,* November 1863). And small bags, made to hang at the waistband, were worn as purses for walking dress: "One of the latest novelties is the Spanish Pocket, a very pretty and dressy little affair. It is worn on the outside of the dress, and is very like a Zouave pouch. It is suitable both for ladies and misses, and, we think, will be a favorite this winter" (*Godey's,* January 1863).

Occasionally a notation is found in a fashion column for small accessories not readily identified in black-and-white photographs: "... crochet ... the bright little roman scarfs now so much in vogue for ladies and children.... scarlet, green, purple, and corn-color, three rows of each and separated by a row of black, two of white, and another of black. The fringe was formed of strands of all the colors in the scarf" (*Godey's,* March 1864).

In a final note on ornamentation, there are many references to both leather trim and metal studs on women's and children's clothing. Such details would be difficult to pick up from a photograph, though they may well be present: "It is a noticeable feature that metal ornaments are introduced into the toilette wherever it can possibly be done" (*Godey's,* October 1864).

Undergarments

The chemisette underbodice, still a feature of women's dress in this decade, was often made en suite with separate and matching long, full sleeves, combining the effect of undersleeves with the familiar chemisette bosom and collar so that a complete shirtwaist seems to have been worn under the dress. The chemisette form was most properly worn under a fitted garment, either one of the fashionable tightly laced Swiss bodices or a summer silk dress with a partially open front and long flared sleeves. The preferred term for the chemisette in the sixties was "Spencer": "For young ladies, most of the dresses are made low in the neck, in order to wear the becoming spencers so much in vogue. These are of muslin, embroidered, or else puffed, the puffs running lengthwise or crosswise as taste may dictate, or else puffed only to form a yoke" (*Godey's*, June 1861).

The corset form that molded the torso for 1860s styles followed the trend of the late fifties and was short, with ample bosom, small rib cage, and sharply flared bottom, and reached only a few inches below the waist. Gussets were inserted at the top to accommodate each breast far more comfortably than in previous decades. The body below the waist was released from pressure. The garment was more heavily boned, not only on seams and darts but in between, for a firmer support and was hooked up the front, although back lacings were still used for adjustment.

The typical chemise of about knee length was still worn under the corset. A contemporary explanation of the cut of the chemise in the midsixties is given by Catherine E. Beecher and Harriet Beecher Stowe in *The American Woman's Home*: "In cutting chemises, if the cotton or linen is a yard wide, cut off small half-gores at the top of the breadths and set them at the bottom . . . six yards of yard width will make two chemises" (357). The chemise was moderately full, and was gathered in by the corset to create a short, full underskirt below it. Chemises had small cap sleeves and, generally, wide curved necklines, though high necklines were present on those intended to show above the neckline of the dress.

The order of putting on undergarments is still the same as in past decades: over the chemise were worn a corset, a plain petticoat (which could be of white wool flannel in winter), a crinoline or hoop of some form, and finally one or two fine muslin petticoats to fluff the skirt and conceal the hoop wires.

By 1864 petticoats were plain and smooth at front, with the gathers drawn mostly to center back, but in 1865 *Godey's* was reporting a trend toward elaborate trimmings: "A trimmed petti has now become the indispensible accessory of a fashionable toilette. . . . Fluted ruffles are exceptionally popular, sometimes two four inches wide, or three of two inches . . . or else the skirt is simply edged with a narrow fluted ruffle headed by rows of tucks, insertion lined with a color, or a braiding design. . . . Bands of blue, pink, or buff cambric stitched on in a pattern . . . a very effective trimming . . . [is] picqué stamped with borderings of bright colors" (*Godey's*, August 1865). The article also mentions "different styles of fluting irons" with which to keep the ruffles neat.

Pantalettes seem to have been adopted by mature women by the late fifties, perhaps because of the undependability of the large hoops in certain circumstances. All were of washable white cotton or linen, and most were finished with tucks and whitework at the bottoms. They were made with the below-knee-length leg sections overlapping front and back at the waist and open at the crotch. Information on the wearing of this garment is scarce, however, since pantalettes were never a part of fashion discussion as they contributed nothing to the silhouette, though they are included in descriptions of sets of under-clothing.

The most familiar feature of women's dress in the sixties is the typical oval hoop, usually made in cage-crinoline style—that is, covered wires that are not rounded out but flat in front are affixed to tapes in order to accomplish the plain-fronted silhouette of the skirt. Hoops of this shape persisted in America almost to the end of the decade, becoming increasingly narrow in the hips.

It is interesting to note that when the hoop was first introduced in Paris in the early fifties conservative American women considered it too risqué; but by the end of the sixties, when Paris finally suggested it be left off, conservative women were afraid that abandoning the hoop would be far too revealing of the shape of the body and refused to do without it. A large part of this reluctance, of course, may well have been simply the economic consideration. In order to do without the large hoops, all the dress skirts in a woman's wardrobe would have had to be recut and made smaller in circumference, or new ones made. During the midsixties, in fact, the wearing of hoops had become so universal and expected that any woman without one was the object of unwelcome attention. Throughout the decade, fashion notes point up the importance of this garment:

> A moderate-sized steel petticoat, and a muslin one—with, of course, a plain one over it—make a muslin dress look very nicely. . . . The best steel skirt we have ever seen has been sent us from the new establishment of Madame Demorest, 27 Fourteenth St., New York . . . though containing forty springs, it is a model of lightness & comfort. (*Godey's,* October 1861)

> Petticoats are now trimmed almost as much as dresses at the bottom. They are usually ruffled, and the ruffles fluted. Crinoline and steel hoops are also frequently ruffled, or at least have all the lower hoops covered with a piece of muslin, as this prevents the shape of the steel showing. (*Peterson's,* May 1863)

> We cannot help remarking, en passant, on the shape of crinoline. It is worn now perfectly flat on the hips, and all the fullness thrown at the back. (*Godey's,* October 1863)

> It has been asserted by some that crinoline is to be abandoned, and we see some hoopless individuals perambulating our streets; and queer oddities they are. (*Godey's,* December 1863)

> . . . in New York, which is considered the Paris of America, hoops are not discarded nor are they worn so small as in some of her sister cities. (*Godey's,* March 1864)

Though the general appearance of lady's dress has changed very much since last year, still all the predictions respecting fashions have not been verified. Crinoline, for instance, which was to have been entirely proscribed, has obtained a new lease, subject, however, to some restrictions. (*Godey's,* April 1867)

Hoops and corsets were widely available readymade:

J. Klein: Hoopskirts for the pew & parlor, carriage—fashionable crinoline, not likely to become displaced as most hoop skirts. French Corsets. (*Janesville Morning Gazette,* November 30, 1866)

And near the end of the sixties even cooks and maids wore hoops, though there is persistent evidence that there were circumstances for which the hoop was not suitable. Women who did manual labor, for instance, or who worked in factories, mostly judged themselves better off without them, and young rural women probably left them off for everyday.

Wraps

Jackets were increasingly worn in this decade, some matching the dresses: "With poplin dresses, paletôts of the same are always worn; these are short with a seam in the center of the back, and are cut to fall in to the figure without fitting it too closely: they are generally bound with velvet or corded with silk—the gimp buttons down the front being very ornamental" (*Peterson's,* June 1863). The paletôt jacket was more accurately a sacque upon its introduction early in the sixties, made to flare gently from the shoulder and hang out over the skirt to approximately hip level. In August 1865, however, there was mention in *Godey's* "Chit-Chat Upon the Latest Fashions" of "a tight-fitting paletôt." This style, very new for the sixties, somewhat resembled the basquine wrap of the fifties, but without a waist seam. Some paletôts toward the end of the decade were close fitting enough that they were worn belted, though then they were slashed at the sides. Many of the latter were of red wool with black braid, but others were of fabric blending with, or matching, the skirt fabric. The fronts of a paletôt, whether a loose or tight style, closed all the way with large buttons or with guimpe "frogs" (knot-and-loop closures formed of braid or guimpe), and the sleeves were either large coat sleeves or slightly flared. The paletôt was always trimmed in a rather military style, with contrasting braid, velvet ribbon, or silk cord. If not made of a fabric to match a dress, in sturdy cotton or part-wool, a paletôt or a sacque might be of anything from a thick tweed to a fur cloth. Black or white wool flannel paletôts are evident in many photographs.

A Spanish- or bolero-style sleeveless jacket worn over the shirtwaist was particularly popular in the sixties. These jackets were very short, no more than waist length (and often shorter), and had rounded fronts. Often of black or red velvetine or flannel, many jackets were also made of fabric to match the skirts. A similar form of this jacket, but made with sleeves, was called the "Zouave." In a *Godey's* August 1865 illustration, a "Zouave Robe" is shown as a matching skirt and jacket over a high-necked white waist with very full sleeves. The skirt and jacket are of a light color, with a trimming of stamped "braid" patterns. The jacket is made waist length with rounded, open fronts, and its slightly flared elbow-length sleeves have rounded slits on the outside seams. All edges of the jacket are trimmed with the braid pattern.

Already in 1861 there were descriptions of an economical way of making an older dress more up-to-date: cutting off a worn bodice, leaving the skirt on its band, and making a jacket of either a Spanish or Zouave style to wear with it over a waist of plain material. The jackets were also made of salvaged fabric. These skirt-waist-jacket combinations were suggested only for young women, and more mature women were expected to adhere to the one-piece dress for casual wear, though similar paletôts and jackets were worn as wraps by women of all ages.

As mentioned earlier, women's wraps were the first garments for women to be mass produced. Most had been imported through the years, but by the 1860s the business of manufacturing women's wraps was thriving in this country. "Not until the census of 1860 was the manufacture of women's clothing deemed worthy of enumeration. In that year mention was made of ninety-six manufacturers who turned out cloaks and mantillas. About fifteen of these were based in New York, ten in Boston" (Kidwell and Christman 63). Fashions in wraps were explicitly described and discussed in the literature of the day:

> Length has in all things taken the place of breadth in the whole style of the figure. . . . Nearly all cloaks & mantles, etc, come to within a few inches of the hem of the dress, and in walking-dresses or coats, they are made in many instances completely to cover them. *(Godey's,* July 1861)

> . . . there is a tendency to shorten cloaks: all the importations are much shorter than the American taste will at present admit; for, as we are told . . . it requires full six months to persuade the popular taste to change materially, no matter what designs rule in Paris. *(Godey's,* November 1861)

The shawl continued as a favored wrap throughout most of the sixties, with many alternatives competing with the rich woven "Indias" for supremacy, though, as noted in *Godey's* in October 1863, there were many kinds of Indias to be had: "The ever-fashionable India shawl, one of the most graceful and convenient wraps, now appears on all the promenades. In no one article is there such a variety of quality and style. They are to be had at Stewart's of all prices, from the convenient little wrap of $50 to the marvel at $2000." The lines of a shawl were thought suitable to the wide, flowing skirts, upon which the folds of the shawl could be carefully arranged. The large-patterned, woven shawls of English and European origin are mentioned in the literature, as are printed ones. Blanket shawls,of plain colors or checks, were still preferred over the fancy styles for traveling. "All the clans from Loch Lomond to John O'Groats house are represented in wraps of various styles . . . trimmed with very deep and heavy chenille fringe, variegated to suit the colors of the plaid. . . . The black and white plaids are not yet discarded" (*Godey's,* March 1864). Many sacque, mantilla, and cloak shapes were worn as well.

Toward the end of the sixties, concurrent with the changes in dress styles, there was a distinct shift in the public's taste in wraps, and the shawl was never again considered the height of fashion: "With the short dresses short sacks or removable basques are indispensable . . . nothing else is adapted to the style of costume. A shawl is absurd, the narrow contracted appearance of the toilette, allowing no chance for the display of drapery" (*Godey's,* April 1867).

A distinguishing feature of wraps made with sleeves in this decade was the prevalence of the curved coat-sleeve style, made large to fit over the similarly shaped sleeves of the dress or jacket underneath and trimmed heavily with cord, braid, or wide ribbon in contrasting colors (mostly black). The open flare in wrap sleeves disappeared in the early 1860s in favor of the coat-sleeve cut.

While long cloaks and wraps were described in the latest fashion information, they required, because of the enormous hoops, a vast amount of material and, thus, were expensive. Not every woman could afford them. Wraps seen in the photographs are mostly the short ones, or shawls. Long traveling cloaks and "waterproofs" were made of cheaper material and were deemed indispensable for every economical woman, and examples do appear in photographs. Interesting references to "dust-colored" linen hooded traveling cloaks are found at this time, presaging the "duster."

Mourning Dress

The custom of wearing black mourning dress—complete with black collar and cuffs and black hat and veil—evidently continued into the decade of the sixties, though it was not until the death of Prince Albert, in 1867, that intense and formalized mourning customs became ultrafashionable. Early in the decade there was some variation appropriate to this dress: ". . . second mourning goods . . . though they are 'only calicoes,' we must admire, in passing, the neat & varied designs of Hoyle's prints, in purple, mauve, & gray, upon a black or white ground" (*Godey's,* March 1861). And "In mourning, the distinguishing feature is a mixture of clear white with black; mauve and royal purple continue to be mingled with black also" (*Godey's,* August 1861).

Reform Dress

The bloomer, so reviled in the early fifties, made a comeback in this decade as alternative dress, though mainly for health reasons. It was still not accepted as street dress by the public, never becoming general enough in use, but it did persist as "sensible" home dress, especially for poorer women working with their husbands on farms and as the chosen style of the National Dress Reform Association, who termed it the "American Dress." In use, the costume was a straightforward dress made in any common daytime style of the period, one or two pieces, but cut off and hemmed just below the knee. The extra skirt material was used to make tubular trouser legs. In the case of rougher materials, these trouser legs could be attached to muslin pantalettes above the knee. (Such costumes are not found in museum collections, as they were no doubt worn out, or not considered important enough to save; little information about their construction can be proven.) Enough short petticoats were worn over the trousers to give a properly feminine outline to the figure—that is, not revealing the thighs and knees. The skirts were made very full. Typically, the American Dress was worn without a corset; instead, "health stays" of a much looser and softer construction were worn. Dress reformers also wore flat-heeled, sturdy boots, not at all like the higher-heeled shoes of fashion. In some photographs of women at health resorts, there is some attempt at elaboration of the costume; the viewer is not to forget that these are "ladies," so hats and bonnets, fine collars, brooches, watch chains, lace jabots, and other accessories are evident.

This bloomer revival did not come out of thin air; it had been an ongoing tradition in the dress reform movement. A National Dress Reform Association had been founded in 1856, and its organ, *The Sibyl: A Review of Taste, Errors, and Fashions of Society,* was published in Middletown, New York, and edited by Dr. Lydia Sayer Hasbrouck. This paper, which featured Dr. Hasbrouck and her crew in the bloomer costume on the masthead, was published until 1865, and was an inspiration to association members all over the country. The costume was not a uniform; rather, its design was left to the ingenuity of the individual, the only suggestions being to corset lightly, if at all, and to strive for simplicity and comfort. For this reason, such costumes generally followed the current styles for day dresses.

HEADGEAR

The dressing of the hair is rightly included in the discussion of headgear in the 1860s, as a new fashion for additional hairpieces dramatically alters the proportional size of the head. The size and shape of hats is correspondingly reduced, the combination giving a particularly effective dating tool for sixties photographs.

The hair net was an accessory particularly important in the sixties. Nets had become useful by the very end of the fifties, when the back hair was released from the customary bun and allowed simply to roll under, and even in the early sixties, when the hair was more painstakingly arranged in a "waterfall" of crimped waves. In the first years of the sixties, nets were often crocheted of black or purple chenille yarns or made of criss-crossed and knotted narrow velvet ribbons decorated with glass bugle beads, silk tassels, or rosettes of ribbon. "Invisible" nets, sometimes made of hair, soon came into more common use: "Nets are now only worn for simple toilet, the invisible ones being the most desirable" (*Godey's,* February 1863).

Throughout the decade, ordinary women, those most frequently represented in our photographs, simply parted their hair near the center and fastened it back from the face with combs, which caused the top and sides to puff. Many kept the hair close to the head and tucked up into a conservative arrangement low on the back of the head, but most rolled it under at back and held it with a net, with all of the back hair hanging at chin level. The net itself was often held at the top of the head with a comb. Frequently a coronet braid was carried around the top of the head, well back from the face, and passed beneath the roll of hair at the nape. The growing size and progressively more complicated shape of the fashionable hairstyles late in the decade significantly altered the scale of a woman's head in proportion to her body size, and this affected the styles of hats and bonnets as well, bringing to popularity a small hat that perched high in front and was directly centered over the forehead and tipped toward the face. The hair was worn in increasingly large, deep arrangements, requiring at times one or even several false braids or sets of puffs and/or curls. Advertisements for such "hair goods" appeared in ladies' magazines and newspapers in the latter half of the decade. Sets of sidecombs were required to hold these masses of hair, and nets, once adequate to hold the simple roll of hair, went out of fashion as the elaborate piled-up styles came in. Women did not universally follow the trend for elaborate hairstyles, which were mostly reserved for evening or very dressy occasions. By the end of the decade, however, any woman with pretensions to fashion had at least a thick braid and a full, upswept hairdo.

Even those women who did not wear the exaggerated hairstyles had to contend with the smaller hats and bonnets. Worn high and centrally placed, they were either perfectly flat or tilted down toward the forehead. By 1868, a low-crowned hat style was shown in the fashion plates, either of turban form or plain with narrow brim. Wide ribbons with fringed ends sometimes hung down the back, and often a small cord was passed under the chin and buttoned. Very small oval hats were popular toward the end of the decade, with elastic cords to hold them in place.

Bonnets were rather high and spoon shaped in the early sixties, becoming much smaller by 1864. In fashion articles women's bonnets were frequently described under the heading "hats," there being less difference in the two forms than at any time in the past, the major difference being the placement of most bonnets far to the back of the head and the use of wide ribbon strings. Curtains, or bavolets, at the backs of bonnets were reduced to vestigial flounces of ribbon or lace, and bonnet sides were equally shrunken in depth. The distinction between the propriety of wearing one or the other form also became less important, and the hat was finally accepted for wear by all but elderly women during this decade.

Fashion commentary on headdress is plentiful:

> The manner of dressing the hair calls for much attention at the present day, and many are the inquiries addressed to us on this important subject. (*Peterson's,* October 1863)

> Most of the bonnets have soft cap-like crowns, though not hanging. The capes are small, so also are the bonnets. The ribbons are very bright, and yellow and scarlet much used, particularly on black bonnets. (*Godey's,* October 1864)

> The genuine Empire bonnet. . . . Imagine a flat square crown, with small front and long gypsy ears tying behind underneath the waterfall. A band of ribbon fastened on top passes down and ties under the chin, pressing the bonnet so closely to the face, that side trimmings are entirely suppressed. Gilt chains on velvet, a rich ornament, or a few flowers, are placed over the forehead. (*Godey's,* January 1866)

The daycap by this date is only seen in the home, for "undress" by fashionable ladies, and for dressy wear by the elderly:

> Coquettish, tasteful caps for middle aged ladies, or for demi-toilette . . . some were of the Corday shape, with coronet fronts, others had long brides or lappets, others were formed of thulle scarfs, entwined together in front, and falling over the neck at the back. (*Godey's,* December 1863)

A particular style of sunbonnet, called a "Shaker," was mentioned and even advertised throughout the sixties, and many remain in museum collections. With deep brims and narrow, elongated horizontal-shaped crowns, Shakers were woven of fine dark and light mixed straw. The Wisconsin diarist Marie Brinker wrote, "Mainly, I knew he had come to get a better look at me, for he had not been able to see my face, owing to the Shaker I wore." And in July of 1860 in the *Janesville Gazette,* McKey and Brothers advertised "Large size shakers, no. 10, 11, 12, 13, & 14, sold for 4 shillings each."

FOOTWEAR

A high heel for women's boots and shoes was advertised throughout the sixties, the heel measuring from an inch to an inch and a half in height. For dress the heel tapered in to a heel cap narrower than its longitudinal measurement. All heels tapered somewhat, those for everyday wear having a more substantial width. Toes were still slightly squared, though more softly than in the fifties, and were a bit narrower. The ankle boot, or gaiter, was favored for walking dress and most daytime wear; small boots either laced up the front, buttoning over in a scalloped flap to the outside front, or had elastic gussets.

Front-lacing boots often sported a silk tassel in front at the ankle. Black patent leather toe caps and heels were common, though not universal. And while uppers were mainly of leather, cloth gaiters were common as well. A sturdy leather walking boot, with a wider-based heel, was favored for walking and day dress for all but the most smartly fashionable occasions.

A dressy evening slipper advertised in the late sixties had a high, pointed back and a one-and-a-half-inch, sharply incurved heel and either a gently rounded, flat, square toe or a blunt pointed one. Large standing tongues and large rosettes or bows of ribbon decorated the fronts. These shoes were made either of cloth or of kid and had thin leather soles.

Men's Fashions

The extension of the railroads and the development of the steamship provided a healthy outlet for the proliferating manufacture of men's clothing during this decade of western settlement. The range of styles, from the flashy and cheap to the finest in dress wear, was calculated to catch the extremes of the market: "Everywhere the lines of transportation extended, Gentlemen's Fashionable Ready Made Clothing was being offered for the inspection of any class of customers" (Kidwell and Christman, 63). And the commercial use of the sewing machine was, again, behind the rapid expansion and the multiple choices. For example, Kidwell and Christman comment that "Brooks Brothers noted in the 1860s that the making of a first-rate overcoat, which required six days of steady sewing by hand, could be done with the help of machines in only three days" (77). Huge workshops fitted with lines of sewing machines turned out men's shirts, and tailor shops utilized machines for the long seams of coats, while still employing hand work for the finishing. In this manner enormous quantities of work and dress clothing were turned out for the wholesale trade. The gentleman's tailor still prospered in large cities, but the bulk of American manhood was outfitted from the rack.

Even given the reasonably low cost of men's shirts and "small clothes," many women with sewing machines recorded the making of these items for husbands and sons. A saving of a dollar or so per garment was substantial in an economy where a working man's income might hover between ten and twenty dollars per month. For women who wanted to make men's suits and coats at home, there were pattern systems available in the sixties, making it relatively simple to fit the garments. But only occasionally do diary entries note the making of a man's coat or trousers. Readymades were advertised widely in newspapers throughout the decade:

McKey & Bros.:
    Suits: Coat, pants, vest: $ 9.50
    Cassimere suit: $19.00
    Beaver overcoat $30.00
    (*Janesville Gazette,* November 30, 1866)

In 1868, the *Gazette* advertised "Men's Good Business Coats" for four dollars, along with "Linen Suits for Men and Boys" and "Paper collars & Cuffs."

As for the styles, men's suit coats came in a range of new shapes. By far the most popular cut was the sack, but even that was available in a new variety of styles. The extremely long, overlarge cut of the late fifties, with its dropped shoulder and wide lapels, most often of black, is the style seen in many early-decade photographs. By mid-decade a more youthful cut was shorter and more closely fitted through the body and had a higher armscye and closer-fitting sleeve. This style, while seen in black, was frequently made up in checks and had a matching vest, both with narrow lapels. The linen sacks seem to have been mostly somewhat longer and were made quite loose with narrow lapels. In some photographs of older, established men, the long frock coat of black wool is still seen.

Vests of the sixties were usually collared, often with the shawl collar. The garment, uniformly long enough to cover the trouser waistband, was mostly single breasted and usually buttoned quite high, though casual photographs show only the top and bottom buttons fastened. In the photographs, a watch chain is typically tucked through a high buttonhole, the watch placed diagonally across the front in a side watch pocket at the bottom of the vest.

Trousers were of a wide, tubular form in this decade and often cut longer at the heel. With no pleats or creases, they had button fly-fronts. Belts were worn, but suspenders (braces) were more common. Trousers could be purchased readymade in a variety of fabrics: from the best, made of European or English wool, to cheaper American materials, part cotton and part wool, such as cassimere, or cotton jean or drill. They were mostly of dark colors, though a pale fawn was popular with fancy dressers, and bold checks were still sometimes seen.

Men's daytime shirt collars did not stand high, as formerly, but folded down lower around the neck and were set off by the narrowest of silk ties with hanging ends. Shirts were most commonly white, but stripes and checks and plaids were available. Work shirts are often seen in the photographs with nothing but the collar band; some of these are retired dress shirts without the button-on collars, and some are readymade work shirts with placket openings at the neck. Thick cotton or wool flannel in plaids, checks, and plain colors was made up into work shirts that were shipped out to retailers all over the nation. For dressier occasions, the detachable dress-shirt collar was stiffly starched and worn with a cravat of wide, usually light-colored silk tied horizontally in a flat bow. For these occasions the shirt had a board-stiff, starched, tucked front. These shirts were uniformly white.

A work smock, or "farmer's frock," is occasionally seen in photographs of the sixties. A closer study of the records of mass manufacturers of "slop" clothing would likely reveal the ongoing manufacture of such garments, but such simple garments were also traditionally made at home.

Headgear

Hats continued to be worn in the multitudinous forms of the fifties, including the silk top hat. In a Charles Oakford and Sons illustrated advertisement in the May 1866 *Godey's,* a narrow cylindrical top hat with a very small brim is labeled "Young Gent's," while a gently outcurved form with a somewhat deeper brim is labeled "Our Style." Every variation in felt hats is seen in photographs, including the cylindrical, tall, shaped hat of light-fawn color of the fifties. The soft felt hat, its crown crushed into a hundred individual shapes, seems to have been favored by railroad workers and farmers, along with an astonishing variety of billed caps. Long after the war was over, the military cap, or kepi, was used as a work hat. There was a preference for small hats during the sixties, especially a very shallow, narrow-brimmed derby shape and a narrow-brimmed hat with dished crown like a "pork pie" hat. As in previous decades, a hatless man was an anomaly, and a man in a photograph is sure to have his hat nearby, merely laid off for the photographer.

A tendency toward chin whiskers is evident in the photographs, a style that is by no means relegated to the old. It seems, rather, to have been often a "coming of age" effort of the very young, although a few beards are seen at all ages. Sideburns are typically cut off short, and there are few mustaches. The hair is cut at ear level in back and is combed from a side part back from the face and down in a smooth style.

Children's Styles

Babies of both sexes were still dressed alike in this decade in extremely long, white dresses with equal amounts of frilling, lace, and tucks. The typical style featured a pointed deep yoke decorated with tucks and insertion and edged with valenciennes lace. Sleeves were either long or short. Long petticoats, still made on a wide belly-band, were worn under the dresses.

At about nine months, children were dressed in shorter clothing in order to give active legs a chance to grow strong. Very little boys and girls were still dressed nearly alike, in short-skirted calico dresses or short sacques. Until about age five, boys were kept in skirts, though their dresses did differ somewhat from those of girls, having what was considered slightly more "masculine" decoration, though it is sometimes difficult to spot the differences. A military trim, lots of braid, tartan plaids, and strong colors may be associated with boys' dresses, while girls' tended to be of lighter colors and more delicate prints. Plain-colored piqué or wool flannel dresses for both were in this decade frequently edged with wide borders of narrow soutache braid sewn on in elaborate patterns. Even little girls' dresses were not ruffled or excessively fluffy at this time, and most had the soutache braid trim. A fine woolen (probably that termed "French delaine" by fashion writers) was a common fabric for both boys and girls. The dresses were made a bit short-waisted and very full in the gathered skirt, with short sleeves sometimes having epaulettes. Binding, piping, and braid were the trim, usually in either black or white. Red, peach, cream, yellow, or tan were popular colors for the woolens, with the lighter pastel colors favored for girls.

As in the past, after the age of nine or ten children's clothing echoed that of adults. Little was written about what children wore, though occasionally a fashion writer devoted a column to their needs; but fashion plates and engravings of elaborately styled garments for children are plentiful. Photographs do not reflect the same usage, however, mainly showing clothing that is more like everyday styles for adults.

> Little girls' dresses are modelled so much after their mothers', that except in the proportionate length of the skirt, one can see but little difference . . . hats, invariably, instead of bonnets. (*Peterson's,* June 1863)

> The fashionable style of dressing little girls from five to ten years of age is exceedingly picturesque. A short, full, bright-colored skirt, composed of either silk or French delaine (more generally the latter) with a black velvet swiss band, and a white bodice, proves a very becoming toilet to them. (*Peterson's,* October 1863)

The engravings show young girls' skirts held out at a fashionable angle, though no mention is found of children's hoopskirts. Crinoline petticoats may have been sufficiently stiff in the short lengths to perform the same function, and, in any case, several starched petticoats were always worn.

The trousers and sacks worn by boys under twelve still reflected women's more than men's styles. The loose sacks were belted at the waist, and the trousers were loose and often full length, although "knickerbockers" were occasionally worn. Smaller boys are often shown in suits of cotton or part wool that consisted of a long-sleeved shirt, often dark, buttoned at the waistband to the long, loose, matching trousers. Littler boys were also often dressed in suits consisting of a full white shirt with trousers and a short jacket, the latter usually fastened at the top only and curving away at the front edges; the Zouave and the bolero style of jacket were both featured. Trimming on these jackets was of a military style in heavy cord or braid.

Both boys and girls wore ankle boots, though they were sturdier than before and had thicker soles. The boots were made like "straights," with little shaping of the sole for either foot, and left and right were distinguished by a closure that flapped over to the outside of the foot. Girls' styles were most often front closing, with tassels at the top of the lacings, and more dainty in the squared toe ends, and they had thinner soles.

Girls wore flat-crowned, wide-brimmed straw hats with ribbon ties, especially for summer, or as they grew older perhaps a small oval hat tilted slightly over the forehead and squarely centered. Small turbans were stylish for better dress.

In contemporary photographs little boys are most frequently seen in very soft, malleable felt hats with flat crowns and rather wide, curled brims. Boys a bit older wore Eton or Morton caps or a "pilot's cap" of dark wool, and boys in their teens wore a shallow derby-shaped hat as well as caps. At about age sixteen boys were eligible to graduate into full masculine attire, complete with a silk top hat of the "Young Gent's" style.

Summary

Women's fashions of the 1860s are distinguished from those of previous decades by the basic changes in the silhouette. Short-waistedness became fashionable in this decade, with lengths ranging from just slightly above the normal waistline to about two inches above it. In dressier costume there was sometimes a waist point, but the back and sides were still short.

Skirts went through several changes in shape, the main difference from fifties skirts being a more tapered fullness. There was a growing tendency to leave the front breadth free of pleats or gathers. The gored dress, with its full-length seams, is a sixties dress, having been introduced in 1859; this style is mentioned in the fashion literature until about 1867.

While sleeve variations abound in the sixties, the one most identified with this period is the coatsleeve shape, a fairly loose and curved-at-the-elbow style used on dresses and jackets throughout the decade.

In men's clothing, the oversize cut, as seen in the long coats and wide trousers of the late fifties, is prominent throughout the sixties, with skimpier sack coats introduced about 1867 and worn by some fashionable young men in photographs. The large cut predominated well into the seventies.

While there are more variations in clothing choices in the sixties, the presence of at least some of these details makes dating easy in this decade.

PHOTOGRAPHS
1860

THESE YOUNG MEN are photographed in an unusually casual manner, probably in a studio setup. Whatever the setting, the pose provides accurate evidence of the easy fit of the sack jacket, the volume of early sixties trousers, and a variety of snappy hat styles.

The gentleman perched on the counter is wearing a light-colored Eton cap over his fashionably short sideburns. His matching three-piece sack suit is of light-colored wool and has the new, looser coat sleeve and wider lapels, and under his white shirt's very small turndown collar he wears a small dark tie. His vest is long, collarless, and buttoned full length. A watch chain falls diagonally from a vest button to the watch pocket.

Of a light-cream stiff felt with matching band, the bowler-style hat worn by the gentleman in the center is fashionably small but fits well down on the head. His mustache adds a rakish touch. A rather high turndown collar is seen on the white shirt, and the generous four-in-hand tie, nearly lost against the white shirt, is of a light-colored silk. The black wool vest has a narrow shawl collar and buttons high with metallic buttons; the coat appears to match.

The bearded young gentleman with his back to the camera shows the frequent preference of unmatched sack and trousers and gives a candid view of the oversized fit. His coat is of black wool and, typical of the sack, has no side or back vents. The light woolen trousers are also loosely fitted, have no crease or cuff, and fall just above the natural heel line. (Black boot heels show clearly enough to reveal the chips and wear.) The small straw hat, with its wide ribbon band and crisp hanging end, is of the shape called a "Nattie" (*Godey's,* May 1866) and is worn perched high on his fashionably full, short hairstyle.

THE FAMILY OF little Katy Macauley Eager marked this portrait "Likeness taken at St. Louis when she was 14 mos. old—October 20th, 1860." Katy wears a dark chintz for the occasion, probably dark red, green, or blue, with small, light, oval spots. Made up in a back-fastened dress, it has a plain fitted bodice and a wide neckline, which is probably on drawstrings so that it could be adjusted to growth and weight gain, and was easy to iron. The simple cap sleeves are edged with double muslin frills and are tied up at the shoulder points to create a draped effect, bringing the frills to a point on the shoulder. These ties were loosened for washing and ironing. The skirt is below the knee in length and has been set to the waist with fine gathers. The seam is piped and another row of piping is set in the bodice about a half inch above the waistline. Katy's short hair has been rolled into ringlets above her ears for the portrait.

MARY BAGLEY POSED for this photograph in 1860, when she was forty-five years old. It is stamped "Kirton, Photographer, Woodstock c. w." Mrs. Bagley is clothed in the conservative fashion reserved for the middle-aged woman; and while not really out of date, she is not in the height of fashion. Rather, she shows what a woman of some means and taste would be expected to wear for visiting or "taking the air." She wears a good black alpaca day dress cut in the broad-shouldered style of the very late fifties, with pleats tapering from the waistfront out to the shoulders. The waist is almost round, though made with a very slight point, and corded, and the bodice closes in front with covered buttons. Set into the dropped shoulders, the extremely large, full bishop sleeves droop from box pleats and are gathered to narrow wristbands. Over its wide hoop, the skirt is plain at front and pleated from side front to center back, where the fullness is either taken up by dense cartridge pleats or in a double box pleat, giving it ample fullness to hang in soft folds over the hoop.

The black frills at either side of the face are ruchings of silk ribbon and lace and belong to a black silk "widow's cap" tied under her chin with a broad black satin ribbon. Under the cap, her dark, glossy hair is combed into the simplest of styles.

DAGUERREOTYPE, 1860–62

Courtesy of the State Historical Society of Wisconsin
(WHi [X3] 35904)

IN THIS BEAUTIFUL portrait, a well-to-do young Wisconsin mother, Frances Adams, poses with her baby daughter, who is probably about eight months old.

The soft black silk dress has the V neckline, soft folds, and open sleeve of the very early sixties, with the upper arm apparently arranged in two puffs and edged at the elbow with black lace. The extremely bouffant undersleeve, with its vertically placed bands of sheer black lace, is typical of those illustrated in ladies' magazines from about 1860.

Mrs. Adams wears her hair simply brushed down and then back into an arrangement very low on the neck, where it is tied with black ribbons. This behind-the-ear dressing, so typical of the sixties, shows off her long dangle earrings to perfection, as well as the little hand around her neck. She also wears a dark bracelet with gold findings, and a spiral gold pin fastens the V neck, where a fine frill of white lace or tulle just shows.

The child wears the delaine dress with soutache braid trim so popular for both little boys and girls. These dresses were often of cream-colored wool with black braid, but peach wool was favored for girls and red for boys. The snug bodice style, with its natural waistline and the slightly flared cap sleeves, was carried over from infant styles of the late 1850s. This short-sleeve style is derived from the favored epaulette oversleeves worn by women as caps for enormous bishop sleeves fashionable from about 1859 through 1864.

1860–64

Courtesy of Valentine Museum (61.1.1)

THIS UNDATED PORTRAIT has "Aunt Lizzie" handwritten on the back, but it is not known whether this inscription refers to the nursemaid or the baby, as it could have been made at a later date.

The young nursemaid appears to be not much more than thirteen in this portrait. She wears the full bishop-sleeved housedress style of the early years of the decade, made in the spotted dark chintz thought so appropriate for servants, together with a small neat white linen collar, which she has closed with a black bar pin. The skirt is held in a smooth fullness that indicates the wearing of a hoop. Her hair is done up in back from a central part and is confined with a flat ribbon bow bound around the crown.

The baby girl is dressed in the extremely long, short-sleeved white dress of the period, with multitudes of tucks and probably lace frills on the yoke and sleeves. A white petticoat fills out the skirt. Her unusually abundant, dark hair is parted in the middle.

DAGUERREOTYPE, 1860–65

Courtesy of Joseph Covais

IN THE COUNTRY or at play, a boy of eight to ten years had the option of wearing his sacque unbelted. This lad wears a linen one with the set-in, extra-full sleeves of the early sixties set at the extremely low shoulder line and gathered into wide, soft cuffs. Made without a collar, this sacque buttons down the front; the rounded corners at the bottom fall over long dark trousers. This garment has been freshly laundered and pressed and is probably not really play clothing but is more likely a second-best garment. For more important occasions a belt, necktie, jacket, and hat would have been added. His hair is unoiled, as were most men's styles by this time.

Ambrotype, 1859–64

Courtesy of the National Museum of American History (C-1566)

The full sacque that was recommended for boys' attire in the late fifties was still worn during the early sixties. This boy's sacque is probably of lightweight wool or a wool blend, in either red or a shade of tan, and is trimmed with broad, black velvet ribbon bands. The sleeves are the only feature altered from earlier styles, now set lower on the arms and gathered quite full into armscyes and easy cuffs.

These sacques are cut flared from under the arms and held in place by broad belts of elastic cloth or leather, usually black, with large buckles. The substantial white collar, standing high on the neck, is embroidered in whitework, and the neckline is finished by a wide silk bow. Typically, long dark trousers, made quite full at the waist, were worn under the sacque, buttoned at the waist to an underbodice of white or tan cambric.

The soft, side-parted hairstyle, cut rather bluntly to show about half the ear, was common among men and boys in the early sixties.

> Puffed sleeves, whether in a straight graduation from the shoulder to the wrist, or two above the elbow terminating in a tight sleeve below, will be worn for the plainer materials, early silks, etc.
> —*Godey's,* March 1861

THIS WELL-FITTED frock shows the fashionable puffed sleeve at its height in the early sixties, presented with snug pointed epaulettes and wide, buttoned gauntlet cuffs of white linen. The dart-fitted, short-waisted bodice and gathered straight lengths of the skirt, plus the extreme width of the hoop, are clear evidence of the early date as well. Also seen here are the effects of the new corset in ordinary use: the breasts are full, separated, and well defined, and the rib cage is tapered firmly to a small waist measurement (the corset being very short below the waist and sharply outcurved).

The woven tattersall check is of wool, or possibly part wool and silk. The fabric has a sheen, and its rather thin, crisp texture creates a light fullness over the hoop and a light puff in the sleeve. It is most likely medium brown or wine with cream checks. A dark leather belt with its large gilt buckle cinches the garment properly at the waist. This is a day dress correct for a schoolteacher or housewife and a proper morning dress for a lady of higher station.

She wears her hair in the popular new style—very low, covering the back of her neck, and probably in a net. Small gold drops are worn in her ears.

1861–65

Courtesy of the Oakland Museum

FOR MISS LYDA LINDSLEY, a schoolgirl of about fourteen, the Garibaldi shirtwaist in plain muslin is just right with a woven plaid cotton skirt and a broad Swiss belt, or "body."

Miss Lindsley's hair, parted smoothly in the center, is done in little crimped ringlets that fall low behind the ears and with a coiled bun at the back of the crown. She has wrapped her black watch cord once around her neck and left the length to fall down the front; the watch is then tucked into the belt. The Swiss belt is formed of carefully "crushed" taffeta, mounted and bound on a boned and stiffened framework, and laced halfway with black ribbon. Beneath it the breadth of the pleated skirt leaves no doubt as to the presence of a full hoop.

A young woman was urged by the fashion literature to stock several different waists, all to be made full in the body and with full sleeves, in white and in plain colors, and then to use the skirts of worn-out dresses to fashion economical separates.

Tintype, 1861–69

Courtesy of the National Museum of American History (C78.26.21)

The unmatched chairs and plain background in this photograph indicate that this portrait was probably taken in a tent or some temporary studio set up by an itinerant photographer. When such photographers traveled out into the country or to small villages, farmers and other working people paid a relatively small fee and sat in whatever they happened to be wearing.

These young working men posed unselfconsciously in their battered hats and worn boots. The man on the left, with straggly chin whiskers, wears a light-colored sack coat over striped bib overalls and has buttoned his light-colored cotton shirt up to the neck. His soft pale felt hat is thoroughly soiled and crushed. His worn boots are pullovers, probably short ones, with moderately high, wide heels of the type always worn under the trouser leg.

The young man on the right wears plain dark overalls over plaid woolen trousers and a striped dark shirt, probably blue, with only a neckband. He has also buttoned it to the neck. The shirt-sleeves are set low and are very slightly eased into the shoulder. His leather-billed cap has a wide band and a high-standing crown. His high-topped shoes are laced at front with hooks and have stacked leather heels (about an inch high and as wide as the foot).

Ca. 1862

Courtesy of the Museum of American Textile History
(Pl.58)

AT THE STEVENS Mills in the Merrimack River Valley, these workers and children (some of whom are no doubt themselves workers) gather to enjoy a break on a sunny day and play a game of chess. By the 1860s a very large percentage of textile mill workers were from central Europe. They lived in mill houses, like apartment buildings, near the works, and at times all family members were employed, with children beginning as early as ages eight or nine.

While details are somewhat blurred, there are several notable features. The most obvious is the woman seated in the foreground; she is definitely wearing a large hoop, which alone makes the photograph noteworthy. Her bright, spotted cotton dress has a gathered bodice, fairly low neck, and very full short flared sleeves with a self-frill at the edge. This sleeve length is unusual in day dress and is probably a modification for work; this is no doubt an ordinary dress with the undersleeves left off. Her hair is styled in characteristic working fashion, neatly and close to the head.

Both of the gentlemen in the foreground wear high black silk top hats with their casual work clothing, a mannerism typical of the period. And it is likely that one or both of the seated men are wearing vests, which were typically kept on even in hot weather, even when shirtsleeves were rolled up and no necktie worn.

The young woman standing in the background against the brick wall wears a calico dress with a dropped shoulder line and short, shaped sleeve caps edged with a self-frill above very full gathered lower sleeves, a style of the early sixties. The child leaning on the fence is dressed in an overshirt, or smock, and one of the boys at center is wearing a pilot's cap. The youngster in the doorway wears over his black vest and white shirt, with its rolled-up sleeves, a suspendered apron that buttons at the waist.

MISS MARY JANE PATTERSON, at age twenty-two, is pictured at the time of her college graduation in 1862. In her 1894 obituary she is credited with having been the first African American woman to receive a Bachelor of Science degree, which she took at Oberlin College with the highest honors.

Miss Patterson is lightly corseted and dressed in the popular Garibaldi shirt, of black or red wool, with (probably) a black and white checked woolen skirt, finished with black silk ruching in two rows at the hem and simply gathered at the waist over a modest round hoop. Her full sleeves are of the extreme "elbow" style shown in the fashion plates for 1862, with the fullness controlled at the dropped shoulder line by box pleats and at the wrist by small pleats or gathers. White soutache braid laid in a lattice pattern, with loops, finishes neck, wrist, and front edges, and a small frill of crimped lace is set inside the throat. A narrow ribbon bow with ends is fastened at the neckline. The belt appears to be a thick black silk cord.

This conservative, youthful style, while it is extremely modest, is very up-to-date and probably not different from that of any of the young women in her graduating class.

Mary's father, Henry Patterson, was a mason and he and his wife, Emeline, had ten children, of whom Mary was the oldest. She was born in Raleigh, North Carolina, in 1840, and her parents moved to Ohio when she was small. It is noteworthy that four children from this working-class family graduated from Oberlin; two sisters and a brother followed Mary's example, and the younger girls both had careers as teachers in the District of Columbia. Oberlin's liberal policy included acceptance of women students and blacks almost from its founding in 1833 and allowed students of lower-income families to work off a portion of their tuition in a variety of jobs serving the college.

Miss Patterson went to Philadelphia directly after receiving her Bachelor of Science degree and taught there at the Institute for Colored Youths until 1869. She left that school to become the principal of a high school in Washington, D.C., and was subsequently placed in charge of the city's large preparatory high school that served black students planning to attend college. The famous Dunbar High School was the outgrowth of this preparatory school.

This unusual daguerreotype was taken at a party celebrating the eighty-fourth birthday of George Nichols, who is seated at center with his wife, Betsy, at his right. Three generations of the Nichols family gathered for the occasion in a sunny room of the Nichols home in Salem, Massachusetts (today the historic Samuel McIntire House). While the Nichols family was important in Salem and lived in a fine house, according to town records they went through many financial reverses and were never extremely wealthy.

Standing, from left to right, are granddaughter Harriet Nichols and her father George; Anna and Henry P. Nichols, husband and wife; Elizabeth P., Lydia R., and Sarah P. Nichols; S. Augusta and John H. Nichols, husband and wife; Charles S. Nichols; and John T. S. Nichols. Seated are: Susan Treadwell Nichols, wife of George N.; grandmother Betsy and grandfather George; granddaughter Charlotte S. Nichols (nearly hidden by the centerpiece); John H. Nichols; Mary Jane Nichols; and granddaughter Martha Nichols.

The wearing of daycaps by three of the older women greatly enhances our understanding of daycap usage in the sixties in that the caps are worn at dinner, as suggested by the literature, and that none are worn by any of the younger women. The caps are all worn well back on the head, and two appear to be brimless. Grandmother Betsy's cap shows frills above the crown that are probably on the edge of a turned-back brim, and the thick side frills of this more old-fashioned style are held close to the face by the broad, sheer ties under her chin. This is not true of the other two, which are worn pinned to the hair just behind and slightly above the ears and which have their ties falling loosely at the sides. The cap worn by daughter-in-law Susan Treadwell Nichols, seated at left, is probably in the form of a lace lappet laid over the head and then gathered up above the ears on either side with ribbons and artificial flowers to flare prettily along the neck.

Details are rather blurred, but several other enlightening elements can be seen. The women's hair is mostly worn close to the head and covers the ears in an everyday style of the early sixties. Granddaughter Mary Jane, at the right end of the table, has a looped, ear-covering style revived from the early fifties, and daughter-in-law S. (probably Sarah) Augusta, standing in the corner, wears short ringlets at her temples.

Under her dress, granddaughter Martha, at extreme right, is clearly wearing a hoop, and we can assume that all of the women present, with the possible exception of the grandmother, are wearing them. Martha's dress, the only one that shows to any extent, is of a typical early-sixties shape for a young "maiden," with its somewhat short-waistedness, full bosom with gathers at the waist, high neck and small collar, and full gathered skirt of printed calico that lies smoothly over its hoop and petticoat. Two of the other women at that end of the table wear dresses made with the "habit" bosom, which is an open V at the neck filled with either white chemisettes or kerchiefs fastened with pins.

Granddaughter Harriet, at extreme left, is wearing a dress with sleeves apparently of the type called a "gabrielle," sheer cotton puffed at several intervals above the elbow and gathered very full into cuffs at the wrist. This, too, is a detail rarely seen in photographs. The sleeve of S. Augusta's dark plaid dress, in the right corner, is stylishly flared and rather long, with an arrangement of puffs at the upper arm. Others' sleeves appear to be of the pagoda style, somewhat short, and, at right, Martha's are worn over very full white undersleeves gathered into frilled cuffs. All of these sleeve styles are summer fashions designed for relative coolness.

The men's clothing is not clear. It is notable, however, that the grandfather wears a very old-fashioned white stock under what appears to be a silk smoking jacket and a close cap. Two of the other men sport Lincolnesque beards.

AMBROTYPE, 1862–63

Courtesy of Historic Northampton (1980.19.10)

SEATED BETWEEN TWO of her friends, Frances "Frankie" French, daughter of John and Frances French of Northampton, Massachusetts, posed for this portrait when she was about twelve. With the off-the-shoulder necklines of party dresses, similar to little children's necklines, and made of silk taffeta, her friends' dresses are of dressier and more girlish styles than Frankie's.

Together the three girls represent nicely the youthful, dressy sleeve styles of the early sixties. The short puffed sleeve on the dark dress is perhaps the most typical; it is set low on the upper arm, with about a two-inch seam closing the bodice shoulder line above the sleeve. The fullness of the sleeve is gathered into a narrow cuff band, which is probably held in place inside by a shorter, straight sleeve lining, which causes the full puff. The sleeve of the striped silk exhibits a double cap flounce, with the short muslin undersleeve familiar from the late 1850s. Frankie's sleeve is actually more up-to-date, having the popular droop and shoulder seam pleating of women's fashionable puffed sleeves, but it has been shortened to a youthful above-elbow length.

It is reasonably safe to assume that Frankie's mother was still making her dresses. This dress appears to have a pleated bodice taken into a yoke and waistband, and with it she wears a black belt. The other bodices are simply gathered into the low neckbands and into waistbands. All three skirts are worn over several petticoats and are about midcalf length. The two party dresses show typical horizontal trim near the hem, one of tucks and one of ribbon bands.

The heavy lockets worn by the two friends are of a type mentioned in fashion articles for women, especially when worn with thick chains, as with the girl in the dark silk. She is also wearing one of a pair of wide, gold link bracelets with black medallions, matching one worn by Frankie; the pair probably belonged to the latter, or her mother, and was meant to be worn as a pair, one on either wrist.

Frankie still wears her hair in the girlish cut, but combed back from the forehead and held with combs at the temple and curled at about jawline level. The variations in youthful hairstyles for girls of about thirteen were numerous; both of the other girls wear their hair snugly drawn back into coronets. The girl in dark silk has unparted hair, and a plaited ribbon cap with a black velvet bow droops at one side.

AMBROTYPE, 1862–64

Courtesy of the Oakland Museum

Bonnets continue to be of the shape worn during the winter, not quite so high in front, but still sufficiently so to admit a great deal of trimming at the forehead. They are very narrow at the sides.
—*Godey's,* May 1963

Wraps are now a matter of no small perplexity. There exists such a variety of styles, that it is difficult to know what to select. The ever-fashionable India shawl, one of the most graceful and convenient wraps, now appears on all the prominades. In no one article is there such a variety in quality and style. They are to be had at Stewart of all prices, from the convenient little wrap of $50 to the marvel at $2000.
—*Godey's,* October 1863

IN THIS SOLEMN portrait, Mrs. Helen Whitney Polache rather glumly displays "falling" shoulders and a properly "artless" arrangement of her pattern-woven shawl. The best dating tool for this ensemble is the spoon-shaped hat, which was at the height of its popularity in 1862. Over her hair, which is carried in waves down from a slightly eccentric part, the bonnet is filled and edged with frilled blonde lace interspersed with small artificial flowers. A small half-wreath of flowers and grasses decorates the outside brim. The back curtain, or bavolet, of the bonnet is visible on one side. She has tied the bonnet's wide ribbon strings under her chin in the approved manner, and her dark, shining kid gloves complete the walking "toilette."

Fort Pulaski, the island fort that protected Savannah, Georgia, fell to the Union in February 1862. That spring, Gen. James B. Barton led an occupation force and took command of the fort. There were both officers' quarters and enlisted men's barracks on the fortified island, which at this time was reached only by boat. It is uncertain how soon after the occupation that some of the officers were joined by their wives; records show that wives visited many camps during times of relative safety, sometimes staying for a few weeks at a time. It is also uncertain whether the wives stayed in quarters at the fort or somewhere in Savannah. Many photographs were made of such occupation activities at the island fort. These, while not sharp images, are historically important.

This photograph of officers and women, probably their wives, taken at the fort's gun emplacements one sunny day in the early sixties, provides an excellent full-length view of a woman's walking costume, a rarity in photographs. One of the young women is shown in her full-hooped dark walking dress, with paletôt jacket, straw hat, and fan. The wide, rounded shape of the hoop is a good indication of a date close to 1862, for by 1865 the skirts were flatter at front and narrower at the top. The crisp, flaring lines of the jacket from the sloping shoulder, the oversize curved sleeve with its deep cuff, and the black ribbon trim are smart fashion details that held from about 1861 through 1866. The hat demonstrates the horizontal, frontal placement so important to the new look.

THE ZOUAVE JACKET style was mostly worn by young women in the late fifties, but in the sixties it was also popular for little boys. The Garibaldi-style shirt was worn by both as well, becoming a favored substitute for the tunic style. Here we see the jacket and shirt styles worn together. The soutache braid trim on this (probably) red wool flannel jacket reflects men's military uniforms and was used on boys', girls', and women's wraps indiscriminately. The Garibaldi is of white cotton and, like most women's shirtwaists, is frilled on either side of the button placket and has a small round collar. A very narrow black silk tie is knotted into a flat bow under the collar ends.

This child, who is probably five or six years old, wears long trousers, which boys often began wearing around that age. They are in a fine woven wool check and, with their loose, tubular legs, are styled nearly like a man's. They may have a fall-front closing, but the fly-front is often seen in photographs of boys by this time.

1862–65

Courtesy of the State Historical Society of Wisconsin
(WHi [X3] 39873)

This photograph was taken at St. Clara Academy, a boarding school for girls founded by Father Samuel Mazzuchelli, a priest and teacher who had built twenty-four Roman Catholic churches in Wisconsin by the mid–nineteenth century. Father Mazzuchelli also established the order of the Sinsinnawa Dominican Sisters, who ran St. Clara's. Young ladies of all ages, many of them from prominent Wisconsin families, stayed at the school until about age fourteen, there learning music in addition to reading, writing, and arithmetic.

While not displaying highly stylish clothing, this portrait is still datable based on the appearance of some details and the absence of others. The hair mostly lies on the neck, confined in snoods or nets, and in one case, at upper right, there is even the Eugénie, a hairstyle of about 1863 named after the French empress. All of the dresses show some version of the bishop sleeve, which is not accurately datable in itself but, seen with the plain bodices, set-in belts, and small collars, can help place this photograph before 1866. After that date at least some of the dresses of these young ladies would have exhibited the false yoke lines outlined with braid or ribbon.

The photograph, taken on a warm sunny day, suggests that simplicity in attire was probably one of the requirements of the nuns. There is no apparent ostentation in dress. All wear good calico dresses, mostly in dark colors, checks, and plaids, but none has a hoop, and most appear to wear only minimal petticoats. Most of the older girls are corseted.

One of the most notable details is the length of the skirts; the older girls (fourteen is known to have been the oldest) wear full-length dresses, and the girl seated at lower left, who appears to be younger, also has a full-length skirt. Skirts for girls twelve and under reach the lower calf, and younger girls' skirts are shorter, though none are as short as knee length.

The (apparently) youngest child, kneeling beside the guitar, wears a smock with very full sleeves over a dark skirt long enough to be caught under her knees. The child seated on the ground near the nun's guitar wears a yoked dark dress with ruching at the neck and either ruching or fringe at the yoke line. The girl standing beside the nun with the guitar wears a small shawl tightly tucked over her shoulders and crossing over in front, where it is probably pulled to the back waist, fichu style, and tied over a checked gingham dress. At extreme left, a young girl wears her paletôt jacket over a skirt and apron.

CARTE DE VISITE, 1862–67

Courtesy of Deborah Fontana Cooney

THIS UNUSUAL POSE features a dress reformer with her husband. Lydia Sayer Hasbrouck, editor of *The Sybil*, the newspaper of the American Dress Reform Association, and a charter member of that group, took her responsibilities very seriously indeed, as suggested by her stance in this photograph, and wore reform dress full time. Her husband, John W. Hasbrouck, must have been in total support of her efforts in this regard in order to be photographed with her in this costume.

Dress reformers did not feel that they advocated anything so extreme as their accusers claimed, and certainly they tried to avoid the appearance of "masculinization." Womanly and pretty accessories were worn, and materials were as fine as for any fashionable costume. Mrs. Hasbrouck and many other exponents of the style lectured on such reform dress and argued its simplicity and femininity, along with its health benefits. The audience they really reached seems to have been confined to those women who performed physical labor, such as women on farms or with small children at home, and who wore the costume only for related tasks. Dress reformers not only never managed to convince significant numbers of women to wear the costume full time, but they were increasingly ridiculed in the press and on the street.

Mrs. Hasbrouck's costume appears to have been economically contrived from a midfifties dress of fine brocaded silk, judging from its very long waist and the sleeve and trimming style. (She would not have cared that it was out of style; another precept of the dress reform movement was a disregard for the changing demands of fashion.) The color of the dress was likely a moss-green and blue, although other combinations, such as brown and blue, were popular. Other than shortening the skirt and fashioning pants legs of the reserved material, she changed the dress only by turning in the fronts rather awkwardly, in view of the trimming line, for ease at the neckline. The bosom is filled with a fine white chemise.

Neat, sturdy boots are worn instead of the insubstantial shoes then in favor. These and the narrow trouser legs provide the only "coarsening" effect of the costume to contemporary eyes. A most feminine touch is deliberately added with the black lace mitts. Her hair, cropped as dress reformers suggested, is still bound in a simple net in a style worn by many women.

In typical sixties fashion, Mr. Hasbrouck wears a long, loose, black sack of fine wool, a matching vest, a neat white shirt, and a narrow black bow tie. His light-colored trousers are soft and uncreased, and his boots the common square-toed pull-ons.

CA. 1863

Courtesy of the Rock County Historical Society
(RCHS4)

THESE TWO YOUNG Wisconsin women present a gentle contrast in their double portrait. Both are wearing the wide hoop of the early sixties, not the more oval and narrow one just coming into style at this date.

The plainer costume, at the right, consists of what is probably the skirt of an older dress, one made of a heavy, light-colored fabric, at least part wool, with graduated black velvet bands at the hem. It is worn over a full hoop, with a snug black belt with a metal buckle at the waist. She wears a very full-sleeved white cotton (or linen) Garibaldi waist under a black silk or velvet Zouave jacket with flowing sleeves, which is trimmed at the fronts and hems and down the outside edge of the sleeves with wide, black ribbon ruching. With her simple hairstyle and the extremely plain, dark parasol, she represents a conservative and economical, though fashion-conscious, young 1860s woman. She most likely made the ensemble herself. With its flat-crowned shape and frontal trimming, the hat she holds is perfectly up-to-date, and it bears a handsome veil of black point d'esprit. It is at this date that the hat begins to be accepted as a respectable substitute for the bonnet, at least until middle age (forty).

The more elaborate costume of the woman on the left has almost certainly been made by a competent dressmaker. It is in the very latest mode and features a new craze: a band of printed ("stamped") black imitation braid embroidery beneath the triple row of black velvet ribbon at the hem. Trimly fitted over the newly curvaceous corset, the up-to-the-minute bodice has jockey points at waistfront and lots of black trim at the yoke line, front, waist, and sleeves. The sleeves are an elaborate version of the fuller coat sleeves, curved to the elbow and wide enough at the cuff to show off the full undersleeves, and are trimmed elaborately: bands of black velvet and lace separate the vertical puffs and edge the sleeve, and there is even a small sleeve cap of sheer black lace. The smart new broad-brimmed straw "flat" is finished with a horizontal side-sweep of black ostrich plumes and is the perfect finish to the latest style of Eugénie hair puffs. An expensive bracelet of cameos encircles one of her wrists.

1863–65

Courtesy of the Oakland Museum

THE ABOVE QUOTE from *Godey's* provides the best
dating tool for this interesting photograph, and
while the cut of the skirt, in straight ungored
lengths, argues for the earlier date, the trim of
pleated ruching of colored silk ribbon near the
hem is a most up-to-date detail of the midsixties.

The bottom hoop near the hem of this dress
can easily be seen beneath its round (trainless)
skirt. The skirt falls over the rather small hoops
with less fullness than usual, even with the side-
front knife pleats at the waistline; this may signal a skimpy cut, though a stand behind her may
be pushing out the hoop unnaturally, thus causing the distortion. The close fit of the bodice indicates that this is a one-piece dress.

This woman's conservatism is evident in her
simple, severe hairstyle as well as in the probably
homemade Zouave jacket. This is the type of
short jacket frequently cut from old black silk
wraps or skirts, thus requiring no actual monetary investment. This example is sewn with
bright contrasting pipings in all seams and
around the edge. Magenta or red silk piping is
often mentioned in connection with black garments in the sixties.

Her most fashionable garment, the black-
and-white checked cape, is not a circle, rather it
is gored for flaring fullness and shows a gathered
neck flounce or hood as it hangs over the arm. A
colored (red?) lining is visible inside the neck and
beneath the hand resting on the newel post. Long,
drop pearl and gold earrings are the only jewelry
visible.

ROSANNA LATHROP, BORN in 1823, is between forty and forty-two years old in this portrait. Dating is best done for this portrait through family history, a thorough genealogy having been done by her descendants. Rosanna and her husband, Azel, farmed a good-sized acreage near Marquette in the Upper Peninsula of Michigan. By the age of forty-two she had borne at least eight children, six of whom survived (four girls and two boys).

Rosanna is known to have made her own and much of her children's clothing; the family was poor and had no money to spare for a seamstress. Yet the new calico dress she wears here has style, with its large bishop sleeves and very full pleated skirt, which is worn over a hoop. Also, despite her rather generous waist size, Rosanna is corseted. Her body simply shows the effects of too many pregnancies to conform to the small-waisted, curvaceous new silhouette. All of the evidence points to the fact that, while still new, this dress was worn for best and, after its newness wore off, for active work around the house and garden.

The glossy new calico appears monochromatic, and madder red, a rosy color, is suggested by the style of the print, a resist pattern of small spots with overprinted motifs of deeper madder. The buttons and ribbon belt, as well as the small brooch, appear to be black. The bodice is cut normally, and she has chosen to use gathers at the belt, which possibly do not extend around the back, since the back bodice was more commonly cut in three pieces, only the center section having a few small gathers at the waist. The narrow linen band collar was a popular daytime choice.

Her hair, done simply, in the manner of all busy women, is worn long and caught in the typical net falling in back.

MARY LATHROP, ABOUT ten years old when she posed for this portrait, was the oldest daughter of Rosanna and Azel Lathrop. Her photograph was probably taken in the Upper Peninsula of Michigan on the same day as that of her mother.

From a farming family, and one of at least six surviving children, Mary did not have many new dresses; in fact the Lathrop children had very few luxuries. Mary's clothing was undoubtedly all made at home by her mother, although probably by age ten Mary herself had begun helping with this work.

Mary's fine-checked gingham dress was purposely made a bit too large, and with large tucks in the hem, to allow for growth; the skirts, to be fashionable, would have been closer to her boot tops. This is certainly a recognizable economy measure, given the growth rate of young girls. Both examples of Mrs. Lathrop's sewing show both skill and economy. The fabrics are not rich; nor are they flimsy and short-lived. They are of sturdy, probably American, cotton and thus washable.

In Mary's dress Rosanna has combined practicality with some pretty and youthful touches. The yoked style gives the illusion that the sleeve gathers are extensions of the bodice, and they are done in the cartridge-pleat manner, all of the gathers standing outward in crisp, small pleats. The dress fastens behind, and its full skirt is well-supported, if not with a small hoop at least with full, starched petticoats. The interesting and quite up-to-date standing collar on the dress yoke is finished with narrow braid.

With her hair brushed back at the temples and smartly curled, and in her puffed long sleeves, Mary looks like any girl of the city, except that for a wealthier child this would have been an everyday dress only, and she would have had more grown-up fashions for dressy occasions.

. . . the dress for the street is generally
looped up . . .

—*Godey's,* September 1863

The custom of looping dresses has now
become universal. . . . Various methods are
employed for looping skirts, such as Mme
Demorest's elevators, hooks and eyes, strings
and pins. The patent pins, however, which
now come of four different sizes, and fasten
somewhat like a brooch, are found very
convenient.

—*Godey's,* August 1865

MISSES THERESE CALLER and Hattie Hubbard of
Chicago pose for this portrait in their smart walking costumes. Their "elevated" skirts are pulled up
in a style introduced in Paris about 1861 as a means
of keeping skirt hems from dragging on the
ground and getting soiled during the winter rains
and spring thaws. When the style is worn by young
girls, whose skirts were already short enough to
clear the ground, it shows the amount of attention paid by the young to fashion fads. Neither of
these girls has the fancy plaid or striped petticoat
really required for the wearing of the "porte-jupe,"
or "skirt elevator." The girls, most likely not yet
fourteen, appear a bit overconscious of the newness of their skirt shapes.

Therese, at left, wears over her adjustable skirt
a matching, double-breasted, short paletôt jacket
with very fashionable details: a double, pointed
sleeve epaulette edged with black braid and matching double-flapped pockets. She wears a high, narrow, dark plush hat, with crown trimming, low
on her forehead and tied under her chin with narrow black strings. A white collar is barely visible
around the ribbons. At the photographer's whim,
her large umbrella ("parapluie" for the rain, as opposed to "parasol" for the sun) has been opened
to form a background for the girls' heads.

Hattie wears a modish "circle" cape of black-
and-white checked wool flannel over her dark
poplin dress. The standing linen band collar belongs to the dress itself. Her big umbrella remains
furled.

1863–65

Courtesy of the Bancroft Library (Catlin, p. 20)

THE DRESS OF this Chinese woman and her little boy is thoroughly Americanized. Since so many Chinese families emigrated to America during the gold rush days of the forties and fifties, it is possible that this young mother was either born in California or came here as an infant.

Like many other sitters in the nineteenth century, the mother keeps her eyeglasses on for her portrait. She wears a neat, probably black alpaca, day dress, fitted over a corset and hoop, giving a smart, up-to-date effect. The skirt, while not gored, flares because of the double box pleats evenly spaced around the waist, with deeper pleats at center back, an acceptable daytime style variant. Hem width is accentuated by two rows of black velvet ribbon, which also trims the square false yoke of the bodice and the cuffs. Narrow white undersleeves can be seen at the wrist.

A black satin band cinches the waist, providing a foil for the elaborate watch chain and fob. The neckline is finished with a trim linen band and a small brooch. Her hair is done in an ultra-conservative style, combed down and fastened tightly into an arrangement around the crown, and there appears to be a black ribbon hanging from the crown down the back.

The little boy is well dressed in his checked skirt and jacket and frilled white shirt. As with all boys under five years, his clothing style echoes that of his mother more than the masculine styles; the Zouave jacket style is identical to those worn by girls and women. The costume is almost certainly of lightweight wool and is trimmed with black velvet ribbon. A growth tuck has been let out of the skirt, probably for this portrait, as it has not yet been pressed out. The tip of one black boot shows on the stool. His hair has been cut and combed to one side, a popular style for men and boys by the end of the fifties.

DAGUERREOTYPE, 1863–65

Courtesy of the International Museum of Photography,
George Eastman House (68:097:25)

THE PORTRAIT OF this five- or six-year-old boy is typical of finer daguerreotypes in that considerable attention was paid to lighting, thus achieving a painterly effect.

The boy is wearing a "pilot's suit" style: long trousers, a matching paletôt jacket, and a tall leather-brimmed "pilot's cap" of the same fabric. The suit is of wool, probably brown, and the jacket has been cut precisely as a woman's paletôt would have been cut, fairly long and lightly flared. The origin of this style is said to have been a man's short coat of the type worn by river pilots. This example is quite long, made to button full length, and has V-shaped vents at the side seams. The sleeves are curved at the elbow, set low on the shoulder, and narrow sufficiently at the forearm so that the small, pointed cuffs just slide over the hands. The narrow collar, front closure, hem, and cuffs are trimmed with the same braid. A high white shirt collar is visible, but the ribbon necktie and the vest that complete the costume are concealed under the jacket.

CARTE DE VISITE, 1864

Courtesy of Deborah Fontana Cooney

Dr. James C. Jackson had this full-length portrait taken in 1864 by "H. Lazier, Syracuse & Oswego, New York," and printed in the form of a carte de visite, probably for purposes of promotion for his health resort, Our Home on the Hill, in Dansville, New York.

Dr. Jackson was a disciple of Russell Thatcher Trall, M.D., who operated the Water Cure House in New York City. The Trall system included hydropathy, gymnastics, diet, sleep, and exercise. By 1854 Trall had established the New York Hydropathic and Physiological School. Students were taken for $150 room and board ($100 in the summer). The students were indoctrinated in dress reform for women, a healthy diet, better ventilation, and control of passions, especially sex. Tea, coffee, whiskey, wine, and tobacco were prohibited, and lean meat was prescribed, but even then only in moderation.

Dr. Jackson began his career as a supervisor of the business department of Glen Haven, a water-cure establishment in Cortland County, New York, purchasing it in 1852. This spa contained a women's department, possibly initiated by Jackson. He is said to have treated six hundred patients without drugs in 1853, operating on the principle "no cure, no pay." His fees for nonresidents were: $1 for advice, $3 for an office examination, and $5 for prescription by letter.

Glen Haven was sold in 1858, and Dr. Jackson purchased, with the financial assistance of F. Wilson Hurd, a health spa in Dansville, New York, in the upland region of the Genessee River Valley, and called it Our Home on the Hill. Dr. Jackson and his adopted daughter, Dr. Harriet Austin, operated this establishment, which became one of the greatest spas and health centers to operate in the United States in the nineteenth century. Patients were segregated by sex in the main house, under the care of two resident physicians and three trained supervisors. Treatments included diet, exercise, and "packing and bathing." Part of the curative process for women at Our Home was the wearing of "the American Costume," a version of the bloomer advocated by the National Dress Reform Association, of which Jackson and his daughter were charter members. The home was large, well kept, and prosperous and had a quasi-religious foundation. Many Quakers, as well as reformers and antislavery activists, were attracted to its program. Clara Barton spent some time there, as well as Ellen G. White, founder of the Seventh Day Adventists.

In his black frock coat, vest, and trousers, Dr. Jackson is dressed similarly to any other businessman of the sixties, yet his extremely long beard and hair and broad poet's collar are not typical at all. Phrenologists of his day would have remarked that his high forehead and penetrating eyes marked him as a visionary.

LUCY J. RUSSELL (1830–92) posed for this photograph in 1864 during her period of residence at the Our Home on the Hill health center in Dansville, New York. She is dressed to take full advantage of the regimen of healthy meals, mild exercise, and walking, which were the main features of life at the resort. Her shape is clearly that of an uncorseted middle-aged woman, flatter in the chest and broader in the waist, by far, than the fashionable figure.

If not made specifically for her stay in Dansville, the dress was cut down from one never worn over a corset, as the full front and waist are of the form used in working dress. The style of the dress is not remarkably different from one worn by any woman at this time, except for its short length and the absence of a hoop. The neckline, trimmed front closure, and full bishop sleeves with their pleats at upper arm are typical of everyday dresses, and the gathered, rather than darted, bodice fullness is not unusual. Her narrow trousers are made of the cut-off (or leftover) skirt material.

The boots she is wearing are similar to those worn by other reform dressers, though the soles appear to be of thinner leather.

ON THE BACK of this photograph is written "Mrs. Phillips, Betts & Prusia, Dansville, New York, 1864." Mrs. Phillips was undoubtedly a resident and patient at this time at Our Home on the Hill.

Her "American Costume" differs from normal day dress in its length, the trouser arrangement, and the mannish boots and has probably been specially made, as opposed to having been cut down from an existing dress. The bodice is unusually deeply pleated into a yoke, in the "infant" style, to create ease. More importantly, it appears not to be worn over a corset and is thus made larger than a normal dress of the period.

The quality of the black fabric, the shape and decoration of the sleeve, and the fine linen cuffs and band are typical of most women's costumes in 1864. Her hairstyle, with the back caught in a full net, is similar to that worn by many women not given to the elaborate coiffures then in style.

CA. 1864

Courtesy of Historic Northampton (1980.19.11)

Nets for the hair are by no means laid
aside; they are still very much worn in
morning dress, and also in evening negligé.
Those made of colored chenille or velvet
are very becoming. They are usually
finished with tassels or rosettes.

—*Godey's,* May 1861

Thanks to those great resources, trimmings, rarely do we see two dresses alike.

—*Godey's,* October 1864

FRANKIE FRENCH POSED for this serious profile
when she was about fourteen. Her bobbed hair
has grown to a ladylike length, and she wears it
rolled into a beaded black crocheted snood, an
exaggeration of the nets of the early sixties, and
fastened at the front of the crown by a comb with
an upright black velvet bow.

Frankie's one-piece dress, of a lightweight
wool or wool blend, is made with the easy coatsleeves of mid-decade and trimmed with black
silk-fringed braid at the front and sleeves. The
placement of the trim down the outside of the
sleeve, at center front, and in a curved line down
under the arm was new and smart in 1864. This
dress was styled with an attached skirt cut in
gores, with the front gore set on plain (without
pleats) and in knife pleats at either side of the
front section, facing toward the back. Deep box
pleats at center back carry the weight and fullness backward to flare into a short train. A
proper, oval-shaped hoop, smooth in front and
flaring under the train in the back, is essential to
the style. This very grown-up costume is probably a full-length dress.

THIS YOUNG LADY, who is about fourteen or fifteen years old, is dressed in a good black school dress and, given her age, is most likely posing for a photograph taken to celebrate her graduation from the eighth grade, all the education most girls had.

The dress, probably made of scratchy but durable alpaca, is cut in the modest, simple style that nearly every schoolgirl would have worn, yet a hoop, a corset, and overpetticoats are required to create this graceful line. The skirt is laid in many narrow pleats all around, turned forward to the center in front and reversed in back. It is not gored.

The one-piece dress has a closely fitted, fully lined and finished boned bodice attached to the finished skirt waistband. The bodice has two long, narrow points at waistfront, called "jockey points," below the many small black buttons of the front closure. The simple white linen band collar is fastened with a small brooch. Long, narrow bell sleeves open near the wrist over muslin undersleeves.

Her hair is done very simply, smoothly combed down in a youthful manner with short ringlets at the sides of the jaw in front of the ears.

Tintype, 1864–68

*Courtesy of the National Museum of
American History (C771.10)*

Perhaps five years old, this young fellow wears knickerbocker-style trousers with his high laced boots. The suit is of a type shown in many mid-decade fashion illustrations for little boys under five; it consists of a short waist-length jacket, with long coat sleeves, buttoned to full trousers with side pockets. A matching belt, widened at front into points, is then buttoned on over the waist-line, closing with buttons in the back. The buttons used on this jacket are little brass balls, and the suit is trimmed in a wide black braid, the belt and collar in a narrower version. A small-patterned silk kerchief is knotted at his throat.

Tɪɴᴛʏᴘᴇ, ᴄᴀ. 1865

Courtesy of the Bancroft Library (1905.16242)

Tʜᴇsᴇ ᴛᴡᴏ ꜰɪᴅᴅʟᴇʀs appear to be between sets at a local dance, though the background suggests that the photograph was taken in a studio. Their readymade clothing is typical of the Western frontier, where men wore shirts and ties, hats, vests, and coats for every occasion. And rather than the shorter dress boots of fashion, men wore their trousers tucked into soft high boots, a habit said to have derived from the cavalry during the Civil War and one continued afterward by men who frequently rode horseback. The appearance of this custom in this photo indicates a rough-and-ready setting.

The man at the left wears a white shirt with the small turn-down collar of the sixties and a narrow tie worn pinned at the neck with a stickpin, the ends curling down in twin spirals. His black wool sack jacket, vest, and trousers appear to belong to a set of "dittoes" made to be sold as a suit. The jacket is cut in the long, generous style of the late fifties and early sixties. The porkpie hat he wears was quite popular with younger men throughout the sixties.

The other man's shirt has a small clip-cornered collar turned over a narrow striped tie loosely knotted and hanging straight. His matching full-cut sack jacket and vest are of the colorful (probably either red and black or brown and black) checks so popular at the time. The vest, which is buttoned only at the top button, has a small shawl collar. Full, creaseless trousers are tucked into the high leather boots. His felt hat is of similar shape to that of his friend, but with a more rounded crown and a snap brim.

Both men wear their hair trimmed fairly short over the temples, a sign of the sixties, though the one at left has curly hair and wears it in a shape fuller than usual. The carefully trimmed mustache on the one man reflects a trend that appears over many decades as a "sporty" aberration.

DR. HARRIET AUSTIN, the adopted daughter of Dr. James C. Jackson, poses in her version of "the American Costume," which is probably also an example of her customary everyday dress, since she was codirector of the Our Home on the Hill spa.

While the ensemble has echoes of the bloomer dress, it differs in its quite masculine trousers and flat shoes. Her black velvet tunic, however, is of a fashionable feminine style for the midsixties. With it, under the narrow, slightly flared long sleeves, she wears good white muslin undersleeves with wrist frills, which match the frill at the neck, to soften the effect. Her black silk skirt reaches just below the knee and is cut as full as regular skirts of this date. There is no hoop, but there are enough petticoats to support the skirt and give a feminine appearance to the form.

Harriet wears her watch rather ostentatiously on a gold chain at the waist, not a usual fashion for women. Her hair is bobbed and either naturally wavy or crimped in a youthful manner and very simply worn. This cut was chosen early in the dress reform movement as the most liberating and simple manner of wearing the hair and as in accordance with a relaxed and healthful costume and life-style.

1865–67

Courtesy of the Rock County Historical Society
(RCHS 12)

THIS PHOTOGRAPH IS of a modest middle-class Rock County, Wisconsin, couple, who could be of either rural or urban background. While Janesville, where the photograph was probably taken, was a sophisticated city, most of Rock County was at this time farming country. This clothing is unexceptional daytime attire of the type worn in every part of the country.

The overlarge bishop sleeve was worn from 1858 until about 1865, several years after it ceased to be featured in fashion plates. This woman has opted to continue wearing this comfortable sleeve even longer; both the false yoke and the gored skirt suggest the later date. Her hair is also done in the tight, above-the-ear style of the later sixties.

The woman's dress is made of an inexpensive and serviceable hard-finish wool or wool combination with a woven stripe. The skirt is cut in a mid-to-late sixties fashion, rather narrow and in gores, as can be seen by the meeting of the stripes at left front, but is still gathered all around in small pleats and set onto a waistband in an everyday manner. While narrow, it is supported by a small hoop that holds it smoothly. The skirt is quite short, a fashion for walking dress in the late sixties. A narrow triple flounce of diagonally cut self-fabric is set on at the hem.

The gathered, front-opening bodice is trimmed with ruching at an artificial yoke line. The linen band collar is of the kind that maintained its popularity throughout the sixties for everyday wear and travel. The full bishop sleeves are only slightly gathered or pleated at the shoulder but are very full at the wrist, thus giving the appearance of an open bell sleeve when the arm hangs straight. The wrist gathers and cuff are visible above the hand resting on her husband's shoulder.

The gentleman is bearded in typical sixties fashion and wears a black wool sack suit with a velvet collar. The sack is oversized and thus probably not very new, as the newer, more closely fitted styles were available readymade. His small starched shirt collar has short turn-downs, and he wears the minimal black tie most frequently seen in everyday use throughout the decade. His square-toed, low-heeled pull-on boots are visibly worn.

1865–67

Courtesy of the Rock County Historical Society
(RCHS5)

THESE TWO tired-looking women with their small children are residents of Rock County, Wisconsin, and though the photograph was probably taken in Janesville, they were likely from a nearby farming area. Their general appearance is one of moderate poverty. Because the bishop sleeve is so moderately sized, this photograph has been dated at mid-decade rather than earlier. The overlarge bishop sleeve finally retreated from favor by the summer of 1865. Such fads in sleeve shape were easy to see and follow, and it cost nothing to modify a newer dress with more up-to-date sleeves.

The cotton skirt worn by the woman at left appears well worn and much washed, but she wears over it a good paletôt jacket of light wool with braid trimming at front, the white linen band of her dress showing at the throat. Her hoop is very evident, as it pushes the skirt up and out in front in a somewhat awkward elipse, buckling the skirt at one side.

The other woman wears the ubiquitous calico dress, made of a dark print, with slightly full sleeves gathered at the cuff and eased into the shoulders. Her skirt is not as full, and two hoop wires show through faintly; there are not quite enough petticoats over either hoop to give a fash-ionable fullness. A white band collar crosses at her throat and is held by a small brooch.

Their hairstyles do not aid greatly in dating, since they represent two styles common for everyday throughout most of the decade.

The child on the lap of the jacketed woman is probably a little boy. His dress is of a dark (possibly red) wool; tucks and braid patterns circle the hem. The skirt is extremely full, and the bodice appears to be buttoned on under the waistband. The high shoes laced over his white stockings are serviceable and sturdy—a boy's shoe, certainly, but not one to be scorned by a little girl growing up in the country.

The only notable dress details of the littlest child are the shoe soles, which are narrow, straight, and square-toed, and that he or she wears a short dress, indicating that the child is at least nine months old.

The lad sprawling on the low stool wears typical sixties boys' trousers, of a light color and with a fly-front, under a dark vest and a Zouave jacket that matches his trousers, but with black-and-white braid trim. His boot soles show blunt, rounded, square toes and slightly tapered one-inch heels.

AMBROTYPE, 1865–68

*Courtesy of the International Museum of Photography,
George Eastman House (69:205:28)*

THIS STURDY LITTLE boy is dressed in a two-piece woolen suit consisting of a bloused top buttoned firmly to full trousers with gathers or soft pleats at front. The shoulders of the blouse are extremely wide and cut low on the arms, more in the manner of ladies' dresses than men's coats, and are of the two-piece coatsleeve cut, rather full and eased into the armscye. The cuffs are snug and buttoned. A small white collar, also related to feminine attire, finishes the neckline. Ball-shaped brass buttons like these, with shanks, were common features of boys' and women's coats in the late sixties.

His soft felt hat has a rather shallow, broad crown and a moderately wide brim, which causes it to appear rather flat in wear. The boy's wavy hair is parted, combed to one side, and blunt-cut at ear level, although a little too long; by contemporary standards, the child needed a haircut.

Ca. 1865

Courtesy of the Museum of American Textile History
(P 341)

FROM THE EARLIEST days of photography, it was common for mill girls to have their photographs taken dressed in their work clothing, often in groups, as though it were something to celebrate or record. The small instruments tucked into a holder at the belt of one and into a buttonhole on the bodice of the other are reed-picks, with which broken warp threads were caught and drawn through the comblike reed of the loom to be tied back in to the warp. In their hands the women carry shuttles wound with cotton weft threads.

While this photograph is dated 1865, it may have been taken a year or two earlier, judging by the moderate sleeve fullness and the tightly skinned-back hairstyles, although it is worth noting that fuller sleeves and hair would probably not have been worn for work around mill machinery.

The high necks, linen band collars, and shoulder seam placement coincide with day dress cuts of mid-decade. The short skirts are another story. In many, but not all, cases women who worked around the looms wore dresses shortened to the boot tops to avoid getting long skirts entangled in the machinery and to give them unhampered, free movement. Some women who worked in the mills, however, actually wore full-length skirts and hoops at work. While no hoops are worn here, both figures are certainly, if only lightly, corseted.

A dark-ground calico, printed with a small monochromatic figure, is used for the older woman's dress, while the other is probably of black cotton chintz, a common material for work dresses because it shed the lint ever present in the mill air.

Their aprons, rounded at the bottom corners and made of light-colored calicos, are typical of those worn by housewives and small children in the late sixties and into the seventies. Those with bibs were pinned in place on the dress. White cotton knitted stockings, probably factory made, are visible above the high, square-toed black boots. The boots have small "high" heels of about an inch or an inch and a quarter in height.

THE SITE OF this portrait may have been a sort of traveling studio, the photographer having brought along a painted canvas backdrop, a few props, some mismatched chairs, and a ground cloth, all of which could be rolled up and put into a wagon for the next day's journey.

These two self-confident young men, while obviously dressed in everyday clothing, are wearing quite up-to-date styles. Their jackets, especially—no longer oversized but fitting rather neatly—show a late-decade cut. The rest of their gear is much worn and scuffed, so it is plain that these men are not dandies but have merely purchased serviceable readymade clothing in the going style.

The man at left wears a matching sack coat and vest. The coat has the braid trim popular from the midsixties, and the buttons and buttonholes rise very high on the rather small lapels. The two-piece sleeve is only moderately full, and the coat is slightly cut away at the skirt fronts. The single-breasted vest is collarless. Striped trousers, which may be of cotton jean, are worn. The striped shirt is collarless and buttoned to the neckband. The neckbands of such shirts had buttonholes all around for collar buttons and separate white starched collars but are often seen in such photographs worn plain. His scuffed boots appear to be of brown leather, in the pull-on style, and have broad, softly squared toes. A dark felt hat, with a rather large crown and soft brim, is pulled comfortably well down above his ears.

The other man wears a shorter sack, with straight fronts, and a matching vest of a muted plaid. A rather large, notched-collar vest is worn over a plain, light-colored collarless shirt. The narrow trousers, of soft wool, fall over worn boots, which appear to have soft tongues lying over the instep with the fronts curled. His hat, while similar to the other man's in its flat-topped, large crown, has a stiffer brim.

FEBRUARY 1866

Courtesy of the Southern Historical Collection
(P3615-819)

LOCATED ON THE Sea Islands off the coast of South Carolina at Frogmore, outside of Beaufort, the Penn School was established in 1861 by the Freedmen's Association of Philadelphia, a Quaker organization, and took as its students the children of ex-slaves from nearby plantations. The children were taught to read, write, and "cipher" and were also very practically trained in social customs and the performance of many common jobs in order to prepare them for living as free people. Boys learned carpentry and other building skills, and girls learned to sew, cook, and clean.

There are many remaining photographs of the students and staff during these early years, from which it is possible to make some deductions. The clothing of the children, by all appearances, consisted of castoffs, probably solicited from Quakers in their many churches.

The boy, Dick, wears a narrow sack coat of 1840s vintage, much the worse for wear and showing the overlarge buttons of that time. He wears the required shirt and tie and no doubt shoes as well, as the children were also taught what was "proper" in dress.

The older girl, Maria, wears a neat spotted dress that not only fits her better but is far more up-to-date than the clothes worn by the other children. The dress is of the modest type often recommended for servants and children and features a prim white neck band. The sleeves are

moderately full on the dropped shoulders and gathered into wrist bands. The skirt appears to be gathered all around. This may well have been one of the dresses made in the school's sewing classes.

Amoretta, the youngest child, wears a combination of misfit garments, beginning with an oversized, faded 1850s basque bodice over a thin, faded dress, from which one of the grow-tucks of the skirt has been let out. Her white petticoat hangs unevenly below the dress and is short enough to reveal the rough, old shoes and white cotton stockings. The children were evidently not allowed to go without shoes at school.

In this portrait Laura M. Towne, one of the first three teachers to teach at Penn School, arriving in 1861, is simply dressed, as befits a Quaker lady, yet still displays fashionable elements of the midsixties. Her full skirt is of dark-colored silk and is worn over full petticoats (no hoop). The short jacket of black silk has a curved, wide coat sleeve with a deep cuff and hangs slightly over the skirt waistband. The jacket's hem is trimmed with braid matching that on the cuffs and fronts, and there are braid frog closures at front under a bow of narrow black satin ribbon. The jacket fronts fall open to reveal a white waist with a narrow band collar. Her hair is done in a simple style, combed down and waved at the temples and twisted into a bun low on the nape.

THESE TWO CARTES de visite were taken of an unnamed family in St. Joseph, Missouri: three-cent stamps on the back of each bear the handwritten date of 1866, with "Uhlman & Rippel, Photographers, Third St., opp. Express Office, and 51 Edmond St., Saint Joseph, MO."

The father poses alone in a stiff wool suit with braid-bound edges and brass buttons, a white small-collared shirt, and the smallest of the popular horizontal neck bows. He wears a common style of well-trimmed beard and mustache, and a heavy gold link watch chain is fastened in a vest buttonhole. Whatever his business, his position in the community appears to be secure.

In the companion portrait, his two little boys pose with their mother. Her clothing is that of a reasonably well-to-do middle-class woman. Speculatively, the mother's glossy straight black hair and her features suggest Native American blood, which would make this a rare photograph indeed, although the displaced Cherokee, for instance, often lived in association with black families, and there was much intermarriage. Her dress appears to be of a lightweight wool or wool blend with sprigged floral patterns in white or some light color. Her handsome sleeves and the yoke line of the bodice are decorated with rows of contrasting satin ribbon. The low yoke line is a late-sixties feature and is entirely artificial; that is, it does not follow the cut of the bodice but is merely applied over the darted and well-fitted shape. A smart, narrow collar of heavy lace is worn with scalloped white linen cuffs. The waist-line is near normal, dropped down from the earlier style, and the pleated skirt is arranged gracefully over a modest hoop. Her hair is done conservatively in a somewhat youthful manner, with a long ringlet behind each ear. The long drop earrings and thin gold watch chain are tasteful accessories.

The boys are dressed alike in braid-trimmed Zouave jackets with tab closures over long-sleeved white shirts, with the frilled cuffs showing below the jacket sleeves. The trousers are buttoned over the shirts at the waist; quite full and pleated, they are worn long. The boys' curly hair is combed into a top section parted off from the sides and back and rolled to the side.

Ca. 1866
Courtesy of the Oakland Museum

Elaborate coiffures still continue fashionable; the principal styles being short frizzed curls, crepe bandeaux, and rolls. Many have adopted the Princess Alexandra style of hair dressing. The hair is carried off the temples à l'imperatrice [the "Eugénie" hairstyle], with two long ringlets behind the ear, which fall on the neck.

—Godey's, September 1863

Skirts are made quite short in front, and all the fullness is thrown to the back, which is made very long. Every breadth is cut slanting at the bottom, and the longest part falls to the back. From the hips the plaits all turn to the back.

—Godey's, April 1864

TWO EXTREMELY FASHIONABLE young Californians pose for this portrait. The standing figure is tightly laced, and wears the newest-style oval hoop, which hangs quite smoothly down the front with its fullness taken to the back, giving a triangular line under her crisp gored and pleated skirt. At least two cotton petticoats over the crinoline were required to smooth out the line to this extent. Black velvet bands are arranged en tablier, or in apron form, at the skirt front, with black silk fringe at the bottom and two matching long, broad sash ends (like panels) fall down the back of the slightly trained skirt. The sleeves are in the smart, tight "condé" style for fall and winter and are trimmed with black velvet bands and tabs at the cuffs and with black silk fringe as an epaulette. Black velvet revers finish the bodice, framing the chemisette front. A black belt encircles her small waist. With this costume, she wears delicate but elaborate drop earrings, possibly of jet, and at her throat a small round brooch over a narrow ribbon bow. The hair is done in the elegant crimped "waterfall," a waved puff raised high on the crown and fastened to the nape of the neck. The fine waves at the temples are probably the result of crimping with a hot iron.

The seated figure wears a no-less-expensive costume, though without the extreme skirt and sleeve. It appears to be of a stiff silk poplin and may be a light tan, lilac, or mauve ("ashes of roses" and "rose sublime" were two of many romantic color definitions used in the sixties). The bodice is finished in the heart shape, trimmed with silk fringe, and worn with a ribbon sash to match the dress. A starched linen band, worn very high at the throat, is closed with a small brooch; the watch chain appears to depend from this point. The sleeves are in the coatsleeve style, but with narrower forearms and extra elbow fullness. Fringe is attached from below the elbow to the wrist in the outer seam, and the cuff is finished with a linen band. The skirt is cut very full and gored, with flat pleats at front and box pleats behind, and is worn over the fashionable flat-fronted oval hoop. Graduated horizontal tucks around the bottom give a crisp finish.

Her hair, into which her companion seems to be placing an ostrich feather tip, is crimped and worn *à l'imperatrice,* daintily set off by large drop pearl earrings.

1866–68

Courtesy of the Essex Institute (14.849)

The taste for solid colors seems to prevail,
and never were such greens, purples,
modes, and garnets as those of this season.
—*Godey's,* January 1863

Mrs. James Babcock of Salem, Massachusetts, was a member of a family of free blacks well known in the community for their excellent catering business.

The narrow, curved, bell-shaped sleeve of her dress dates from about 1866 and was cut to curve at the elbow on the inner seam, causing the sleeve to hang to the front, much as the plainer coat sleeves did. Unlike bell sleeves of the fifties and early sixties, these hang nearly to the wrist and curve up sharply at the inseam to show the cuffed undersleeves.

The bodice is cut in an earlier style, but the manner of trimming is distinctly late sixties. Buttons began to have more importance at about this time and were frequently quite large and often cloth or crochet covered. Trim became fanciful toward the midsixties, sometimes, as in this case, consisting of strips of narrow ruching following the boned front darts and with matching trim on the skirt. A pinked, pleated self-ruching finishes the open sleeve edge, and the white undersleeves show slightly. A typically small white lace collar is worn. The hoop worn to support this skirt is probably of the correct, narrow, flat-fronted shape for the date, but it is held unnaturally by the iron support against which she is braced. The dress could have been in any of a number of rich colors popular throughout the decade.

Mrs. Babcock's hairstyle is even more up-to-date than her costume; it has been carefully done in a short fringe of ringlets behind and below the ears and is dressed with a coronet braid and soft rolls at the temples.

CARTE DE VISITE, 1866–70

Courtesy of Deborah Fontana Cooney

This photograph, by L. D. Johnson of Vineland, New Jersey, is of Mrs. Mary E. Tillotson. Mrs. Tillotson was a charter member of the National Dress Reform Association, whose constitution was drawn up in 1856.

The clothing adopted by Mrs. Tillotson for this occasion is not quite as drastic as it seems at first glance. While she has, indeed, left off the intervening knee-length skirt under the long tunic, only the trousers and the sturdy, low-heeled boots have any masculine appearance. The tunic she wears is identical in all respects to one featured in *Godey's* in April 1866 as the bodice of a croquet dress worn over a normal full-length skirt.

The dainty collar, with its standing frill of crimped lace, is finished at the throat by black and white lace ends under a rosette and is similar to fine, expensive collars shown in *Godey's* for May 1862. It is quite feminine, as is the hat she holds over the cloak draped over the back of the chair. This hat is one of those half-bonnet styles, with ribbon loops over each ear and a white ostrich plume "thrown over the crown," meant to be worn with fashionable walking costumes. Her hair is done in truly up-to-the-minute rolls and ringlets.

She carries a scrolled paper in one hand, perhaps a copy of the National Dress Reform Constitution she so whole-heartedly supported. According to historians, Mrs. Tillotson maintained her connection to the Dress Reform movement all of her life, obviously in the face of much public ridicule. The front page of the *Daily Graphic,* a New York evening newspaper, is given over on Saturday, January 24, 1876, to a series of unflattering cartoons of a dress reformer's convention evidently just held in the city. Mrs. Tillotson is the subject of two of the caricatures, one labeled "Mrs. Tillotson/Vice President of the Asst/20 years ago," showing her as an attractive young lady wearing an 1850s hairstyle and bloomer dress, and another showing "Mrs. Tillotson/20 years later," which depicted her as an unattractive old woman in the seventies dressed in a version of the tunic with pleated flounces and a long ringlet hairstyle. An even more pointed thrust is made at the movement in this article with the caricature bust of an unnamed woman in a short haircut and eyeglasses, labeled "Not particularly good looking, but so intellectual."

Skirts are worn as ample and full as ever, and are generally gored to throw them out at the bottom.

—*Godey's,* October 1861

We find also a charming assortment of fancy jackets, most of them sleeveless, but finished on the shoulders by an epaulette.

—*Godey's,* June 1866

A very convenient style of Garibaldi waist for morning wear is of muslin or alpaca. It is made with two box plaits corded into a band at the throat. At the waist there is no band; it is drawn at the back with a drawstring which ties inside. The rest is kept in place by the skirt which is fastened over it. It can be trimmed with braiding or cord.

—*Godey's,* June 1865

EMILY HILL AND Rose Gaylord of Florence, Massachusetts, pose here, at about age sixteen, in youthful versions of skirt-and-waist styles not easily traced either through the fashion plates or existing collections of historic clothing. The most obvious clue for dating is the shape of their hair, which is wide at the temples in late sixties fashion. But a more subtle clue is in the smooth front of Rose's skirt; by this date gored, narrow-hipped styles began replacing the full skirts.

Emily, on the left, wears a fine muslin Garibaldi with rows of drawn cord transversing the V-shaped yoke and forming soft puffs between them. The front closure is accentuated in the photograph because of the watch chain, which hangs from behind the brooch closing the linen band collar. The shirtwaist is full in the bosom, and the sleeves are cut full and eased into the low armscye for a soft effect. Her skirt is simply gathered all around and is of a plain light-colored material, probably cotton, and is well supported by a hoop and several full petticoats. Hidden by her arm is certainly one of the snug, rather wide belts preferred for such styles, possibly one of elastic. Her hair is done in a most grown-up deep puff at the crown and waved and curled deeply at the temples in the latest fashion.

Rose wears a skirt and Spanish jacket made of matching plaid cotton material, but the jacket has been quilted and the centers and lines of the plaids overembroidered in black, to go with her black brooch and the jet buttons of her waist. This waist is of a simpler style than Emily's and is therefore more suitable for wear under the bolero-type jacket. The extremely high band collar of starched linen is most becoming. The skirt of this costume is cut in the newly approved gores, with a center-front seam but no pleats or gathers in the front whatsoever; all fullness is concentrated at the back. The hoop worn with this skirt is narrow at the hips, oval and flaring at the back hem. The waistband is wide and snug, and no belt is worn over it. Rose wears another version of the wide-temple hairstyles made popular by the Empress Eugénie of France; this is a youthful adaptation with a thick roll high at either side, rather than the deep waves, and with the back hair falling in a few curls at the nape. A flat white bow is pinned at the top of the crown.

STEREOPTICON VIEW, CA. 1867

Courtesy of the State Historical Society of Wisconsin
(WHi [X3] 37029)

GEORGE T. LINDEMAN, a photographer from Milwaukee, traveled the state of Wisconsin taking, and selling, stereographic views. This scene he entitled "American Farm Yard in Winter," which he additionally labeled "Taken West of Milwaukee."

Here, far from any exclusive reform community or health spa, we find the "American Costume" in everyday use by a woman obviously dressed for utilitarian purposes. The shortened skirt and the appearance of little or no corseting are evidence of an independent mind, suiting the needs of frontier life. The woolen checked dress, with its ruching trim and elaborate sleeves, almost certainly started out as a long dress, worn over a hoop, to be worn to church and town.

Most women did not use the bloomer dress as their only costume. They were not, in fact, making a statement by wearing the style; rather, they were choosing safe, comfortable adaptations so that they could perform hard, active work efficiently. This garment is considerably looser and wider in the waist than normal; it was probably let out when made into a working dress. In its original use it was worn over a corset. The worn apron of gingham check was possibly cut from an old dress.

On her head this young farm wife wears a black wool "fascinator," a bonnet knitted or crocheted of wool yarn and edged with loops across the crown and at the ears. It is tied under her chin, without a bow, with wide, white-edged, dark ribbon. Her long hair hangs in ringlets below the bonnet.

The little boy is dressed in a suit made with a long-sleeved shirt buttoned to long, full matching trousers at the waist. The sleeves are of typical coat-sleeve style, set low, and the shirt has a small collar. He carries a soft black felt hat with a fairly wide brim and a wide dark band. His well-brushed blond hair is blunt-cut at ear level and combed to one side.

His father wears an old frock coat over woolen or denim trousers, well soaked and soiled at the cuffs. His light-colored vest may be a knitted one. He sports a full beard and mustache and wears a fur cap.

TINTYPE, 1867–70

Courtesy of the National Museum of American History (C69.25.4)

THIS THIN YOUNG man, in a new black wool suit of the late-sixties style, has grown a rather impressive beard, even though he is probably not past his midtwenties.

The shorter sack coat appears to have been buttoned at the top at times, as it hangs from that point suggestively. The sleeve has the deep elbow cut typical of this date and is narrowed considerably at the wrist. While it appears as though the young man is without a vest, he probably wears one nearly open under the coat, closing at the lower buttons only. The commonly worn starched white shirtfront and small standing collar, with the extremely narrow black tie, are almost clerical in appearance. The trousers show the width of the generous cut of the sixties with the "break" over the front of the boot and the slight drop to the heel. He wears the typical square-toed pull-on boots.

Most dashing is the spanking new hat, which is a Brighton style (as pictured in a Charles Oakford and Sons advertisement in *Godey's* in May 1866), of stiff black felt with a wide black silk ribbon band.

July 1868

Courtesy of the Valentine Museum (1563)

BABY HEUSTIS COOK, shown here with his nurse, was the son of Richmond photographer George Cook, who took this record portrait of his baby son and his son's nurse. Heustis himself grew up to become a noted photographer of Southern life.

But the attractive and neatly dressed nurse is the focus of attention in this photograph. Her bold, black-and-white-striped dress, with its directional treatment in the yoke bands, is of a most current fashion for morning dress. The small round puff at the top of the sleeve is a stylish addition that has no basis in pure function; it is cut on the bias and perfectly set in. The sleeve below it is perhaps somewhat looser than the fashion, which is generally shown as very snug below such puffs. This adaptation, however, undoubtedly made lifting and caring for a baby easier. The bodice of the dress is gathered into a waist so neat and small that it is obviously fitted over a proper corset. Snow white linen is worn at the throat, as is a cameo brooch. Her hair is done smoothly in a net in a simple manner followed by most women for everyday.

The attire and grooming of this highly visible servant reflects the pride of the Cook family in its home and position in the community; house servants appeared as extensions of the family's means and taste. As the child's nurse, this woman would ideally stay with him, in the background, all the years of his growing up and remain with the family to care for any future children.

A soft, dark, woolen shawl over one shoulder cradles Heustis's head as he reclines on his nurse's lap. His short-sleeved, fine muslin baby dress has a very long skirt with many narrow tucks and is trimmed at the yoke and sleeves with whitework embroidery. Several long white petticoats fill out the long skirt.

GLASS-PLATE NEGATIVE, 1868

Courtesy of the Oakland Museum (12.50)

AFTER THE WAR, A. W. Russell, already well-known for his Civil War battlefield photographs, became the official photographer for the Union Pacific Railroad and recorded the progress of the line with many views.

This dated shot, taken at Echo City, Nevada, shows the new plank end-of-track office building, which was taken down and rebuilt as the road moved west, the crew staying in one locality as long as it was practical. The clarity of this image and the variety of men's garments provide an excellent overview of men's ready-to-wear clothing at the end of the decade. The variations in the cut of jackets are particularly apparent.

In the doorway stands Dan Casement, payroll chief for the road. The men with him are his clerks, the large number apparently necessary in order to keep operations, and the huge crew of workers, moving efficiently.

The young man at far left, probably either black or Native American, is well dressed in a sack coat, quite short, cut away to round fronts and with narrow notched lapels. The sleeves are quite narrow and are set into a near-natural shoulder line. The coat is shaped but not closely fitted, a reasonably new cut. His light vest is waist length and snug enough to show transverse wrinkles. It is buttoned to the neck with brass buttons and has a narrow turndown collar. A trim white shirt collar and neat striped tie just show above the vest. The black, rather stiff felt hat, its crown slightly pinched, has a firm, rolled, bound brim. His black boots appear exceptionally well cared for.

The seated man to his right wears a black slouch hat and is dressed in matching light-colored plaid wool vest and trousers, with a generously cut black sack with a shawl collar. A narrow black tie is nipped into a small bow under a starched white collar. The single-breasted vest is below-waist length and only casually buttoned, apparently at the neck and waist, in a popular offhand style. The uncreased trousers are tubular in cut, the backs longer than the fronts. His well-worn pull-on boots with their broad squared toes and sturdy soles and heels are clearly visible.

In the next chair, the man wears a well-worn outfit consisting of a black homburg hat and a sack suit of black wool made with shawl collar and bound edges. The jacket is medium length and has very slightly rounded front corners. The vest, unbuttoned, has rounded corners and reaches below the waist. All edges, including pockets, are bound. Under the vest the shirt is of fine horizontal stripes or checks; the collar and tie are hidden under his beard. Well-worn and dusty boots extend from rather narrow trouser legs, uncreased and clearly showing their machine hems.

The man standing behind him, against the door frame, is without facial hair and wears the small, dapper round hat mostly seen on young men for the next fifteen years or so. The short, semifitted sack and narrow trousers are of recent cut and similar to the suit at extreme left but with wider lapels. The single-breasted, waist-length vest, appearing so much darker in the picture, is probably of silk, as it catches the light differently than does the black wool. He wears it fully buttoned, to show off a heavy watch chain. His boots reveal that they have received more attention, that they are newer, or that he has a more indoor job than the other men.

Dan Casement, in the doorway, wears light-colored trousers, uncreased, with rather wide tubular legs with the bottoms cut longer at the heel. His long, cutaway, wide-collared sack coat is worn over a matching vest buttoned only at the top and at the waist. The shape and cock of his homburg hat are highly individual, as is his extra-long full beard. His worn, soft boots are in need of polish.

A thoroughly dished-in black felt hat and a shirt without coat or vest mark the man sitting to Casement's left as very much an individual. His shirt is very loose, blousing over the trousers, and has a tailored sleeve with a pleat at the cuff. His brush beard just covers the common narrow black tie. Most remarkable, however, are the trousers with black braid down the seam, which may be of military issue. Many men, including the photographer himself, had migrated directly from military service to the new railroad in search of jobs. Many of Russell's images taken for the Union Pacific show men wearing parts of military uniforms, both Union and Confederate.

In fact, the second-to-last gentleman seated on the right wears what could be Confederate gray trousers, complete with military braid. With them he wears the ordinary shawl-collared black sack and black vest over the white shirt and narrow tie. The full mustache and outstanding white hat may denote a different background or different taste from the other men.

And at far right, the gentleman in the broad-brimmed wide-awake hat wears pin-striped black trousers with his moderately cut sack and vest. His worn boots are evidence that this part of the country was dry, dusty, and hard on footgear.

What may seem remarkable in this photograph is the almost universal adherence to coat, vest, tie, and hat in a situation far from urban refinements. The prevalence of this custom is borne out by all American photographs of men throughout this decade, no matter what the situation.

A. W. RUSSELL frequently took photographs of settlers as the Union Pacific Railroad pushed westward. This extended Mormon family, the Ashtons, was brought together outside their small, sod-roofed log house and photographed while the crew was working out of Kaysville, Utah, in August 1868.

The simple clothing of the Ashton family is adapted to life in such a home on (probably) a working sheep ranch. Yet the women's dresses, though plain, are not made in total ignorance of fashionable cut. Rather, they represent acceptable day dresses of some three to five years earlier and in fact are the same plain styles retained everywhere for active work.

The striped dress on the woman at far left has a neat, curved coatsleeve finished with black ribbon, and the calico dress worn by the woman standing to the right of the door, at the churn, shows the extremely full sleeve of the early half of the decade in an unusual extension of its period of popularity. To the right, the seated woman with the child on her lap wears a similar style in a darker color with a small white collar.

Mary Ashton, standing at left in the doorway, has the most unusual costume; she wears a short sack, possibly with a set-in waistband, of colored calico over a darker calico skirt; this smocklike everyday garment was called a "Josie," and while it is not found in photographs in any numbers, it was a common workgarment throughout the nineteenth century in all parts of the country. None of the women wears a hoop, but, from the form of most of the skirts, full petticoats are evident.

Both little girls wear dresses of striped fabric similar to that used in the dress worn by the woman standing at the spinning wheel, and all of them may either have been made from wool spun and woven at home or from one bolt of goods. The children wear bib aprons of colored cotton. The barefoot boy at right wears a dark jacket that buttons at front with bright buttons and mid-calf-length trousers.

Samuel Ashton, seated in the doorway, wears well-worn high boots, with the trousers tucked in, and a faded (probably blue) work shirt, which is partially buttoned over a darker shirt underneath, and a dusty slouch hat.

The entire family appears surprisingly well-groomed and presentable given the environment and the circumstances.

AN UNIDENTIFIED YOUNG girl, about sixteen years of age, poses for "G. D. Morse, Photographer, 315 Montgomery Street, San Francisco." It is her hairstyle that provides the best date for this portrait, and the costume details confirm it. Her hair is done in a popular youthful style with clusters of long ringlets held at the sides by combs and with a smart little hat, proper only for very young ladies, tilted straight over the forehead.

Checks, especially of black and white, were extremely popular in 1868, and the yoke effect in black velvet ribbon had been smart fashion since about 1866. The late-sixties cut is well displayed by the arm held across the lap: small at the armscye, with a definite curve, larger through the upper arm and elbow, and tapered to the cuff.

The short-waistedness of the late sixties is graphically demonstrated in the belted dress, and the fitted bodice shows the expected curved corset line. The belt is quite likely one of elasticized black mesh with a large metal buckle, of the kind mentioned for boys' smocks and ladies' dresses in the late sixties. The high, plain linen collar is closed with one of the black brooches so popular at this time, made either of bog oak or jet, and the thick black chain necklace and earrings are probably of the same material. The skirt is well supported with petticoats, not extremely full, and is probably gored, although it shows waist gathers. She wears a hoop under it, though this is the extreme end of the popularity of the hoop.

Mrs. Evatt of San Francisco sits for her portrait at the studio of "W. H. Cook & Co., Successors to James Dorr, 28 3rd St., San Francisco." Mrs. Evatt, who appears to be in her midthirties, wears a somewhat too-girlish hairstyle. This ringlet fashion, so popular with young ladies in 1868, is formed by parting the hair in the center and bringing the side hair straight to the back, where it is held by combs. Then the hair is parted down the back and pulled toward the ears at either side and held with side combs; there it is set in long ringlets in a high position, with braids forming a crown. Long earrings usually accompany this hairdo. While we might assume that this hairstyle was not acceptable for women of Mrs. Evatt's age, a few other photographs show fortyish women wearing it as well.

Mrs. Evatt wears the closely fitted style of the last two years of the decade, probably of wool, in one of the popular stripes trimmed with narrow white-edged black velvet ribbon in yoke fashion. A rosette of this ribbon is pinned at waistfront. The bodice cut and the rather narrow, gored skirt with its deep flounce help date this portrait close to 1870. The large buttons are also a feature of dress about this time. The relatively close-fitting coatsleeves, with their fitted cuffs and full caps, also speak to the late date. The figure shows clearly the effects of the short, curvaceous corset of the late sixties, which emphasized the bosom.

Large gold cuff links and a very long gold watch chain are worn, the watch brought up and tucked above the button just below the yoke line.

Ca. 1869

*Courtesy of the National Museum of
American History (83.7983)*

IN A CHARMING gored dress of heavy cotton, this eight- or nine-year-old girl poses with her wax-bonnet doll. The girl's hair is brushed back and done up at the back of the head in one of the plainer late-sixties styles, and the dress has many features that aid in dating.

First is the fabric. Based on numerous surviving examples, seen and handled, this dark cotton can confidently be said to be of a heavy weave with raised woven stripes crossing at the plaids in a darker color. The general coloration of this heavy material is often brown—a medium, slightly reddish, brown for the squares and a deep-brown, woven, raised cord crossing at the centers. The border squares in such combinations are usually of cream with some orangish-yellow.

The cut is also an excellent guide: the skirt is plainly gored and finished at the hem with a bias flounce with a heading, a treatment seen into the early seventies. The skirt is set into a wide, straight waistband, and the bodice, which has a deeply shaped yoke, is slightly gathered into it. The close, round neckline is set off by a small frill of white lace. The narrow sleeve is still in the two-piece style, though much narrower than formerly, and is finished with a bias self-ruching. A bit of white stocking and black boot top can be seen beneath the skirt flounce.

The doll is dressed in a "princess feather" hat (actually molded in one with the wax head), which dates to the late sixties as well, and wears a white shirtwaist with jet buttons, a short-sleeved open jacket, and a light-colored skirt.

LATE 1860S

Courtesy of the Library of Congress
(LC-B-8171, 152-A)

THERE IS ALWAYS poverty, and any treatment of clothing habits for a given period should include the results of having no money for clothing. Because there is no body of evidence, a photographic study cannot do this well: few portraits were taken of people who could not pay for them. After the Civil War, when the Deep South was thrown into such a state of bankruptcy, curiosity led some photographers to make tours and record in photographs the devastated land and people. This is such a photograph, possibly one taken as a part of a series meant to provide illustrations for a lecture.

The black families of the South, forcefully disengaged from their former owners after the Civil War, at first did not have the resources to find gainful employment, nor did even the most sympathetic planters have money with which to pay them, nor was there any real business set up that needed workers. At best, for many years poor black families relied on seasonal jobs as field hands.

The clothing of this family is not datable as a whole. While individual garments suggest certain periods, one can only speculate on how long they may have been worn. The garments themselves are almost certainly castoffs and cover a broad span of years.

The dress of the standing woman holding the baby consists of a small-print calico skirt, probably cut from an old dress, and a white shirtwaist with the sleeves rolled up. The apron is either of a light, plain color or is a badly faded piece of calico.

The dress worn by the woman standing at right has a short basque bodice cut in a fifties fashion and trimmed all around with a dark contrasting frill. She wears it with a mismatched spotted skirt cut short for ease in walking. A whitework-trimmed fifties-style petticoat shows at the hem over man's work boots. The seated woman wears a striped cotton skirt under her apron, together with a white shirtwaist and a buttoned jacket, with the sixties-style sleeves pushed up nearly to the elbow.

The standing man wears a white, probably cotton, vest of a late-fifties cut, fairly long and made with a narrow shawl collar, with many small buttons down the front, and cut straight across at the bottom. His shirt is white and is worn with the collar open. Over it he wears what may be a gray uniform coat from the Rebel army. The seated man wears jeans that appear to have been worn all through the war, probably the last of his slave-issue clothing, with an open shirt of common make and a loose sack coat that is ten or fifteen years out of date.

The children's clothing does fit them, though it is in poor shape. The boy kneeling at front wears a passable roundabout jacket and wide-awake hat.

CHAPTER FOUR

The 1870s

And now a word about those samples you sent me. I thought the cashmere very pretty indeed. The material of the green dress is just such as we once called moreen, and was used almost exclusively to cover a chair, cushions and sometimes used for window curtains. We would as soon then have thought of wearing mosquito bar for a dress as that. So much for the ups and downs of fashion.

—Susan A. Brown, December 21, 1879

*A*t the beginning of the decade the country was still in a postwar recession, which became a depression in 1872. The lack of money and jobs undoubtedly affected fashion, but such a trend is difficult to trace through photographs. The fashions were still published as usual in the American magazines, and people were still photographed in clothing that resembled the styles in the fashion plates. Still, poorer people may well have worn their good clothing a few more years before being able to purchase a new style during these hard times.

The fashions themselves did not change enough in the first three years of the decade to actually require new purchases; this phenomenon was due not to the recession in America but to the troubles overseas. The Franco-Prussian War (1870–71), which resulted in the loss of the Alsace-Lorraine to Prussia, caused much hardship and suffering throughout France and actually interrupted fashion communications for a time, the only such occurrence during the sixty-year period of this study. American fashion writers apparently did not say much about the war and its effects, but it was discussed in depth in English magazines. In 1870, in an unsigned article in *The Young Englishwoman,* a fashion writer bemoans the current conditions. She begins by pondering the "incongruity" of the French having always set the styles for English ladies, though she admits to a fondness for French taste. She then traces the history of French fashion supremacy, finishing with the observation that

No serious interruption of communication has taken place, until the eventful year of 1870, and certainly no autumn fashions are attainable now. How long the intercourse will be suspended it is impossible to guess at. On the score of humanity alone, it is to be hoped that Paris will be spared the horrors and devastation which have fallen upon so many of the thriving towns and villages. . . .

Though Paris is mute for the present, and l'ordre du jour is very far from favorable to the fashions, we still get many ideas and a large quantity of material from France. (600, 608)

Yet American magazines continued providing fashion plates, culled from earlier French offerings, and discussing styles at length. It was patently important to American writers, and to fashionable American women, that the latest word was from *la belle France*—no matter how stale. When commerce was resumed, the new French line was immediately copied.

Many other factors, however, went into the formulation of American fashion in the seventies. The availability of the sewing machine and the success of American fabric makers were critical factors, and equally important was the development of a system of standardized proportional measurements, which made possible the cheap production of both patterns and readymade clothing. Added to this, vast improvements in transportation and marketing were developed during this decade. There was, consequently, by this time no hamlet too insignificant or removed to receive the pattern catalogs and ladies' magazines or to have available a selection of fabrics, pattern systems, and sewing machines, almost as soon as they were available in the Eastern cities.

Jensen and Davidson suggest that the sewing machine was not so much the cause as one of the results of the changes in the clothing industry. They note that sewing machines could have been developed at least twenty years earlier than they were, as a number of people were already working on models in the 1820s. These attempts were discouraged because of economic reasons; in the early days mills did not have the capability of producing the vast amounts of fabric to make the machines viable. It was also felt that too many seamstresses would be put out of work, without the possibility of very great profit to the manufacturers (37–38). Developments of the sewing machine were made during the fifties and sixties, and by the 1870s all of the variables were in place to make it profitable to install machines in every factory. The many women displaced from their jobs were then employed, at reduced wages, to sew undergarments and shirts and to do the hand-finishing on machine-made garments —a very good deal for the manufacturer.

A side effect of these combined events was the virtual end of the era of the small dressmaker. By 1880 in Philadelphia alone there were 80 percent fewer dressmaking and millinery establishments than there had been in 1860, and there was a parallel increase in readymades during the same period (Jensen and Davidson 49–50).

Home Sewing

Owning a sewing machine was a matter of some social importance among the middle class, and there was no shame in claiming the manufacture of one's own nice clothing. Jensen and Davidson's demographic survey of the owners of sewing machines reveals some interesting comparisons: families that owned sewing machines actually spent slightly more on readymades than nonowners, and 59 percent of church-going families owned machines, a somewhat larger percentage than for nonchurch-goers (38). These facts suggest that there was a relationship between the moral perception of self and family and the desire to be fashionably dressed. The conclusion to be drawn from this is that upwardly mobile families whose standards included cultural and religious training perceived certain material possessions as markers of their comparative respectability. The ability to have new clothing from the continually changing offerings of current fashion, with their built-in obsolescence, was one of the most important of these symbols. "Women across the nation could now make fashionable clothing without specialized training. Moreover, they were expected to keep up with fashions or suffer social ostracism" (Jensen and Davidson 12).

Women also used their sewing machines to add to their incomes. In the reminiscences of a woman earning $30 per month teaching penmanship in Neilsville in southern Wisconsin in 1871 is mention of a sister who had set up business as a milliner in Waukesha: "She was good at making over old hats. She could reshape any old straw hat, mend it and make it look like new. Besides she had a sewing machine I had bought for her the year before. Very few women possessed such a machine and as ruffles on dresses and underwear were the height of style at the time, she got the hemming of ruffles, for which she charged a penny a yard" (Brinker 202).

A sewing machine could be purchased for approximately $64 by 1870 (they cost about $12 to make), yet not every family could afford one, as the average annual wage in the seventies was $500 (Jensen and Davidson 37). A woman herself generally made far less; the township of Vienna in Dane County, Wisconsin, paid $1.75 per day to its teacher during the school term, and in 1879 a young woman signed a three-month contract to teach school in Madison, Wisconsin, at $18 per month. Still, many women whose incomes were low did buy machines, and married women persuaded their husbands to do so for them; some determined to take in sewing to make a living, some hoped that their own clothing savings for the family would account for the cost, and some mainly wished to own a machine as a symbol of respectability, hiring local seamstresses to use it for them. Jensen and Davidson's list of priorities for the family woman at this time is enlightening: first, carpet the floor; second, keep the children at home and out of the factory; third, buy a sewing machine; and finally, buy a parlor organ (38).

The social importance of the sewing machine is not to be denied, yet its direct role was to provide more people with more and better clothing for less money. Because American women everywhere now had access to good fabrics and had learned to cut and sew, no fashion, however new and elaborate, was denied any of them. Their individual boundaries were limited only by the amount of time available and their degree of skill, given that they could afford fabric. The latest news about making fashionable garments was printed monthly, and patterns were eagerly exchanged. In addition to the amount of published material available to her, the home sewer often relied on the advice of knowledgeable friends, sometimes through correspondence:

> I liked the material of your dolman, and I want you to be sure and tell me what it would cost. That is, the bare cloth, as I have a cashmere dolman lined like that that I never liked. It is trimmed with fringe for which I paid $1.00 a yard. I thought I would like to get a new dolman and have cut a later style, and take that cashmere and with some black silk then make Anna a dress. Now I want to purchase something for piping. What shall it be and what color shall it be? I want you to tell me and do not wait, please, several years to reply, because while I am waiting, she will outgrow the material. I send to New York for anything I want in the shape of fancy silk. (Susan A. Brown, December 21, 1879)

Advice on what ladies were to wear and spend was also available in fashion magazines and newspapers. In "A Woman's Wardrobe," in the November 1877 *Prairie Farmer,* Jenny June gives her list of indispensable items:

One silk dress:	$65.00
One woolen costume:	$35.00
One indoor dress:	$15.00
Summer dresses, making, trimming, & belongings:	$40.00
Two wrappers:	$10.00
Shoes, including slippers:	$20.00
Hats for summer and winter:	$15.00
Underwear, corsets, and hosiery:	$25.00
Cloak, shawl, and some other outside garment:	$25.00
Total:	$250.00

> This is a very bold estimate, and the prices are such that good material could only be secured by having the garments at least partly made at home. (Helvenston 112)

The personal records of many women reveal that the sewing machine was extremely important to their daily lives, though it did seem to enslave them rather than give them more leisure time. "In reality the sewing machine did not save time. Rather, as with other so-called labor-saving devices for the home, it increased expectations" (Jensen and Davidson 35).

To a certain extent interpretation of fashion information varied locally. There is persistent evidence that women living in smaller communities sometimes were behind the very latest fashion fads, but usually this was because they knowingly avoided details requiring too much work or styles too rich for their social lives. Such women may also simply never have bought new garments reflecting every nuance of fashion, reasoning that their clothing was already adequately up-to-date, and a new color or shape or way of wearing a garment that had taken hold in the cities would not be enough to justify a new expenditure. And there were, certainly, some lags in perception; in order to keep up with such trends, it required that some observant person from the local area made frequent visits to centers of culture. For example, on a visit to Milwaukee in 1871, one young woman from the small nearby village of Germantown experienced a slight culture shock:

> When I had put on my new black dress, she thought it was very nice and becoming but it needed just one thing—a bustle. Not having one she would make me one. She found a piece of white goods, filling it with newspapers and putting strings to it and I put it on. It seemed all right except that it shortened my dress in the back, which she said it couldn't be helped and wouldn't be noticed with my coat on. I couldn't see why it was necessary to go in style to church, but after getting there I would have felt very much out of place if I hadn't been fixed up. (Brinker 201)

The successful establishment of Madame Demorest, initiated in the 1860s by Ellen Louise Curtis, catered to an elite clientele and proved that women everywhere would eagerly pursue fashion information and buy patterns. Used by dressmakers for wealthy women, and of course by some talented women sewing for themselves, the Demorest catalogs of fine fashions and dressmaking systems continued to increase in popularity in the 1870s. Several of the popular fashion magazines, including *Godey's, Peterson's,* and others, furthered the business in a less specialized way, filling orders for patterns and materials and printing fashion advice and information while often referring their readers to *Demorest's.*

The pattern-making operation already set up by Ebenezer Butterick became far larger and more successful than *Demorest's* in the seventies. Aware of the profits to be gleaned from such an effort, and with a knowledge of textile production and an acknowledgment of the possibilities of mass use of sewing machines, Butterick had begun to mass-produce patterns for men, women, and children in the 1860s. By 1871 the Butterick Company was producing twenty-three thousand patterns daily, and in that year alone it sold more than six million patterns, for which the profit margin is said to have been very large (Jensen and Davidson 12). Butterick and his patterns revolutionized how people selected and acquired their clothing, giving the common person as wide a range of style choices as the wealthy. Not surprisingly, the most visible result was the proliferation of fashion choices and the elaboration of detail.

A summer 1873 Butterick Catalog (found in the State Historical Society of Wisconsin collection) is stamped "The Friendly Buckhorn/

Rindlisbacher Bros./26 N. Main/Rice Lake, Wis." Rice Lake was at this time a very small northern Wisconsin town, mostly populated by the families of lumbermen. Thousands of Butterick's small catalogs were mailed to retailers, rural and urban, in every part of the country, including even such small communities as Rice Lake. In this issue patterns for every kind of garment worn by women and children were offered, along with some for men's underclothing, shirts, and smoking jackets. A small sketch and a number defined each article, along with short descriptions, measurements, and prices, which ranged from ten cents to forty cents per pattern.

Readymades

The production of readymade clothing for women had already increased enormously by 1870. The profit from the production of readymades in America in 1860 totaled seven million dollars, increasing in the next ten years to thirty-two million (Jensen and Davidson 28). While most of these garments were for men and boys, women's items became increasingly subject to mass manufacture in the seventies. In addition to cloaks and other wraps, readymades of the seventies included tunics, sacques, jackets and suits, which fitted loosely enough not to require personal tailoring. These garments were either of silk or light wool; the wearing of a black silk skirt with a bodice of a different color and fabric had become very fashionable. Cotton wrappers, actually long morning dresses of inexpensive printed goods and relatively unfitted, were also good subjects for mass production. Women's readymade skirts and suits were advertised, as were linen "dusters" and coats for traveling. On July 2, 1877, for example, the *Janesville Gazette* advertised readymades at Smith and Bostwich:

Flannel Suits:	$8.50
Ladies Skirts :	.37½ to $1.25
Linen & Cambric Suits:	$1–$9
White Vests & Dusters:	$1

Another Janesville Store, Echlin and Foote, simply announced in the *Gazette* on July 6, 1877, that they had readymade clothing for sale.

Readymades did not completely take the place of home sewing, however, because of the new expectations of having more variety in dress; a woman could elect to purchase the more utilitarian items cheaply off the rack and thereby save her premium clothing dollar for custom-made garments, or for good material to sew at home, and thus be better dressed.

Territorial Settlers

Lands to the west were opening up and inducements were great to settle the new territory. Americans and immigrants alike were attracted to the land to be had merely for "proving up," and many families undertook the long and difficult trek west. The information available on the importance of clothing, or more importantly fashion, in the lives of these settlers is meaningful. As in every period of hardship and work, records show that women abandoned all pretense of fashion while on the trail and while setting up the homestead, planting the crops, and tending stock. Some women lived and died in that state, never gaining enough leisure to reach for cultural or frivolous improvements. And for others it was only much later, and for their daughters, that their feminine instincts were finally awakened in this regard. For many women the comforts of "civilization" came in the form of lengths of calico and silk and the patterns they received through the mail. It was generally felt that a woman might excusably wear men's clothing, or some coarse substitutes for womanly dress, while doing the chores, but she should still dress "properly" for church and for the many dances and picnics on Saturday nights and Sunday afternoons. Daughters born to these families were usually expected to dress fashionably, if economically, on all public occasions.

It is worth noting that, according to Helvenston, the Native Americans with whom settlers came in contact did wear some adaptations of clothing learned from or given by whites, but that the native people, seemingly by choice, did not as yet follow fashion changes. The women of the Plains tribes, those most often encountered by the wagon trains, are reported to have worn along with their blankets either a long, loose wrapper of bright calico or a loose chemiselike blouse of calico over a gathered skirt (175–76). In Kansas the government issued eight yards of cloth to each tribeswoman annually, but by making dresses with only about six and a half yards, most of them saved some of the new cloth for barter. Many settlers recorded reminiscences about trading for pieces of this "government calico," and because much of the calico was of identical pattern, they could frequently gather together enough cloth for a dress by trading with several of the Native American women, even though the colors were usually very bright and gaudy (Helvenston 93, 175–76).

People living in western cities did, however, keep abreast of the latest fashions. In 1870 the editor of the *Wichita Eagle* wrote,

> The style and intelligence of the people who are setting up the homesteads and building up the frontier towns of Southwestern Kansas are often a subject of remark by those just in from the east on tours of pleasure or business. It is no uncommon thing to see in Wichita, in lumber wagons, as neatly and fashionably attired ladies, as intelligent men and women, as can be pointed out in the streets of more pretentious cities east. The great majority of those living on homesteads in this section of the state are people of refinement and taste—splendid people, who will make this valley a paradise ere many years. (Helvenston 162)

Yet it was often a long time before there was enough leisure or money available for most women to indulge themselves or their daughters too greatly. Emeline Crumb wrote in her reminiscences of Kansas prairie life that as a young girl she was "so tired of washing and ironing that same one piece dress, it was a relief when the pony ran against the gate post and tore a huge hole in the skirt," and another Kansas woman, Mrs. D. M. Valentine, remembered ginghams: "Heavy, coarse, and really ugly ones" that nevertheless "served their purpose well . . . never wore out" (Helvenston 80). In other memoirs women wrote about the despised denim and calico and sometimes even converted wagon covers, cheesecloth, and flour-sack fabrics they were forced to wear during the hardest years (Helvenston 81). Mary Hudson, writing in 1876 in the *Kansas Farmer,* defended her interest in fashion even though she was unable to afford it for herself: "Because I must wear calico, must I also be deprived of the pleasure of admiring the beautiful attire of my more fortunate sisters? Can we not admire a fine picture or garden, or landscape, though we do not possess them ourselves?" (Helvenston 163).

In 1874, Ellen Baxter suggested making a "ladylike and nice dress" that would still be practical as a working dress:

> The skirt is to be just long enough to clear the floor, and is finished with a deep Spanish flounce. The waist is a blouse; a drawstring is in place of a belt, and below it the cloth extends three or four inches, forming a sort of skirt, finished by a narrow ruffle. When a white Swiss frill is basted around the neck, it will be a pretty as well as comfortable working-day dress. At times, when it would be more convenient if shorter, it can be looped by fastening together hooks and eyes which are to be sewed on each seam a short distance apart. (Helvenston 127–28)

Older, out-of-style dresses were usually pressed into service as work dresses, as Mrs. Marion Bucknell described in a letter to *Kansas Farmer* in January 1879:

> Short dresses are the thing for working in, and gingham is very good and serviceable if you are going to make new dresses, but what shall we do with dresses that are not nice any longer, yet are good and whole but faded? I cannot afford to give them away nor put them in the rag bag, so I take off superfluous trimming, shorten the skirt if need be, and make work dresses of them, and when they will no longer do for that, rip the skirt up and make 2 or 3 long, wide work aprons of them. (Helvenston 107)

Records indicate that for the most part only the plainer fabrics were found in western shops. Mary Hudson wrote of her delight at seeing the "magnificent" dry goods displays of some of the merchants at the Kansas City fair: "It is really a treat to those of us who see little of the sheen of satin and the frosting of lace" (Helvenston 87).

People in the rural Midwest had, perhaps, better and closer shopping facilities than those in the West, but they record similar experiences in producing and caring for clothing. Jessie Campbell Menzies, a farmer's wife living outside of Janesville, in Rock County, Wisconsin, kept a diary that is almost solely an accounting of her efforts to keep her family clothed from 1877 through 1881. A sample period in 1877 reads as follows:

1/15: Susie pitched down her red dress & I done some patching.
1/19: Susie & I sewed on my dress and I cut out a new "waste" [sic]
1/23: Went to Jansvl. and took chickens. Susie got some triming [sic] for her dress. I cut out my skirt and fixed over wrapper.
1/24: Susie finished my overskirt.
1/25: Susie stitched my skirt.
2/17: Went to Center to get a dress fitted.
2/19: Susie cut out a wrapper for herself.
3/7: Bought a piece of Janesville Cotton.
3/22: Stopped at Mrs. Carters and paid her for making my dress.
3/29: Went to Jansvl. and had our pictures taken.
4/17: Susie cut out my wrapper.
5/3: Susie fixed my hat and I cut out coat and pants for Willie.
5/17: Bell & I washed the wool & bags.
6/15: Finished Bell's bask [sic] and cut out and partly made over her skirt.
6/23: Went to Jansvl, got Bell a white dress and a lot of things for myself.
. . . .
10/20: James & I went to Jansvl. I got a pair of everyday shoes and a piece of sheeting for Susie and a twilight for Bell & me.
. . . .
1/8: Susie made a flannel shimmie for herself.

Women's Fashions

Much that was newly fashionable in England and America in the 1870s was due to the wave of national esprit that swept France in the years following the Franco-Prussian War; the couturiers who influenced Paris fashion made capital of current patriotic sentiments, designing new lines for women's dress using historic elements. Designers played loosely with details of French historical costume, limiting themselves not at all to those of the revolution, and in photographs it is common to see a "Louis Quatorze" sleeve, a "Louis Quinze" vest, a "Josephine" waistline, and even a "Velasquez" hat illustrated in the same fashion magazine—sometimes on the same figure—and often with a "Marie Antoinette" coiffure. Fashion writers stated that these styles had all been "improved" and "brought up to date" to suit the tastes of modern women; in most cases the "improvements" made the relationship to actual historical models fairly tenuous.

The bustle form was the most typical feature of dress in the seventies, causing more change in the look of the skirt than just the back protuberance. Because of the emphasis on the back of the costume, the sides of the skirt were drawn ever further in and back, so that the frontal silhouette also changed dramatically in aspect. Never before had there been so rapid and dramatic a transformation in a woman's silhouette; the wide, rather plain sweep of skirt over full petticoats, which had been the standard for forty years, within just a very few years gave way entirely to an elongated, narrow form that was crossed and gartered around the lower body with every kind of trim and protruded (in varying degrees and areas through the decade) at the back. The overskirt, often pulled up at the sides and carrying its own load of trimming, was present in varying forms throughout the bustle period.

For the first four years of the decade, women's costumes mostly consisted of a short-waisted, fitted basque bodice with a short hip-length peplum that was trimmed at the back waist with deep pleats and bows, an overskirt draped to an "apron" front and with an arrangement of puffs on the hips and at the back, and a long, very full, flounced skirt called an underskirt. For the first two or three years of the decade, full petticoats and a crinoline and a substantial bustle of some sort were used to support this early-seventies style. Waistlines were at first very short, and by 1873 the bustles were set extremely high and were almost horizontal, with the overskirt elaborately draped over them. This shortness of waist was not true of late-seventies bustle dresses.

During the decade's early years, written descriptions of fashions claimed repeatedly that the dress should cling to the form and be very narrow, revealing the figure. The writers used a relative standard here, however, since the skirts were still quite full at the hem at this time— "The skirt is made slightly to touch, and very narrow, not more than three and a half yards round" (*Peterson's,* May 1873). The impression of narrowness was from the frontal view, which was extremely close to the figure.

Fashion writers considered the early seventies quite permissive as to style, within certain parameters: "Fashion is lenient; almost any style of costume may be adopted that suits the style of the wearer, if only a few rules are observed: one is that the dress must fall flat, close in front; another, that a ruffle, in the same shape, must be worn at the neck, and that the hair is worn close to the sides of the head, and high on top" (*Peterson's,* April 1874).

Beginning in 1874, as waistlines began to lengthen, the two-piece dress was the most popular form, with a very long jacket bodice, alternately called a tunic, a sacque, or a cuirass, depending on nuances of cut and style.

The cuirass bodice, that fits the figure closely, is very high, with long basque, and has the effect of being moulded to the body, is always made of a different material from the dress. This cuirass bodice is frequently worn over the bodice of the dress. When the sleeves are of one material, the bodice is of another. The sleeves match the trimming. (*Peterson's,* April 1874)

. . .

The make of the waists of dresses is as varied as the trimmings of skirts. The cuirass, or armor, or corset-waist, as it is indiscriminately called, is very much worn; but it shares popular favor with many other styles, for it, above all other corsages, should fit perfectly to look well. (*Peterson's,* April 1875)

Some of the long bodices buttoned down the front, and some were worn hanging straight and open, in sacque style, over vests nearly as long. Even these long sacque bodices were closely fitted at back and sides, and the cuirass style was fitted throughout, with the snug fit extending quite low, though in the beginning of their popularity even cuirass bodices were made full enough at the hips to go over some skirt fullness. By 1877 the fit was carried more narrowly over the hips, the upper skirt fullness vanished, and the bustle disappeared.

Upper garment length grew to astonishing proportions during the seventies, sometimes to such an extent that the skirt beneath all but disappeared, the elongated top developing into the popular polonaise. The polonaise was contemporary with the long jacket style until the end of the decade. Both were cut in long gores without waistline seams. Descriptions of polonaise costumes usually refer to the parts as "underdress" and "overdress." A one-piece, full-length, trained dress cut in the same manner as the polonaise was also popular during the era of the narrow, trained skirt. Such a dress, cut in full-length gores, was introduced in 1875 by Worth, whose Paris couture dressed the royalty of Europe. Worth named the style the "Princesse," after the Danish princess Alexandra, who married Edward, Prince of Wales. The term "princess style" in reference to a gored dress does not predate this event (Helvenston 171).

The influence of high fashion was insidious in the 1870s. While photographs of older women taken during the first half of the decade often show them wearing an old-fashioned dark dress with a plain full skirt, within the same photograph may be seen younger women and girls in distinctly up-to-date bustle dresses, even if the setting is a simple farmhouse. Even the older women's dresses are not fashionless; they merely represent a fashionable cut of a few years past. During the latter half of the decade, the dresses of these older women often appear properly narrower in outline and show the newly fashionable pleated-flounce trim, though they are still much plainer than those of high fashion and are usually black. While photographs of rural women provide most of the evidence for this deduction, nineteenth-century custom decreed that it was nicer for all "old ladies" to dress conservatively and to leave high fashion to the young: "But really elegant and well-bred old ladies do not follow the fashion in this way. At sixty, ladies should, and usually do, preserve a certain uniformity of dress, at least in color and fabric. They are not excluded from changes in form, but they select the simplest and avoid the fanciful and above all the youthful" (*Demorest's,* January 1877).

The colors favored for all dress in the seventies changed along with the attenuation of shape, becoming gradually confined to deep tones, especially for day dresses. By 1878, the palette was distinctive:

> Light colors have disappeared, even from cambrics, percales, and other thin cotton fabrics . . . we have dark indigo, and leaf shades speckled with minute patterns in a different shade, or in India colors . . . the impression being strong in favor of dark tints for day wear, no matter what the fabric, while light ones are absolutely confined to rich stuffs and to those diaphanous materials, which are only suitable for indoor and evening wear. The great feature of modern dress is this harmony of tone. Browns are not worn with greens, but only with the self, or a strictly complementary color, and this last, which may form a contrast, is not obtruded, but is used for bows, or the lining of bows, revers, or flounces . . . (*Demorest's,* January 1878)

A benchmark of seventies styles was the use of several different materials in one costume:

> Polonaises are usually of a different pattern of material from the petticoat, but the sleeves and sash are often of the color and material of the petticoat. Sometimes, where basques are worn, the plain, solid color is used for the petticoat, basque, and sash; the overskirt and sleeves being of the figured material. The bodices are all finished at the top with collars of the same material, laid flat in front, but standing upright, and wide, at the back, either plain or in full box-plaits. (*Peterson's,* August 1874)

Cotton dresses, now even for dressy occasions, sometimes consisted of three patterns of fabric with shared colors, often using plain, plaid, and stripes as various parts of the dress. Most often the skirts were of the dark, plain shade and the overskirt and bodice of a lighter mix, with either or both used in trimming all three pieces. Trims were most often of rows of small pleats, called "kilting," or of ruffled flounces of one of the fabrics. For more elegant occasions, wool dresses were frequently trimmed with a blending color in silk, and silk dresses were made of two or more compatible colors. Directions for making up one of the new costumes included the advice to remake the skirt of an old silk dress for the underdress: "An old silk, re-turned, will always look better, and make a more elegant costume, than to have the skirt of the same material" (*Peterson's,* December 1874). "Re-turned" here means turning the dress inside out after ripping out the old construction and cleaning the material.

Many dresses, even cotton ones and wrappers, and especially the one-piece princess styles, were trained throughout the decade. While there were objections to it, and for periods during the decade "round" skirts did become fashionable, the train was an inconvenience that stylish women gladly suffered for its "gracefulness and beauty." The statement made by a trained dress was definitely one of ladylike leisure. But those without such pretentions could dress fashionably enough throughout the decade without wearing a train.

Writers of fashion information for women kept insisting that even cheaper dresses could be up-to-date: "There is no reason, why a delaine, calico, or common water-proof dress should be less elegant or less fashionable in cut, than a silk dress, or a velvet one" (*Peterson's,* May 1874).

WRAPPERS

Along with dress styles, the form of the wrapper, or negligé dress, altered substantially over the decade:

> Morning wrappers are mostly made with the double Watteau fold behind, and may be worn flowing loosely, but is [*sic*] in best taste when belted by a band passed beneath the watteau fold. A pretty and simple mode of trimming, is to scallop the wrapper all around, letting the scallops fall over a side plaiting of silk. It is buttoned all up the front, a button being placed in each scallop: the belt is made of silk, and is fastened at the left side with loops and sash ends. (*Godey's,* March 1873)

Many of the kinds of wrappers available readymade late in the seventies are described in the spring 1879 issue of *Ehrich's Fashion Quarterly*. Selections range from a $1 "Loose sacque Wrapper, of dark standard Prints, trimmed with rufflings of the material" to a $13 "Elegant Wrapper of Ladies' Cloth; trimmed with rows of braid, and a box plaiting round the bottom. In Ruby, Navy Blue, Seal Brown, Black, Gray, and Eugenie Blue." Others range from $1.25 to $6, from calico, rep or flannel, with the $6 style made of "Fancy Stuff." Some versions are described as "Gabrielle" and "Full Gabrielle" in cut, referring to the gored princess fashion by the same term as that used in the sixties for the gored dress.

MOURNING

Mourning dress was still de rigeur for the upper classes in the seventies and was therefore followed in varying degrees by the middle and even working classes. As usual, fashionable cut and fit was expected during mourning, and the nuances of various stages of mourning were expressed by gradually lightening the weight of "crape" and veils and admitting more light-colored trim and jewelry. Whole sections of etiquette books were devoted to such dress, though it did not get much play in the fashion writings. *Godey's* proclaimed in March of 1873 that "For light mourning it is unnecessary to give any hints. We may, however, state that purple is not now worn, black, white, and gray being more fashionable."

ACCESSORIES

The English manner of interpreting Paris fashions was admired in America, and English fashion publications were widely circulated.

American and English discussions and selections of style elements at this time were therefore quite similar. An English fashion commentator wrote in 1870 that "The reign of the plain linen collar is now indeed past. With the open dresses, a variety of chemisettes in lace and embroidery have been introduced in the female toilet, and even with high dresses the plain collar is no longer worn; it is exchanged for delicate ruffles of muslin, tulle, or lace, which are certainly far more becoming to the face and complexion. Ruffles to match are worn around the wrists" (*The Young Englishwoman,* April 1, 1870).

Separate fichus, frills, neck scarfs, and cravat collars were featured in American fashion periodicals, most standing high on the neck but some falling away from a V- or square-shaped neckline. In 1870, a wide pelerine collar is illustrated; made in one piece and with a neckline squared front and back to slip over the head, it is of muslin and has parallel rows of puffing and lace flounces. For 1873, "The favorite collars are fraises made of plaitings of either open-worked batiste or of muslin trimmed with Valenciennes lace, or all of Valenciennes, or all of tulle illusion. As the hair is worn so high, these frills look very ornamental around the throat. The sleeves consist of plaiting, opening towards the wrist; they are usually made of batiste, with an open work hem" (*Godey's,* April 1873). Muslin bodices with sleeves, set on a waistband, were popular and, in chemisette fashion, were to be worn under the open basque or jacket styles. Cuffs of these bodices were wide, either of double crisp frills of linen or lace or of linen with pleated lace edges, and showed below the jacket sleeves.

The most ubiquitous accessory in this decade seems to have been the black velvet neck ribbon, which was worn in widths from a quarter to a half inch and was long enough to tie at the back of the neck in a bow with long strings. Either a brooch or some type of charm was attached to the ribbon at the front. Large lockets or cameos were also worn on substantial gold chains; some were imitation cameos, with the heads often carved of jet or of stone surrounded by jet. Long strings of large jet beads were popular as well, and in some cases they were long enough to loop once around the throat and hang down the bosom.

Earrings often matched a necklace and were very long in the early years of the decade, with many dangles and bobs. From about 1873, when the hair was done closer to the sides of the head, the fashion turned to more slender, single drops. The extreme upsweep of the hair in the late seventies made a heavier button earring more popular, often a large pearl.

Wide gold bracelets were worn, sometimes in pairs and sometimes many at a time on one wrist. In photographs these appear to be decorated with engraved designs, but they were sometimes set with cameos. Bracelets with charms or bangles were favored by young girls.

Decorations for the hair usually consisted of elaborate combs, but not those with protruding tops. Large, elaborately curved combs of tortoise or horn often had silver tops decorated in repoussé or engraving. These were worn either at the temples or at the very top of the crown, where they held back the coronet of curls or braids.

The form of the glove changed early from the gauntlet style of the sixties to a longer, narrower form: "Gloves are worn long on the wrist, sometimes with six buttons. Those known as Gant de Suede, are most popular. Lace mitts come with long fingers, and are very fine" (*Peterson's,* May 1874). Furs were indispensable to high fashion in this decade. "A fashionable set of furs consists of a long boa and a muff. Collars and cuffs are not worn, the latter not at all, the former only where extra warmth is required, or for elderly ladies. . . . Black furs are at present the most fashionable fur" (*Godey's,* March 1873). Other furs mentioned in winter fashion articles were fox, expecially the black and silver varieties, and black sealskin, of which were made the long winter sacques, either plain or bordered with some other fine fur. Chinchilla was much used for trimming woolen costumes.

Handbags do not get mentioned frequently in the literature, though they are seen in the fashion plates as rather small, flat pouch shapes usually with chain handles. These pouch bags were often attached to flat metal hooks for hanging at the belt, chatelaine style. "The chatelaine bag appears to have become an indispensable addition to all morning costumes. The most economical plan to adopt, is to select a black velvet one, and to have your monogram embroidered on it. Such a chatelaine, or 'aumoniere,' as it is called, can be worn with almost any costume" (*Peterson's,* October 1874).

WRAPS

While not the high-priority article in the seventies that it had been in previous decades, the shawl remained a valid option as a wrap for utilitarian and evening dress, though it was replaced in fashionable street dress by the jacket or coat. *Ehrich's Fashion Quarterly* lists nearly a full page of shawls in its winter 1879 issue in what they term "goods of every quality and price, from the most expensive Camel's Hair to the cheapest Shetland." Among the Shetlands are listed several hand-crocheted shawls "In solid colors, or plain centres with colored borders. Prices: $4.00, $5.00, $6.00, and $8.00." Chenille squares are mentioned as new. Under "Real India Shawls" are listed "Camel's Hair India Cashmeres, long or square, new and elegant designs, small or medium Black and Scarlet centres. . . . Price, each, according to quality, $60 to $250." Others listed are "Paris, Vienna, Berlin, and Paisley Brochés" in prices from $8 to $15, and Beaver Shawls, Scotch plaids, Berlin Diagonal Shawls ("very novel"), and shawls of silk broché and of plain wool. It is interesting to note that the colors in the Scotch plaid shawls are black, Oxford gray, drab, brown, and blue—not at all the brilliant palette of the sixties' tartan plaids.

Much more popular than the shawl was the small, more or less fitted, wrap of the seventies, the dolman, which was quite prominent in contemporary fashion literature. "Wraps should always follow the outlines of the dress, so as to fall loosely over the puff of the skirt; but are made quite flat in front, falling closely to the person" (*Peterson's*, October 1874). The dolman had no proper sleeves but was cut and fitted over the shoulders so that the low arm slits allowed only limited vertical movement. It was a wrap designed to set off the bustle, as it invariably had tapes at the inside back waist that tied in front, snugging the wrap to the small of the back. The "skirt" portion was made with either slashes or pleats below the waist to allow it to extend and fall gracefully over the bustle in back.

This wrap style had a varied but prolonged popularity throughout the decade. Dolmans were made in a variety of fabrics, in silks or woolens, all elaborately trimmed around the edges with fur, feathers, pleated ruchings, ribbons, or chenille loops. They fastened close to the throat with hooks and eyes. *Peterson's* advised that "The most convenient dolmans for wearing at all times and upon all occasions, are those made of very fine black cloth, and embroidered all over in the vermicelli pattern with silk, mixed with vermicellis of soutache" (*Peterson's*, October 1874).

But the jacket was by far the most popular wrap of the seventies, and it had many forms. Many of the new outdoor jackets were boxy and short, in the early part of the decade particularly, and some, called "masculine," or boyish at least, in inspiration, were unfitted at the waist and somewhat resembled the paletôt garment of the past decade.

> The English walking-jacket again appears, made of warm, rough cloth, nearly half an inch thick. It retains its jaunty shape, fitting like a gentleman's coat, with high shoulder-seams, double-breasted fronts, coat collar, and three back seams, far apart at the waist, but no postillion plaits. Coat-sleeves and pockets, with flaps, complete this trim, tidy and withal masculine-looking jacket. Children's and misses' jackets are shown in precisely the same shapes just noted. (*Peterson's*, November 1873)

> The small, cloth jacket now worn, are [*sic*] very much in the style of gentlemen's garments; they cross over in front, often have pockets at the sides, and invariably a small one in front, in which the watch and a flower are placed. (*Peterson's*, December 1873)

In the seventies the term "paletôt" was reserved for a longer, semi-fitted jacket that was often slit at the back and under the arms. Many short overjackets of the early seventies also had side and back slits, around which the trimming was placed. Some of these were worn belted.

In the last few years of the decade, jackets were extremely long, some even below hip length. They were increasingly made of material other than the dress, especially sealskin, but often formed a suit with the two-piece dress underneath. Elaboration of trim and detail gave limitless variation, with lapels, cuffs, and other details frequently in a different fabric from the body. The sacque jacket was worn throughout the seventies, vying in popularity throughout with the dolman and the shawl: "Sacks are cut in every style—with tight sleeves and with flowing ones, tight in the back, and then again without any seams. The Dolman does not seem to take as well as at first predicted" (*Peterson's,* May 1874).

Long, fitted woolen coats were popular in the last few years of the decade, when skirts were extremely narrow and the bustle extension was practically nonexistent. This was the first time in many years that such a fitted long overgarment had been possible; the new narrow dress styles accepted a long, slender wrap as long as the back was arranged to accommodate the newly reduced back bustle and trimming of the dress skirt. A double-breasted, gored coat with triple shoulder capes is featured in *Peterson's* in 1878, and several other versions are also seen. The coat sleeves of these wraps appear rather loose and not so curved as in the sixties, and they are invariably trimmed at the cuff. These long wraps, even though they had sleeves, are sometimes called "cloaks" in the advertisements.

Undergarments

The one element of style commonly recognizable in the 1870s as typical is the bustle. The bustle was supposed to have been derived from (and was frequently referred to as) the pannier, the eighteenth-century sturdy cage support that held the skirt in an unnatural bulge on either hip, like the donkey-baskets for which they were named. Only one cage support, of course, was required to hold the heavy back draperies of early-seventies dresses, but the term "pannier" appeared sporadically throughout the decade in fashion descriptions of bustle styles, sometimes referring to the bustle itself and sometimes to the side-drape puffs of the drawn-up overskirt. "Tournure" was an equally well-used term for the bustle.

Bustles were not a new idea in nineteenth-century dress. A bustle pad had often been used in past decades to support skirts, but done so inconspicuously, hidden under very full skirts. In the early seventies, on the contrary, the outer garment was arranged and decorated to make an obvious feature of the bustle, the central feature, in fact, upon which all the lines of the dress depended. Even in 1877 and 1878, when no bustle protuberance was worn, the back of the costume was accentuated and trimmed to be the predominant view.

Short bustles of stiffened ruffles, wire or cane cages, or muslin puffs boned to hold their shape were produced to be worn under a tied-back petticoat with back fullness for the styles of 1870 through about 1876:

> All dresses are worn bouffant at the back, and are arranged to look very flat and slender at the sides. The skirt is tied back over the tournure, which should be long and narrow, and consist of twelve steel springs encased in muslin, and kept in place with elastic bands. This bustle should add nothing to the breadth of the hips, but is required to push the skirts far out backward, and is long enough to support them half their length, making them flow out gracefully in-

stead of falling in below a projecting pouf at the waist as they have recently done. (*Peterson's,* September 1874)

By 1876 many women had given up wearing the large, high bustle and were sporting the longer-waisted, more low-fitting costumes decreed by Paris. These costumes still required some support at the back for a fashionable appearance, but the fullness was placed very low, sometimes just behind the knees. The "Paris Tournure," as illustrated in the April 1877 issue of *Peterson's,* was a flat muslin garment with a starched arrangement in back stiffly held to below-hip length but puffed out at the bottom. It was to be laced around the body so that the back was formed "merely of a deep, double box-plait, perfectly tight-fitting, to which is added two flounces, very full and stiffly starched." A set of five tapes tied at front held the tournure close to the body nearly down to the knees, where the large, stiff flounces directed the back-fullness of the skirt. The form created is typical of 1877 and 1878, when no rear protrusion whatsoever was evident in the outline of women's dress. This condition did not last very long, however: "Paniers are, as yet, seldom seen, though some of the imported dresses are strewn with them; but they will certainly be the fashion, before long, as crinoline, or tournures, or 'bustles,' (the thing is known by all three names) are already appearing, though very modest in size, at first" (*Peterson's,* February 1879).

The alteration of the womanly form from that of the late sixties to the late seventies was considerable and was accomplished, after the bustle, mainly through changes in corset shape. The change was gradual: for the first three or four years, the very short-waisted, full-busted corset style was worn, not changed much from the late 1860s type. Beginning about 1874, the corset became more and more heavily boned, and the line lengthened, especially at the front, although a short corset was still advertised. The newest bodice style, the cuirass, demanded a longer line, and the long corset became extremely fashionable as the decade progressed, gradually changing to the extremely drop-busted, hip-length type of the late seventies, with its exaggeratedly long, small waist. In wear, this corset was carried over the petticoat so as to reduce bulk under the slim dresses. Tight-lacing was often so extreme under these fitted dresses that a two-piece steel "spoon busk" was developed for the front of the corset to pull the front in more tightly and smoothly at the natural waist. Such a corset required up to forty stays (Brown-Larimore 90–91).

During this decade whalebone stays were gradually replaced with those of buffalo horn and, later, cane or steel. Stay materials were put to a real test in the late seventies, and the "unbreakable" corset was developed late in the decade to counteract the frequent cracking of corset stays at the waist from too-tight lacing (Brown-Larimore 122–23).

The corsets themselves were treated as fashion items in the seventies and were made in many colors, black being a favorite, though scarlet, red, gray, drab, and white were also popular. A satin corset to match a silk dress (the close-fitting dress styles slipped neatly over a satin underbody) was a fashion plus adopted by such women as could afford the frivolity.

The petticoats of the very early seventies were still multiple and still mostly of white cotton and ruffled at the hem, as in the late sixties, although petticoats in colors to match dresses, and in silk, became quite popular later in the decade. The crinoline, while disparaged, was sometimes retained in the first two or three years of the decade in order to support the skirts' abundant trimming, though by 1871 crinolines were considered unfashionable. By 1876, the fashionable skirt was so narrow that petticoats were not starched and were worn only one at a time. In that year, a new petticoat style was developed that made it possible to have the upper slimness but to retain bottom and back fullness; the fronts of these styles were plain and ungathered and much fullness was taken to the back, where it was variously treated for back emphasis. Such a petticoat might have either a full-length set of stiffened flounces down the back, a partial length of rows of puffed crinoline gathered to the waist, or simply back fullness to go over the bustle, fitted with a set of tapes to fasten under the bustle pad. Many were trained. The fronts of all petticoats were plain and ungathered, and many were equipped with ties to fasten behind the thighs in order to hold them down to the body in front and to force the fullness to the back. Many were made with a deep hip yoke. Petticoats always had thick flounces at the hem so as to "throw out" the skirt from the feet, though by 1877 these flounces were no longer starched.

While the familiar chemise was still a part of the wardrobe, for wear under common housedresses, it was not suitable under the newer styles. The smooth fit of the cuirass bodice demanded more elimination of bulk. The shaped underbodice, or corset cover, therefore became popular during this time. It was so closely molded to the figure that it required a front closure, as it could not be slipped over the head. This garment was made with the same cap sleeves and wide, shallow neckline as the chemise and was generally finished with whitework and lace.

Underdrawers, made with legs to just below the knee, were worn and also frequently combined with the corset covers to form "combinations," or "union suits," which were cut to fit closely to the body under the cuirass bodices. Seams were generally full length, requiring no waist seam, and the garments closed down the front. Necklines were still wide, sometimes drawn on cords, and sleeves were still short caps.

MATERNITY ALTERNATIVES

As in previous decades, the wrapper of the 1870s could be made so as to be expandable for pregnancy, not a difficult feat, since the Watteau fashion was often worn loose in any case. The one-piece wrapper was easy to make, though readymade wrappers of many shapes, some quite full, were available at low prices.

While special maternity clothes, or even patterns for such garments, were not provided in the 1870s, information concerning healthful dress alternatives was available:

> The dress should be loose and comfortable, nowhere pressing tightly or unequally. The word enceinte, by which a pregnant woman is designated, meant originally without a cincture,—that is, unbound. . . . Stays or corsets may be used, in a proper manner, during the first five or six months of pregnancy, but after that they should either be laid aside or worn very loosely. Any attempt at concealing pregnancy, by tight lacing and the application of a stronger busk, cannot be too severely condemned. (Napheys 174–75)

Headgear

Both hair and hat fashions changed as much through the decade of the seventies as did dress styles. At the very end of the sixties, and into the seventies, fully dressed hair was done in chignons, frizettes, and puffs. Just at the turn of the decade, the late-sixties fashion of dressing the hair à l'ingénue, in girlish long ringlets, was followed by many women, mostly younger ones. A fashion for "careless" locks then became popular up to mid-decade, featuring softness and tendrils around the face and waves and curls hanging behind a large, loose topknot held by a comb. In 1876 there was a sudden fad for short, frizzed bangs, which remained in favor well into the eighties. This style created a softness for the forehead under the hats and bonnets, which tended to be worn well back on the head.

A bonnet style that was quite small and had neither curtain nor strings was popular in the early years, complementing the specially high, wide hairstyles. This style was part of a conscious emulation of the late-eighteenth-century French court hairstyles, à la Marie Antoinette. The hat was at that time merely a decoration to the head, perched high on the hair. This exaggerated style disappeared by 1874.

> Bonnets and hats are decidedly larger, and, consequently, infinitely more becoming than the ridiculously small headgear perched high at the top of the head, to which we have of late become accustomed, but never reconciled. The drawn velvet bonnets, lined with light-colored silk, which are presently coming into vogue, take us back quite a couple of decades, made in black, in brown, and in prune velvet, and lined with pale-blue or pale-pink silk; a flower is placed at the back, and falls upon the chignon. . . . Strings and even curtains are again to be seen on the newest bonnets. (*Peterson's,* March 1874)

> The new bonnets are not bonnets, but merely round hats, with strings. They are odd, with large, square crowns with curious brims turned-up somewhere, either back or front, one side or the other. They are worn very far back, leaving the front of the head entirely bare. (*Peterson's,* May 1874)

In order to suit the high ruffs, and general style of dress, the hair is worn higher on the head than it was six months ago. The bulk has changed its position. Instead of being massed as a chignon at the back, it is combed up from the nape of the neck to the top of the head, and there arranged in light puffs and curls. Heavy frizettes have disappeared, but false hair has by no means followed their example, for there is quite as much, if not more, worn than at this period last year, only it is managed differently. It is prepared in long switches, which are all hair, and can be twisted into a coil and pinned, either as a coronet or as a Josephine knot, into loops, bows, or puffs—in fact into twenty different styles, and it is infinitely more natural-looking than the stiff, formal chignons which were pinned on in one solid mass at the back of the head. Curls of all sorts and sizes, from the short, frizzy ones to the stiff, round ringlets, are mounted on long hair pins, and studded about the coils and puffs. Thick ropes, made of two tresses of hair twisted together, are newer than plaits. The front hair is usually crepe[d] in long, natural rippling waves, and, where it is becoming, the front parting is made at one side rather than in the center; the side hair is no longer combed straight upward from the temples, any small side locks being turned rather toward the face than away from it. (*Peterson's,* March 1874)

Birds are again used for bonnets, and especially for hats, though there is scarce a perceptible difference between the two. (*Peterson's,* November 1874)

By 1877, there were every variety, size, and style in both bonnets and hats, but bonnets had become narrower.

Bonnets are all close-fitting to the sides of the head, and trimmed entirely according to the tastes of the wearer. Hats are of every variety, from the large, wide-brimmed garden hat, and the stylish Gainsborough, wide and flopping on one side, and turned up closely on the other, to the English walking hat, which fits the head closely, is usually turned up on both sides, and looks as if it meant business. (*Peterson's,* August 1877)

Lamballe bonnets, and Gainsborough hats, modified to suit all faces, are the most worn; but if the hat is rather large, and turned up on one side at least, and the bonnet is rather high, and close-fitting to the head, any kind of head gear passes that is becoming; fruits and flowers are used in profusion . . . (*Peterson's,* September 1877)

By 1878, hats and bonnets were still substantial but not overlarge—that is, not increasing the width of the head. This was the year in which a new style of bonnet was introduced, the capote: a narrow, high shape with a "crushed" fabric crown often made to match a costume.

The introduction and fashionable vogue attained by that class of bonnets which consist mainly of a soft crown, has stimulated the fashion of costumes, of which the bonnet forms an integral part, being made of the same material as the dress. This is not only the case with silk and velvet costumes, and silk and wool, but also with the rougher tweeds, bourette cloths, and particularly plush fabrics. (*Demorest's,* November 1878)

Ladies who can afford to match their costumes do not, of course, confine themselves to black velvet; their suits of wine-color or bronze are accompanied by bonnet to match, and, in fact, nothing can be conceived more incongruous than a black bonnet in conjunction with the fine dark shades in costume, the beauty of which is the preservation of perfect harmony. (*Demorest's,* September 1879)

Footwear

Late-sixties shoe styles featured a high "Louis" heel—sharply incurved and with a broad heel seat—for dress. A slipper form with this heel shape, quite high, carried over for dress wear in the early 1870s. Long tongues and buckles were a part of the design.

But a change came in the seventies. A new, lightweight kid boot, with rather broad, low heels, became very popular at the beginning of the decade. The boot was usually open in front and buttoned up the outside edge, coming slightly above the ankle. For dress, and even in some sturdier styles, the fronts were open in some manner to show the stocking, either with scallops, points, or straps at the buttonholes. Most of these boots were black.

The fashions in boots and shoes are undergoing a considerable alteration, inasmuch as the high Louis V. heels are suppressed, and are now rarely seen, except with evening toilets. Walking boots are made with broad, flat heels, that conduce to the comfort as well as to the health of the wearer, as we are convinced that these high, slanting heels which fashion has imposed on us for the past few years are far from comfortable, and promote, to a great extent, an awkward gait. For day-wear boots are made of unglazed kid, the only ornament being a festoon of black-silk stitching. Useful boots for ordinary occasions are made with square toes; but for dressy toilets the corners are rounded off, which makes the boot look smaller. (*Peterson's,* February 1874)

Silk stockings are now almost invariably worn, because the popular boots are a compromise between boots and shoes, the front being opened and barred across, with kid straps fastening in the center with buttons; these straps cover the instep, and are considerably higher than the ankle. The boots are always of dead, not glazed kid. (*Peterson's,* September 1874)

Black silk stockings are more fashionable than any others just at present, and there is a great variety in them; some are open-worked, some are studded all over with flowerets of various hues, and some are of widely-contrasting colors, the leg being violet and the foot white, with fine violet stripes; in others. . . the foot is scarlet, and the long alternate stripes of scarlet and white. These silk stockings are worn under shoes with high heels and fancy buckles, and they generally correspond in some measure with the toilet being worn at the time. (*Peterson's,* August 1877)

Fashions for Men

The cut of men's coats and jackets continued to be less oversized in the seventies, with sack jackets, the most popular style, becoming shorter and more close-fitting with narrower sleeves and lapels. At the same time, older styles reminiscent of the early sixties, including some extremely loose, long sack shapes, are seen in photographs and were still sold readymade at that time. The sack jacket was still worn mostly buttoned at the top button only, falling open to show the vest and the watch chain. Black was still worn by the majority of men of all classes for daytime, but plaids and checks were extremely popular for casual jackets and suits, some of which were made of part or all cotton or linen. And while black was still the most important color for the dress suit, some light trousers were shown with black frock coats for daytime, and morning trousers were striped. A very long frock coat was featured, often with a wide shawl collar, for dignified day dress for important occasions.

As in the past, the wearing of a vest was the rule, even for the most casual attire. A farmer in shirtsleeves and jeans would still wear a vest over his work shirt. The dressy vest was most often made to match the suit, although there were the usual fancy silk jacquard vests in rich colors.

Shirts had a little more color than before, in stripes and plaids on white, and were mostly made without collars, the manufacture of separate collars and cuffs having become most efficient. Troy, New York, was the center of this industry. These collars and cuffs were all of heavily starched white linen or cotton. A proper wardrobe of these handy items, six collars and six pairs of cuffs, was supposed to last a "gentleman" for about one year, the benefit of having the white linen detachable pieces being that the shirt would not need such frequent laundering. Shirts of the seventies were mainly made with attached band collars perforated with buttonholes for this use. The bodies of shirts were of many colors and patterns other than white: blue, red, black, or gray stripes were popular, as were small plaids in those colors on white. Some patterned shirts had inset white pleated bosoms; some were made plain. All white dress shirts seem to have had the inset bosom, more or less elaborately pleated and frilled.

The favored necktie of the seventies was rather wide and tied in a loose knot rather low at the throat, with square ends overlapping. It was made of silk, generally striped, and was fully lined, sometimes appearing slightly padded in the photographs. Older or more conservative men often wore black ties, some narrow and tied in a small bow, as in the sixties.

Hats came in every style known in the past decades, and even the ordinary working man was just as likely to be seen wearing a black derby as a soft felt hat or one of the many cap styles. The high silk hat was more rarely seen in daytime but persisted for evening wear.

Furs became very popular for men's winter garments at this time, especially for caps, which were most often made of sealskin or otter. Both of these pelts were also used in making gloves and as trim for overcoats, in a border or facing for the entire coat. Overcoats, as well as short double-breasted jackets, of sealskin were worn by both men and boys.

Generally boots and shoes lost the squared toe as a more rounded form became common. Black leather was still the only choice, but there were patent-leather dancing slippers, glazed-calf dress shoes, and dull cow- or horse-hide boots to choose from. But the favored boot was still the short pull-on. On September 29, 1871, the *Rock County Recorder* in Janesville, Wisconsin, ran an advertisement by J. Talbot for "Men's Sewed Boots: $3, Kip Boots, $3.50."

A man's complete wardrobe could be purchased readymade throughout the seventies no matter where he lived. If he had money, he may have had his suits tailor-made, but fine-quality suits could be purchased off the rack or ordered to size from the factory. Every price range was available for purchase, as was every garment, from the smallest article of underclothing. It was still possible to have one's suits made nearer home; tailors were available even in small cities. On March 21, 1879, the *Janesville Daily Recorder* advertised men's suitings at $20 to $25 and pants from $4 to $5. E. T. Foote announced on the same page "Shirts made to measure, at $1.50–$2.00" and a "Coat & Vest: $18–$30." Foote's also advertised that they carried Stetson hats at $2.50, men's linen collars at .20 per pair, and half hose for .10.

Children

Styles for children in the first three years of the decade appeared much like those of the late sixties. For very little children, both girls and boys, this meant the Gabrielle style for best, a flaring gored style, most often of lightweight wool, with trimming of soutache braid patterns and usually a back bow or belt set rather low. Skirts were very full and held out by several petticoats. Colors were varied, with red, peach, and creamy white predominating. For boys, especially, plaids were often used, either for the full costume or for trim; the tartan kilt was an extremely popular choice. For everyday, little children and slightly older girls wore cotton dresses with bodices and skirts gathered to a band at the natural waist. These had either short puffed sleeves or long ones either gathered to a band cuff or made straight. The "sailor suit" was equally popular for both sexes, with skirts for girls and either knickers or long trousers for boys; with the sailor suit, in fact, very little boys often were put into long trousers. In any case, the middy blouse, trimmed smartly with braid, had a sailor collar, and with it black silk ties were worn.

> Sailor suits for girls, similar to those worn in fall, are again being made up in twilled washing flannel, either pink, creamy white, or navy blue. They are made with the sailor blouse, sailor collar, pockets, sash, and

plain skirt; and are trimmed with wide white braid, or else bias bands of cashmere. (*Godey's,* April 1873)

A sailor suit, for a boy of 4 years, is made of striped flannel, or plain navy-blue. Blouse, with under-vest, collar, and cuffs, of plain cambric, to match the suit in color; black or white braid, or a row of each, may be used for ornamentation. (*Godey's,* April 1877)

For summer, a popular color scheme for a young girl's house frock in 1877 was white and sky-blue bunting; another popular choice was of white picqué embroidered in white. The fabrics for girls' dresses, especially later in the decade often followed the dark color schemes of high fashion. References in 1877 fashion articles to fabrics for girls include navy blue percale piped with turkey-red chintz or checked claret and blue woolen goods.

A penchant for quaintness is evident at the end of the decade:

Children are dressed very picturesquely this season. Their quaint caps and bonnets, high boots and long stockings, the white lace trimming on their dark frocks, and the bright touches of color in their neutral-tinted costumes, helps to a very artistic effect. Little red, Phrygian caps, ornamented with red feathers, are worn with white flannel or bunting costumes, the stockings also being red. All sorts of quaint capes and collars are added to frocks and coats; the double round collar, the lower one two inches deeper than the upper, being the most popular. These are generally seen on coats and ulsters; dresses being trimmed rather to simulate a deep square, and enriched by upright insertions and outlined with lace. (*Peterson's,* September 1879)

By 1874 even little girls' frocks emulated those of fashionable women, made short-waisted and with the full complement of bustle puffs, overskirts, sashes, and trimmings. This form persisted through the first two years of the change to cuirass styles (1874–76), but by 1877 all girls' dresses were made with the long, gored cut, any sash or waist treatment taken down to the hips and all fullness banished. Extremely wide sashes were tied around the low waistline for both little boys and girls, and a bow was formed in the back that was sometimes actually wider than the body. These sashes were often of wide ribbon but just as frequently of contrasting cashmere or plain silk, and, in the case of cottons, of the fabric of the dress. One little boy's dress was described as being navy-blue linen trimmed down the back with vertical bands of Hamburg lace and was shown with a very wide matching ribbon tied very low in an enormous bow at the back.

Summary

The decade of the seventies ushered in numerous changes in silhouette, color, and surface decoration. The silhouette goes from very full in the first three years to increasingly narrower styles, and from a high bustle placement to one very low, behind the knees, and then to none at all. The proliferation of embellishment and the greater restriction of movement required in women's fashions represent, in fact, a step backward in any progress toward freedom in dress. A parallel development of simple, unbustled, plain cotton dresses for housework is notable in the catalogs, so that a woman had choices for everyday, but the photographs indicate that the restrictive high-style clothing was worn by all for best.

At the same time, men's clothing became much more relaxed. A businessman was no longer required to dress as rigidly as before, and in fact the form of the modern business suit may be traced to the sack suit of the seventies.

As always, conformity to these guidelines reached even the poorest farm, if sometimes in a naive interpretation, indicating that the force of social pressure was as strong as ever and that American know-how was keeping up with demand.

PHOTOGRAPHS
1870

༄

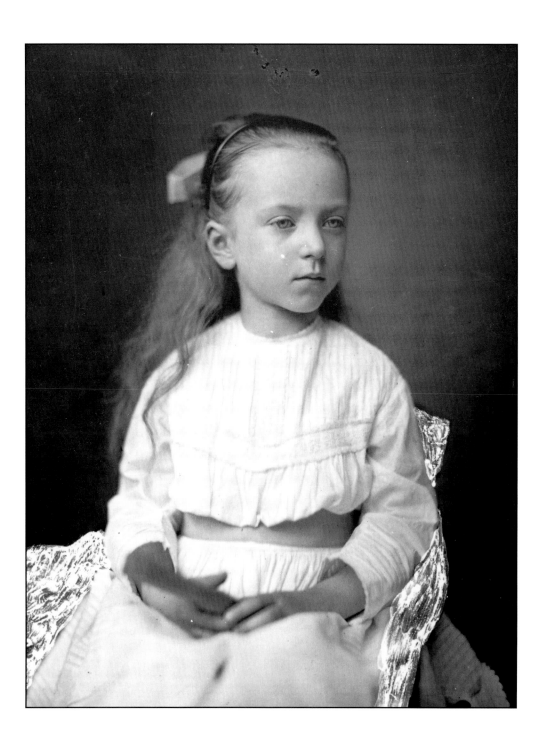

THIS ETHEREAL PORTRAIT, taken at Mathew Brady's studio in New York City, is labeled "Miss Waugh." It is one of Brady's exceptional, atmospheric portraits. (The "tinfoil" effect around the chair may be from some attempt to alter the film.) The child is posed in a summer dress style worn around the turn of the decade: one-piece, with bodice and skirt gathered into a yoke and waistband. The pointed yoke was especially popular in 1870.

The shoulder line of this fine white cotton dress is rather high, though still slightly dropped, and the sleeves are narrow but fairly loose and are a little short on the arm. The neck is high and close, and there is a very narrow white scalloped edging, which also trims the sleeve edges. Whitework and tucks trim the cuffs and yoke. The skirt is finished with wide bands of small horizontal tucks, for fullness, and a pastel ribbon serves as a sash.

The *Alice in Wonderland* look of this hairstyle is created by tying back the hair and holding it off the high forehead with long, curved combs, then tying a pastel ribbon in a wide bow at the back of the crown.

THIS GROUP PORTRAIT features, at top center, Nina Linn Sturgis, and, at lower right, her younger sister, Ella Marie, with their classmates and teachers from the Convent of the Sacred Heart, Manhattanville, New York City, taken in 1870, the year of Nina's graduation from this exclusive school.

This mixed group presents an excellent cross-section of proper female dress for a certain age and economic class at the beginning of the decade. The girls in this photograph are from wealthy homes—the Sturgis girls the daughters of a brigadier general—and their clothing reflects the latest fashion plate information for persons of their age. The teachers, less affluent and wearing conservative clothes a year or two out of date, nevertheless follow the latest styles in hair dress and accessories. Nina's dress is particularly up-

to-date, with its short-waisted fit and elaborate skirt.

Beginning at far left, the teacher is wearing a properly conservative, late-sixties-style black alpaca one-piece dress with a small collar of plain white linen. The dress appears to be slightly trained, since the black braid trim disappears at the fold near the hem, where more length is buckled under. A comparatively high shoulder seam is emphasized by narrow trimming over the generous coat sleeve. Her hair is done simply with the very large chignon of the late sixties and early seventies. Small jet earrings are worn, as well as a very narrow black velvet neck band, and a flat ribbon bow pinned at the throat. She wears a ring on her forefinger and a wide gold bracelet, with a stone or cameo in a rectangular mount, on one wrist.

The girl standing beside her, probably younger than Nina, has her back hair "falling" and temple puffs frizzed and parted in the center, a style popular about 1870 with young girls, and what is probably a dark ribbon bow is set high on the back crown. She wears a dark woolen one-piece dress, with the soft bodice fullness often seen in youthful styles, with a deeply pointed white linen collar and a black silk ribbon at the throat. The seventies proclivity for cuff trimming is evident in the double row of very large buttons. White linen bands show at the wrists. The skirt, visible below the teacher's book, has a fringe trimming just below the knee set on with piping in small scallops. This may be the edge of an apron-fronted overskirt.

The young lady seated in the chair is wearing a short black wool jacket that has very full coatsleeves tapering to narrow cuffs and a black overskirt that has an apron-draped front with ruffled self-trimming falls over a matching underskirt. A small white linen collar and cuffs are worn, as well as the ubiquitous narrow black velvet neck ribbon, whose ends fall in a loose bow at the back of the neck. She wears small, conservative drop earrings under the fashionable chignon.

At center back is Nina. Her well-made one-piece silk dress is of a dark, lustrous, heavy material with silk fringe trim in a V-shaped yoke under velvet ribbon bands. The soft coatsleeves are set down from the shoulder point, but only moderately low, as was the style. A small frill of pleated lace, probably Valenciennes, is tacked in the neckline and is most likely matched by cuff frills. A bow-shaped gold pin is fastened at her throat. The shape of the bodice reveals the short, rather high-busted, short-waisted corset popular from the late sixties until about 1874. The full overskirt, made with side puffs, a deep, high bustle, and a puffed apron front, is bordered with rich striped ribbon. A plain black velvet ribbon encircles the neck. She wears long drop earrings.

Another popular form, worn by the girl standing beside Nina, has the bodice and skirt made of different fabrics. The basque-style bodice of black silk is buttoned high to the throat, where a white linen collar is fastened with a small black jet brooch. It is trimmed at the hem by a full double frill of black silk bound with a bias-covered cord of the striped silk of the skirt. The large buttons are covered with the skirt fabric.

While little can be seen of the detail of the dress worn by the young lady seated at the table (facing right), it is of black silk satin and has the linen collar and cuffs proper for schoolgirls. A black ribbon is tied at the throat, and a bustle effect is clearly seen at the back.

The teacher at far right shows the fluted bretelle-like shoulder trim—a feature of 1870 fashion plates—set well above the seam line of the sleeve, along with a fine whitework collar and a light silk neck bow. She, too, wears the popular black velvet neck ribbon and appears to have matching ribbon tied around the chignon. Her dress appears to be of black alpaca and shows a modest bustle pad.

On the floor in front, the child at left is wearing a dark dress, which may be of a navy-blue or wine color, with a deep, pointed yoke of white with dark stripes and a drooping neck bow falling free of the dress. The collar is a standing white band. White buttons close the back bodice. The cuffs of the slightly short sleeves and an underskirt beneath the scalloped overskirt are of the striped white goods. Her hair is done with a center part with short waves over the temples and ringlets falling from the back of the crown, and a ribbon band is worn.

The second child is Ella Maria Sturgis. She wears a dark silk overdress, fitted in the bodice and belted over an underskirt of white, or some light color, trimmed with bands of the dark silk. The coatsleeves are narrowed on the lower arm but set into the slightly dropped armscye with some ease. The overskirt is drawn up at the sides, where it is fastened with pointed tabs of the light material, which also bands the cuffs. A white linen notched collar is fashionably cut, coming to a V in front. Her curly hair, held from her face by a light ribbon tied around the head, is held back by combs at the temples and falls in ringlets down her back.

Seated at center is a young woman with a light ribbon tied in a bow in front of the chignon. Her black bodice shows mainly at the neck, where a fine lace collar and dark ribbon trim the throat. She wears a lighter-colored skirt that has a pleated flounce about six inches in depth and is finished at the top by tacking down a fold of each pleat.

IN ABOUT 1870 the three Gordon children of Savannah, Georgia, posed together for this portrait: from left to right are Alice, Juliette, and Willie. Juliette, born in 1860, was nicknamed "Daisy" by her family and grew up to found the Girl Scouts of America.

While the girls' dresses have the full coat sleeve, puffed overdress, and full skirt of fashion, they are extremely plain and economical in style as compared with those seen in the fashion plates. The Gordons, at the time of this portrait, were not exceptionally wealthy people.

The girls are dressed in identical homemade dresses cut of one bolt of cotton plaid and trimmed with narrow braid. They are of the kind "made with two skirts," according to the fashion books for 1870, where they are most often shown in silks and wools, with the bodice and overskirt in one fabric and the underskirt in another. In this case, the style was probably accomplished by making the bodice and overskirt in one piece, with a separate underskirt on a plain muslin waist. These dresses differ from women's everyday cotton dresses mainly in their soft fullness at waistfront and, of course, skirt length. While the plaid fabric and braid trim are similar to those used in women's cotton dresses, the scalloped edges are a feature usually found only in children's fashions at this time. Their boots and stockings are black, and the sashes are of colored, possibly red, cashmere or plain cloth. Extremely narrow lace edges the necklines.

Willie wears a black or navy suit, possibly of cotton velveteen. The sack-style jacket is buttoned high at the neck over a snug white collar and is worn with knickerbocker-style trousers. Knickerbockers had become more and more popular for little boys during the latter half of the sixties. The cap is sailor style, with a hanging ribbon, and the ankle boots are worn over white stockings.

ALICE WARNER HUIT is eighteen years old, according to the handwritten note on the back of the photo, as she poses for this portrait at "Woods Gallery, Odd Fellows Building, Marysville, California."

She is dressed up in her bold plaid basque, ribbons, and jewelry. The costume is of a heavy silk and is trimmed with ruched self-puffs at the upper arm and the cuff of the curved coat sleeve. A narrow frill of lace is tacked just inside the edge of the cuff. No collar is showing, but the wide silk neck ribbon is arranged in a flat bow with widespread ends, with the loops pinned down at the center by an oval brooch. Jet beads are doubled around the throat and hang over the ribbon ends, and another, smaller, brooch is worn at the front of a black velvet neck ribbon, which appears to be encircled by a strand of small white pearls.

Alice wears her back hair in a padded roll held by a coarse black net to fall low on the neck; and from a center part, waved temple rolls are drawn high at either side. A white ribbon bow is arranged to lie flat on the crown, with ends hanging to the back. The hairstyle is modest for this date. Long earrings, probably of loops of jet beads on gold findings, hang to the collar line. The pair of rings she wears may include a band of jet.

Agnes Lennox Babcock, a very fashionable young lady, appears to be under twenty years of age in this portrait.

She wears her hair tightly drawn back and arranged in a long twist wrapped around the head and under the back hair, which falls low on the back of the neck, in a highly conservative fashion still popular from the late sixties. Her long earrings, with their many appendages finished with faceted jet balls, are quite smart and new for the seventies. She is also wearing the black neck ribbon popular with young ladies, in this case with a gold ornament in the shape of a padlock looped over the ribbon.

The small oval straw hat, a youthful fashion carried over from the previous decade, was highly popular in the early seventies and is worn far forward on the brow in the latest manner. The hat trimming is modishly small, confined to a tiny ostrich plume and an eccentrically placed flat flower with buds on the shallow crown with its narrow velvet ribbon trim.

The silk, or silk-and-wool, dress is monochromatic and has a soft turned-down collar of the same material. At the throat, Agnes wears an inset standing white linen band, and the dress front is finished by an artfully arranged puff of silk ribbon, with a brooch having a dependent chain and a faceted jet ball to match the earrings.

THE FREEMAN TWINS, Adi and Ida, are pictured here on or near their sixteenth birthday, February 11, 1870. The twins were born in Buffalo to a Brothertown Indian woman whose maiden name was Towne. Their father was Captain Freeman, and the family lived about half the year on his packet boat on the Erie Canal, where they had a passenger and freight business, and the other half in Buffalo. Undeniably, the twins' dresses in this portrait indicate a family of some means.

With its two views of the same dress, this double portrait is ideal for showing off the extreme early-1870s style. The identical dresses, either of heavy silk or a lightweight wool mixture, show many of the very latest fashion details for the winter of 1870. The self-ruching that follows the curved, slightly belled sleeve from shoulder to wrist is particularly noticeable in the fashion plates for this season. The very full, high bustle arrangement is done at the back of a one-piece flared tunic overdress, which is finished with two self-flounces and falls over an elaborate underskirt featuring alternate panels of buttoned-down pleats and vertical puffing. The whole shows the typical "upholstered" look preferred by ladies in the early seventies.

The extemely short-waisted corset sets the bodice style here: it is at its most curvaceous, and the full, high bustline it creates is accentu-ated by some bodice fullness, which is shaped by released darts. The dresses are short-waisted to emphasize the line. The girls have added frilly lace collars with wide matching bows and are wearing softly fringed dark silk kerchiefs beneath to set them off properly. Ida, at least, is wearing a long strand of (probably) jet beads, and both girls have long drop earrings.

Their thick curled hair perfectly suits the styles of the late sixties and early seventies, when many women had to purchase separate hairpieces to keep in style (though Adi and Ida were known to complain frequently about their naturally curly hair). The twins' hairstyle is fashion-plate perfect for 1870: well up off the face, drawn high to the back above and behind the ears, and long "lovelocks" falling over the shoulder and down the back.

Hats like the pale-colored straw on Ida's lap were worn at the center of the forehead, almost flat but tilted lightly forward on top of the mass of hair, and usually had an arrangement of ribbon puffs under the turned-up brim at the back, which lent the name "settin' hen" to the style. The wide ribbons were worn down the back over these puffs. The hats could be tied under the back hair with narrower ribbons, though hat pins became popular at this time to obviate the use of such ties.

Carte de Visite, ca. 1872

*Courtesy of the State Historical Society of Wisconsin
(WHi [X3] 45282)*

THESE FOUR YOUNG ladies, perhaps fourteen to fifteen years of age, posed for this group portrait, which is stamped "Plumb and Loomis Portage City, Wisconsin." They are dressed in somewhat different styles, all quite up-to-date though youthful. The girls are probably in their best dresses and may be posing for their graduation from eighth grade, which is all the schooling many small-town girls received. In tiny Portage City these girls may well represent the entire graduating class for that year. Boys were frequently taken out of school earlier, as their help was needed on the farms.

The girl standing at left wears the most girlish style, with its loose bodice simply tucked into the skirt and with the long, flared sleeves introduced again in 1870. The sleeve flounce is matched to those on the skirt, and there is a matching bustle flounce at back. The standing frill around the back and sides of the squared neckline is of lace. A heavy chain of black links holds a watch, and a looped gold brooch is fastened at the ruching on the dark neckline, where it holds a fall of dark ribbon. While high contrast in fabrics is a feature of seventies dresses, the color plan of this costume is unexpected; when two colors were used in one garment, the bodice was usually made of the lightest color.

The other standing girl wears a striped silk dress. It is impossible to see the bottom of the basque bodice, but there is a suggestion of it where her hand crosses her body. Light, sheer lace outlines the V neckline and fills the neck at the throat, standing in back in a frill, and fine black lace accents the shaped corsage. The coat-shaped sleeves have a deep cuff, trimmed up the seamline at the back with a small frill and edged at the wrist with the light lace. The overskirt hangs in an apron front.

The girl seated at left front wears a woolen dress with a basque bodice that fastens at back and has two points at front, a very popular fashion. It too displays high-contrast fabrics, probably shades of tan and brown. The shaped yoke is covered and edged with fine black lace, and a small silk scarf is knotted and pinned around the neck, where a white frill shows. The loose coat sleeves, with their deep cuffs, are banded in a dark color to match the skirt bands, and the cuffs are finished with lace frills. The skirt is made without an overskirt but has four contrasting narrow bias bands of the dark fabric sewn on with a braid at the top edge of each. Plain, worn button-boots with modified squared toes and thin soles show beneath the skirt.

The young lady seated at right wears a dark silk, or silk-and-wool, dress even more up-to-date than the others, in the high-waisted, bustled polonaise fashion. The coat sleeves have the wide cuff line marked by self-ruching and are finished with a lace frill to match that at the throat. A fringed and patterned wide silk ribbon is pinned to flare over the bosom, and a heavy-linked black necklace falls over it. The apron of the overskirt is seamed and gathered at the sides to fall into a pouf where it hangs longer in back. It is edged with a self-flounce. The underskirt is separate and has two flounces of graduated depth. This girl is also well corseted.

All of the girls have their hair upswept at the temple and crown and have small tendril bangs, and all but one have the back hair falling in waves. The girl standing at right wears instead a loop of braids behind the crown with one long curl hanging over her shoulder. All wear small, slender drop earrings.

IN THE EARLY 1870S, while most blacks were far from affluent, many made good livings as cooks, porters, dressmakers, or servants. A great many young women were expert seamstresses and either had their own home businesses or worked for sewing shops. And many young African American women worked in the factories that produced readymade clothing and there learned to operate the steam-powered sewing machines. Though these working people were, for the most part, able to afford some good clothing, it is certain that they were still forced to economize.

The bracket date for these two photos is suggested by the open bell sleeves, not shown in fashion plates after 1873, and the slightly narrower shape of one of the skirts, which had begun to narrow by 1874.

The woman standing wears a small hat of a type seen in 1870 and 1872 in *Godey's,* with high, narrow trim, that sets off her long ringlets. Her black silk jacket is made in a "habit front," open at the bosom and close fitted in the bodice section, and falls open over the skirt front. This style was particularly popular from 1870 through 1873. The white lace frill of the dress sleeve beneath is visible at the cuffs of the open sleeves. The V neck and rather wide lace collar are accentuated by a low-placed rosette puff of light-colored ribbon, fastened as usual by a brooch and with flat ends hanging in the front.

The woman seated at left is dressed in a made-over costume. Her outdated skirt, too full even for the late sixties, has a strangely interrupted Greek key border near the hem and is supported by a full, wide hoop. Judging from the shape and trimming, the skirt was probably salvaged from an 1862 dress. Over the skirt she wears a long, black silk overdress with very full, open sleeves edged with white lace. The collar, of white embroidered linen, again emphasizes the V-shaped neck, slightly standing at back and spread in points at the front, where it is set off by ribbon ends held by a brooch. She wears her hair in a low puff, probably held by a net, and topped by a flat bow with ends hanging to the back.

The young woman on the right wears the most up-to-date costume: a black silk three-piece dress, notably narrower in outline, trimmed with black silk lace over white ribbon bands. The basque bodice is fairly short and hangs over an overskirt with an apron front, the sides of which are pleated up to the back section, and the join is covered with a strip of the trimming, which then follows the overskirt as it falls lower at the back. The flared sleeves of the basque are trimmed to match, and fine white muslin frills have been added inside the wrists. A good white collar outlines the shallow V at the neck, and a choker of beads encircles her throat. As with the other two women, she wears a gold watch chain.

The young man is quite nattily dressed for his portrait, wearing a dark (probably black) woolen sack suit of the newest cut, a collarless single-breasted vest, and a white shirt with stiff collar and cuffs, with just enough cuff showing to be smart. His jaunty bow tie is quite youthful in effect. His dull, calf shoes show the somewhat rounded-off squared toe of fashion. A good woolen overcoat lies over the chair, and he has elected to keep his rakishly tilted fedora hat on his head for the portrait.

IN A RARE MOOD, this woman, "M. McDaunt," according to the label, sat for her portrait in her corset cover. Mathew Brady, who made this portrait, was a renowned photographer and ran a respectable studio, so the purpose of this outrageous, daring pose is open to speculation. Was M. McDaunt an actress? Was she a good friend of the photographer who agreed to sit for one of his "artistic" poses taken for the sake of the art? Or was she a famous "lady of the night"?

Whatever the reason, this photograph provides a rare, detailed look at a beautifully fitted underbodice fastened over the corset, which gave it shape. The underbodice was made with deep darts and without a waist seam and was cut to flare generously over the hips, where the body was released from the snug corseting. The full bosom is accentuated by the V-shaped deep yoke, composed of alternating vertical bands of puffing and insertion, and the lace trimming, probably Valenciennes, has been carefully starched and frilled. The cap sleeves, very short, are of bias bands of the puffing and insertion and trimmed to match the yoke, and more frills finish the neckline. The garment buttons down the front and is worn here outside the dress skirt. Made of fine cotton, this fancy corset cover is prob-ably a part of one of those three-piece sets of French lingerie sold in the finer department stores, with drawers and a petticoat to match.

On the front of the undergarment, she wears a large gold link brooch—from which hangs a watch chain of rigid gold links—strung with a large stone ring and a wedding ring. This, too, is an unnecessarily flagrant detail. She is also wearing other jewelry, as though she were fully dressed: cabochon drop earrings and a pair of matched gold bracelets of intricate design.

Very little of the dress skirt is visible, but it appears to be of wool, to be deeply puffed at the back, and to have a pleated vertical ruching (just seen below the arm, where it doubtless outlines an apron-front effect).

Her hair is done in the carefully disheveled-looking style of the early to midseventies, a style that was meant to appear soft, youthful, and natural; it is drawn back from the forehead and up to the crown, behind the ears, and shows the "accidental" tendril bangs of the latest Parisian style. For the portrait, Miss McDaunt has left the back hair flowing, though she probably usually wore her hair in a large, loose puff at the back of the crown.

In ink on the back of this photograph, this boy is identified as "Percy Russel (1867–1948)." It is also stamped "Carte de Visite by J. Davis Byerly, Frederick, Md. 1873." It is rare enough to find such accurate documentation with any photograph, but to find one with such a revealing display of the intricacies of boys' clothing was a real joy.

This young boy is not dressed in typical everyday dress; instead, this pose provides us with an unusual view of his better clothing. Percy is sitting without his jacket and necktie but still in the dressy style of outfit that requires these finishing touches (as though he has come home from church and made himself comfortable). We can see clearly how the shirt buttons to the trousers, with many sturdy buttons and buttonholes at the waistband. The trouser, in this case, is made with a drop seat, and the legs are quite generously proportioned over the hips; it is almost certain, from this fullness, that these are knickerbockers.

The shirt is only slightly oversized, is boldly patterned with dark and colored stripes on white, and closes with dark, shining buttons. It is probably gathered to its own waistband, where the buttons are attached to join it to the trousers. The long sleeves are moderately narrow and attached at a dropped shoulder line similar to that used in women's shirtwaists. The sleeves are gathered into narrow cuffs.

While Percy has managed a very casual pose, even leaving off his soft silk necktie, he shows evidence of having "spruced up" for the photograph: his fine hair has been dampened and combed carefully flat in a deep side part. It more than likely fell much more loosely and naturally across his high forehead on a "normal" day.

GLASS-PLATE NEGATIVE, 1872–73

*Courtesy of the State Historical Society of Wisconsin
(WHi [D31] 527)*

338   DRESSED FOR THE PHOTOGRAPHER

Andreas Larson "Andrew" Dahl came from his native Norway to Dane County, Wisconsin, in 1869 at the age of twenty-one. At some point not long after his arrival, he began traveling the countryside around Madison and small towns in the area, photographing families and their homes and farms. Dahl especially liked to photograph his friends, the Norwegian immigrant families, out of doors on their new farms, often from enough distance to show their fine new houses to advantage. Many of these immigrants were, by this time, successful farmers and enjoyed sending these group portraits back to Norway to show old friends evidence of the good life in America.

The first actually documented pictures taken by Dahl date from 1873, although he certainly experimented earlier. Early in the seventies, he posed this extended family in front of the home of Sjur Recque, a local farmer, in Springfield Township, Dane County. The women's full skirts, the long overskirt, and the one short flared basque place the date near 1873.

Martha Recque, seated at left, is wearing a very smart dark calico dress fashionably made (probably at home) with a long overskirt, which is not pleated up at the hips but falls gradually longer behind and is arranged in a bustle puff at the back. Edged with a wide border, the overskirt lies over the quite-full skirt, which is supported by petticoats. The snug bodice, well fitted over its corset, is made with coatsleeves. It buttons in front to a high neck, where a small white collar is finished at the throat by a knotted tie. Her hair is brushed high into rolls, nearly straight up from the temples, and is fastened behind in a knot. This pretty costume and hairstyle would pass inspection in any city situation.

Seated in the center, Mari Recque Lee wears the ultra-conservative "best black alpaca" of middle-aged women and with it a trim white linen collar and small white tie. The skirt is very full, in late 1860s fashion, but not supported by hoops and is probably at least a few years old. Mari's wavy hair is simply taken back into a low coil, possibly of braids.

Brita Recque Quale, seated at her right, wears a similar dress, but one with the double black velvet ribbon yoke demarcation of about 1868. A white linen collar and a short, nicely finished white apron complete the costume. Her hair is pulled back severely, probably in a coil of braids.

Nels Lee and Ole Quale, seated facing each other, are dressed in similar worn sack suits of the old-fashioned oversize cut. Ole wears a large, soft-crowned, black hat. Both men have full beards. Louis Quale, standing in the back, is wearing a newer, closer-cut sack coat over his light trousers, and his round-crowned black felt hat is typical of the period.

Standing next to Louis, young Anna Marie Recque is dressed in a smooth-fronted, flared basque, which is worn over an overskirt bordered with a flounce and a band of trimming to match that on the basque. The hair is swept back and hangs from the crown, where it is held by a net. A white scarf or tie is knotted at her throat.

The little girls are dressed in similar cotton everyday dresses with leather belts and big buckles. Both have deep flounces at the hem, are loose through the bodice, and have long coatsleeves. The dress on the girl at right has a puffed overskirt. The farmhands, whose only notable clothing is the common soft, dark hat, stand in the background with the dog.

GLASS-PLATE NEGATIVE, 1872–73

Courtesy of the State Historical Society of Wisconsin
(WHi [D31] 746)

THIS GROUP, WITH its strong facial similarities, may be one of Andrew Dahl's Norwegian families, though his subjects also included "Yankee" families from the area. Because of the positive identification of hoops under the dress skirt of at least one costume, this photograph probably predates the documented 1873 beginning of Dahl's work. Even the middle-aged and elderly left off hoops before 1873, whether or not they still wore the skirt that had once required the hoop.

The woman holding the small child wears a carelessly mismatched tunic, or perhaps overdress, and skirt. The outfit is entirely innocent of fashion pretensions, being one of those chance combinations dictated by economic necessity, yet it does have datable fashion details. The bodice of this garment is loose and has a front opening, necessities for nursing mothers, and may have been made in a loose tunic shape for the last months of pregnancy. Its carefully cut long, rounded skirt front, matched trimming, and full coatsleeves are also similar to most late-sixties overdresses. The dress is worn with the usual deep, white linen collar, a small brooch, and a dark belt.

During the last months of pregnancy, when a woman's ordinary clothing no longer fit, a loose overdress such as this was often worn over a skirt with a drawstring waist. But this young mother has worn one of her regular summer skirts. Made of sturdy cotton, in dark stripes, it has three flounces of slightly gathered bias at the hem, a style of skirt often shown in *Godey's* in 1869 with a matching overskirt and basque. Her hair is frizzed and done fashionably in puffs above the temples with long ringlets, mostly reduced to waves, falling behind the ears.

The child, most likely a boy, is dressed in a short, gored calico dress with Greek key trim in white braid, over white stockings and high black shoes.

The little girl in the foreground wears a dark tattersall-checked cotton dress with a full bodice and skirt gathered to a waistband and long coatsleeves. The dress fastens down the back and has a growth-tuck above the hem. White drawers with whitework trimming show below the knees, where her knee-length white stockings do not meet the pantalettes. Her very high boots of black kid lace up the front. The child at center wears a white or pale cotton dress, similar in cut to the little girl's check but with a pale ribbon sash so extremely wide that it causes the dress to appear short-waisted.

The seated gentleman has an antiquated full beard and mustache. He wears a sack suit of black wool, definitely not new, with a collarless, single-breasted vest. His extremely small, conservative black bow tie is all but hidden by his beard.

The lady seated in front is wearing a very old-fashioned hoop, probably made necessary because her "best black dress" has not as yet been shortened so that it can be worn without such support. The dress, a conservative "old lady's" fashion of about 1869, is made of good black silk, or silk and wool, and has an overskirt edged in a box-pleated ruche. She wears a light lace bow tied at the throat and fastened with a large brooch.

Her hair is thin and unfashionably skinned back from the face.

The little boy in the high chair wears a short gored dress similar to that worn by the baby but of black or navy-blue wool with braid trim. Drawers show at the knee, and his chubby legs are encased in white stockings and high black boots. He holds what appears to be a stereopticon viewer.

In back, the young, beardless man at left wears a much more fashionable collar and necktie than that of the seated, older man, with the relaxed look and larger scale of the early seventies. His fitted black wool sack suit is also highly up-to-date.

The shorter woman at center back wears a black skirt and white shirtwaist with the standing white linen neckband of the late sixties. A light-colored ribbon is tied at front and pinned with a dark brooch. Her hair is held above the temples with combs and falls in long, loose waves and ringlets.

The taller woman wears a bodice of some dark fabric, alpaca or silk, with probably a lighter-colored skirt that is perfectly smooth in front and cinched with a wide black belt with a prominent buckle. A small white starched collar, a soft bow of wide black silk ribbon, and a long strand of black jet beads finish the costume. Her hair is in the same general style as the other women, and she wears a flat bow at the crown, which would have ends hanging down the back.

The boy standing at right is possibly thirteen. He wears a black wool sack suit with black velvet collar over a good white shirt and black silk tie. This is very adult attire for someone his age and is possibly his confirmation suit.

ANOTHER ANDREW DAHL group portrait, taken outside a brick home in Dane County, shows a group of young people, probably members of the same family. The open bell sleeve, introduced in 1870, was still shown in *Godey's* for summer dresses in August 1873, but thereafter disappears from the fashion literature. Such sleeves, worn by three of the young women, plus their short basques and many-flounced skirts and their ringleted hair combine to provide strong evidence that the photograph was taken close to 1873.

It is immediately apparent that four of the girls have dresses made from the same striped cotton fabric. The older girls' costumes are identical, being made with the short basque and open sleeves finished with narrow self-ruffles. Starched white undersleeves with frilled edges are tacked inside the sleeve cuffs. Both girls wear lace lappets crossed at the throat under the white collars and held by cluster brooches; this fad is much discussed in fashion books in the early seventies. Their hair is identically done, parted in the center and rolled high at the temples with a high chignon puff behind a comb and very long side ringlets falling over one shoulder.

The littler girls wear identical frocks as well, made loose in the bodice with the coatsleeves quite open at the cuff and edged with self-ruffles, apron fronts similarly edged and mid-calf-length underskirts with three bias flounces. White stockings and very high black boots show neatly beneath the dresses, and black belts are worn. Small flat ribbon bows finish the plain necklines. The children wear their hair simply pulled back from a center part and held by silk ribbons, which then hang straight down the back.

The young woman at back wears an interesting dark wool basque with a ruffle set at the hem that is headed with contrasting black-and-white braid. It is also made with the long, open bell sleeve, and the cuffs are edged with a self-ruching of the same contrasting braid trim. A light skirt is worn under the jacket, and a small, triangular silk scarf with fringed edges is knotted around the neck under the white collar frill. Her hair is done quite smoothly at the forehead and hangs in controlled ringlets behind her ears.

The tall young man with the chin-whiskers wears a black wool suit with wide revers over a shawl-collared, single-breasted vest. A watch chain stretches across the vest to a watch pocket. His necktie, two inches wide, is of black silk and is tied in a small crisp bow. He holds a soft black felt hat in one hand.

The youngest child is possibly a girl, since the boots are higher than those seen on little boys and more like those of the older girls. The dress, not an indication of sex, since it was commonly used for both boys and girls, has short puffed sleeves, a bodice and short skirt gathered to a waistband, and two growth tucks.

The boy, perhaps twelve or so, wears a pale, natural-colored, hip-length sack jacket of linen. The notched collar is set high, with buttons and buttonholes close to the top, and a white tie is worn with the snug-collared shirt. An unbuttoned black vest shows under the jacket, where a bit of shirt peeps through. The dark trousers are without creases and appear to be of corduroy. The tubular legs are worn over square-toed, pull-on boots. He holds a flat-crowned black straw hat.

The girl seated at right, who is perhaps thirteen, wears a dark, woolen, two-piece dress with velvet trim at the bodice front and cuffs. The short basque bodice is worn over a plain skirt that was probably made over from a sixties style. A wide white silk ribbon is tied in a spreading bow at the throat. Her hair is worn in a childlike manner, fastened with combs at the temples and falling in waves down the back.

GLASS-PLATE NEGATIVE, 1871–73

Courtesy of the State Historical Society of Wisconsin
(WHi [D31] 763)

ANOTHER NORWEGIAN IMMIGRANT couple, photographed outside their home by Andrew Dahl, displays the pride with which these new Americans dressed their American-born children.

The short basque of the older girl's dress and the dart-fitted and bustled tunic overdress on the other are adaptations of fashionable dress used in juvenile styles in the very early part of the decade.

But while the girls are both dressed in the latest style in dresses, the mother is wearing a style about five or six years out of date, and this, her "best black dress," is worn without the hoop that used to support the full skirt. The dress, apparently of sturdy black wool alpaca, is of an everyday late-sixties style and has a set-in belt. The coat sleeves are trimmed with button-down pleats at the shoulder and a row of braid at the outside seamline below the elbow, and made narrow at the wrist. The skirt is gathered all around and is very full; a rock has been placed on the bottom to keep it from blowing in the breeze. A plain linen collar with rounded points is fastened by a very small brooch at the neck. The hair is done in a no-nonsense tight bun worn low on the crown in back.

Both girls, the older probably twelve and the younger about ten, wear homemade plaid cotton dresses cut from the same bolt of material in the correct style for their ages. The older girl's bodice is cut in a short basque with darted fronts falling in deep points over the overskirt, which hangs in a short apron front that is not draped where it joins the back. The longer back section is puffed into a bustle shape. The underskirt is plain and gored and comes to the boot tops. The basque, sleeves, and overskirt are finished with black velvet ribbon and a bias piping of the plaid. A good lace collar, with sharp points, is set off by a rich, dark ribbon with colorful floral embroidery and a small dark brooch. Her hair is worn in the popular corkscrew curls with a dark ribbon at the coronet.

The younger girl is stylish in a gored and darted tunic overdress with its long back puffed up into a bustle shape. The coatsleeves are finished with black velvet ribbon and a white frill, and the tunic is edged by a black silk ruffle. A bit of white stocking and a high black boot just show under the midcalf skirt. A double strand of light beads outlines the small neck bow under the flat white collar. Her hair is twisted into rolls at the temples and hangs in curls and waves down the back.

The father wears muttonchop whiskers, not usually seen at this date in America, and his sack suit, worn over a shawl-collared vest, is of the older, looser style. The small black necktie and his worn pull-on ankle boots are equally conservative.

AFTER THE GIRLS and women picked the hops, it was customary to have a celebration of the harvest. Andrew Dahl, whose shadow may be seen at center front, recorded this celebration for posterity. No one picking hops would be likely to wear her best or most recent dress, yet these workers, particularly the attractive young woman at far left, wear fairly good cotton dresses and have their hair becomingly done. The dresses would probably have been at least one or more years old to have been worn for such work. Both of the dresses that can be clearly seen are of the style of 1871–72, with flared, knee-length overskirts with no side draping. When new, each would have been supported with very full petticoats.

The woman at left wears a dress with the long overskirt of about 1870, cut flared and falling to about knee length. The overskirt is slightly longer at back and hangs over a deeply flounced and slightly trained skirt. The underskirt is gently and evenly full, as though it is supported by more than one petticoat; a bit of trained white petticoat may be seen at the back of the skirt. A small white collar and a neck bow finish the costume in rather dressy style. On her piled-up hair she wears a small, flat hat that she has decorated with hops.

The woman at right wears a dark calico dress that gathers into a waistband and has an apron overskirt bordered, like the sleeves, with contrasting braid. This skirt is also of the very early part of the decade, as the underskirt is flared and not yet draped at the side seams. The skirt hangs limply because it is probably worn over only one everyday petticoat. There are no puffs or ruffles, only a very simple white linen collar.

The women and girls all carry great wreaths of the hop vines; some wear garlands around their necks and in their hair, and several wear sun bonnets.

Glass-Plate Negative, 1873–79

Courtesy of the State Historical Society of Wisconsin (WHi [D31] 92)

POSED BY ANDREW DAHL in their Sunday best, this elderly Norwegian couple exhibit their ethnic heritage. The general habit of immigrants in this country was to shed any vestiges of "old country" attire as quickly as possible in order to look as American as their neighbors. The typical photographs of older immigrants show them in dark, plain, slightly out-of-date clothing, no different from that worn by any other older "Americans"; their traditional clothing, of which this is a sample, was carefully put away and treasured and only taken out and worn for special occasions.

Not particularly festive dress, these are peasant garments of a type whose style did not change greatly in Norway for decades. The man's coarsely woven white cotton shirt, only the collar of which shows, is almost certainly of the loose style and has a T-shaped construction with placket front. The vest, of black wool, is collarless and plain and buttoned very closely up the front with many fancy brass or pewter buttons, a special Scandinavian feature. His frock coat, while twenty years out of date, was still at one time at the coat of general fashion and not an ethnic costume per se, and almost certainly it was the one he had worn in Norway. In fact, most ethnic or folk costumes are made up of some older garments with quite recognizable fashion details, with regional differences added in decorations, special shirt and cap styles, and other accessories, and then worn for many years without change.

The woman's plain, striped cotton dress is probably also one that was worn before coming to this country. Apparently made of indigo-dyed (at home) coarse cotton, it is clearly an 1860s cut, having the typical dropped shoulder and curved coat sleeve, front closure, and full skirt. It has been dressed up with a narrow standing band of white lace at the neck, and the plain, gathered skirt is worn without a hoop. Fabric aside, any older woman in this country might have worn a similar garment at this time; the dress is in no way different because it originated in another country. After all, the fashion information in both countries came from the same source.

Her white cap is similar in shape to daycaps worn in this country in the 1840s, though its carefully fluted brim is of a very different character. Cap brims in many local regions of Norway were heavily starched and crimped with special irons that produced these regular, rounded flutes. The entire brim of this cap has been done up with this kind of iron. It is in this kind of detail that folk costumes from different parts of the "old world" can be differentiated.

THIS GROUP PORTRAIT gives the impression of a plain, working-class family. Perhaps it is the fault of the photographer, but the awkward pose, with the women seated with their feet flat on the floor and knees slightly spread, makes the skirts appear cheap and limp. The effect is heightened by the sober, stiff pose and dour expressions. The bright flowers in the women's hats are an amusing contrast.

The three older women all wear imitation cashmere shawls, and all four wear their new-style hats and bonnets set well back on their heads in the approved fashion. Their hair is parted and severely pulled back, and any puffs or chignons are concealed by the hats. Without any softness at the temples, the hairstyles are extremely conservative.

The girl at bottom left wears a black silk jacket of the new, longer shape over a black silk skirt and scalloped overskirt. A broad black neck bow is topped by a smaller white bow, with narrow folded collar points above that. The little boy is wearing long trousers of cotton in light stripes, a hip-length sack jacket to match, and a white shirt with a ruff collar that frames his face.

The woman seated at the right wears a dress of bold contrasts with three wide flounces, each headed by two bands of black ribbon and edged with another, which dip to points at center front. The bodice, composed of both the light and dark colors, has shoulder bretelles. A lace scarf is tied in a bow at the throat, and a printed shawl is thrown over one shoulder, its dark-colored center surrounded by a bright paisley-style pattern. A shawl, of any type, was not the high-fashion choice of wrap in the early seventies, though they were much used by the middle class.

Other than their shawls and hats, little can be seen of the costumes of the two women standing at back, except that the dress worn by the woman at the right is of a dark silk with a fine black stripe. Both women wear long, slender drop earrings.

The young man has a shadow of a beard and is dressed conservatively in white shirt and black suit jacket and a small dark-colored silk bow tie.

Glass-Plate Negative, ca. 1873

Courtesy of the State Historical Society of Wisconsin
(WHi [D31] 395)

All dresses are worn bouffant at the back, and are arranged to look
very flat and slender at the sides. The skirt is tied back over the
tournure, which should be long and narrow, and consist of twelve
steel springs encased in muslin, and kept in place with elastic bands.
This bustle should add nothing to the breadth of the hips, but is
required to push the skirts far out backward, and is long enough to
support them half their length, making them flow out gracefully
instead of falling in below a projecting pouf at the waist
as they have recently done.

—*Peterson's,* September 1874

WHILE NO DATE is given for this Dahl photograph,
the dress styles of the two women at left show the
still rather full skirts and short basque jacket bodices of the early part of the decade. The slender,
open bell sleeves date from 1870–72, and the dark
dress has the long, flared overskirt shape of 1870.

The woman at far left wears a dark dress, probably wool, with a gored, flared overskirt arranged
in a back puff with a long hanging drape. Its
sleeves are long and open in a bell shape, showing puffed white undersleeves. The underskirt is
not worn over a hoop but is very full. It is slightly
trained and has no trimming around the hem. A
light-colored silk scarf is puffed at the throat into
a full, soft bow.

The light-colored dress worn by the woman
standing next to her is cut in a newer fashion; its
narrower overskirt has a more pronounced lift, a
set of gathers at the side seams, and a plainer
apron front, with the back lying over the dropped
tournure. The underskirt is still a bit full but
hangs gracefully in toward the body. The very full,
light-colored neck bow may be one of the lace
lappets, tied around the neck. The hair is curled
and fastened fashionably high on the crown and
falls in the popular long ringlets at back.

Even the older woman at center wears a dress
with an overskirt, though it is not pulled up at
the side seams into the fashionable drape and is
more like the tunic overskirts of the late sixties.
It is of dark silk and edged with self-ruching over
a plain underskirt that appears to be worn over a
hoop. Her no-nonsense hairdo is probably attributable to her middle age.

The little boy seated at front wears a dark
jacket, buttoned to the throat, with matching
trousers, and a small white collar shows. The
pork-pie hat he holds in his lap is of straw and
has a black band.

Most of the men are wearing black sack suits,
and their cut is still generous and fairly long. The
farmhand standing at the gate is dressed in very
worn trousers, possibly jeans, but still wears a
long-sleeved shirt, a dark wool vest, and the ever-
present hat, this time a wide-brimmed straw for
field work.

CA. 1875

Courtesy of the Oakland Museum

IN THIS UNSTUDIED pose, two teenage girls in Oakland, California, enjoy a cool day on the porch of their home; they are relaxing in full sunlight, and extra wraps are in evidence. The important details placing this photograph after mid-decade are the long jacket style, the draping of the narrow overskirt, and the elaborately pleated and puffed flounce on the visible skirt. Skirts in the early seventies were much fuller and not so heavily trimmed.

The girl standing is about twelve or thirteen, and she wears a very fashionable costume: the new, longer open jacket and, probably, under that a long vest front to match. The coat sleeves are finished with the popular wide cuffs, which are decorated with knife pleats and a piped band. White cuffs show at the wrist. Visible are a frilled white collar and a white silk neck scarf tied with tasseled ends. The jacket is trimmed with self-piping, bands, and pocket flaps and has a notched collar. The overskirt is cut round and draped up at the hip to form an apron, and the back is shaped in flat puffs hanging low. The apron front is finished with cording and puffs of self-fabric. The underskirt, which is just ankle length, is a fine example of midseventies finish: it has a knife-pleated deep flounce stitched down over the hemline, topped by a self-ruffle that is puffed at the top. A sturdy, wide-heeled walking boot shows clearly. The hair is worn pulled to the back of the head, where it is held by a braided section tied with a large bow, and rolled into long curls below. Short, curled bangs show at the forehead.

The girl in the rocker wears a white shirt and a dark wool two-piece costume consisting of an open-fronted jacket with black and white ruching trim at front and down the arms. The jacket sleeves are neatly edged with starched white undercuffs. The skirt is finished with two deep flounces headed by the same ruching. Over her lap she holds a patterned blanket, and a striped and fringed shawl hangs from the back of the rocker. The hair that shows is bound around with a black velvet ribbon and is somewhat puffed at the crown.

THIS YOUNG COUPLE posed at the studio of Plumb and Loomis in Portage City, Wisconsin. The occasion is not noted, but the young lady seems to be displaying a ring on one hand, and the two are dressed well enough for a wedding picture. The date is determined by the tightly curled fringe of short bangs, which began as a fad at mid-decade. Elements of the dress that corroborate this date are the deep cuff of the sleeve, the tablier trim, and the narrower skirt.

This dress was quite likely made by a seamstress and is as attractive and well made as any city dressmaker might have produced. The fabric is a heavy silk, perhaps part wool, and it is cleverly puffed down the tablier, at the side fronts, around the skirt back, and at the bustle. It is a one-piece garment, quite narrow in the skirt, and has the long bodice newly fashionable, with several darts at either side fitting the front. The sleeves are smartly tucked and narrow on the lower arm and have white lace cuff frills. A similar frill interfaces the V neckline, which is further enhanced by a falling dark lace band and a nosegay of small flowers. Her hair is done in a very smart chignon at the top of the head, tightly curled bangs, and the back hair flowing. Long earrings complete the picture.

The young gentleman's sack suit is cut in the latest fitted fashion and cut away at the front to reveal a double-breasted matching vest and a fine gold watch chain. Both coat and vest have the latest wide, rounded collar. A wide white shirt collar is set off by a figured silk tie knotted casually and spread wide under the fronts of the vest. The matching trousers are tubular, uncreased, and quite narrow and long. The boots show the rather narrow, rounded-off square shape. The young man is beardless and wears his curly hair in a deep side part (the high wave is probably unavoidable given such thick hair); most hairstyles at this date appear somewhat more slicked down.

THIS PORTRAIT OF William B. Rutledge (1825–1917) is marked "Deputy P.S. Marshall under President Abraham Lincoln," but no information is currently available on such a deputy post. (The Illinois State Historical Library says Rutledge was never a member of Lincoln's cabinet.) Neighbors of Lincoln's in New Salem, Illinois, the Rutledge family is mainly remembered for Ann, William's younger sister, whose name is associated romantically with Lincoln's and who died in 1835. Some time after the Civil War, William Rutledge moved out to Oakland, California, where this photograph was taken and where he died in 1917.

Mr. Rutledge wears a readymade and inexpensive suit of corduroy, probably of a warm-brown color. In typical midseventies style, the sack jacket is loosely cut, though not oversized, with the sleeves set nearly at the true shoulder line. Buttonholes run all the way up one lapel, with buttons to match on the opposite edge. A collarless matching vest is buttoned all the way, except for the bottom button. Loosely tubular, unpressed trousers match the coat and vest.

A wide-striped shirt is buttoned right up to the soft collar, which seems to call for a necktie but is worn without one. A large woolen shawl of a dark, paisley design is thrown over the folding camp chair in which the sitter is posed, which could mean either that it was worn by Mr. Rutledge or that it was a cameraman's prop.

Courtesy of the Museum of New Mexico (14264)

THE ORIGINAL CAPTION for this Bennet and Burrell photograph reads, "Rustlers of New Mexico." While we do not have a precise date for the etymological shift in meaning, the term "rustler" was originally a synonym for "hustler" and had no negative connotation, only later becoming a term exclusively applied to a cattle thief. If the sitters captioned this photograph themselves, surely "rustler" held either the original meaning or was intended as a joke. With all the guns in evidence, a spoof does seem possible.

Some hispanic influence is evident in the clothing of these three men, as was often the case near the border. They all wear forms of Mexican-style large hats; the man on the left wears a sombrero, the man on the right wears a smaller version of the sombrero, and the man in the center wears an odd wide-crowned shape. The embroidered shirtfront on the man at left is also of a hispanic style, and a certain dashing look to the mustache may also reflect a Latin American influence.

Otherwise the men wear businesslike clothing—dark, patterned shirts, vests, sack jackets, and wool trousers—that would have been seen anywhere in the country. Existing photographs show that these everyday garments were as common to the "Wild West" as to the East.

Their boots, the Wellingtons in general use throughout the West, are worn with the trousers tucked in, a protective method adopted when riding. The straps over the instep hold spurs. The guns are tools of the trade, necessary to protect animals and other property from predators, animal and human, yet it would have been adequate to wear only the pistols in their holsters and to show the rifle merely leaning against the wall; to have the guns presented at the ready seems a part of the purpose of this photograph.

GLASS-PLATE NEGATIVE, 1876

*Courtesy of the State Historical Society of Wisconsin
(WHi [D31] 555)*

ANDREW DAHL PROBABLY set up his own camera to take this photograph of himself, posed on the back of his horse, "Curnel," in front of the State Capitol in Madison. The photograph was taken in the fall of 1876, when Dahl had just returned from the Centennial Exposition in Philadelphia.

He wears a dark wool suit of the new cut, with the short sack jacket and narrow trousers, with a rather large-collared white shirt and a soft, black tie. His black felt hat is soft and tall-crowned and has a narrow brim.

The friend holding the reins wears a shorter-crowned soft black felt hat and a black knee-length overcoat over what may well be military trousers, apparently of blue with black braid down the outseam.

The other gentleman wears a long sack, rather old-fashioned by this date, of black wool over black trousers, and his hat appears to be the same type as Andrew's.

ANDREW DAHL PHOTOGRAPHED this University of Wisconsin class of 1876 outside of the Main Hall. The class is, surprisingly, nearly an equal blend of men and women, and this portrait offers a fair mix of clothing types.

Without going through the individual costumes, several things are immediately apparent. First, the young men are all wearing white shirts but sport a wide variety of neckties, including one or two pale silk bow ties, at least one long dark silk knotted tie, and several ties that appear to be knotted and have their ends drawn to the sides under the collar ends. The men are all clean shaven, and their hair is cut at ear level but left full on top, with side parts. All may be assumed to carry hats, as evidenced by the tall homburg-style black felt lying on the grass near the young man at lower right. Their coats range from long, loose, conservative sacks, as seen at center, and medium-long frock coats, like that at lower left, to the chesterfield-style sack with its velvet collar, at upper right. Menswear catalogs at this time feature all of these styles.

One common factor of the women's dress is the use of a necktie, whether of lace, silk, or ribbon. Several of the ladies wear the basque jacket, and the puffed apron overskirt may be seen in at least one pose. Many of them wear one-piece black dresses of conservative cut and material. Hem plaits and bands are evident on several of the skirts worn by the women in the front row. Two women wear white waists, and one of these appears to be a basque that is confined at the waist with a black belt. One even wears a bibbed white apron of the type that is pinned to the dress in front.

There is great disparity in hairstyles, with many girls wearing their hair severely brushed back from a center part and knotted snugly at the back of the head and others showing soft waves over the temples. None have flowing hair at the back. Three, at least, grouped toward the left, appear to wear small hats. Every line points to the same kind of corseting, which controls the rib cage area and spreads the bosom in a broad curve.

In order to suit the high ruffs, and general style of dress, the hair is worn higher on the head than it was six months ago. The bulk has changed its position. Instead of being massed as a chignon at the back, it is combed up from the nape of the neck to the top of the head, and there arranged in light puffs and curls. Heavy frizettes have disappeared, but false hair has by no means followed their example, for there is quite as much, if not more, worn than at this period last year, only it is managed differently. It is prepared in long switches, which are all hair, and can be twisted into a coil and pinned, either as a coronet or as a Josephine knot, into loops, bows, or puffs—in fact into twenty different styles, and it is infinitely more natural-looking than the stiff, formal chignons which were pinned on in one solid mass at the back of the head. Curls of all sorts and sizes, from the short, frizzy ones to the stiff, round ringlets, are mounted on long hair pins, and studded about the coils and puffs. Thick ropes, made of two tresses of hair twisted together, are newer than plaits. The front hair is usually crepe[d] in long, natural rippling waves, and, where it is becoming, the front parting is made at one side rather than in the center; the side hair is no longer combed straight upward from the temples, any small sidelocks being turned rather toward the face than away from it.

—*Peterson's,* March 1874

CHARLOTTE "LOTTIE" MIGNON CRABTREE was at the time of this portrait a budding young actress, certainly under twenty years of age. As a young professional person who had more money to spend on clothing than the average woman, and who had more to gain through maintaining a well-to-do appearance, Miss Crabtree may be surmised to have been exceedingly current in fashion at all times. Examples of her promotional cartes de visite, made throughout the last quarter of the century, remain in collections all over the United States. Her home was in San Francisco. It is the frizzed bangs and the contrived disarray of the hairdo that most readily date the portrait at 1876, but the sleeves of her costume are equally datable.

Lottie's costume is made in a youthful, softly fitted style with quite narrow sleeves that have the new high shoulder line and sophisticated cuff treatment. The collar is narrow and straight and trimmed with a black velvet ribbon border and a standing frill of fine pleated illusion matching that in the cuffs.

A faddish necklace of huge gold links with a locket or cameo is worn with slender multiple drop earrings and two very large diamond rings. Her hair is done in frizzed bangs and pulled back at both sides, rather loosely, to fall in ringlets down the back. Her use of kohl on the eyes and brows and of lip rouge is noticeable in this portrait; makeup is excusable in the nineteenth century only for stage purposes, and occasionally for evening wear.

THE 1876 DATE of this portrait of the two Schrantz boys is based on their known birth dates. Michael was born in 1863 and must be about thirteen in this picture; Martin, born in 1872, looks to be about four.

Michael wears a black wool sack coat with a fine pinstripe, almost certainly designed and made for an older man. It is cut with the wide, rounded lapels popular in the early years of the decade, with cutaway fronts, and is piped all around. It is worn over a double-breasted, shawl-collared vest and a white shirt with a white tie, which does not show. The wool trousers are only a shade too long, falling in folds to the worn boots. The black felt hat fits him rather well. At his age, he is no doubt a farm hand for his dad.

Sturdy, pugnacious-looking Martin wears a short, rounded black jacket, meant to be buttoned to the neck, with a small round collar. Tattersall-checked lining can be seen at one side, and a white handkerchief peeps from the breast pocket. Over his white shirt, he wears a V-necked vest on a plain waistband, matching the long trousers that tuck into his copper-toed boots. His small derby-style black hat bears some emblem on the band.

CARTE DE VISITE, CA. 1876

Courtesy of the State Historical Society of Wisconsin
(WHi [X3] 43705)

THIS VERY YOUNG lady has been posed in a manner calculated to best display her fashionable dress and hairstyle. The date is established partly by the style of the hair—the corkscrew curled bangs were big news in 1876—but real corroboration is found in the length of the overskirt, which extends at least to the knee, where a rosette is fastened at the side-front seam and a narrow hem ruffle may be glimpsed.

The woven cotton plaid of the dress is in smart, dark tones, possibly dull greens or indigo and red, and the enormously wide sash is probably a heavy red silk ribbon. The full coat-sleeve style and dropped shoulder of the seventies are here exemplified, with the piped deep bias cuff showing clearly with its button and buttonhole trim and white cuff facing. A rather large collar of coarse white lace, a girlish fashion, is centered by a rosette of the lace at the front, and a gold chain encircles the neck.

The child's face is well-framed by the contrived tiny ringleted bangs, the tiara comb holding the back hair into deep side puffs, and the glistening corkscrew ringlets of the back hair.

The cuirass bodice, that fits the figure closely, is very high, with long basque and has the effect of being moulded to the body, is always made of a different material from the dress. This cuirass bodice is frequently worn over the bodice of the dress. When the sleeves are of one material, the bodice is of another. The sleeves match the trimming.

—*Peterson's*, April 1874

THIS YOUNG BLACK woman wears the smart, longer basque of contrasting material newly fashionable in 1876, probably of wool and silk, in the contrasting colors so much in vogue. She is also wearing the new, lower-busted long corset, over which the cuirass bodice is properly fitted. The jacket cuffs are smartly and deeply trimmed and worn over stiff linen undercuffs. Cuffs and basque are edged with fine silk fringe. A standing white ruff frames the neck, and a black lace scarf is tied to puff at front. The basque is trimmed with black velvet ribbon and black buttons.

A very narrow, extremely long, tied-back overskirt is flattened at the sides with tabs of black velvet piped with the skirt material and at the back is draped into the popular flat puffs. The hem is finished with long black chenille fringe beneath ribbon and braid bands. A slightly trained underskirt of a third color, perhaps gray, has a balyeuse of accordion pleats under a box-pleated flounce edged with black ribbon.

Her hair is brought high at the top of the head, then back into a mass of curls, and bangs fringe the forehead in the approved manner.

CARTE DE VISITE, 1877–79

Courtesy of the State Historical Society of Wisconsin
(WHi [X3] 43707)

THIS PHOTOGRAPH OF siblings in their nicest new clothing is dated mainly by the long, narrow overdresses with their low bustle arrangement, a late-seventies style.

The oldest child, standing at right, fully displays her fashionably cut dark woolen dress with its princess lines and flat tournure. The dress worn by her sister is made the same, both echoing contemporary ladies' styles, except for the bib-front trimming of pleats and the extra-large lace collars so popular for girls. The overskirts, skirts, and sleeves are finished beautifully with piping and "kilted plaits," and the sleeves display very grown-up frills. The whitework pantalette edges beneath both dresses reveal a few inches of white stockings. Both girls wear soft kid boots, probably red, with flat, low heels and softly squared toes. Their hair has been carefully divided and curled into long ringlets from the point where it is held together at the back of the head.

The brother wears a dark wool suit, buttoned high to a small collar, and, barely showing, a white shirt collar inside. His high boots are visible, so the pants are likely to be knickers. His hair is cut exceedingly short and is worn slicked down, a fad that began for boys near the end of the decade.

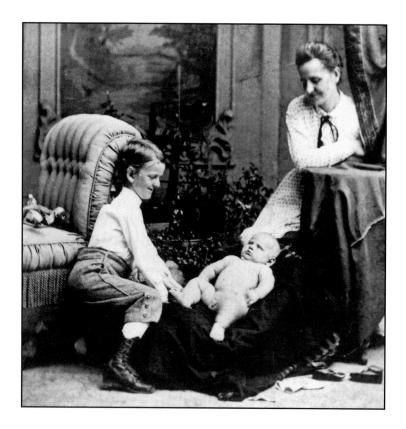

THIS CHARMING SCENE was taken at home on a hot summer day in California. The long overskirt of the mother's dress fits smoothly at the sides, is parted at center front, and falls without bustle support down the back, nicely dating the photograph to post-1877.

Her very plain summer calico dress is finished at the throat with a frill of white lace and with a narrow black silk ribbon bow. The coatsleeves are looser than they appear and are set into the low shoulder seam with no extra fullness. The young mother is relaxed in her summer cotton and wears her hair stylishly, brushed up smoothly from face and neck and into a back chignon.

The older boy wears a typical long-sleeved shirt with a standing white collar, and his short trousers provide an excellent look at the style worn by boys in the seventies; they are short (above the boot tops), somewhat oversized, tubular, and have button plackets at the side vents. These are of a light-colored, lightweight wool and are made with a welt seam down the sides, side pockets, and a very wide waistband. No suspenders are worn, and it is probable that the shirt buttons to the waistband of the trousers and that the wide band is a belt over the buttons. White cotton stockings are worn with the high kid boots. The boots' side-button closures and one-inch heels are clearly visible.

Baby brother represents a warm-weather clothing tradition that spans not only decades but centuries.

THE LONG, GORED polonaise, with no bustle fullness whatsoever, appeared about 1877 but was worn fashionably only through 1878, when the bustle began its return. This photograph was taken when the style was a bit out of date. but this is to be expected in a woman's dress made over for a teenage girl; the collar and hat represent juvenile styles of 1879–80.

The costume is of silk, probably brown, with a small woven figure. It is typically closed down the long front by many small buttons of mother of pearl and tortoise shell with either incised designs or silver picqué. The neck is finished by a small dark silk ribbon, over which a gold chain and a cross are hung. The skirt line of the polonaise is cutaway at front and falls to corners at the hem, and the fronts are edged with black silk fringe with jet beads, a style much too adult for the wearer. The skirt back, of the kind worn totally without bustle support, hangs in flat puffs nearly to the hem. The sleeves are of the narrower coat-sleeve style and have cuffs edged with a flounce and an underfrill of white, emphasized by the matching black jet bracelets.

The underskirt is puffed at the front, where it shows beneath the polonaise, and is finished at the hem with a flounce and at the sides and back with three flounces. The proportion of underskirt to polonaise has been changed by cutting down the underskirt to fit the younger wearer.

Courtesy of the Roger Schrantz Family

JOSIE AND LUCEY SCHRANTZ, sisters of Michael and Martin, pose for the camera a few years later in a makeshift setting, possibly in their own home at Random Lake, Wisconsin, where their farm was located. As this photograph testifies, mothers and daughters alike knew about and desired pretty dresses like those they saw in the fashion books and, for special occasions, were able to have them.

The girls' hair has been recently washed and rolled up in rags and left in fat shining curls, rather than being combed into a more stylish shape. Almost certainly their hair would usually, for any but this momentous occasion, have been worn hanging rather long and tied back from the face with a simple ribbon. Instructions found in ladies' books suggest braiding girls' hair at night and combing it out in the crimped waves every morning.

Their dresses are of a type that was available readymade, even through mail-order, for very little money, though they could have been made at home. They appear to be of cotton sateen. The color may be black, but could just as likely have been of a deep wine or dark brown color. The dresses are identically styled, with the long tunic stitched and piped at the hem and closed with many small bright buttons.

These were called "girls' tunic dresses" in the ads and were made in two pieces. Beneath the tunics, the skirts were set on a sleeveless bodice of plain cotton cambric and probably had an upper skirt section of the lining material as well. Four slightly gathered flounces give the skirts the controlled fullness of fashion. The lowest flounce here may be set under a growth-tuck so that it could be let out next year; it is substantially narrower than the three above but would ordinarily be the same size.

Both girls wear sashes; the sash at left is of light-colored silk with fringed ends and is tied in a bow at one side. The older girl wears a silk sash that matches her dress and ties in back. The wide white collars rise high on the neck and are probably of heavy cotton or even linen and have a deep crocheted frill around the edge. A small matching frill finishes the sleeve cuffs. Their buttoned boots have modified square toes, and although they are high, they do not reach to the dress hems. Their stockings are black.

THIS YOUNG WOMAN was photographed in a new-style walking dress at the Saurman studio in Kansas City, Missouri.

The 1878 shape starts with the corset, the lines of which may be clearly seen in this portrait: very low in the bust, narrow in the waist, and with control extending down over the hips and stomach. The sitter is perfectly dressed for this silhouette; her smartly cut cuirass bodice fits like a glove over the new-style, narrowly cut skirt.

This dress is probably of linen and has wide revers, cuffs, and a skirt band of woven plaid. The bodice sleeves, according to the latest style, are cut closer to the arm and are much higher at the shoulder, though still slightly dropped. The bodice closes with closely set small buttons. At the throat, a standing frill of white lace is finished with a white silk bow, and a dark ribbon bow is worn at the low V neckline.

The skirt is trimmed with broad transverse tucks above a wide band of the plaid, cut on the bias, and is decorated low at center front with a dark silk bow to match that at the neckline. A deep self-flounce at the hem is bordered with a bias band of the plaid. The latest derby-style walking hat, extremely narrow of brim, is set at a rakish tilt. Black walking boots complete the smart costume.

CARTE DE VISITE, CA. 1878

Courtesy of the Chicago Historical Society
(IChi-03599)

POSING HERE FOR her portrait is Chicago's first news girl, Nettie Milsson. With her cheerful, competent appearance and neat dress, Nettie competed with the more numerous newsboys, probably selling papers in her home neighborhood.

Her two-piece cotton costume is made in the bustleless cuirass fashion of 1877–79. The bodice is hip length and fitted, with the long vertical trimming of the cuirass style, and is worn belted (common among young girls). The deep cuff trim and small self-collar are also datable to 1877.

The overskirt is very long and narrow and is edged at the hem with a bias band of stripes. The underskirt, which has almost certainly been shortened to fit Nettie, is finished with a deep gathered flounce of the dark dotted fabric, which has been trimmed at the heading and hem with similar bias bands. Her overskirt is proportionately longer than in fashionable women's dress, as it overlaps the upper bias trimming of the skirt flounce. Shortening the underskirt has pulled the flounce underneath the overskirt. Black walking boots show under the shortened skirt.

A black straw hat, worn in a businesslike manner, and a pair of dainty earrings and a ladylike lace jabot, complete the picture of a cheerful young entrepreneur.

POSING AGAINST A painted backdrop at the photographer's studio, these two women hold the shuttles that mark them as "mill girls." While most of their clothing is covered by the bibbed aprons, enough shows to place the date at the very end of the decade. The dress on the woman at left is sufficiently exposed to enable us to identify it as one made in about 1878; it has the long overskirt that draws up at the center and is worn over a flounced underskirt. The use of a printed calico with stripes of another calico for trim is also typical of this period.

The armscye is only moderately low, and the sleeves are fairly loose, with neat white linen cuffs tacked inside the wrists. A good, rather dressy white frill stands inside the neckline, and a silk ribbon is knotted at the throat and fastened with a brooch. Her extra-short skirt and sensible walking boots, and tight, close knot of hair are unfashionable concessions to having to stand and work for long hours with dangerous machinery. Her apron, however, with its heart-shaped bib that pins to the dress, snug waistband that fastens in the back, and shaped skirt, is quite nice and has been carefully washed and starched. The entire apron is edged with purchased whitework edging. Such aprons are typical of the seventies.

Her companion's dress is not so readily identified, though the standing white collar and soft neck ribbon are typical of the seventies. A small hem flounce of this sort is typical of working dress for many years, most usually appearing on cotton skirts that are not too full and are simply gathered into a waistband. The light-colored calico apron worn over it has a narrow bib that rises over the shoulders in wide straps, probably to button to the waistband at the back. It is longer than the other and made straight and not at all full. And while it is not apparent, these women doubtless wore firm corsets and certainly at least one petticoat.

Tintype, 1879–82

Courtesy of the National Museum of American History (C 77.8.6)

The best means of dating this photograph is by examining the girl's dress. Her long, fitted jacket bodice and the skirt's distinctive flounce are typical of the last years of the decade. The boy's sack jacket is another gauge; it is of the really skimpy cut associated with the eighties but which in fact was available for several years in the late seventies.

The young lady, eleven or twelve years old, wears a cotton plaid dress cut in the extremely long jacket style and with the close-fitting long sleeves of the very end of the seventies. She wears with it a very wide hand-crocheted collar, a juvenile fashion of the late seventies and early eighties, with a small ribbon bow and a choker of beads. The skirt is finished with a bias flounce and a puffed band and ends at midcalf to reveal the childlike striped stockings and high-buttoned boots of a young girl. The costume is topped by a dashing white straw hat with a domed crown and a small brim turned up on one side, trimmed with dark ribbons and daisies. Her black hair is cut in straight bangs.

The boy, likely her brother, wears his narrowly cut sack jacket buttoned only at the top button, over what is apparently a white jersey. His black woolen trousers are cut extremely high and are probably made over from a man's trousers. Very worn boots complete the picture of an active boy in unaccustomed finery.

CHAPTER FIVE

The 1880s

A very great and radical change is taking place in fashions, which it is impossible properly to estimate because it is still in progress, in fact, has only just begun, and will take perhaps half a century to fully develop. . . . fashion in dress has been (formerly) determined by the caprices, the tastes, the necessities of the royal rulers of nations, and a priviledged class who surrounded their persons, and basked in the sunshine of their favor. [These are] . . . hardly now entitled to any more respect than the example of anyone would be, occupying prominent position . . . [the revolution] found its expression in the representative idea embodied in paper patterns of the fashions, fashions for the millions, and the millions accepted it, and millions more are ready for it.

—*Demorest's Mirror of Fashions*, February 1880

*T*HERE IS NO doubt that a revolution in women's dress actually did begin in the 1880s. It is most interesting to observe that such a revolution could take place during one of the most elaborate and restrictive periods of high fashion in the century. In part, of course, the very restrictiveness of fashion contributed to a reform movement; but it is more complicated than that. What really happened in this decade is that work dress followed the fashions to a degree and was thus given a status never attained before. Both in the paper patterns and in ready-to-wear, working dresses were available in a multitude of acceptable styles at very little cost, and those styles altered along with the high fashion, even if only in a modified manner. In this respect, the 1880s did truly usher in the modern era in women's dress.

By 1880 women formed a large percentage of the retail sales force in the developing department stores; they served elsewhere as "type-writers," secretaries, receptionists, and telephone operators; and vast numbers of them worked in the mass-production of textiles and clothing. Consequently, there was a tremendous demand for acceptable clothing styles for working women, styles that were less complicated, easier to wear, and simpler to care for.

Even among women not in the job market, a change in life-style was taking place, with a new emphasis being placed on physical health and sports activities. Especially among the relatively wealthy, who had the leisure to ride horseback or play tennis and golf, more and more women were participating in this trend. Thus, among the leaders of fashion, socially acceptable clothing choices for active wear were in demand. Like all high fashion trends, this one also reached down into the working classes, making possible the purchase of easy-to-wear jerseys and skirts.

The rise of the department store and the continuing success of mail-order shopping, both occasioned in part by the availability of so much mass-produced clothing, had great impact on the democratization of fashion in the eighties. Because of this trend, both high fashion and everyday styles became relatively easily and cheaply attainable. What had been true of men's clothing styles for many decades was now true of women's: mass-production and availability had created a stronger tendency toward the standardization of dress, assuring that regional differences across the entire nation were even further obliterated.

Newspaper advertising also became more sophisticated and widely published in the eighties, having an undeniable effect on both clothing choices and the fashion industry. For example, in 1884 Milwaukee's Montgomery & Ward store placed advertisements in the *Janesville* (Wisc.) *City Times* for their "Buyer's Guide," which could be had by mail. A tremendous increase is also noticeable in the number of engraved illustrations of clothing items in advertisements, whether local or not. Both the broader advertising and increased illustrations were happening nationwide.

In the economy of the 1880s, the rise of the pattern industry was as important as the growing ready-to-wear trade. The immense reservoir of available fashion information, pattern systems, patterns, and fabrics made the eighties an ideal time for the home seamstress. The comparative complexity of fashionable dress and the range of activities demanding acceptable alternatives had brought about a need for many different kinds of dresses, thus providing an economically sound reason for home manufacture of at least a portion of the wardrobe. During this period, even many women of substantial income made their own common dresses and those of their daughters, perhaps hiring a seamstress to do the more tedious work. And at least one firm offered a package deal that promised to simplify this task: "LADIES' UNMADE DRESSES—we furnish the material, uncut, the Patterns, Trimmings, Lining, Buttons, Sewing Silk, Thread, etc.; in short, everything required to complete the Costume. A Lady thus secures the exact quantity of material required, has an accurate and fashionable Pattern, and best of all knows beforehand what her dress will cost her" (*Ehrich's,* Fall 1881). *Ehrich's* priced these packages at $1.10 for the cheapest cambric dresses and up to $25.65 for silk and brocaded satin in colors. There was plenty of home-sewing advice: "No economies can be used in cutting, lining, or trimmings except by that useful and almost extinct class of dressmakers who used to go round from house to house, and often made christening and bridal robes for the same family" (*Demorest's*, May 1882).

There were women in every town and city who cut out garments for home sewers, made at least the hard-to-fit bodices, did only the fussy trimming details for some, or made complete costumes for those who could afford it. A woman doing only remodeling and finishing would call herself a seamstress, and one who was more accomplished in the art, a dressmaker. A business card tucked inside the diary of Chicago's influential Mrs. J. J. Glessner reads:

> Lizzie J. Benson/Seamstress & Dressmaker
> 176 W. Indiana Street, Chicago
> Terms $1.25 per day.
> Work done at home or elsewhere, as desired.
> Orders by mail promptly attended to.

A list of referrals includes Mmes Glessner, Avery, Cutler, and Sprague. Mrs. Glessner mentions a "Lizzie" several times in this diary in 1881, saying, for example, on May 12, "My dresses came from NY and were dreadful looking. I tried them all on—had Lizzie fit them."

Because of the increased availability of the home sewing machine and the proliferation of pattern systems for precision fitting, the pattern business had by this time become so large that it could reach into every home and was, accordingly, patronized by rich and poor alike. Patterns came in sizes and therefore needed little adjusting. It did not matter whether a tailor or seamstress was employed by the wealthy or whether a poorer woman did her own cutting and sewing; identical styles were dispensed and consumed in a manner that helped create a national norm.

Women of modest incomes not only sewed their own and their family's clothing, but they spent endless hours revamping outdated fashions to conform to the latest changes. In January 1888 the *Ladies' Home Journal* commented on this situation in an article entitled "Economy in Buying, Refurbishing, Remaking and Mending": "It is so seldom that women earn money that they do not count their time as worth anything."

In an August 27, 1884, letter to the *Kansas Farmer*, a Kansas farm woman named Agnes Weir wrote about her method of keeping up with the seasonal changes of clothing for her family, and the letter was published:

> In summer I look over the winter clothing, sort out such articles as can be repaired for further use, and fold away the perfect garments that need no mending. Take down a list of such articles as will be needed to replenish each individual's wardrobe for the coming winter. After the week's ironing and mending is over, I begin on the winter clothes that need mending and do each week what I can until they are all done. Then I look over my scraps and receptacles and see if I have anything I can make over to save buying new material. After I

have made my selections I know just what I will have to buy, and thus get all our winter clothes ready by fall. In the winter months I adopt the same plan with the summer clothing, thus keeping one season ahead. (Helvenston 96)

Annie Gorham Marston's diary is an eloquent testimony to the hours spent by a young rural Wisconsin mother in providing and caring for the clothing of the family. From January 1 to May 31, 1885, Annie bought material and made one night dress, one white embroidered skirt, one calico skirt, one sack, and one flannel sack; remade one bunting dress and a brown skirt; mended "Ben's coat, pants and drawers," a quantity of stockings and underwear, and her "Mother Hubbard" dress. She bought material as well, taking to the seamstress for at least partial construction one brown gingham plaid dress, one polonaise of "bourrette cloth," and one seersucker dress. And, of course, meanwhile she "Churned, ironed shirts, skirts, and collars until I was tired out," made a jet-bonnet from some trimmings, and "washed woolens to put away for summer, did mending and worked on scarf."

High-style costumes, which changed throughout the decade, were complicated and elaborate in construction, but day and casual or sports dresses were comparatively simple. The division between the wearing of high style and simple dress was along the lines of use, and not always along the lines of income or class. With the new patterns, nearly every woman could provide herself with a stylish dressy ensemble; and if she then made or purchased several grades of less dressy clothing, she could save her best ensemble for suitable occasions and appear properly dressed at all times. Photographs of working women in walking dress, for instance, compare favorably with those of upper-class women dressed for a like occasion.

Sources of Inspiration

In spite of all the protestations to the contrary, Paris was still the source for high style in the eighties. Famous women who had their gowns designed by Paris couturiers were widely copied: "Actresses are still the leaders in fashion to a considerable extent. The model of Ellen Terry's Portia dress, in the trial act, is utilized for the popular tea gown. . . . Sarah Bernhardt in 'La Tosca' has inaugurated a reign of terror for stout ladies. Her gowns in the latest creation of Sardou have settled the styles for the winter" (*Dakota Republican,* January 1888).

New American fashion magazines reached the public in the eighties, all featuring descriptions and plates of the French fashions. *Demorest's* publications were especially popular, including, besides the monthly *Mirror of Fashions,* the *Quarterly Illustrated Journal* and two semiannual publications, *What to Wear* and *Portfolio of Fashions.*

No one who purchases paper patterns of the "fashions" can afford to be without the "Portfolio," a large folio of 64 pages and 800 illustrations, which photographs all the leading styles with such clearness and distinctness, that the full effect of the most intricate as well as the most simple costumes is obtained . . . no lady who makes clothing for herself or others, or who buys it, can afford to be without our "What to Wear . . ." (*Demorest's What to Wear,* Spring/Summer 1880)

While the writers of these articles covered high fashion thoroughly, often describing fine costumes "seen at Worth's," the general direction of these publications was toward a median line of dress for ordinary women.

> There is very little to complain of in the fashions of today even by the most inveterate grumbler, for there is no fashion that is unwise that is obligatory. In fact, day fashions, fashions for the street, impose upon all women a simple, short, sensible dress, if they will wear it, and permits them to envelop themselves in a straight, protective garment, which requires no more care or thought than a man's overcoat. It is true that there are dresses with long trains, and masses of ruffles, accompanied by bodices cut as small as possible, and sleeves which are gossamer or no sleeve at all. But it is not necessary that all women wear such dresses, and as a matter of fact they don't. Only a very small minority wear very costly dresses, and out of this a still smaller number have them made with tight bodies and short sleeves, or without sleeves. (*Demorest's,* January 1881)

Women's Fashions

In common with the beginning of every decade, there was no sharp demarcation between the styles of 1879 and 1880. The silhouette was narrow, with little or no fullness provided by petticoats and with the skirt back only very slightly enhanced with padding. Because of the vertical emphasis and the elongated lines caused by the prevalent corset form, the cuirass bodice and the gored polonaise remained in favor. Most bodices were at least hip length. A popular alternative in this period was found in the jersey; a high-necked, machine-knitted woolen sweater, once a man's casual garment, the jersey was adopted by women of the eighties and worn fitted snugly over the skirt to the hips. The sleeves were made very tight and somewhat short on the wrist, in line with the sleeve of current fashion. Polonaises, generally gored from the shoulder and frequently reaching nearly to the hem flounce of the underskirt, were still popular. The one-piece princess dress, like an elongated polonaise with a slight train, also carried over from the seventies and was fashionable for more formal attire. And, as always, directions for making adaptations of these styles were plentiful in the literature. "A simple way to make lawn for indoor wear is with skirt and rather long sacque, the latter edged with white lace, and trimmed down the front with bows of white ribbon . . . easily made by the most inexperienced needlewoman if she possesses a good sacque pattern— that is one modern in style, well cut in, high on the shoulder, and well-shaped, somewhat shortened sleeves. A single flounce is quite sufficient for the skirt" (*Demorest's What to Wear,* Spring/Summer 1880).

At the same time, common dresses for housework and everyday wear were still being made in the three-piece style, though with a somewhat shorter basque: "A very useful way of making plain cambric or dark blue check, is with two skirts, and sacques of medium length, trimmed with a cross-band stitched on flat, and edged with a contrast which forms a narrow doubled fold. If the fabric is plain, a brighter check may be used for the piping; if it is checked, a red, or old-gold (solid) piping would be in order. This is not a new style" (*Demorest's What to Wear*, Spring/Summer 1880).

Another style was often worn by very young women. A fifteen- or sixteen-year-old Iowan wrote in her diary about making herself a basque with a pleated yoke, "the fullness thus obtained shirx [shirred] as far as desired." The long sleeves were tucked at the top in three-quarter-inch tucks and shirred at the bottom, leaving fullness over the elbow. She joined the underskirt, which showed below the basque, to an underbodice and added special details: "an underskirt and waist together . . . no sleeves . . . I embroidered the belt." Later that same year, she and her mother cut out a navy-blue "brilliant" dress for her with a "Real pretty overskirt, looped up high on the sides and coming to the pleat ruffle of the underskirt, and where it shows in front and at the side putting on shirred pieces" (Miss Gillespie, July 29 and November 1881).

From the beginning of the decade, inexpensive alternatives were available readymade, in stores and through the mail. For example, an 1880 *Ehrich's* summer quarterly advertised two grades of calico housedresses, at $1.70 and $2.25, and a fine two-piece walking costume "of Swiss organdie, and Languedoc lace," selling for $20.00 or $22.50 "with train skirt." Similarly, *Demorest's What to Wear* (Spring/Summer 1880) featured gingham and cambric dresses "for the country," which were to be made "as complete dresses, with round waist and simple overskirt," a style often shown in catalogs. Such dresses are seen in many photographs of women at home during the eighties; most of these are one-piece housedresses, the bodice fullness gathered into a waistband, with gathered skirts and a flounce of varying width at the hem. These dresses made in summer cottons have rather narrow bishop sleeves, with narrow self-cuffs and very slight gathering at the shoulder, and often plain neckbands and yokes of self-fabric, sometimes with frilled trimming. Dark washdresses, possibly of wool, are even more plain, with simple round necklines, tight sleeves set very high on the shoulder, round waists, and plain, rather skimpy, gathered skirts, sometimes cut at ankle length for mobility.

In essence this perceived need of having two or three alternatives, even for common dress, was general throughout the decade, with stylistic changes evident even in work dress as fashions dictated. Changes in cut might include, for instance, skirt fullness, which, even in the most common dresses, increased after 1882: "The skirts are wider, and the puff at the back larger. The full effect is usually given by the cut and the rich folds of the material used. Small horsehair pads are sewn in the back breadths only" (*Peterson's,* December 1882).

Changes also occurred in fabrics and color choices. A distinctive fashion in dark-colored silk, velvet, and wool walking dresses became popular in 1882, and the rich colors used in them began the 1880s trend for dark colors, even in calicoes. These walking dresses included a fitted, tailored dress and a wrap to match and required that a soft hat be made of the wrap material (thus, the home sewer had as much access to the fashionable mode as anyone). "The great art, now, in a street or visiting-costume, is to have every part of it—dress, bonnet, cloak, and muff—to match precisely in color, though they may all be of different materials. The gloves alone are permitted to form a contrast; and these are almost invariably now of undressed kid, in various shades of tan-color" (*Peterson's,* April 1882). The favorite colors were dark, often a rich claret or deep purple or copper and gold shades. A silk costume with a wool wrap might have had a matching velvet or plush trim, and the hat might have been at least partly of the velvet or plush. Even twelve-year-olds had similar outfits, according to a young diarist, the daughter of a Janesville judge:

> Jan. 1, 1882: Hat is garnet plush poke with cream colored plume and strings.
> Jan. 9 : After school mama and I went to Miss Shaver's, dressmakers. I am having a green dress made with gilt buttons and plush collar, cuffs, and pockets.
> Feb. 5: Elsie and I both had cloaks alike and pokes, hers trimmed blue and Roman pearls to match and mine with garnet. (Pritchard diary 1882)

> In summer, the tendency toward dark colors is mitigated, and there is a distinct preference for white: Cotton dresses are so beautiful in design and color that they are made up as fancifully, in many cases, as the foulards and more expensive goods. White dresses are unusually popular, and are made so elaborately, in many instances, that silk would be less expensive; we now speak of nainsooks, cambric, etc. (*Peterson's,* June 1882)

By 1883 the tournure, or bustle, had returned to fashion in the deep, high line similar to that seen in 1874, and side panniers, pulled up high into puffs with deeply folded apron drapes, were popular. The bustle size reached its climax in 1886, as the short corset also returned; thus, the fashionable body was confined sharply through the rib cage and released just above the natural waistline into a nearly horizontal deep bustle in the back and fuller hips at the sides, and the bosom was raised very high again. The broadened hips were fashionable from about 1883 through 1886, briefly replacing the slender frontal silhouette. Stylish dress during this period featured a variety of shorter and shorter basque bodices that conformed to this line—all very tightly fitted, some cut up in a curve at the hips, some short all around, and some pointed, but most had long rounded points at front. Many bodices of this period had tight sleeves cut short on the forearm and featuring cuffs or half-cuffs.

Beginning about 1887, the huge bustle seemed simply to deflate and fall in on itself, forming a drooping set of deep folds down the back and causing the skirt to hang straight from the hips as seen from the front. The overskirt was at this time frequently set on as a separate length of material with one straight edge hanging free. The front was pleated into the side seam high at one side and draped diagonally across the body to a low set of hip tucks on the other side, and the back was arranged in several low-hanging puffs. Some of these skirts omitted the drooping puffs and took up the fabric with box pleats at center back. The free straight edge of this kind of overskirt, as often seen in photographs, fell straight down behind the opposite side seam. This style appeared in everything from wool and light, printed fabrics to the cheapest ginghams. Many common "round-waisted" day dresses had this kind of skirt, as evidenced by a number of photographs, and it was also common in two-piece costumes of better material.

By 1888 many daytime and walking dresses featured long, box-pleated skirts that hung straight, not flared, but with plenty of material. The apron drape, still often present and frequently shown over such a box-pleated skirt, rose to a band of flat folds high across the belly, often with the outer edges pleated into the waistband at side fronts rather than into the side seams. In the back there were long drooping folds and still some bustle support. And at the end of the decade, a new kind of skirt—one that was so narrow as to interfere with walking to some extent and that had its weight tied back behind the thighs—was highly fashionable. The skirt had an interior arrangement of steel and tape for handling the back fullness, which was a fashion necessity. A formal style, its materials were usually fine wools and rich satins and brocades.

In eighties photographs all bodices appear corset-fitted, many with very high standing collars. Similarly, sleeves are set very high, with the armscye cut somewhat in from the point of the shoulder in back, and are extremely tight—though at times there seems to be some release in the sleeves of dresses meant for active wear—and still cut short of the wrist bone. In the last year or two of the decade, an applied shoulder-cap is frequently seen. Looser, sometimes even puffed, upper sleeves occasionally appear after 1887:

> Caps or jockeys upon the tops of sleeves are improving to the appearance of a lady whose shoulders are too low for perfect symmetry. Frequently these decorations are made of contrasting and more decorative goods. It is in the varying and fanciful shapes of sleeves that the most noticeable novelties of today are seen, and, certainly, after the prolonged reign of those that were tight-fitting—and which are still by no means unfashionable—puffed, loose, and open sleeves are a refreshing relief to both arms and eyes. (*Delineator,* October 1887)

Artistic Dress and Other Alternatives

Fashionable women longing for change, for looser sleeves or some other relief for the eye and body, were ready for the introduction of

"Artistic Dress" and, to a degree, were responsible for a small wave of partisanship for this fad. Proponents of the style looked to England for inspiration; in that country, picturesque gowns drawn from the paintings of such artists as Velazquez, Rembrandt, and Rubens were worn as an expression of freedom from the dictates of fashion by a certain class of women interested in the arts.

Oscar Wilde was, for example, a great English proponent of this "artistic" style for women. On April 14, 1882, Mrs. J. J. Glessner, a wealthy Chicago society woman, went to a meeting of the Decorative Arts Society Board. The members had invited Oscar Wilde as the guest speaker for the meeting. Wilde had been causing quite a sensation in the United States with his 1881–82 tour to publicize the "artistic" Gilbert and Sullivan operetta *Patience* and in his efforts to foster an artistic dress movement. Mrs. Glessner was not impressed. She wrote in her diary, "he is a great fool and humbug—he wore rough cloth baggy trousers, a gray velvet jacket and vest, patent leather shoes, a gendarme blue silk necktie and handkerchief, a dark green coat with heavy fur collar and cuffs, a brown hat of peculiar shape, lemon-colored kid gloves stitched with black, carried an ivory cane, had his overcoat thrown back, his long hair parted in the middle and falling about his ears . . . he told us we should not wear artificial flowers."

Nevertheless, the essentially English artistic movement did gather some impetus in this country from Wilde's visit, though primarily (but not exclusively) among residents of the larger cities. "Artistic" teas, soirées, plays, and musicals were arranged as showcases for the wearing of such gowns. With them were worn the natural, loose, "carelessly bound" hairstyles and natural flowers pinned on the dress and hat, the chief favorite being the sunflower. Further aims of the movement included artistic pursuits of all kinds and the artistic decoration of the home. The movement survived, to a degree, into the nineties.

The wearing of such dress never became a real trend or caused a reduction in the excesses of high fashion, which it was designed to do, but it did influence to a certain extent the design of everyday comfortable dresses for the home. For example, the wrapper of the eighties shared some features of artistic dress, being generally trained, sometimes having the graceful "Watteau" set of back pleats falling from the shoulder, and often having picturesque long sleeves.

More than ever throughout this decade, a wrapper was worn over the uncorseted, or lightly corseted, form as acceptable dress, even for mixed company. Women's diaries often mention making wrappers of calico or flannel, and readymade wrappers were among the first items available through mail-order catalogs. In 1880 *Ehrich's Fashion Quarterly, Purchaser's Guide and Manual of Shopping* offered wrappers ranging from "dark calico, lined to waist, trimmed down front and on sleeves and pockets" at .90; a "Half-tight wrapper trimmed with bands of colored border, and lined to waist," at $1.50; and cashmere, wool flannel, and serge "demi-train" wrappers for $5.50 to $11.50. In 1886, *Ehrich's* offered quite similar wrappers, the only difference being a much deeper tournure, in accordance with the fashion. Seersucker was a popular fabric choice.

One wrapper, the "Mother Hubbard" style, featured the familiar square yoke and gathered bodice of the true Mother Hubbard; but rather than falling free, it was fitted to a snug waistband or belted. The typical Mother Hubbard was a free-falling, long-sleeved cotton frock gathered into a yoke. Photographs taken in the eighties show a similar type with the front fullness taken into long tucks that reach below the waist. These styles were typically worn unbelted around the house, especially for pregnancy. The Mother Hubbard was acceptable in the eighties as morning dress, but for the house only; its use as dress for hot-weather comfort, however, was almost universal. In fact, it was not long before it was worn farther and farther from the front door, sometimes causing shock and dismay. Mary Dodge Woodward, who had accompanied her adult children to settle near Fargo, North Dakota, wrote in her diary on June 3, 1885:

> I have cut out the dress which Nellie sent me . . . were I farther west, I should not dare to make it "Mother Hubbard," as the paper says that in Pendleton, Oregon, that type of costume is prohibited unless worn belted. Bills to that effect have been posted in the town, ladies who violate the ordinance being fined heavily. The alleged reason is that such garments scare horses, cause accidents, and ruin business. (Culley 165)

Another woman, Helen Boyden, kept a travel journal as she went west from Chicago to visit Pikes Peak in 1887. At one stop on the prairie, she recorded that "The toll gate is locked and an enormous fat woman comes out and opens it, a Mother Hubbard fits her quite snugly." A small drawing of this remarkable woman is included in the journal, and it shows the typical square yoke of the garment, its long sleeves, and the fullness quite taken up over the large body.

Reform dress, while still discussed, was not too influential during the eighties:

> The majority of women are fast settling down to some permanent ideas in regard to dress, and it could be done much better and more rapidly if it were not for ignorant would-be reformers, who know nothing of the subject, but are possessed with the antiquated notion that fashion is folly, and their particular hobby wisdom, and keep hammering at it, totally oblivious of what has been accomplished, and of course giving no credit for it. (*Demorest's Review of Fashion*, January 1881)

ACCESSORIES

Fans were popular accessories for visiting and party dress in the eighties, though little commentary on them is available, and they rarely show up in photographs. In April 1882 *Peterson's* mentions in passing that "Ostrich-feather fans are still the rage, and are carried to more preposterous dimensions than ever." Fans of all types were quite large. Japanese paper fans were especially plentiful, for, as with the other decorative arts, there was a fascination with the artistic, oriental decorative techniques that suited the aesthetic sensibilities of this period.

Parasols, too, were fairly large, and available in a wide range of styles: "Lace parasols, either covered with ruffles of Spanish or Chantilly lace, or with the cover made entirely of Spanish lace over colored satin, are much in vogue this fall. . . . Umbrellas made for ladies use are of medium size, the handles being perfectly plain and smooth, and in live ivory, with the owner's initials or monogram in colored letters at the top" (*Peterson's,* September 1882). Muffs are also evident in photographs and seem to have been almost taken for granted as part of outdoor dress. Beaver, black otter, and monkey fur were the popular muff skins in 1888.

Jewelry styles tended toward novelty in the eighties. Humorous subjects were featured in lapel pins, such as mice or rats on a fence, a pig looking through a fence, or a tennis racket and ball: "Jewelry is now nearly always limited to ear-rings, a handkerchief pin, and sleeve-buttons in the street, and instead of ear-rings and pin forming a set, as formerly, it is usually the case that the pin is a fanciful design executed in silver, or oxidized metals, and having no relation to any other ornaments worn" (*Demorest's,* November 1880). The fashion column of the *Dakota Republican* on February 9, 1888, reported on a marvelous variety in such pins, charms, and pendants: a miniature oil-paint tube of silver, tiny enameled opera-glasses, an oxidized silver figure of Punch, a silver sounding rod and a coil of ropes, a paint brush with a gold handle and a red and white enameled brush, and a coil of gold ropes bearing a gold lizard with diamond eyes.

UNDERGARMENTS

Body modification in the high fashion of the 1880s was extreme. The torso was rigidly reduced in a manner that altered from an elongated line in the early years to a high, curvaceous, shortened line later on, and the lower body first expanded below the waist, beginning at the rear with the bustle, extending to the hips by mid-decade, and then deflating by 1887 to a drooping, narrow shape.

The corsets, crinoline cages, and petticoats required to form and support these changes in shape make an interesting study. The hip-length, low-busted corset of the late seventies persisted through the first two or three years of the new decade, giving the correct form to the long bodice styles and narrow-hipped skirts. When, in 1882, some of the Paris styles began to have a higher-busted fit and panniers began to reappear at the hips, a new style of French corset was a welcome change. It was much shorter and fuller in the bosom but had a correspondingly smaller rib-cage dimension. The bosom was raised significantly, while the waist was greatly shortened at sides and back, though extending down at front into a curved, thrust-out belly section with a boned point. A short, flared basque extended around the sides and back. Stomach and hips were no longer confined or altered by this corset shape, and petticoats were again put on over the bottom of the corset.

Attempts at corset reform were rampant in the eighties. "Madame Clark's Hygeian Corset" is pictured in 1886 as generously cut and longer and fuller over the abdomen, with short sides and laces at the hips. There were further protests as to the effects of restriction on the unborn, and attempts to introduce expandable corsets for gestation were more or less successful.

Petticoats, having been for so long narrow and unstarched, became fuller and more important during the middle of the decade, and those intended for wear with trained dresses often also had trains and arrangements of flounces down the back. Most were still of white cotton, though drab cambric or colored flannel were at times used for everyday, and colored silk ones matched evening dresses. Mary Dodge Woodward mentioned in her diary on January 7, 1887, that her son, Walter, bought her "a felt petticoat and a Dutch calico gown, both very handsome" (Culley 165). A petticoat was made to be worn over the bustle in order to conceal its structure and smooth the lines under the dress; thus, in mid-decade the petticoat had to be made much longer in back, even for wear under "round" skirts, because the huge bustle structures took up so much length.

It is problematical whether every woman wore bustles; there are many photographs of women at their housework or other work wearing housedresses not designed for a bustle, and it may be true that some older women never adopted any form of it. Even those who wore the bustle probably did not wear it with every type of dress, though afternoon and walking dresses did for the most part follow the form and dresses for dinner and the theater definitely required it. Though the bustle was apparently, judging from personal records, worn in some form by most women for best dress, there is evidence that some wore more moderate styles of bustle than the extremes of fashion dictated. Bustles advertised in *Demorest's* in 1883 vary greatly in size and shape, though all are relatively small constructions of wire that fastened around the waist with tape. One alternative bustle shape, the "Paris Tournure," was pictured in several publications as a nearly flat structure of muslin, enhanced with stiffened ruffles, and as hanging down the back to midthigh, with ties at the front to hold the structure firmly around the body. This understructure gave a definite, firm line to the skirt without going to extremes. *Ehrich's* displayed a great variety—twenty-five different styles—of bustle offerings in 1886. Two resembled the Paris Tournure, one was made in the same shape but with twelve stiffened ruffles, and two forms employed stiff pleats, one a vertical and one a deep crescent shape. One style was formed of graduated puffs of stiffened material. Wire forms included one "hip extender" and one wire bustle pad on a cloth front. A curvilinear form made of cloth and steel, called "The Princess of Wales Bustle," sold for .75. Obviously, many sizes and shapes were popular for bustles, with the more extreme forms reserved for the most elaborate dress occasions.

Drawers and corset covers of cotton were sold separately during the eighties, but the machine-knitted "Vest & Drawers in One," which was advertised in *Demorest's* in October 1880, remained popular as the "union suit" for cold weather, and, as in the seventies, there were lighter, fitted cotton versions for wear under the long sacques and polonaises.

The elaborately tucked, embroidered, and trimmed corset cover of white cotton was never more popular than in this decade, and silk versions were made for evening dress. This garment fastened down the front and had shallow cap sleeves and a wide shallow neckline often fitted with drawstrings so that it could be adjusted to expose the shoulders if desired. The knee-length chemise, designed to wear under the corset, was still in use as well.

WOMEN'S WRAPS

The long, rather narrow style of coat that became popular when skirts narrowed in the late seventies is a strong feature of the early eighties. The narrow shoulders and skirts of fashionable dress lent themselves to this columnar form, and deep vents and pleats in the coat skirts allowed room for walking. Coats and cloaks were often double-breasted, and the most usual form of collar was high and straight and worn buttoned to the top. Shoulders were set-in and narrow. Coat styles remained similar throughout the decade, though by mid-decade the back was necessarily styled to fall over the deep bustle. In the fall of 1880 *Ehrich's* advertised "coaching ulsters" —long, narrow, double-breasted traveling coats—for $8.50 to $11.00. *The Delineator* reported in October 1887 that "Long coats and short jackets with hoods are elegant in the new heavy-weight woolens."

Both fur and fur-cloth were frequently used in eighties wraps: "Fur is a good deal used on the half-long coats, this winter; it is put on in very wide bands, the cuffs and pockets being ordered to correspond. But fur is thus used on every-day costume merely. For visiting suits, the fur-finished plush is preferred, as being much richer" (*Peterson's,* January 1882). The *Dakota Republican* of Vermillion ran a column on ladies' fashions on February 2, 1888, that included the comment "It is a lively competition between the comparatively old-fashioned seal-skin cloaks and the newer, more picturesque wraps that reach to the ground." Sealskin jackets and short cloaks had been in use since about 1876, coming into favor with the introduction of the long cuirass bodice and the polonaise.

The jackets of the seventies all persisted into the eighties for common wear, most often double-breasted, sometimes with open lapels and sometimes with the high straight collar. A thick, heavy English wool was used to make warm, straight, quite boyish, double-breasted jackets. A half-long jacket, worn well below hip length, was a more mature and dressy style and frequently a subject for fur trimming.

The "waterproof," commonly referred to in contemporary literature, was mainly a tightly woven woolen cloak or cape with a hood, although in the spring of 1880 *Ehrich's* advertised a lightweight version called a "gossamer waterproof" that was made as a circular cape of rubber-treated gingham.

The shawl was still in evidence as a utilitarian or evening wrap and was available, in fact, in more versions, and more inexpensively, than ever before, while at the same time the "real India Valley" shawls were offered for $60 to $200. Shawl sizes offered by *Ehrich's* in the fall of 1885 included 35-inch, 40-inch, 47-inch, and 52-inch square "shoulder shawls," two-yard square shawls, and four-yard long shawls. An astonishing variety in style and price began at .50 for a 35-inch woven square and went up to $1.50 for a crocheted Shetland and $2.25–8.00 for a "Paris Broché" (square or long with black or red center) and for French cashmeres with crimped fringe, which came in blue, pink, gray, tan, ox blood, cream, or cardinal. "Reversible Persian" and "Imitation India" shawls were also available.

Hair and Headdress

The large and interesting hats of the late seventies persisted into the new decade, along with, almost from the beginning, some peculiarly eighties innovations:

> Autumn Bonnets: there is a revival of bonnets. Hats are still to be seen but the bonnet has come to the front, with the new fall styles, perhaps because it shows more of novelty, and therefore of attraction . . . the picturesque and the artistic had been almost exhausted in hats, and a revival of the "granny" styles in bonnets was really all that was left to produce a sensation, and it succeeds. The material most popularly used in millinery is plush, plush plain, plush striped, and spotted, what is called "leopard," or "tiger" plush. In the high combinations of colors, such as bronze, gold, and garnet, peacock blue, bronze, and gold, the effect is of course very striking, and it is enhanced by the tropical splendor of the many-hued feathers, and the richness of the gold lace, and ribbons used in trimming. . . . Felt appears . . . as turbans, or English walking-hats for young ladies. (*Demorest's*, November 1880)

And by 1882 the fancier early styles had become "old hat."

> Hats are far less exaggerated in style than they were last season. The immensely large Gainsborough and Rubens hats are no longer worn by the elegant ladies, but only by eccentric ones. The poke shape has almost entirely disappeared. Wide-brimmed hats are still worn, but in a very modified form, the Holbein shape having the preference and being really picturesque and graceful. In the matter of coiffure, the hair will be worn a good deal lower on the neck than it has been for some two seasons past, being arranged in loosely-looped braids, sometimes intermixed with curls. The style of dressing the front hair remains unchanged [in curled bangs]. (*Peterson's*, January 1882)

Bonnets have scarcely altered in shape since last year. The small capote is the most usually becoming to those that have passed their youth, though women of all ages still wear the large bonnet. (*Peterson's,* April 1882)

Bonnets are now almost Universally worn in the capote shape, though some few pokes and large hats are seen. (*Peterson's,* May 1882)

The "Poke" of a medium size, or the small Princess bonnet, that in many cases is so small that it looks as if it was only a fancy material on which to attach a bunch of feathers or flowers, are equally worn. Hats are usually turned up on one side, but the small turban or "pork-pie" hats are popular, especially for young ladies. (*Peterson's,* October 1882)

The favorite bonnet is the capote. Strings are now totally out of style for fall dress . . . capotes in white or scarlet, or electric-blue cloth, with brims in black velvet or black astrakhan, with black velvet strings . . . for demi-toilet. (*Dakota Republican,* February 9, 1888)

The distinctions among all these styles are often difficult to separate, especially since the fashion plates refer to simply "hat" or "bonnet." But the styles seen most frequently in photographs are of two main types. The most common is a bonnet shape, with or without strings, that is extremely narrow and vertical, has no appreciable brim, and has trimming high at the center front only. This style runs through the entire decade and becomes exaggerated in height toward the end. The other general type is the proper hat, with one or another kind of brim, though within this type is found a multitude of forms and sizes. Brims range from quite wide in the summer to narrower and with one side or the back turned up during fall and winter. Sizes range from the modest top-hat shape to the flat-topped pork-pie and a miniature derby. In photographs, decorations can be so lavish that they often obscure the outlines of the hat structure, which is quite frequently of felt. Trims often consist of combinations of plumes, ribbons, and lace that surround the entire head or of ribbon puffs or plumes simply placed at center front or at one side only. Flowers are not as prevalent as these kinds of decorations. Beginning about 1887, an extremely tall felt hat became popular. The tall crown, while flat, was tapered. These hats appear in late-decade photographs in dark felt with very little trim, perhaps only a ribbon or sometimes one or two small ostrich tips. Their dimensions appear to be about seven inches high at the crown, with a top about five inches in diameter. A similar style, usually smaller, and often of fine straw, was advertised earlier in the decade; one example was a narrow-brimmed, moss-green straw that was worn forward on the head; it had a crown standing about six inches and was three inches in diameter at the top. The trim included small flowers at the front and a nose veil of green.

Various styles of knit headgear were advertised for women during the eighties, including small caps, a "medieval style sleighing hood," a pointed cap called a "toboggan," a "Normandie" bonnet with a double frill around the face, and plain or beaded "fascinators," which were described and illustrated as loosely knitted zephyr wool head scarves.

FOOTGEAR

Shoes were made in many styles in this decade, but the ankle boot is most frequently seen in the photographs, as worn with walking dress. The boot now rose quite high on the ankle and was generally buttoned at the outside with a scalloped edge. Heels were generally low, quite wide, often even flat, but small one- and one-and-a-half-inch curved heels were also worn. Boot toes were basically oval and narrow or a bit squared off at the tip with rounded corners. Ladies' "French Kid Boots" were advertised in the R. H. White and Company catalog for the spring and summer of 1883 at $4.00–8.50 unglazed and $9.50 glazed. Similarly, "Curaçao Kid" boots, with no heel, were advertised for $1.50. A flat-heeled, unglazed kid boot not differing substantially from that worn by boys and men is frequently documented as having been worn by women who lived and worked on agricultural homesteads in the newly settled west. Even coarser adaptations were necessary in terribly cold, snowy, or even muddy weather. For example, Mary Dodge Woodward wrote in her North Dakota diary on January 7, 1887, that "Walter has bought me a pair of wooden shoes, without which I could not get along here" (Culley 165).

Shoes for dressier wear all had higher heels, and many were made with several straps over the instep, as in the late seventies. A rather plain pump was also fashionable, and strap shoes with huge buckles and tongues were affected with formal dress.

Stockings came in many colors and were meant to match or blend with an outfit: "The finest hosiery is exhibited in plain colors, such as the new blue-green, India red, the olive shades, heliotrope, pale pink, garnet, pearl, blue, and brown. These are in thread clocked with silk, and also in solid silk" (*Demorest's,* March 1881).

Men's Styles

By 1880 all vestiges of the old, oversized, loose sack coat had disappeared from favor, and the short sacks were much more narrowly fitted, with narrow sleeves set high on the shoulder. A few styles of sack coat, for older men, were cut longer, but even they were narrow. Lapels were extremely narrow and small, as the coat was made to be closed high at the throat, barely showing the necktie. Even a photograph of a poor, elderly man no longer shows the oversize coat style. During the decade a cut-away jacket front was introduced that allowed the bottom of the vest, and therefore the watch chain, to be exposed to view even when the jacket was fully buttoned. This jacket had only three or four buttons and was intended to be buttoned all the way to the top.

All varieties of coats were still made, and a man could purchase frock coats and long morning coats in the more expensive lines, but the sack is virtually the only style seen in photographs and, therefore, must be taken to have been universally acceptable as day wear. Most appear to be black, although some pattern occasionally shows and other dark colors were certainly worn.

Shirts in photographs are mainly white, with collars either of the stiff, standing style, popular late in the decade, or a medium-sized turn-down style. When the former, the necktie may be seen wrapped all the way around the neck, having no collar to cover it. The more usual turn-down collar is worn with a wide variety of ties, many of them rather wide and soft and with a large knot, often in very light-colored silk, but also in colors and patterns. Black ties appear to have been equally popular, most about an inch wide and tied in a bow with ends.

Trousers were at their narrowest in the eighties, still without creases, somewhat longer at the heel, and breaking long over the instep. While black trousers seem to have been the rule, an occasional pair of boldly striped pants appears in the photographs.

Boots were apparently favored for day wear, usually short pull-ons, and were still always of black leather. The toes of those seen in photographs are broad and squared off with rounded corners and broad heels.

A youthful-style hat, resembling the shallow-crowned felt derby worn by schoolboys, with both side brims curved smartly up and a dip over the forehead, is seen on young men throughout the eighties. The soft felt hat is frequently seen in photographs in gray and beige, as well as black, and shaped with a crease and with the soft brim variously bent. A stiff, deep-crowned black homburg was extremely popular with dressier daytime suits. The straw sailor shows up in leisure-time photos, and a full range of caps is shown for casual dress.

Children's Styles

Babies of both sexes were still clothed in dresses in the eighties, very long and elaborate ones until about nine months and then short ones for crawling and walking. The dresses for little boys were said to have been a bit more plain and "boyish," but there was usually little difference until about age five. At this time, little boys were often put into short trousers beneath the dress skirts or into kilted sailor suits or tartan plaid kilts. The clothing of little girls from age five became much more elaborate, at least for "dress," and was flounced, ruffled, and lace trimmed. Both sexes wore fairly large white collars, often of lace but more frequently of white linen, and both wore soft silk neckties, the boys' usually of black.

Little girls' dresses followed women's fashions to a certain extent from about age six or seven, even to the semblance of a bustle shape. This is especially true of the early eighties, when the polonaise was considered such a practical costume and the long princess lines were comfortable and becoming. Waistlines for girls' dresses in the first half of the decade were therefore all long, either with a skirt sewn to the low waist seam or with a separate skirt on a cambric underwaist worn under the long tunic. When the extreme bustle was fashionable for women, there was more material puffed and draped as panniers and puffs for young girls, but in no case was there a bustle structure per se. When, later, the skirts narrowed and the bustle descended into drooping folds, girls' skirts did likewise.

The colors, and even to some extent the rich materials, of women's styles became popular for young girls as well; consequently, dark, sober colors and the sheen of silks and velvets are seen in the photographs. Fad styles, such as the vest or waistcoat of the late eighties and the high band collars, were reflected faithfully in girls' dresses. Skirts were worn short, but below the knee, until about age twelve, when they might be made somewhat longer, nearer the boot top; at about age fourteen or fifteen the skirts reached the same relative length as those of women. Girls also followed the fashions in wearing long, fitted coats, sometimes with quite pronounced bustlelike fullness at the back in order to accommodate the back fullness of the skirts.

Ingénue touches were included in teenage girls' dress, sometimes as late as age sixteen, and generally consisted of a youthful collar treatment, meaning a very large heavy lace collar and/or the use of smocking or ruching around the shoulders and yoke. A looser bodice form was required for girls, as well, and tightly fitted, boned garments were not proper until age sixteen.

Black, or at least very dark, stockings were apparently worn by most children for their photographs, the colors of the past decade having gone out of fashion. "Children's hose are hair-striped and in modest colors, not at all showy for everyday wear. Flaming red and yellow are reduced to the cheap counters, and are selling at quarter price" (*Demorest's,* March 1881).

Highly polished calf-skin (the best being of glacé kid) boots that were somewhat higher than the ankle and that mostly buttoned at the outside were worn by both boys and girls throughout the decade.

Girls wore bonnets and hats that were miniature versions of some of their mothers' styles: "The favorite bonnets for little girls are pokes or gipsies, which make them look like diminutive grandmothers. The smaller the girl, so long as she can walk, the larger the bonnet" (*Demorest's,* March 1881). Older girls wore the felt hats, some tall and some in the pork-pie shape, that were seen on young women for daytime. All of the knitted hoods, fascinators, and caps were also worn for appropriate occasions. Late in the decade, a thick, fluffy, knitted beret with a large topknot was popular with young girls.

Boys seem to have worn short pants more in this decade, with some wearers as old as twelve. These pants were narrow and fitted, coming to just below the knee, where they often had button plackets, and were most often accompanied by matching jackets. The jackets were usually square bottomed, single-breasted, and buttoned to the top. Full-length stockings, which must have required garter belts, extended up inside the pant legs. Boys in photographs wear the Eton and other English schoolboy caps, peaked caps, straw sailor hats, and even sometimes the shallow dome-crowned hat that resembled a minia-ture derby; very little boys, like their sisters, often wore bonnets and, when a bit older, wide-brimmed straws.

Summary

The new options in dress in the eighties and the methods for their acquisition come together to produce the most confusing selection of alternative styles yet seen. Some of these are plain, but most are elabo-rate. This is a decade during which there were more really divergent alternatives to fashionable dress and more vivid changes in fashion-able dress itself than at any time in the latter half of the nineteenth century.

Most characteristic are the commonsense alternatives for working women and housewives that were so various and so different from, and yet so related to, high fashion. The importance of this new, wider range of acceptable styles of dress is definitely that the working woman and the active, health-conscious woman had more input, with every-thing no longer dictated from overseas. Articles in American periodi-cals that addressed the fashion and dress question were more than ever aimed at the multitudes, rather than at the favored few, the twin objects being both to make it possible for the poorer woman to have fine fashion and for all women to have such sensible dress as was re-quired by their life-styles. And yet there was no real easing of fit in women's clothing; a corset, tight sleeves, and restrictive long skirts appear in all photographs of working women, no matter how "simple" the dress style. Progress in this area was slow.

This decade, for instance, displays thoroughly the tyranny of the corset in its many forms. The vertical emphasis in women's styles of the early eighties—exemplified by the hip-long, tight cuirass, polonaise, and even the jersey—blossomed briefly but fully from 1884 through 1886 into the most "upholstered" look of the century, with the greatest ever proliferation of surface texture and detail in fashion-able dress, only subsiding in the last year or two of the decade into the more tailored look of the nineties.

Yet, through the mediation of an acceptable plainer type of every-day dress, common to all economic levels, a woman of the eighties was able to have more relief from the restraints of high fashion than ever before. Even more importantly, everyday and certain "artistic" dress styles began slowly to influence fashion by the end of the eight-ies, signaling the end of the despotism of the corset. The time of mass-produced, simpler, and easier-fitting garments was at last in view.

The plain, rather somber and repetitious clothing of 1880s men throughout, still based on English prototypes, was in direct contrast to these elaborate changes in women's dress, yet in effect shows the same process. It was the mass production of men's garments, begun long ago, at the beginning of our sixty-year period, that had promoted this universality of garment styles that were both easy to make and generally easy to wear.

PHOTOGRAPHS
1880

There is the widest latitude in bodices, basques, and sleeves. Coat basques take the lead of the basque styles, but the cuirass is equally well worn and the deep casaque, which is drawn smoothly over the hips and shirred up in front, from which it is draped away, is perhaps the most popular mode for washable materials and secondary toilets.

—*Demorest's*, March 1881

THE "CASAQUE" OVERDRESS, a distinctive style of the first two years of the eighties, is distinguished by its long, slim shape and symmetrical drape. Together with the generous coat sleeves, reminiscent of the past decade, the style pinpoints the early date of this photograph, and the corkscrew bangs confirm it.

This young woman is smartly dressed for a formal portrait in her polonaise casaque of heavy silk, with the puffed bodice front of darker (but certainly blending) silk satin. The front of the bodice is closely fastened with stylish, highly decorated buttons, a distinct fashion feature of the early eighties. The overdress is cut in a slim princess style, and the back will be shaped and puffed into a very low drape, but without infrastructure for any exaggerated bustle effect. The overskirt at this time always rises at the center-front hem either in a gentle arch or in a shallow inverted V, is trimmed all around, and is generally accented at center-front with a puff or a bow. The hem of this example is finished with piping and a wide silk ribbon over silk chenille fringe. The coat sleeves are elaborately trimmed, with the entire lower-arm portion covered with puffs and pleats. A thick white lace frill finishes the cuffs, and a fringed white silk scarf is tied in a soft bow over the fluted collar.

The skirt worn beneath the long polonaise is of a lighter, though blending, colored silk. It is finished with hand-stitched rows of puffing over a knife-pleated flounce like that of the cuffs.

Popular in the 1880s were corkscrew curls worn around the face, the hair being cut short over the temples and forehead and curled tightly with a hot iron. The back hair is worn in a small knot or coil high on the crown, but not showing at the top of the head.

*Courtesy of the Rock County Historical Society
(RCHS 6)*

All dresses are made short that are not
intended for very dressy purposes.
—*Demorest's*, March 1881

AGAIN, THE SYMMETRICALLY draped skirt front
and the coatsleeve date this photograph. The
crimped bangs and the bodice are other confir-
mations. Long, pointed basques of this sort were
mentioned in *Demorest's* as early as 1879 and continued to be featured in fashion illustrations
through 1882.

This dressy example is apparently made of a
heavy silk, or silk and wool, and features a finely
pleated self-frill attached by the outside edge to
the one-inch black velvet ribbon trim set down
the side fronts, facing toward the neck and front
of the basque. The coat sleeves are set high, but
still quite loose, and have the popular broad
wrapped cuff style held over from the seventies.
A knife-pleated frill at the cuff edge matches that
of the basque front. The front closure, with its
close-set, rather large, bright buttons, is concealed at the top by a twisted dark silk scarf, worn
around the neck frill and laid at front over a jabot of white lace.

The long, narrow overskirt is drawn up very
slightly at center-front into a balanced drape and
then taken back and brought up to a small puff
at the rear. The overskirt is bordered with the
black ribbon trim and a band of the fine knife
pleats. Three flounces of interrupted pleats with
black velvet tabs interspersed make up the
underskirt, which is at least three inches short
of the floor in the manner of the early eighties.

The flat knife-plaitings are going out of fashion, shirred or gathered ruffles and box-plaitings taking their place.

—*Peterson's,* April 1882

Heretofore, ladies who were slender have been desirous of adding to their apparent flesh, but of late years this is not always the case. "Lengthened sweetness" is now a mark of high fashion. Ladies who are so fortunate as to be tall and slender, emphasize it in every way by the cut and style and make of their clothing. The preponderance of the art and esthetic idea has something to do with this tendency. For this reason draperies continue to be preferred placed low on the skirt, and in flat or irregular folds. Drapery bunched up over the hips, or just below the waist, reduces the apparent height and increases the apparent bulk.

—*Demorest's,* March 1881

WHILE THIS OVERDRESS is still in the narrow casaque shape, the short, tight sleeves proclaim the date as probably the winter of 1882, barely before the comeback of the bustle. The hair, too, with its softer, fuller shape, marks the advance into the decade.

In a well-fitted dress of dark, checked wool, possibly a deep wine and black, this young woman is the picture of the modern girl of the eighties. Her princess-cut tunic is one of those with a few transverse tucks taken in the skirt, low at center-front, to cause it to drape prettily, and it is edged at hem, sleeves, and neck with fine black lace. The narrow skirt beneath it is finished with three rows of fashionable puffs, leaving a smartly deep flounce at the hem. The tight, just-below-elbow sleeves and the tiny, shoebutton-size buttons are in the very latest mode. A fashionably fluffy hairstyle is just obscured by the felt hat with its ostrich feather laid horizontally across the crown and its tuft of ribbon. The chignon at back is worn in a soft, youthful style, hanging low on the nape.

The young man with whom she is so familiarly posed wears a closely fitted, double-breasted frock coat with silk piping and covered buttons, neatly buttoned to the top over a turn-down small collar and scarf tie. The sleeves are fairly loose but are cut very high into the armpit in the newest style. The cuffs of his starched white shirt show smartly below the jacket cuffs. The black felt derby-style hat, with its extremely narrow, jaunty brim, is typical of the period for young men and sets off the newly fashionable short haircut. The light trousers worn with this outfit are belled over the foot, where surprisingly worn black shoes and white socks show.

THIS HANDSOME GROUP photograph, entitled "Presbyterian Church Choir," was taken in Watsonville, California, by "Heliographic Artist Chas. W. J. Johnson." The close-fitting sleeves of most of the women's dresses and the variety of skirt treatments place the date at 1882. The long overdresses, while quite different from one another, are similar in general shape, all having a center-front trimming and symmetrical drape. The date is further verified by the amount of both vertical and horizontal trimming on the skirt worn by the woman seated second from right.

The costume on the woman at left is very dressy, probably made of striped silk with velvet trim, sleeves, and underskirt in either shades of plum or brown. A high band collar is filled with a white neck frill, matched at the cuffs. Her knees are turned sharply toward the center of the picture, bringing the center-front trim of the striped overskirt, with its looped ribbons, almost out of view, but the side seam is visible, giving a partial view of the soft bustle. Chenille fringe hangs from the edge of the long overskirt.

The comparatively simple black (wool?) dress on the next woman left of center is made with a very plain casaque overdress that is buttoned closely at bodice front and finished at the edge with a wide band of silk with a large bow at the raised center-front hem. The narrow underskirt of this dress is finished with a deep flounce of interrupted knife pleats trimmed with matching silk ribbon bands. A high, straight collar is set off with a lace neck frill and a black ribbon bow and gold brooch. Frills fill the flaring cuffs.

The next woman is dressed in a costume of similar make but with the addition of much shirring and trimming. A black silk band pleated into rosettes is used nearly everywhere possible: at neck, sidefront seams, cuffs, tunic border, and flounce, and a fan of knife pleats edges the short sleeve. The sleeves, while fashionably short, are not tight and may represent an alteration to keep an older dress in style. She wears a gold necklace and watch chain and a bracelet.

The young woman seated at right is probably the youngest and is certainly the most plainly dressed in a dark wool, back-fastening, hip-length cuirass tunic very simply edged and trimmed. This style had been favored by young women for several years by this date, and the garment is probably not very new. The separate overskirt is treated like the casaque fronts, tucked up at center-front and finished there with ribbon loops. The flounce of the underskirt is a simple undecorated border of box plaits. Even the neck and sleeve trim are plain, although there is a good silk ribbon necktie and a round locket. Trim, glossy, square-toed button boots show enough that the dress can be seen to be fairly short. This girl is also the only one to wear the tightly crimped hair.

The three gentlemen all wear black wool suits, though the styles are very different. The gentleman at left has a rather formal, wide-lapel version of the sack, with expensive bound edges. At center can be seen the more informal sack coat, and at right a long, dressy, double-breasted frock coat is worn. All of the men's neckties are narrow and black, tied in a bow under wing collars, and all of the gentlemen have short haircuts and facial hair.

IN THE HEAT of an August day, young Richmond lawyer Lewis Dandridge Aylett poses for the photographer outside his office, where boards have been laid down on the rough earth to support his office chair.

Everything about his attire is typical of the eighties: the small, exuberant hat; the buttoned vest; the close shirtsleeves; the wide tie under the turn-down collar; and especially the very long, narrow, tubular trouser legs. The sack jacket that completes this suit will be cut close under the arms, narrowly fitted to the chest, and fairly short. His chin-whiskers, trimmed chops, and mustache represent the latest fad for young gentlemen.

Spring 1882

Courtesy of the Essex Institute (7518)

Skirts are very close-fitting in front and at the sides, notwithstanding the introduction of tournures at the back.

—*Peterson's,* October 1882

MISS PANCHARD, WHO was employed for many years by Miss Bray at this dress shop in Salem, Massachusetts, either purchased or inherited the shop sometime after Miss Bray's death, somewhere around 1880, according to Salem historians. This photograph is said to have been taken soon after this event. But the long, narrow polonaise, with its low drape and tight sleeves, helps date the photograph at a year or two later.

This plain black dress is probably made of alpaca, a long time standard fabric for clerks, seamstresses, teachers, and older women because of its practicality. It was thin but sturdy and long lasting and it tailored well and presented an unassuming front. Its only drawback was a tendency to become shiny with age.

The smoothly fitted short basque is slightly shorter at the hips and back to allow for the returning side drapes and bustle, but it does not as yet have the abrupt flare at the hips that comes about in 1883 when bustle fullness increased substantially. It has closely fitted sleeves, set high on the shoulder, and finished with black velvet cuffs that match the velvet "falling" collar. A collar of this type is featured in *Godey's* in 1883. A narrow white linen collar and cuffs are inserted. The long, apron-shaped overskirt is drawn up in folds at either hip, which lie quite flat so as not to widen the figure from the front, and form a distinct pouf at the back. The underskirt, very slightly trained, is narrow and finished with a deep pleated flounce.

Equally interesting are the calicoes and ginghams displayed in the window; while dark grounds predominate, as might be expected, one or two are light, with dark dots or florets. The two upper pieces are probably shawls, one in vivid stripes on a dark ground, the other a border print on a light ground with light fringe. An early spring season is suggested by the textiles on display and by the open door.

THE FOUR CHILDREN of the relatively prosperous farmer Anson Cook of rural Boscobel, Wisconsin, were brought into town to have this group portrait taken. Anson Jr. is standing at back and seated (left to right) are Effie, Lily, and Edith.

Anson is neatly dressed in a lightweight sack suit of wool or a wool blend. The jacket has a very narrow lapel and a breast pocket with contrasting binding. The collarless vest is similar in form to casual vests worn by men; it has a low pocket matching that on the jacket. A white shirt, and probably a white necktie, show at the neck. The hair is cut short, to fall softly above the ears, and parted far to one side.

The older girls wear very good dresses of dark-colored silk taffeta, perhaps wine-red, made with tunic bodices. While they may well have been locally made, dresses similar to these in quality were by this time available in shops or through mail order. The details are similar to those of women's dresses, but there are several differences, beginning with the bodice. Girls' frocks fasten down the back and are not molded to the body. Their coat sleeves are cut in a similar manner and set at the tip of the shoulder, but in children's styles the sleeves are looser. On the other hand, the cuffs, side gores, and tunic hems are finished with bands of interrupted knife plaits, in imitation of adult styles. The plain, rather narrow skirts mimic the bustleless mode of women's styles but, for children, are made separately on slip bodices. The skirts are trimmed to conform with the bodice. Fine lace cuff frills like these are also worn by women, but the heavy lace collars are definitely a juvenile style; women's collars at this time are mostly confined to small standing bands, and when of wider styles are of finer lace. The girls' glazed kid boots are buttoned at the sides and well polished.

These young ladies are quite up-to-date in their hairstyles, as well, with side hair skinned back into twists or braids and little corkscrew curls across the forehead. These curls are extrapolated, without doubt, from fashion-plate figures, though such illustrations in no instance show the isolated, corkscrew technique; the soft, feathery appearance of frontal hair in the plates was evidently easier to admire than to emulate. By 1883 nearly every head in the fashion magazines shows short, crimped front hair.

Little Lillie wears a princess-style dress, possibly of silk but more likely of cotton sateen, with cuffs and hem finished in knife plaits. Her sleeves are even more generously proportioned for her size than the older girls' and are set equally high at the shoulders. A sleeve ruff and large lace collar make her as fashionable as her big sisters. The bold-striped stockings she wears are, by this date, worn only by very little children. The sturdy, rounded-square shape of her boot soles and heels shows clearly.

MARIETTA STOW, WHO was born in 1830, is shown here in her 1880s version of reform-style dress, "American Dress," which she used as a plank in her campaign platform as a reform candidate for the vice presidency of the United States, running with presidential candidate Belva Lockwood. The team ran twice, though this portrait was probably made for the first campaign in 1884. The narrowness of the skirt, and its tightly wrapped appearance, were features of the early eighties. The original dress was an older one that Mrs. Stow would not have hesitated to cut up into this kind of costume. She did not wear reform dress in private life.

Mrs. Stow was a well-known, if controversial, figure in California and national politics in the eighties. She already had a long history of public works by the time this photograph was taken. Beginning in Washington, D.C., as the young and well-to-do Mrs. Bell, she worked with Mary Todd Lincoln in an association formed to aid poor shop girls. Widowed young, she next worked to raise money for the orphans of the Civil War and traveled the country lecturing about her experiences in Washington and taking pledges from the audience. Her sympathies had always led her to work for disadvantaged women.

Her treasurer during this period was Mr. Stow, a San Francisco hardware merchant, whom she married in 1866. It was when he died in the 1870s that she found that the probate court had appropriated not only the money she had brought to the marriage from her earlier union but all of the joint fortune of this marriage, and she never gained it back, though she made herself a highly literate nuisance in the California courts. She originated an equal rights marriage property act, labeled the Stow Bill, which failed passage many times.

In 1880 Marietta entered local politics, ran for governor of California in 1882 and for vice president, under the Equal Rights party, in 1884 and again in 1888. On October 27, 1884, the *Oakland Daily Evening Tribune* jokingly commented on the Lockwood-Stow ticket's costume, asking, "Why don't the Democratic party propose to join its forces with Belva Lockwood? She might add a little 'bustle' to the flattened Democracy."

The costume in which Mrs. Stow poses here, similar to ones she wore for her lectures and public appearances, is contrived from a dressy garment of about 1882, with the top of the draped silk skirt cut off and the entire skirt raised. The complex horizontal folds, chenille fringe, puffed bustle section, and pleated flounce of the skirt are left intact. A bustle support is not worn, but the cut and drape of the skirt are otherwise identical to those of fashionable dress in about 1882. Over this elaborate skirt she wears a black velvet long basque with white lace scarf and frills, and a gold watch chain is worn in masculine fashion. Beneath the skirt she wears what appear to be black satin trousers of the same leg form as men's. On her feet she wears flat, sturdy boots with tapered toes.

THIS WELL-DOCUMENTED Heustis Cook photograph of the first lampshade switchboard at Richmond, Virginia's Southern Bell Telephone and Telegraph Company must be dated close to mid-decade because of the fairly large size and shape of the bustle.

A relatively clean and "ladylike" job for women, the position of telephone operator allowed the wearing of good daytime clothing, and dress choices were made on the basis of both comfort and "proper" appearance, plus utilization of somewhat older dresses if desired. The clothing of these two operators explains a great deal about the attire of working women in the eighties. No social gap separates these women to any extent; both girls no doubt have similar wardrobes but have made different choices for this work day.

The bustled dress, one of those called a "tailor-suit" in the trade, because male tailors so often made them, is of a crisp, lightweight, part-wool fabric, judging by its texture. This style was considered extremely plain and even "masculine," in spite of the elaborate draping. The cut of the bodice is clearly visible in this back view; the shape of the side-back pieces may be seen, and there is apparently a center-back seam. The extreme snugness of the bodice, its up-to-date short, flared basque skirt and box-pleated "jockey," or "postillion," are plainly shown. The narrow sleeve shows both its two-piece cut and the high armscye of the eighties. A typical high, straight collar is filled with a linen band.

The apron overskirt has made its comeback by this date, and is shown with the front length pulled up into pleats at the side back, so that the front falls softly into an "apron" of folds that just reaches the top of the underskirt flounce. The back breadth hangs square and straight at the bottom, well over the deep, pleated flounce, and is tacked above into puffs over some supporting structure. The underskirt has the broad pleated flounce of fashion, with the upper edge of the pleats tacked down into decorative folds.

In direct contrast to this modestly smart costume is the printed cotton housedress of the girl in the chair. The set and tightness of the sleeve and bodice and the narrow band collar with its frill are perfectly smart for a post-1883 date, yet there is no bustle effect. The skirt is simply gathered to the waist seam in an old-fashioned manner that will be general for housedresses for many years to come; no concession whatsoever is made to the current mode of drapery in fashion for dressier styles. The fabric is a calico print, probably monochromatic. A white dimity apron, tied around the waist, protects the skirt front from soil where the knees press against the wires and plugs.

Both women wear their hair as simply as possible in order to accommodate the headsets, both opting for a coil of braids low on the back of the head. There are signs, however, of cropped and curled frontal hair.

TINTYPE, 1884–86

Courtesy of the National Museum of American History (C68.12.7)

THIS PORTRAIT WAS probably taken at the home of this modest working-class family, who, wearing outdoor clothing, appear to be dressed for some special occasion. Note that the family dog is even included in the portrait.

The young lady at upper left wears a tailor-suit of mideighties style with an open neck in which the high collar of a white bodice shows. It fits poorly, with many transverse wrinkles, and may be homemade. The jacket collar is probably of curly lamb cloth, a popular trimming for wool suits and coats. Fashionable details include the closely spaced buttons and the skin-tight, somewhat short, sleeves set high on the shoulder. Her hand and bare wrist are visible between the boy's head and the dog's, holding an arrangement of flowers and ribbon bows. The dark fabric extending at left behind the boy's head is probably a plain shawl held over her arm. Just between boy and dog, the drape of the skirt front may be glimpsed, and beneath the boy's chair it is possible to see that the skirt is very narrow at the hem and somewhat short of the floor. The wide-brimmed, deep-crowned straw hat is of a youthful style often mentioned in the fashion literature and frequently seen in photographs. The colored satin ribbons are softly puffed and draped at front and form the only decoration.

The young gentleman at the back is dressed in the usual short sack and vest of black wool cut in the latest narrow style, and his white shirt has a straight, high, stiff collar, around which his striped dark tie may be seen. The flat-crowned hat of black felt, a "pork-pie" style, is also black. The trousers are of a lighter wool with a woven stripe.

The seated, older woman wears a printed long shawl with a border of the print around a dark ground color; the printed ends fall over her lap. Her plain dark suit, worn over a black under-bodice with a high collar, is set off by the white linen collar insert. The high-crowned little capote bonnet, with its soft crown and frontal decoration, is typical of the date. The folds of shawl and skirt are confused at her back with the low, curved arm of the chair with its heavy fringe.

The seated older boy's curly hair is unruly under the small cap. His short jacket, with its soft collar and high-buttoned front, and the narrow, dark trousers are typical wear for boys, and almost a match for his younger brother's. A flower is stuck carelessly into his buttonhole. Both boys wear white shirts and ties. The straw sailor hat worn by the boy sitting on the floor is mentioned frequently as the perfect hat for a young boy of ten to twelve years.

May 1885

Courtesy of the Neville Public Museum

THE STUDENTS OF the Pine Street Elementary School in Green Bay, Wisconsin, make a fresh and appealing impression on the occasion of their spring photograph. Among the children may be found almost every current variant of ordinary dress.

The young teacher serves to demonstrate a workaday version of the short-basqued fashion of mid-decade. The curvaceous corset has definitely formed the figure, and the short basque skirts stand out roundly in high style. The bodice has the firm, melonlike roundness and fit of fashion, and the sleeves are smoothly and fashionably snug and set at the proper height on the shoulder. It is in the skirts of this black alpaca dress that we see the adaptation for active, daily work. They are done very simply, in all-around loose pleats and without any draping of the front or bustle arrangement at the back. They hang double, however, with the overskirt at the popular length. A soft black knitted scarf is worn hanging from a knot at the throat, and the hair is done simply in waves off the forehead. The whole represents a conservative approach to fashion, quite proper for a teacher and easily worn through several stylistic changes without giving a dowdy appearance.

It is useful to observe, first, the things about the girls' dresses that are similar. The most obvious are the large collars worn by most of the girls. They are all of rather coarse white construction; some appear to be tatted or crocheted, some to be of lace. They are all rounded in shape, even when worn over the squared and braided yoke of a sailor dress. Also, with only two exceptions, the dresses are of very dark materials. Most of the fabrics appear to be woolens, though there are apparently some sturdy cottons. As to shape, while there are many closely fitted jacket styles of bodice, a more up-to-date form is obvious in the blouson, which hangs well over the waistline in several instances. Several girls wear long tunic overdresses. The skirts of all the dresses may be seen to come well down the lower leg, leaving not much space at the boot tops. Stockings appear to be all black. Three of the girls wear pinafores, two with narrow straps and one with wider frilled ones. There is a charming variety in hairstyles, variously held back from the face, ranging from rather long, straight bangs to center parts to back-brushed, all apparently with the long back hair hanging. But there are no hair ribbons in evidence; when worn, they always hung to the back of the head.

The boys have relatively monotonous garb, owing to the prevalence of black, and the dress of the older boys can be seen to imitate that of men. The youngest boys wear white collars over short, fitted dark jackets, as closely buttoned as the girls'; most of the older boys seem to be wearing short dark sack coats. Several very dark shirts are apparent. The hair, like that of men, is cropped very short, leaving just enough to comb to the front or off to one side.

1885–86

Courtesy of the California State Library (21,209)

THIS PORTRAIT OF a large and happy group of Californians is intimidating in its detail. In spite of the rugged-appearing terrain, none of these people is in hiking or camping dress, and it is safe to assume that they have come out on a Sunday drive or train ride to some favorite spot.

The deep bustles shown on most of the women's skirts, the extreme curves of the corseted torso, and the distinctive hip-length fitted jackets all date the photograph to the mideighties. While the scene is casual, the "dressed-up" appearance of this group in general argues against their having worn out-of-date styles on this outing.

Especially noteworthy is the back view of the young lady at center front, since photographs usually show such skirts only from the front. The very drooping lines of the bustle pouf and the large amount of material fastened up to form it are clearly demonstrated. A similarly made skirt is shown on the standing figure at far right in the second row, in a frontal view, with the long bustle drape showing behind the hip and the transverse lines of the drapery showing on the front. The contrast and form of this figure's light-colored basque jacket is notable.

All four of the ladies' jackets in the foreground have round, longish, fitted basques and are quite plain, with narrow fitted sleeves. The checked example is worn as an open jacket over a suit with a habit front. The skirt of this sitter shows its construction well, showing that the long pleats were at times stitched down from about the knee to just above the hem and that the back breadth was treated similarly to that on the standing figure.

Little can be made of the compressed folds of the dotted skirt of the seated woman, except that the pleated double flounce is dagged, or pointed, and the bustle draperies are bounteous.

The variety of women's hat styles alone is perfectly marvelous. They range from the top-hat types, some with very tall, narrowly tapered crowns, through the childlike straw sailor to the vertical, pointed capotes, a turban shape, and a few little tip-tilted, brimmed hats with plumes and bows. The rearview of the hat in the center is very clear, showing it to have a light straw frame and rather broad brim and a crown of soft, dark fabric contorted into a crushed crown and loops with a large curled plume. A crisp ribbon bow finishes the back. This style is described in fashion literature as a "capote."

Two women's coats can be clearly seen, both shaped close to the body and having narrow sleeves and straight, high collars. The one at center top is double-breasted, and its skirt is draped into a bustle effect in back. The woman in the second row at the right wears a short elbow-cape of black fur or fur cloth over her light jacket.

All of the gentlemen wear the sack suit, in its various expressions, most of them of matching pieces. Most also wear the homburg hat, although a flat-crowned "pork-pie" style is seen on the young man near the center top, and a rakishly upturned light felt is worn by a gentleman at left. All these gentlemen look like substantial businessmen, in their starched white shirts and variety of neckties. Only one man, probably the youngest, is without facial hair.

1885–89

Courtesy of the Huntington Library (151,31)

PACKING ROOM S.CAL. PACK⸻CO.⸻L.A. CAL

THIS CREW AT the Southern California Packing Company in Los Angeles is made up mostly of women. The photograph is given the late bracket date because of the uniformly tight sleeves and bodices; no fashionable clothing would be expected here, yet the short-waistedness and close fit of bodices and sleeves follow the popular cut of mid-decade.

Unlike working men, women did not have the option of wearing loose-fitting work clothes, and there was no popular relaxed cut at this time except for the Mother Hubbard, which was not proper for wear in public. In spite of the greatest variety of clothing types yet seen, women worked at home and in the factories in clothing cut to preconceived lines of beauty, then minimally adapted for washability. Mostly this entailed merely leaving off the overdraperies of the skirt. Few allowances were made for more comfort, especially in public.

The central figure does actually wear what may be either a cotton wrapper or a trained cotton dress, possibly a readymade. It is smoothly pieced and fitted over a firm corset through the back of the bodice and has the very tight sleeves and high armscye of the very late eighties. The back-skirt fullness is gathered at the lower back in a row of cartridge pleats in the manner of a wrapper train.

Every woman who can be seen wears the same uncomfortable-looking tight sleeves and has the same closely fitted bodice, and the only other visible skirt is close to floor length.

Mrs. A. L. Adamson of Richmond, Virginia, posed in this elegant costume for Mr. George Cook at his studio. The shape and set of the large bustle dates the portrait nicely and gives us an amusing hint of the probable conversation between sitter and photographer; the bustle is more the subject of this portrait than the woman. This sitter is from a Richmond family quite prominent at the time, a family that would be expected to dress in the latest and best.

This professionally made dress is composed of a boldly striped satin, likely dark-brown velvet stripes on copper, and a coordinating plain satin. The precision of fit is evident in the nearly wrinkle-free tight sleeve and the melonlike firmness of contour in the bodice. The nearly nonexistent basque flare extends in back flaps, or postillions, almost horizontally over the immense bustle pouf. The pose reveals the precise cutting diagram of the bodice back, with its dropped-back shoulder seam, high armscye, and intricate piecing under the arm. The mid-1880s corset shape is equally evident. The ends of a white silk neck scarf or ribbon fall in a soft bow at the back of the neck.

The satin skirt is shaped in a short, draped apron front that is carried around the hips to the side-back seam, but the pleats are taken into the waist seam itself and not into the side seam as before. The deeply tacked bustle pouf is formed of a separate breadth, thickly pleated into the waist seam and tacked into puffs over a free-hanging end, which will fall free over the top of the underskirt flounce.

Mrs. Adamson wears her hair slightly puffed and shaped in a vertical roll called a "French twist," with the frontal hair fashionably short and curled.

STEREOSCOPIC VIEW, CA. 1886

Courtesy of the California State Library (21,207)

IN THIS FAMOUS "Scene at Ocean Beach–San Francisco Cal." can be seen the most extreme silhouette of the eighties—the deep, high bustle of 1886 and a bit of what was worn beneath it. In the background, at right, is the celebrated Cliff House.

The waders, probably teenage girls, are fully dressed, complete with bustle poufs and hats, and must hold up their dress skirts as well as petticoats out of the surf. The girl standing in the background on the wet beach facing the camera is using her short petticoat, left hanging, to shield her upper legs from view, while she holds the rest of her dress up in a bundle. Her upper legs and knee-length drawers are silhouetted by the sunlight on the water.

The ladies at left show full street dress, with no concessions made for either sand or sun, other than the parasol. The costume in the foreground is a dark tailor-suit with a flared basque jacket over a draped overskirt, a bustle back, and a full-length skirt. The hat, of a type shown in *Godey's* in 1885, is tilted forward and sits high, with floral trim bunched at front. The rather large hat seen in the background has a vertical accent, a medium brim, and flower and feather trimming at one side.

Ca. 1886

Courtesy of the Southern Oregon Historical Society
(1716)

THIS LARGE GROUP, posed while on an outing in the Oregon hills, provides a broad overview of everyday dress in the mid-1880s and is a testimony to life-style in many ways. While certainly older clothing would have been worn for such an outing, a "not-before" date can be set by the tight sleeves and short, fitted bodices of many of the women's dresses. Unfortunately, aprons cover some skirt fronts, but the seated woman near the tree at center has a high bustle drape at the hips, which argues for the 1886 date, and a bustle drape shows on the figure standing near the tent as well.

The mix of clothing ranges from Sunday-best to casual. While the gathering consists only of women and little children, it is probable that some menfolk are off fishing or hiking; the tents give evidence that this is an excursion to last at least a full day, as opposed to a simple picnic.

Most remarkable from a modern point of view are the women's hats; only one or two of the ladies are bareheaded, and several of those appear to be holding hats. Few of the hat styles appear to be suitable to a day in the woods; for the most part they are very smartly shaped and trimmed and would be quite proper for wear in town. Outstanding among them are the tall, truncated cone–shaped crowns seen in both hats and bonnets, with their flat tops; the young woman standing in front of the tent wears a light-colored bonnet with such a crown, with an ostrich tip curled at the very top. Bonnets are distinguished from hats at this time by a lack of brim at the back. One hat, that of the woman at far left, standing beside the tent, is identical to a man's soft dark felt fedora.

While all of the hats, regardless of brim size, are squarely placed on the head, the one worn by the lady in the center has an eccentrically placed brim. None of the brims, even those of the wide "picturesque," or "painter's," styles, is drawn down to shade the face, though one woman wears her small-brimmed hat tilted forward over her forehead. Most of those women not wearing hats have their hair in the large chignon at the top of the crown with short, softly waved hair over the forehead and temples.

The children's hats, which are seen in varying sizes, are wide brimmed and uptilted, the boys' and girls' styles being indistinguishable.

Also notable is the presence and the form of the corsets that shape the bodies under the various costumes. Even the oldest woman wears one, and the fit appears to be firm and tight and wide at the hips and full in the bosom in mid-decade style. The woman at center back is so thin and tall that the bosom is not repositioned by her corset, which may mean that she is wearing a looser style on this outing. The unrelenting, smooth fit of the other dress bodices indicates the prevailing look.

The one woman in plain clothing who seemingly has a loose bodice is actually wearing one of the short, straight little woolen "English" jackets, as it was called in the literature, over her fitted dress. Closer to the center, in the back row, one young woman wears a dark shawl around her shoulders, obscuring the lines of her dress.

The most obvious aberration is the presence of the loose cotton Mother Hubbard dresses; two of the women wear this style, most prominently the one standing at left front beside the buggy and the little child. Since a smaller baby is in the buggy, it is a reasonable assumption that this particular dress has served as a maternity garment for this young mother and is now being worn during the nursing stage. The sleeves of these Mother Hubbards are narrow and quite close to the arm and set very high at the shoulders in the style of all other dress sleeves. The yoke, from which the dress hangs in gathers, is in this case curved, and the fullness of the dress body below it appears to be taken in with stitched pleats down to the waistline. The dress is made comfortably short, at about boot-top level. The other girl wearing such a dress is at center back, standing in front of a tree and behind other figures that cut off a full-length view of her costume. This dress, apparently of a dark, checked gingham, is made with the close-set sleeve, and has white frilled edging on the small collar. The straight yoke line and front pleats show clearly. Like the other, it fastens in front.

The only other figure worthy of note is the young girl at right front in the wide sailor hat. She wears a typical long-waisted girl's dress of dark plaid with plain dark sleeves, a pleated skirt, and the ubiquitous heavy lace collar. The costume is front closing.

1886

Courtesy of the Neville Public Museum

THE TEN GRADUATES of Green Bay High School, class of 1886, posed for this annual school portrait with their teacher. The proportion of girl students is very high; in this small city, with its surrounding farmland, most of the boys likely dropped out of school in order to work at home.

The girls, probably about thirteen to sixteen, are very nicely dressed and reflect the middle-class nature of the city. Their clothing is unremarkable, and, like their hairstyles, exhibits the wide range of choices available at the time.

One very common dress style is that of the girl at lower left. Her two-piece costume is of a windowpane check, probably in brown and cream, and made with a perfectly plain underskirt. The bodice is closely fitted and carried to a modest length at the hips, where there is a short, pleated, draped "apron" front at the top of the skirt. The sleeves are snug, without being too painfully so, and fall somewhat short of the wrists, as do all of the girls' sleeves. A low standing collar is filled with a standing white linen band, and an ombre-shaded ribbon bow decorates the neckline. The bodice fronts and the cuffs are of plain, dark fabric. This costume is probably made of a fabric that is at least part wool. The young lady's flat bangs are really quite up-to-date.

The girl at center front wears a fashion much discussed in the literature but rarely seen in the photograph; it is a "redingote" style. As it is used here, it consists of an overdress attached at the shoulder and armscye seams in front and probably in the back as well. There are pleats at the neckline that cause the garment to hang softly, and its skirt is apparently curved back at the hem. The fabric appears to be a printed wool challis, and cuffs are made of it for the dark underdress, which has a standard, short, closely buttoned bodice. There is a small ribbon collar at the neckline. The color of this dress is quite likely a deep red, with the print in blending tones.

The variations in the skirt styles of the remaining dark wool dresses are typical of the mideighties. The two at lower right are quite similar, though the overskirt on the right is pulled up more sharply to the opposite hip; a double set of box plaits at the hem of this skirt is similar in scale to the knife-pleated flounce on the other. White band collars show slightly, and one girl has a lace-edged white handkerchief pulled to a round frill from the upper-bodice closure.

The black wool dress worn by the taller of the girls standing at back is elegantly made and suits its handsome wearer. The nicely fitted bodice has a box-plaited flounce of its own and is worn over a closely flounced matching skirt. The other girl in the back row wears her fitted basque over a plain gathered skirt of matching black wool and has her white handkerchief tucked into the upper front.

The dark woolen dress on the remaining seated figure has a knee-length, softly draped overskirt over spaced and carefully tacked knife plaits. The rather large metal buttons are a touch probably owed to a mother who saved and reused buttons and lace from older dresses, for they are of a type more popular about four years earlier.

All of the girls wear high black shoes with moderate heels, oval toes, and thin soles.

The three boys all wear the typical skimpy sack jackets of the eighties, of various dark-colored woolens, buttoned at the top button only and showing matching vests buttoned closely underneath. Their shirt collars are small and close and the ties inconspicuous. The male teacher wears a much-worn and abused frock coat and black wool trousers and exhibits the beard so often affected by authority figures in the eighties.

TINTYPE, 1886–87

*Courtesy of the National Museum of
American History (C76.4.7)*

THREE YOUNG PLAYMATES, perhaps eleven or twelve years old, obligingly pose in someone's backyard dressed in their coats and hats, thus providing a rare look at outdoor clothing. Two of the coats show evidence of some bustle padding of the dress underneath, and it is readily apparent that the coat skirts are cut to make the most of this detail. Both bustle shapes are rather high and deep, and a date of 1886, corresponding to the deepest bustle shape for women, is suggested.

The coat worn by the girl at left is smartly composed of a light-colored wool with a darker V-shaped long front panel and hood. The welt-seamed pocket relates to boys' and men's jacket pockets of the period. Her hat is a junior version of the narrow-brimmed, vertical styles worn by women, with all the trimming running up the center front and extending above the crown, and her hair is fastened in a ponytail. The flat shoes tie at the instep and are worn with dark stockings.

The coat on the middle girl is the simplest, having a large patch pocket at the hip and a high collar. It has extra fullness in the form of gathers concentrated at the back but no bustle allowance. It appears to be narrowly double-breasted. Her hair blows in fairly long, uncurled bangs, and is fastened at the back of the neck to hang straight under a tilted small hat, with one brim turned up and a plume at the back.

The girl at right wears a coat that has a matching capelet for added warmth and is well-bustled and quite flared in back. This style is often shown double-breasted in the fashion plates. She wears one of the popular shaggy tam-o-shanters, with a huge pom-pom at the top, over her long hair, which is held by a black bow at the nape.

All of the girls wear flat-heeled shoes that lace at the instep and have fringe tassels on the laces.

THE HANDWRITTEN LABEL on this Truman D. Keith photograph reads: "Cow &c. on Fruit Ranch, Fresno, Cal., June 27, 1887." The woman holding the cow wears a good example of the common cotton printed housedress of the eighties; the apron appears to be made of the same printed material. Both are neatly starched and ironed, and the dress, which is buttoned firmly to the high neck, is worn over a corset and has long sleeves. Even such casual dress as this is usually finished with a hem flounce; not only does this produce an attractive flare, but it keeps the skirt out from between the feet when walking.

In the background stands a woman dressed in a simple dark cotton printed dress or wrapper. She is wearing a pith helmet, good for working in the orchard, and is holding a large straw sun hat.

THE CAPTION ON this Truman D. Keith photograph reads: "Returning from work, Fresno, Cal., July 8, 1887." Pictured are a couple who have been working in the groves of a fruit ranch, he with a large hoe and she with pruning knife and clippers.

The woman is dressed for moderate weather in a medium-length black basque jacket, no doubt of a light-weight material, which flares attractively at the hips and is obviously worn over a corset. She wears over the black tie at the throat a fresh white neckerchief. Her skirt, with its deep flounce, is simply gathered to a waistband and is made of polka-dotted dark cotton. The pith helmet is her protection against the bright California noonday sun—and falling fruit.

The overshirt worn by her companion has a double-breasted placket with white buttons at either side. It, too, though no doubt of cotton, is dark. The trousers are probably jeans. A soft felt hat is his protection from the sun.

This KEITH PHOTOGRAPH is labeled "Teachers, Belmont School, Belmont, Cal." As educators, these six people would have been uniquely visible, and their dress and deportment had to meet at all times the public expectation of moral leadership. They are, therefore, conservatively dressed, though in good materials and suitably current fashions.

The most noticeable feature of the gentlemen's appearance is the prevalence of facial hair, with the men displaying all four of the popular expressions: the full mustache, the walrus, the Vandyke, and the full beard. The three gentlemen standing have similar stiff, narrow, standing collars. The neckties are not discernible.

The woman at lower left wears a mid-decade-style bustled costume of striped wool, probably white on black. The short, pointed basque is trimmed with black braid in scrolls at the bodice front and probably with jet buttons. A white

silk scarf is tied in a large soft bow at the very high collar. The slightly eased narrow sleeves have pleated cuffs and are faced with stiff linen cuff bands. The skirt is softly pleated at front and finished at the back in a deep bustle pouf. There is no draped apron, though there is probably an overskirt. Her erect posture and the trim fit are due to a good corset.

The older woman wears an up-to-date dress, apparently of black silk taffeta with black velvet sidefront vertical panels tapering to the waist. The collar is fashionably high and faced with a white linen band, but the overlarge buttons may have been saved and reused from an earlier dress; such buttons were popular about 1882. A large cameo does something to soften the appearance. White bands face the cuffs. The fit of the torso and the softly draped apron front affirm the presence of corset and bustle.

Ca. 1887

Courtesy of the California State Library (20,505)

FAIRLY ACCURATE DATING is possible for this portrait because of the costume of the lady at left. While the photo may have been taken a bit later, she is dressed in a readily recognizable 1887 fashion: a vest-suit of dark wool with the open jacket (probably just fronts sewn into the side seams) fastened at the throat with large, linked gold buttons, the vest being closed with smaller, flat metal buttons. A stiff white collar band is decorated with a small gold pin at the neck. The skirt shows the newest style, as it is quite full and consists of wide-spaced box plaits under a high, almost horizontally draped, snug little apron front that finishes in back with a long bustle drape. A white handkerchief is tucked into the apron folds.

The much younger woman at right wears a printed silk of some dark color with cream reserves and with cuff tabs of filet lace. A scalloped white lace fichu circles the neck in a wide band over the high collar and reaches to a deep point on the bosom. A girlish cluster of looped moiré ribbons decorates one shoulder. The bodice is snugly fitted and waist length, and the skirt is simply gathered at the waist, with one tuck near the hem.

Both women wear their hair in the newly fashionable, though hardly flattering, flat parted bangs with the back hair severely tucked into a twist behind the crown.

The boy seated between these two women is perhaps twelve or thirteen years old. His rather formally buttoned sack jacket, broad polka-dotted tie, and fresh haircut indicate an event of some importance. He is dressed in short pants and wears rib-knitted hose and laced boots.

Vests and vest effects were never more popular than at present.
—*The Delineator,* October 1887

IN THIS NICELY dated portrait, Lavinia Strange poses at the Jordan Studio in Washington, D.C., dressed in an expensive and stylish, well-appointed costume. The costume consists of a dark wool suit composed of a fitted basque jacket over a draped overskirt and a shaped underskirt. The jacket, while still very smart for 1887, is of a style that remained popular for several years; it is similar to one featured in *Godey's* in March 1885. Well fitted and nearly horizontal all around the hem, it is quite long, with its skirt stiffly flared and standing out away from the overskirt slightly at the hem. It is either slit or pleated at back, to accommodate the high bustle, and gently rounded out over the overskirt drape at front and sides. Very small buttons, possibly of jet, close the front. The curve of the 1880s corset is well displayed in this pose. The sleeve is particularly evocative of the fashion plate of this date: set high on the shoulder and quite tight on the arm, with very little ease, and made just a bit short at the narrow wrist, where white linen cuffs extend about an inch. Jet buttons finish the cuff opening. A silk kerchief is knotted around the neck.

The overskirt, too, is in the latest style; it is gathered quite high into a draped apron and puffed at the back into the extreme, supported bustle shape, from which the length falls long and square nearly to the skirt hem. The front breadth of the underskirt has broad transverse tucks.

The gloves she carries are of natural, tan kid, the type considered most correct for day dress in the eighties. And her jewelry is quite tasteful: either a wedding or engagement ring, a brooch or heavy cross at the throat, modest gold earrings, and a black watch cord.

Gingham and cambric are better made, and fitted, as dresses, so that they can be worn on the street, and there is no better way for the country than to make a complete dress with round waist, . . . [and] a simple overskirt . . .
—*Demorest's Mirror of Fashion,*
Spring/Summer 1880

JOHN CAMPBELL BURGE was an active photographer in Arizona, New Mexico, and El Paso from 1885 to 1891, and his photographs captured the social scene from all angles, including common ranchers and working people. This portrait is chiefly dated by the style of the mother's dress, which shows the slightly flared skirt with false side panels, and a suggestion of the flat, pressed-down bustle drape of about 1887. This family, perhaps not well-to-do by contemporary standards but reasonably well off, is possibly of Hispanic descent.

The wife wears a simple daytime dress, either homemade or readymade, of cotton gingham plaid and cut with a round waist. While quite slight, she is obviously properly corseted. The bodice is well fitted, darted at the front with at least two darts, and fastens with a double set of small, light-colored buttons. The narrow (but not tight) sleeves are worn just a bit short, have no cuff frill, and are set high at the narrow shoulder in proper form. The narrow band collar, simple in itself, is made quite dressy and high by the insertion of a crisply fluted white neck ruff. The skirt is slightly flared, indicating its late ori-

gin. It is made with a simulated divided overskirt, which is outlined by a wide whitework border at fronts and hem. The back panel is set in flat pleats to form a long bustle drape, which extends down the side seam in a pressed pleat. A flounce of knife pleats finishes the hem.

Her hairstyle is rather mixed, with the frizzed longer front hair showing the popular trend but with heavy braids carried low at the nape. Most women by this date are beginning to wear the back hair in a cluster of curls or rolls directly on the top of the head.

The child, perhaps two or three, is dressed in a homemade cotton plaid dress, slightly mismatched at the bodice front, made with a low waist and a box-plaited skirt. The dress is quite short. The long sleeves are loose, and the cuffs and collar are edged with a looped white braid. A whitework-edged short petticoat and plain white drawers show above the long stockings (probably red) and the typical high, shaped, kid boots with their outside button closing.

The father wears a neat, well-pressed matching sack suit of wool tweed, probably gray, properly buttoned at the top under the small collar and lapels. It is cut in the short, close-fitting style most popular at the time. A handsome gold watch chain and fob hang from the middle button of the single-breasted, waist-length vest. A crisp white shirt with a small turn-down collar is set off by a narrow black ribbon bow tie. Mustache and full, short beard are worn in the current fashion. His worn boots have thick, serviceable soles and high heels and appear to have buttons on the outside of the ankle.

In this multiple portrait can be seen a group of young women from a small northern Wisconsin town, all neatly corseted, dressed, and coiffed. They possibly form a graduating class.

These women all show a conservative treatment of the costume just after the collapse of the deep bustle of 1886. All wear wool, most in black, and two wear fine woven stripes. The new silhouette is best seen on the figure at the right, where the skirt is taken into the waistband at the sides in pleats, has hanging folds down the back, and is covered at the waist with a short, fitted, nonflaring basque with a long pointed front. The skirt at extreme left shows an apron-front drape and displays a bit of the squared jockey tails, or "postillions," of the black basque. All of the visible basques are short, all smoothly fitted over corsets, and each is decorated and/or closed with close-set, small buttons. Each has a very high round collar finished with white, most in a frill of lace but two with linen bands. Diagonal closures, a new fashion, are seen on two of the basques.

Each of the young women wears her hair in a full, shining roll at the top of the crown and has the front hair variously cut short and curled. Only the woman at left rear wears earrings, but jewelry is worn by all. A wide gold chain with pendant is worn by three, and four have bar pins (one with a locket pendant), and a narrow gold bracelet is visible on one girl's wrist. A gold watch chain is worn by the girl second from right in the front row; it lies across the upper bodice, with the small watch hanging from a separate bar pin.

VERA DAVIDSON OF Madison, Wisconsin, and her little brother, Leo, pose here in their new bonnets.

The bonnet shape worn by these two children is the capote, which was a feature of ladies' fashionable dress from 1886 and was copied in children's styles almost immediately, where it was called "picturesque." The crown for children was quite often of puffed velvet, velveteen, or plush, as here, though for ladies it was often of a fabric to match that of a wrap or dress, which might be of satin or sometimes even wool. Both bonnets are probably of a deep maroon, a favored color, but could even have been black.

Vera's long plaid cloak is of the Kate Greenaway style, full-length with puffed sleeves over a narrow forearm, and double-breasted with buttons down the front. Greenaway's books and illustrations in Empire-revival style were the inspiration for much "artistic" children's clothing during the late eighties. This long coat is made with a combed-angora-fur collar. The bonnet is edged with mixed lace, over a pleated underbrim, beneath the gathers of the brim and the high crown. It is tied snugly under the chin by a ribbon bow.

Leo's bonnet is considered a bit more masculine, with its plain helmet shape, dark ribbon ties, dark crown, and matching ribbons. His coat is also reminiscent of Kate Greenaway's popular illustrations: it is extremely full, quite long, and apparently has two skirts hanging from a very high yoke. It is made with fancy, puffed upper sleeves and with narrow lower sleeves trimmed with dark embroidery.

Ca. 1887

Courtesy of the California State Library (21,205)

For ordinary [boys'] wear, the school "derby," the straw "Sailor," the broad rough-and-ready, half turned up from the side, are the most popular.

—*Demorest's,* March 1881

THIS INTERESTING OUTDOOR scene shows two California families, or more likely one extended family, of some means. Their dress is pleasantly varied but on the whole quite formal for an outing in the woods.

The gentleman at left wears a fitted black wool sack suit, its hip-length jacket firmly buttoned all the way up to the small lapels and its narrow sleeves set high at the shoulder. Two bound pockets are set low at right front. He wears a standing white shirt collar and small necktie. The trousers are tubular, of striped fabric, and fall very low over the instep. His soft black felt fedora hat is the only item seeming to relate to casual attire; he is otherwise dressed properly for most business duties. His mustache and beard are of late-eighties form.

The other gentleman appears to be dressed for golf. His striped knickers and dark knee-hose are worn with black-and-white golfing shoes. Either the light-striped jacket does not quite match the trousers or it has been washed less. It is of the sack form and is worn over a white shirt with a soft white tie. A straw hat indicates that the season is approaching summer; spring is suggested by the wildflowers pinned to the ladies' corsages.

The women present strong contrasts. The lady at left wears a draped bodice with long puffed sleeves and an extremely high collar, a combination of details not seen in the fashion plate until 1887. A large brooch closes the collar. The skirt of her dark dress is broadened out at the hips because of the high-draped apron front. The narrow waist is snugged by a matching ribbon sash. Her hair is fashionably rolled up, and short bangs are seen under the large, jaunty hat. The rather wide-brimmed, tilted felt is made with a tall crown decorated at front with a ribbon rosette and at back with ostrich plumes.

The woman near the center wears a checked wool costume of a style new in 1886. The bodice is well fitted, with a long, rounded frontal point and a basque skirt nearly vanishing at the hips. The habit front of the jacket reveals the white insert and small collar. A thickly draped, short apron front is drawn back to meet the extreme bustle shape, and the back breadth falls free beneath the poufs. She wears a high-crowned black capote, one brim turned sharply up and the front down, with a distinctly vertical emphasis in the ribbon and plume trimming.

The black dress worn by the woman at right, with the child on her back, is cut in a very recent mode; it is made with a short, pointed bodice and a skirt that is pleated into the waist and drawn to one side in a full-length drape. The fabric of the long drape is taken into the back waist seam, creating the long folds that extend down to the hem and show at the opposite side. The hat is like a small, narrow black silk top hat with a stiff brim and a black ribbon rosette on one side.

The sailor suit on the oldest boy is quite likely readymade. It is probably of navy-blue cotton twill, trimmed with white braid, and worn with a black silk neck scarf. The middy is set on a waistband so that it blouses. The long trousers have braid down the outer seams. His straw sailor hat is trimmed with a ribbon nearly matching the striped bib.

The little girl next to him wears a striped cotton jumper dress with a set-in belt at the natural waist, gathered bib and skirt, and braid trim. Her black stockings and high side-button boots are typical for everyday wear.

The smallest standing child, who could be either a boy or a girl, is wearing what is probably a sleeveless pinafore, with a broad, flounced collar, of white or a very light color, over a long-sleeved, pleated white dress. The stockings are probably red and the high shoes black and side-buttoned. The hair is worn in long ringlets, a style common at this time for little boys.

The jacket worn by the girl to the right is typical of everyday wraps for both women and girls; it is a double-breasted, straight-cut style and is worn over a white, or light cotton, dress that appears to have a natural waistline. She wears an overlarge plumed hat with this costume.

The striped double-breasted jacket of the seated boy is made like the standing girl's. It is worn with corduroy knickers and black stockings, topped off with a small peaked cap of plaid wool. The younger boy behind him wears a navy-blue sailor suit, probably also readymade, complete with a bosun's whistle on its white cord. His trousers are full length. The broad-brimmed sailor hat is of straw and may be red. His curly hair is cut in bangs and falls below his ears.

The girl seated on the blanket wears a polka-dot dress in sailor style, the bloused middy falling over a pleated skirt. The dress could be blue or red, or even pink, and is trimmed with white braid and a white ribbon bow. A smart hat is worn over her heavy bangs.

The toddler riding "pick-a-back" offers a look at the short trousers that were worn under little boys' frocks and a better view of the white cloth hat also worn by the other little child. The black stockings and buttoned boots are the same as those of the older children.

JUNE 1887

Courtesy of the State Historical Society of Wisconsin
(WHi [X3] 36722)

Gerhard Gesell was the proprietor of a portrait and commercial studio in Alma, Wisconsin, from 1875 to 1906. His work, several hundred original prints and dry-plate negatives, captured and preserved much of the daily life of this northern Wisconsin community.

For example, here Emma Protz, Clara Tester, and an unidentified friend seated between them (probably Emma's sister, Julia) were photographed by Gesell sometime in June 1887, when they joined six other women at a Schuetzenverein "shoot." The Schuetzenverein, a traditional target-shooting society for men, like those found in Switzerland, was established in Alma in May 1863. Only on special occasions were there "ladies' shoots," and special targets were set up for them. Nine ladies were invited to shoot in 1887.

These three young women have a most efficient and capable appearance as they pose with their specially made Schuetzenrifles, but in no manner is their clothing imitative of men's. Two of the girls even wear flowers. All three dresses are made in the latest fashion, with the extremely short basque bodice and the one-sided draped skirt, with its front swept from left to right and pulled high on one hip. A back view would show the typical baggy, low poufs of the current bustle effect, with a straight edge hanging along the left hip to the hem in back. The small felt hats worn by this trio may have been special schuetzen hats, since they are all alike, but actually the shape and style is one frequently seen with ladies' walking dress.

At left, Emma wears a light wool suit that has the ultra-fashionable dark velvet trim and tucked front with the smart new applied cuff at the top of the wrist. The collar, of black velvet, is fashionably high. The bangs are short and curly. She is wearing her shooting mitts.

The friend in the middle wears a neat, sprigged dress of lightweight wool or cotton, the basque flaring prettily over the side drape, with a high white collar and bow at the throat. This girl also has short bangs.

At left, Clara is dressed in a frequently seen style, one made perfectly plain in the bodice, smoothly fitted, and closely buttoned in a short, pointed basque shape with very tight sleeves just missing the wrist. It is probably of lightweight wool.

This group photograph may have been taken by young Heustis Cook, who did much of the outdoor photography around Richmond, Virginia, for the George Cook Studio. While details are difficult to see in this photograph, the diagonal drape and low bustle effect make the skirts the most effective keys to dating.

With so many young people, it is difficult to tell what sort of group this is, but the black woman at left holds keys and so may have been a housekeeper for the building shown. She is dressed in a bodice, probably a hip-length basque, of checked gingham, with an unmatched skirt of light calico with a hem flounce. A lighter apron is worn over the skirt. In spite of the workaday attire, the hat and keys lend her an air of importance.

The girl at upper left wears her hair in a large puff without bangs. The beaded cascade on the bodice is placed to one side in a manner not much seen until the second half of the decade. The flat-waved longer bangs on the next girl, and her contrasting bodice-front trimming, are later elements, showing in fashion plates by 1887. In her lap she holds a very wide-brimmed, deep-crowned straw hat in a youthful style, with silk flowers piled high.

The tall hat of the fan-wielder, with its curled ostrich plumes, is probably of felt. Her shorter sleeves are a smartly stylish touch, as are the wrist-length stitched gloves.

The striped basque on the next girl, with its matching high-collared insert, tops a matching skirt with an overskirt panel that is in the split form, the front draping to the opposite hip and the back hanging in the long bustle folds.

Such a bustle can just be seen on the skirt of the black suit at upper right, and a plastron of pleated silk, a quite new detail, decorates the bodice front. This small "capote" hat, with its puffed silk crown, is typical of most of the eighties.

The woman seated at center front wears a wide black hat with the brim turned up in back, which is very new. Her black wool skirt has the expected long, diagonally draped overskirt. Bodice details are somewhat confused by the square of the shoulder-strap bag, but we can see the dark pointed cuffs of the narrow sleeves.

Seated in the very middle is a young woman in mourning dress, still with the crepe veil pinned to her rolled-back hair. The very high collar, bodice insert, and trimming are completely black, and a black parasol can be seen below her knee. The fashionably draped skirt of her black dress lies in folds over her lap.

Even the cotton dress of the black woman standing at right, probably hired help for whatever institution is represented, has the long, diagonally draped overskirt and hanging back panel of post-1887. The dress has a medium-length basque jacket and is made of a woven cotton gingham plaid with the ankle-length skirt having a wide bias band at the hem. She wears with it a patterned neckerchief and a black straw hat and, rather ostentatiously, round spectacles. Her boots are of worn leather.

The young gentlemen are all nattily dressed, with highly polished pull-on ankle boots and dark sack suits. The neckties are all of light silk, tied in large loose knots with the long ends tucked into the vest; all are worn over starched standing collars. The hats vary from the two smooth black homburgs at left to a straw sailor and a black slouch.

1887–88

Courtesy of the California State Library (4444)

It is always a difficult matter to dress little boys well, between babyhood and the knickerbocker age, but the pretty kilted dresses, which are simple and childlike, and yet essentially boyish, solve the problem.

—*Demorest's,* June 1882

This photograph, labeled "The McFarland Ranch, near Galt, Sacramento Co.," shows an extended family, probably with two employees standing at right. The portrait is datable mainly through the style of the dress worn by the second woman on the right, which shows the asymmetric drape, lack of bustle, and contrasting fabric fashionable in late 1887 and 1888.

The woman at her left wears what is for the time a very plain dark dress, possibly of cotton sateen but more likely of silk, with a simple overskirt draped up slightly at one side and a plain underskirt with a small flounce. Capable, hard-working hands show under the slightly short, tight sleeves. The baby on her arm wears either booties or moccasins and black stockings. The little boy at left front, in surprisingly short hair, wears a dark kilted skirt with matching jacket, apparently of wool, with a wide white collar.

The polka-dotted dress worn by the next woman is of an 1886 style and thus is at least a year old, though very neatly fitted and fresh looking. The short, long-fronted basque jacket and the short apron drape are familiar from those years. The curly-haired toddler wears an unre-markable frock that is made rather long-waisted and with loose, long sleeves and a gathered skirt. The child is most likely a boy.

The up-to-date side-draped dress on the next woman is definitely an 1888 style. The high dark velvet collar and the matching dark bodice front and skirt accents all speak to this date. The light fabric appears to be a silk moiré.

The woman at right is almost certainly an employee, possibly the cook. Her printed cotton working dress is of interest because of the yoke and the full, easy bodice front, though the sleeves are still the long, snug ones of fashion. The plainly gathered skirt is finished with three tucks so that it hangs fashionably in a flare.

All of the women wear their hair precisely at the tops of their heads in rolls or curls, the very latest fashion, and all, even the cook, are well corseted.

The man at right is probably a field hand. His loose cotton shirt is worn without a collar and buttoned to the throat, the long sleeves neatly buttoned at the wrist. He wears dark jean trousers with work boots. A broad straw hat is his protection from sun and rain.

1887–89

Courtesy of the San Francisco Public Library
(MC Cab)

THIS YOUNG LADY, perhaps sixteen, is pictured toward the end of the eighties. Her long hair is worn fashionably, pulled into close waves at the sides and low at the back, where it is simply laid in a coil of braids, and the long bangs are laid flat to the head and pushed into wavelets.

The juvenile style of her dress is marked by the smocked bodice and double collar, with the undercollar ruffled. A fichu and bow of white-work is attached at the throat, and a crisp white linen collar band is folded in points inside the neckline. She wears crystal beads and a chain, which hang over the point of the neckline, and cameo drop earrings.

GLASS-PLATE NEGATIVE, 1888–90
Courtesy of the Museum of New Mexico (76778)

THIS YOUNG GENTLEMAN posed for J. C. Burge at Deming, New Mexico, where Burge operated a branch studio under W. A. Gilmore during the last two years of the decade. It would appear that this portrait was posed especially to display the sitter's proudest possessions: a pearl-handled revolver, a heavy watch chain and fob, and a cameo pinkie ring.

He is dressed in cheap readymade clothing that might be seen anywhere in the United States at this time: a skimpy, checked seersucker sack jacket and matching vest, probably in the most common brown-and-tan combination; a pair of striped pants, chosen without a thought for coordination; a white shirt with a stiff, plain, standing collar; and a narrow black silk necktie. The walrus mustache and side-parted short hair are hallmarks of the late-eighties date.

1888–91

Courtesy of the Valentine Museum (1384)

HEUSTICE COOK RECORDED this group, which seemingly represents only a part of the lineup along a railing somewhere near Richmond. They are all well dressed for what is obviously a special occasion.

The young men all have hats, though most have them in hand. The sweeping crown on the figure at center back belongs to a large black sailor-style hat, worn well back on the man's head. Spanking white shirts, silk neckties, and good black sack suits are worn by all the men, and all but the man at center back have their vests fully buttoned.

The women are dressed in a range of styles, the latest datable details being the very dark contrasting vertical trim on two of the bodices and the plain, full skirts on several of the costumes.

The seated girl at right front wears a light-colored woolen outfit with a short, fitted bodice that has the heavy, contrasting braid trim of about 1887; the long, tight sleeves, set high on the shoulder, end at the wristbone. The skirt has the long draped front so frequently seen in the late eighties. A small standing collar is set off by a silk scarf looped to one side. The smart accessories include a leghorn straw hat with black band and black silk mitts. (Mitts, while not often seen in photographs, did make a brief comeback during the eighties.)

The young woman standing at left wears a one-piece light-colored cotton print, very simply made and well fitted, with a colored ribbon sash. A bar pin and watch chain are worn on the bodice. This simple unbustled style is seen everywhere as day dress throughout the eighties, especially among the very young, the elderly, and those women who do active work. Her small bonnet is crowned with contrasting ostrich tips. She holds the arm of another young woman just out of range of the camera, whose skirt is formed in the side-sweeping, long drape of the late eighties and who wears a close-fitting dark basque bodice with a long front point. A narrow capote bonnet can just be seen, trimmed directly at front with white flowers.

Standing at center is a woman wearing a costume economically contrived either from two older dresses or one made with the silk bodice of an older dress and a soft printed skirt of new material. Vertical panels of dark (velvet?) material frame the front opening, which is concealed by the twist of the white chiffon scarf. A trim poke bonnet of straw sets off her face, and a dark silk ribbon sash may be seen falling down the skirt front.

The woman at right wears one of the dark, printed challis dresses, made with a short, flared basque jacket (which is too large for her) having velvet trim at fronts and cuffs. A large frill of white is seen at neck and wrist. The small bonnet with its upturned brim is somewhat out-of-date and not fully trimmed.

Legs akimbo, the woman sitting on the grass wears a striped wool skirt, evidently of fairly plain cut, with a black bodice, which may be of wool jersey, that closes only partially over the bosom. A white shirtfront and band collar show underneath. A little straw hat is tilted at a jaunty angle. The little girl standing at right shows the change from long waistlines back to normal ones that children's dresses reflect toward 1890. She too wears a hat, a black straw sailor with the typically upturned brim.

THIS TWELVE- OR thirteen-year-old girl, photographed by T. G. Mernin in East Las Vegas, New Mexico, wears a dress that could be her first near-grown-up style, which appears to have been adapted from an older woman's dress. The asymmetrically draped overskirt dates this photograph to about 1888, but since the dress has been made over there is a likelihood that the date for the photograph is a year or two later. For a poor family, hand-me-downs were the only alternative when a daughter reached the age for more adult clothing.

The adjustments made to this dress are obvious in the front of the bodice, which appears to overlap farther than originally intended. The short basque fits properly through the shoulders and most likely was not shortened, but the bosom and waist evidently needed to be taken in; the tucked panels were never meant to be pulled so out of shape. The wide, gathered collar and the ribbon rosettes, both youthful touches, were no doubt added during the remodeling.

The overskirt may be the original length, but has apparently been remade; the mismatched plaids in the seam near the front probably indicate some tampering with that side of the skirt. The underskirt, with its short box-plaited flounce, is at the proper boot-top length for the girl's age and it was probably shortened at the waist.

Her severely pulled-back hair and flat, curled bangs testify to the fact that this young lady is well acquainted with the fashion of the moment.

GLASS-PLATE NEGATIVE, 1888–90

Courtesy of the State Historical Society of Wisconsin
(WHi [V22/D] 1468)

THIS YOUNG GIRL poses in her rather grown-up dress in the studio of Charles Van Schaick in Black River Falls, Wisconsin. Very girlish in form and appearance, she is nevertheless wearing a perfectly fitted adult style for the last two years of the decade.

The costume is of wool, pale blue or another pastel, over (probably) a dark-blue or deep-red velvet. The pointed bodice front is of the velvet, and the jacket is closed over it with three wide pointed tabs and buttons. A small white frill sets off the high collar. The skirt is draped from pleats at the waist at the front to expose the velvet underskirt on one side. On the opposite side the length is taken up into bustle folds in back, and the edge hangs straight to the hem beneath the folds. The dress is so new that the crease made in doubling the fabric over the bolt is still evident down the center front.

The hair is pulled back from the face and done in a small arrangement high on the crown, another (probably recent) grown-up innovation. Neat black boots show beneath the fashionably short skirt.

CA. 1889

Courtesy of the Valentine Museum (1281)

IN THIS GROUP portrait we see a reasonably well-to-do family posed on the porch of their Richmond, Virginia, home, complete with its suspended canvas swing-chair. The late-decade date is best illustrated in the dress of the mother and oldest girl, which show the dark contrasting trim and slender lines, especially the mother's fully pleated underskirt. The mother's flat, waved bangs are another telling detail.

The familiar sack suit worn by the father appears to be made of a lightweight material, either a thin wool or a wool-linen mixture, and is somewhat out of shape. Such jackets, not being lined, were subject to sagging if worn much, especially in high heat and humidity. The vest, with its extremely small shawl collar and high closure, was the style of choice for most men by the end of the decade. The beard and mustache are also excellent indicators of the late date.

Both little boys at front wear knickerbocker suits with boxy hip-length Norfolk jackets buttoned to the neck and soft ribbon ties. Their large, starched, white shirt collars are brought out over the jackets, and the shirt sleeves show smartly at the wrists. Black stockings and polished boots give them a Sunday-best appearance.

The mother wears a stylish dress of two fabrics, the dark pleated wool or silk skirt partly covered by the pattern-woven silk overskirt at one side, which shows its vertical pleats and the beginning of the sweep of drapery around the long bustle folds at back. The short, fitted bodice is inset with shaped vertical panels of the skirt fabric at the sides, and numbers of jet buttons close the front. Cuffs of the skirt fabric and linen inner cuffs finish the somewhat-eased sleeves. The neckline is quite high, consisting of a dark high collar and a white linen insert. Her hair is done in the parted, down-plastered bangs currently in favor.

The littlest girl wears a coat of striped wool with a rather short waistline, very narrow sleeves, and a triple-flounced and scalloped skirt with matching trim on the fronts. The skirt fullness is smocked at the top, and the fronts hang open. A deep bertha collar of white lace is attached. Her thick, straight bangs and short hair are typical for little girls at this time.

The oldest child wears the smart vest-form jacket over the bodice insert, which consists of a pleated front and high collar of a dark fabric. The body and sleeves are of the printed silk overskirt fabric. The bodice is smartly short in the sleeves and cuffed with the dark material and is closed over the bosom with a pointed tab with buttons at either end. The black pleated underskirt may be seen near the hem, and the long overskirt is fashionably drawn up to one side, where it undoubtedly reaches into long bustle poufs and ends in a straight drape at the opposite side in the back. High, polished boots, buttoned up the sides, are worn over black stockings. The thick straight bangs are again apparent, and the back hair hangs long.

The brother whose hand she holds is dressed in his Scottish kilts with a dark jacket and vest front trimmed with buttons. His neck bow is of black silk, and his collar indicates that a white shirt is worn. His stockings seem to be falling down over his boots.

Glass-Plate Negative, ca. 1889

Courtesy of the Museum of New Mexico (76514)

J. C. Burge took this photograph of Main Street in downtown Kingston, New Mexico, with a few of its citizens posing out of doors for the occasion. The picture is full of details of clothing habits in the West in the late eighties. It is notable, first of all, that this is a relatively small, and fairly new, Western town. Most of the frame buildings have one story and are almost makeshift in appearance; yet the community can obviously support at least one dressmaking establishment, as well as an "Opera-House." As a footnote to these observations, it is interesting to see that the ladderlike frames in front of the dressmaking shop protect newly planted trees. All of these details, not least the dressmaker's shop, illustrate the determined effort to maintain familiar cultural standards, which included "proper" dress.

Obviously, women's dress in this frontier settlement includes correct corsets, stylish hats, and fashionable clothing. Skirts are worn in up-to-date late-eighties fashion: generous in girth and less encumbered by extra draperies. One woman wears the new, full, pleated skirt, made perfectly round except for an allowance at the back for a slight bustle pad. The standards for acceptance of these new styles may be taken to be those of any city in the nation, large or small.

The three women at the dressmaking shop may all be seamstresses, and the lady in the rock-ing chair may possibly be the owner of the shop. Her dress is quite stylish with its dressy overskirt, extremely high collar, and lozenge-shaped bodice fronts of velvet. A pleated short flounce is attached at the edge of the skirt, and ankle boots are worn.

The only other dress that provides much detail is the dark wool worn by the woman standing on the street at the corner post of the Occidental Hotel. The bodice of this closely fitted two-piece costume has a long point in front and no basques. It is fastened with close-set buttons down the front, and narrow white cuffs show at the rather short sleeves. The skirt shows the free-hanging medium fullness of the late eighties set into the all-around pleats.

Only two elements of women's dress are effectively displayed on the upper porch: the tall, flat-topped little hat, a style popular from about 1887, and the checked gingham of the cotton house-dress on the figure seated at the front corner.

The only clearly notable detail of men's clothing is in the cut of the light trousers on the figure standing in front of the porch; they are distinctly longer at the heel, flaring very slightly at the back to accommodate this cut, and quite narrow and tubular above.

W. J. SMITHERS had this full-length portrait taken in the Johnson Studio in Sioux City, Iowa, in 1889. His attire for the occasion is up-to-date, representing a common style of rather flashy readymade clothing for men: a morning suit with striped trousers and cutaway coat. Although the extremely short, slicked-down hair is a good clue to a near-nineties date, an even better indication is the coat's sack style, which is cutaway in the newly popular slant and has only one button, which is placed high, and a very narrow notched collar and lapels. The object of this coat style is to reveal the bottom of the vest and show off a watch chain, which does not seem to be an issue here. The coat and vest are of a subdued, dark woven check, most likely in brown shades, topstitched all around and with welted pockets.

The trousers are of a bold stripe and are cut in the rather narrow tubular fashion, with the front just breaking over the shoe and the heels cut longer.

The new, shaved-up haircut, the stiff white shirt, and the narrow bow tie, together with the pocket handkerchief and boutonniere, denote some rather formal occasion.

Tintype, ca. 1889

Courtesy of the National Museum of American History (C84.618.9)

VERY NEAR THE end of the decade, these four housemaids, dressed in their working clothes, posed together with the household cat. The change in treatment of the frontal hair that marks the entrance into the nineties is quite evident in these four variations. The bangs are no longer cut short or curled in individual corkscrews; in fact, one woman wears her hair parted in the center, her growing-out bangs making short waves at the temples; the seated woman at right wears deep bangs waved flat to the forehead; and the other two wear short frontal hair curled back for some distance on the crown.

The skirt worn by the woman seated at the left is another giveaway as to date; the overskirt panel extending on a diagonal just over the hem flounce is brought up to the opposite hip in shallow folds and leads to the sagging bustle folds at back, leaving the opposite end of the skirt panel to hang straight down behind the left side seam. The tight, midforearm sleeve and the contrasting satin trimming on lighter-colored wool also confirm the date.

The two girls standing are wearing cottons, and both have typical late-eighties neck treatments: one a black silk ribbon bow over a starched collar insert and one a fold-down collar of coarse lace over a standing dress collar. The dress on the woman seated at right is of black wool, possibly alpaca, with the high collar of the late eighties. Three of the girls wear long checked gingham aprons with rectangular bibs pinned to the dress; the other girl's apron has strap sleeves and fastens in back.

This image shows clearly the desire and ability of all classes to wear what is fashionable.

1889–90

Courtesy of the California Historical Society (20,508)

This photograph is of a large, extended California family of Hispanic descent. The extremely high capote bonnet worn by the oldest lady is the best evidence of a late-eighties date. Further evidence is found in the construction of the light-colored skirt at right, still one of the relatively complicated styles of the eighties, with its low-hanging back drape falling down one side. Both men's and women's hairstyles speak to the late date as well; they are high, forehead-revealing, and close to the head at the sides, with no hair worn in front of the ears. The men's hair is typically oiled and worn tight to the head.

The matriarch best illustrates the dignity of the occasion, in her heavy black silk with its extensive jet passementerie and tablier of black lace flounces. Her fashionable bonnet and tight black gloves complete the formal effect.

Grandfather is the image of the patriarch in his trim beard and good black suit. Only he and one older son wear the frock coat; the younger men and boys wear the sack. Where neckties are not apparent, they are of light-colored silk, tied flat and laid under the high vest front so as to be almost invisible in the photograph.

The woman at left wears a cuirass bodice with a hip peplum and back drape, in dark wool, and the bodice is finished with a military braid lying in loops over the bosom and shoulders. Around her neck she wears a dark, printed silk scarf. The wristbone-length sleeves have a slight flare, revealing the shortness of the tight, shining kid gloves with their heavy black stitching. The matching skirt is plain and gored and still slightly draped from the bustle pad.

The girl at far right wears a nearly identical dress, but buttoned in a double-breasted fashion and trimmed with black passementerie. She wears a corsage of roses but no gloves. Over her curled hair she wears a small bonnet covered with crushed cloth and lace and with white ostrich tips. Her plain skirt hem reveals laced boots of black kid with pointed toes.

The littlest boy wears a light-colored suit of brocaded wool, with huge buttons on the straight jacket, over a kilted skirt. His wavy hair is cut in childish bangs in "Buster Brown" style.

Both of the women standing are wearing short, fitted basque bodices, and their skirts show the elongated draped fullness over the small bustle pad at back, with pleating into the waistband, typical of the late eighties. One wears a puffed neckcloth, and the other has contrasting passementerie trim. Their hair is quite differently done from the others'—the one still frizzed in too-long bangs, brushed up high; the other in plastered-down bangs.

CHAPTER SIX

The 1890s

Oh, for some prophetic insight into the costuming of the woman of twenty years hence! Will she be a hybrid sort of creature like one of the fabled monsters and in her raiment suggest both sexes? Are we to be so developed by the Delsartean school of expression, the calisthenic and athletic training now so much in vogue, that we will come to the wearing of garments that reveal rather than conceal the muscularized limbs and in our untrammeled worship of beauty and form cast aside all modesty and garb ourselves in raiment that shows the contour of the figure? Artists declare that it is only the manly figure which should be defined, and that a poetic air of mystery should pervade the garments of womankind. Every man sensitive to feminine influences has felt a pleasurable tremor when he hears the frou-frou of a woman's skirt, which brings with it an air of graceful femininity, and suggests daintiness and fascination. Are we to be so athleticized that we will disdain all fripperies and wear the garments once considered as the prerogative of our husbands and brothers? We are trembling on the verge of a revolution in dress. What the future holds for us is an unsolved mystery.

—*Godey's,* April 1896

*M*ANY CIRCUMSTANCES CAME together in the nineties to ensure that American people could not only have more clothing per capita than ever before, and in greater variety, but that there was a universal understanding of style. Life-styles were changing. The dictates of fashion became much more lenient, and there was a greater demand for plain, functional dress that was less expensive and easier to make. Advertising contained more illustrations and increased in volume. Mass production increased. Department stores proliferated. Retail catalog outlets were developed, and "the Post Office's rural free delivery system, which started as an experiment in 1896 . . . was the greatest boon imaginable to firms that used the Post Office for delivery of packages" and thus made shopping by mail viable (Kidwell and Christman 164).

The advent of Montgomery and Ward in the seventies had initiated the megalithic catalog, a consolidation of hundreds of specialized catalogs, and in 1893 Richard Sears launched the great Sears and Roebuck Company. Once the Rural Free Delivery system was in effect, after 1896, catalog shopping boomed. Besides contributing to the demise of the small-town general store, this kind of shopping quite naturally created its own market for more and more goods, and the tastes and needs of American people inevitably continued to evolve in order to meet (and influence) the supply. An escalating ladder of modern consumption was under way.

Home Sewing

The styles of the nineties were greatly simplified from those of the previous decades, and both patterns and pattern systems were so abundant that sewing was simpler and more pleasant than ever before. Even though mass production had brought the cost of readymade clothing down, many housewives still saved money and were able to have more up-to-date clothes because of sewing at home. A wonderful addition to the wardrobe was the shirtwaist, which, in particular, because it required so little fitting, was commonly made at home, even though readymades were plentiful. The separate skirts were also relatively easy. A cotton housedress or wrapper or a Mother Hubbard could be made up in a day. Children's wash clothing was often still made in the home as well. As before, a seamstress could make these everyday articles of clothing from cheap fabric and save her major clothing dollar for better readymade garments for herself and her family.

Fashions for Women

Women's clothing choices increased drastically again in the nineties; American women had much more to say about what they wore. Healthful outdoor exercise, even swimming and bicycling, became normal feminine activities during this decade and brought with them the desire to have less constraint in everyday clothing. Corsets loosened, and the larger feminine figure was no longer deplored quite so thoroughly: "Abnormally small waists are surely going out of style . . . the English journals are once more protesting against the custom of tight-lacing and so should we! Compared with the previous generation who thought anything above an 18" waist clumsy, we are a race of Amazons" (*Janesville Weekly Gazette,* January 16, 1895).

There was even some change in the progress of fashion information; while the haute couture of Paris still served as the beacon, the Parisian penchant for tight-laced, exaggerated female curves was resisted in this country by many women who did not strictly observe French dictates. English styles, more common sense, were actually described in American fashion articles in terms that led to their acceptance as fashion and not merely as workable alternatives. Both styles survived side by side and in practice had many details in common, most notably the sleeves. Even the English-style "tailor suits" were made with the spectacular sleeve styles of the nineties and followed the fashionable silhouette.

Still, the new craze for English tailoring did initiate a remarkable new look for American women:

> Tailored suits, consisting at first of jacket, skirt, and vest, were advertised occasionally in the catalogs of the 1880s. Bloomingdale's offered nine choices, for example, in 1886. By the 1890s, they appeared more frequently, sometimes in the form of blazer and skirt. Often the term "man-tailored" was used. . . . Man-tailored suits were distinguished by the use of heavy materials and by details associated with the construction of men's suits, particularly the collar. Since dressmakers weren't familiar with the tailoring techniques involved in stitching, padding, and pressing men's coats, a man-tailored suit did, in fact, have to be made by a male tailor. . . . The tailor-made suit, which had a removeable jacket, was worn with a waist, and thus began the new demand for shirtwaists. By 1891, shirtwaists were offered as separate items of apparel to be worn with just a skirt, a great boon to the working woman, who, with one skirt and a selection of shirt-waists, could appear to have many changes of clothing. Shirtwaists came into use first as summer garments, but continued into general use for all seasons as women found they could be adapted for all occasions—shopping, afternoon wear, and even informal evening wear. "The separate skirt with a well-made waist presents always a trim appearance." (Kidwell and Christman 137–45)

A small Wisconsin newspaper confirms this appraisal at mid-decade: "The Shirt Waist and blouse have much to do with the trim and dainty appearance of our young women as they go about the house, instead of the old wrapper, ready made silk waists are being sold at wonderfully low prices. Almost anyone can afford to look neatly dressed at home" (*Janesville Weekly Gazette*, February 27, 1895). Readymades made it possible, in fact, for the working woman to follow the latest trends in skirts and shirtwaists, and even to have nice, dressier garments for reasonable prices. The variety of her clothing options in the 1890s, even at the economy level, was wide.

The shirtwaist followed every new fashion in dress bodices, including an assortment of "masculine" shirt styles, and changed in style whenever a new sleeve shape was "in," which was quite frequently. Colors and materials ranged from white cotton, some with woven or printed stripes or figures, to pastels to deeper-toned cotton with white collars and cuffs, to soft, dark silks with frills and puffs. Fabric patterns were typically used to accentuate the shirt shapes; in the summer of 1896 *Godey's*, speaking of cotton shirtwaists made with the large leg-o'-mutton sleeves, said that "Waists have the body stripes running up and down, and the sleeves crosswise." As the advantages of the separate waist became obvious even for dinner dress, waists were made in soft, sometimes sheer, black silk crepe or satin, which, when worn with a heavier black silk skirt, gave the impression of an elegant and dressy gown.

The distinguishing features of 1890s shirtwaists were the extreme narrowness of cut of the bodice shoulders, the presence of thick gathers or pleats in an always-enlarged upper sleeve (varying during the decade as the shape of the sleeve changed), and fullness of some kind over the bosom and down the front. The back of the shirtwaist was usually shorter than the front, seamed down the back, and fitted, often having tapes inside that tied in front, to hold the back close to the figure. In tailored cottons, the front fullness was generally controlled with pleats, and in softer fabrics with puffs and gathers. Collars were usually high on the neck, many severely stiff and straight, though a surplice style was popular in silks for evening wear, when it was permissible to bare the neck.

There was much more coverage of fashion information during the nineties than ever before, and the articles and ads were well illustrated. Women's columns in the popular periodicals, and in newspapers as well, followed all the fashion trends and interpreted them for their readers. One such trend was nostalgia: "we are historically, if not correctly, gowned. With the usual perversity or good taste, call it what you will, of woman, the ages have been mixed up and the sleeve of one time is joined to the bodice of another; the skirt belongs to still another era, and the drapery, or decoration, may be of this time and this day. The result is decidedly picturesque, and, if to the eye of the student it seems mosaic, it is by no means lacking in artistic effect" (*Ladies' Home Journal*, December 1890).

The Ladies' Home Journal in October 1891 showed dress styles that were extremely long-waisted at front and had loads of gathers from neck to waist point and also many fitted, hip-length overblouses belted in a deep V at waistfront. With their long sleeves gathered very high on the shoulder, but narrow on the arm and standing in sharp puffs, these dresses were considered quite "natty."

Jordan Marsh, of Boston, issued a catalog in 1891 showing women's suits with such a sleeve style and bodice shape, all with extremely high, straight collars. These collars quickly became de rigeur in tasteful dress, with *The Ladies' Home Journal* even declaring that "To permit one's neck to show in daytime is bad form" (August 1890). The sleeves of the new suits were somewhat eased, from a very high puff at the shoulder, tapering gradually and cut just a bit short on the wrist. Prices for these made-to-order suits ranged from $28.50 for tricot or cashmere to $25.00 for fine cashmere or Henrietta cloth and up to $35.00 for faille silk. In 1892 and 1893 B. Altman's catalogs illustrated similarly styled costumes, with larger sleeves, announcing, "Ladies Dresses Made to Order."

It is interesting to track the nineties waistlines. Beginning with the long-fronted style of 1890, waistlines rose until, by mid-decade, most dresses had either round waists near the normal waistline or, at most, a moderate front point with the bodice having upper-front fullness that was held fairly close at the diaphragm. Waistlines stayed at the normal level until late in the decade. In 1898 a new, lower-busted silhouette suddenly became fashionable in better dresses, and it was emphasized by frontal-bodice fullness all the way down to the newly lowered waistline, even hanging over it slightly.

By this time many bodice fronts were of contrasting, soft material to dramatically accentuate the new puffed line. Late nineties garments were made in plain but rich silks and woolens, with the bodice fronts in bright silks of woven or printed patterns. Most such dresses had soft bishop sleeves of the same silk as the bodice fronts.

But it is the sleeve and its changes that give the best dating tool for the nineties. The leg-o'-mutton sleeve was for some time the shape of choice, sometimes thought of as the only choice, which it certainly was not. At first, in 1890, the sleeve remained very tight on the upper arm, and a puff was set vertically, high on the shoulder. Photographs show that even cotton washdresses and blouses sported these new sleeves within a short time of their introduction in the fashion literature and through 1891. It was a short-lived, transitional style, however, as it turned out, as such moderate sleeve shapes were not much to be seen in the plates after 1892, when the puff expanded around the upper arm.

An easier sleeve had been introduced in 1890 fashion plates, showing the upper-sleeve puff expanded outward and allowing some fullness down to the elbow, which style was called a "gigot," meaning "leg of mutton." This at first was a gentle shape, not extravagant in its use of material or effect. It is featured inthe descriptions of suits and in many fashion notes: "The 'gigot' sleeve . . . is made over a coat-shaped lining fitting tightly from the elbow to the wrist, with the other material fitting smoothly over it until at the top, which is cut wider and longer, gathered over the top of the lining, and the fullness tacked here and there to keep it up" (*Ladies' Home Journal,* January 1890). This relatively modest sleeve shape was also transitive, evolving rapidly into ever and ever wider styles. The ladies' fashion column for J. M. Bostwick and Sons, in the *Janesville Weekly Gazette* said in July 1892 that "Balloon sleeves are even larger than last year." By 1893 the sleeve had grown to a very full, drooping puff held by a close forearm, and it was said to be a revival from the 1830s, though with narrower shoulders in the bodice:

> A stylish leg-o'-mutton sleeve is close-fitting below the elbow and very full near the shoulder. It is to be hoped that women with broad shoulders will choose a more moderate form of gigot sleeve. Quite in accordance with the amplified, stiffened skirts are the drooping, puffed sleeves, which are likewise a revival of the same period [the 1830s]. In those days of quaint modes, dress shoulders sloped abnormally below the shoulder-line, and this condition was emphasized by the drooping sleeves. The fashionable woman of today protests vehemently against a return of the exaggerated length of the shoulder, and is content to adopt only the drooping sleeve, which is far more graceful and picturesque. (*The Delineator,* July 1893)

The drooping sleeve persisted through 1893 and into 1894 but by 1895 had become much stiffer and wider. *Godey's* described the popular sleeve as wide and very flat on top with "a distinct inflation as they approach the elbow" (November 1895). Such sleeves required about a yard of material each and were so heavy that the shoulder seam was lengthened somewhat to carry the weight. By 1896 the sleeve had reached its apogee, extending almost horizontally from the shoulder. The ideal by this time was to have no drooping lines in the upper sleeve, which meant that some internal support was necessary; this was accomplished by flatlining the upper sleeve with a stiff crinoline or fibre chamois, a leathery fabric, before pleating into the armscye. At least one type of wire sleeve-hoop was actually patented in 1896, just before the demise of the huge sleeve style. The height of an extreme fashion detail always carries the seeds of its decay; already in 1896, some sleeves were shown that displayed less fullness at the top: "The sleeve is gradually displaying a disposition to cling to the arm, the fullness receding to the top; one of the latest models is a tight-fitting coat sleeve, reaching well above the elbow, with a not very full puff above" (*Godey's,* January 1896).

After 1896, a wide range of smaller puff styles were seen at the shoulder and upper arm, along with many variations in bretelles and other shoulder-enhancing trimmings on the bodice. In 1897 some suits and dresses were made with a nearly straight sleeve having only a slightly puffed top, but by 1898 the most popular style was a long, tight sleeve with a small, full, ball-shaped puff set very high on the upper arm, made either of self- or trimming material. The shoulder breadth of the bodice cut was correspondingly narrowed again.

Throughout the entire decade, the bishop sleeve maintained its popularity right along with the mutton-leg shapes, particularly for lightweight materials, especially cotton shirtwaists. The volume of the bishop sleeve increased steadily in the first half of the decade, and by 1896 it was thickly gathered into both shoulder and wristband; after this date, and through the end of the century, it declined in volume, like the mutton-leg styles.

Sportswear and leisure demands created a market for good, durable, smart outfits. Cotton denims, duck, whipcord, and linen were freshly treated in crisp suits for golf, tennis, and the seashore, and these and hard-finish woolens were used for bicycling and walking suits. White or navy-blue were the preferred summer colors, but red or white picqué was considered very "snappy," according to fashion writers. Sailorlike braid trim was featured on deep square "sailor collars," and long black silk "sailor" ties were worn at the neck.

Novelty woolens were used for dressier suits. *The Ladies' Home Journal* in November 1893 also listed soft suitings, smooth-faced cloths, and "rather heavy bengalines." Small-check stuffs (wools) were suggested for general wear, made up in tailored fashion. But these sporty styles were not all-pervasive: "Rich black satin makes the most elaborate

Spring toilette . . . counted the most fashionable of all materials," according to *Godey's* fashion editorial in May 1893. Other colors for spring, according to the same article, included wood tints for suitings, also grays, ecru to white, soft, dainty greens, and "decidedly dark blues." High contrasts were common: black with turquoise, old-rose with dark green, wood brown with dark blue, baby-blue with bottle green, or gray with deep brown—the key was "very dark for contrast." In its suggestions for winter 1896 *Godey's* stated that combinations of black and gold, green and brown, black and silver, or crimson and blue in either wool and velvet or silk and velvet "are liked by almost everybody and are considered always in good taste." The editor also admonished, "All of us who are wise, possess a black gown." *Godey's* suggested in the summer of 1896 that piqué and duck be used for suits; "dark and light blue, striped, figured, and dotted, white with colored dots, and other pretty combinations."

The silks used for dresses during the era of the large sleeve were of many types and colors, but there was a tendency for delicate, wandering motifs and for warp-printed, misty combinations of colors in very lightweight weaves and "straggling designs" in sheers. Oriental effects in prints were extremely popular as well. Silk dresses in these prints very often were trimmed with solid colors in satin or velvet, and there was a distinct fad for the crushed cummerbund of contrasting material. When a silk costume was made for dress, with the puffed sleeve ending just below the elbow, it was popular to finish the edge with a hanging frill, made either of lace or of contrasting material. Some special-occasion dresses had the lower sleeve made tight to the arm in lace below the silk puff.

The trim of nineties dresses was often concentrated on the bodice; contrasting fabric, usually velvet or satin, and lace or braid were the usual additions, along with surface treatments such as puffs, frills, gathers, tucks, pleats, and fancy collars, and this became even more common toward the latter half of the decade. "Neck-dressing is an all-important thing nowadays; the officer's collar with crushed band, and the flaring Valois are alike fashionable. . . . the stylish Valois, made of velvet or lace, and wired to make it stand out, frames the face most becomingly. . . . Jet, as a trimming, can not be superseded, and splendid passementeries in bold conventional patterns are used on both black and colored weaves" (*Godey's*, January 1896).

Skirts, too, changed during the decade. *The Ladies' Home Journal* claimed in August 1890 that "Skirts are made so plainly nowadays that all of the dressmaker's ingenuity is taxed to have novelty about the bodice." Even the plainest skirt, however, was by no means straight; the predominant shape in the early nineties was a swooping tulip or bell form, very wide at the hem and smooth over the hips, from which it flared dramatically. Women were advised to use the waist and skirt as an economy measure in dressing well:

A woman who is not a butterfly of society may be quite well-dressed by purchasing three new gowns each season, the last year's ones doing duty as second-best. For instance, she must have one new and well-fitted tailor gown for the street, one reception and one dinner or ball gown; a black silk skirt with three silk-and-chiffon waists will supply all the necesary changes, and a little ingenuity will do the rest. Full, round skirts should be four-and-a-half to five yards wide, and just now it is stylish to drape one side slightly, by pushing the fullness up near one hip and fastening a large rosette there under the fullness. . . . Wear a small pad bustle [a narrow pad at the center back of the skirt where fullness was to be concentrated] if the figure requires it, and one steel twelve inches long, placed twelve inches below the belt [cross-wise], or two drawing strings, fourteen and twenty-four inches below. (*Ladies' Home Journal,* January 1890)

Following the plain skirt, there has come the sheath-like garment that is almost as difficult to walk in as was the old-fashioned tied-back. It must be cut with great care, for it is absolutely plain, and at the front and sides it is fitted as carefully as a riding-habit and fits almost as closely. Of course, these skirts will only be developed in heavy cloths, and the woman who likes to look jaunty and has a good figure will be at her best in this simple skirt with a close-fitting coat and a fetching bonnet. (*Ladies' Home Journal,* October 1890)

The handsomest skirt fronts are "broken" in front by a few plaits run in the bell, which makes them more becoming to stout and thin figures than the close-fitting bell, sheath, or fin-de-siecle shapes that reveal the contour of the form. (*Ladies' Home Journal,* October 1891)

In the November 1891 issue, *The Ladies' Home Journal* gave a scale pattern for making the popular "French" skirt, a sweeping, one-seam, near-circular style with three darts at each hip and deep box plaits at the back, where the skirt was about six inches longer. This cut gave a smooth, close fit around the front of the figure with a flaring hemline that was said to be particularly effective in heavy materials. The skirt required forty-five-inch fabric and was cut on the crosswise fold, so the fabric had to be ninety-seven inches long if a slight train was desired. For a round skirt, a ninety-inch length, doubled, was sufficient. Another type of skirt was defined in a local newspaper column as having many gores from the waist: "The umbrella gores that we see so much are always fitted at the top and closely gathered or plaited in the middle of the back. Trains and demi-trains prevail. The demi-train is still seen on the promenade, and it is to be hoped it will soon be abolished, for it is untidy and disgusting" (*Janesville Weekly Gazette,* July 1892). In July 1893 *The Delineator* described a change in skirts: "The fullness in one of the new swelling skirts is confined in box-plaits at the back . . . the folds are . . . always rolling." A little later in the same article it reads: "Early nineteenth century fashions are copied in the new Empire and 1830 skirts as faithfully as fin de siecle tastes will permit."

In October 1898, a *Gazette* article said that "Some of the latest skirts are twelve yards around the foot and contain twenty-four yards of goods." *Godey's* maintained in January 1895 that

> Skirts continue to retain their fulness [*sic*], and are made in divers ways; the panel front of a different material with overlapping sides, has taken well; the front made of a straight width, folded over to form a very wide box pleat, is new and stylish, as is also the panelled skirt, where sides of a different material or color are set in; the latter is an excellent method of renovating skirts which need additional width. Most women prefer the skirt closely fitted on the hips, although a few of the recent models show a fulness adjusted to the figure by a few flat pleats, which flare widely as they approach the foot.

By this date, all walking skirts were made to clear the ground completely, and it was considered bad form to have skirts touch the floor. By 1898, and through the end of the century, skirts were increasingly subject to a continuation of the bodice trim, with sweeping curves and scallops of braid or lace placed diagonally. The fashionable skirt form at this time was a tulip or vase shape, which clung to the "hourglass figure" at least to below hip level, and often to the knees, before flaring dramatically at the hem. Some everyday skirts actually followed this line, but the no-nonsense skirt type worn with the everyday shirtwaist, as seen in photographs, was still flared from the hips for ease in walking. Gathers around the waistband, even in summer cotton skirts, were not common near the end of the decade, but instead there were gores, panels, or stitched-down pleats, often with an eccentrically placed vertical line of pleats or folds running the full length of the skirt.

Undergarments

The corset form, as might be surmised, was more a matter of dissension in the nineties than at any other time in the century. It had by this time been firmly established that freedom of the body, exercise, and fresh air leads to health, and so for the first time there were healthful and attractive alternatives to the tight corset. Yet really high fashion was based on extreme tight lacing. Adherents to tight lacing, and there were many, could offer up no real logic to support their argument other than preferred appearance. Many manufacturers advertised corset alternatives. In June and August 1890, several were advertised in various ladies' books as being "endorsed by Annie Jenness-Miller," a popular writer and exponent of exercise and clothing reform. Jenness-Miller suggested several types of corset under her own name, including "The Best Corset Substitute," a "Compromise Bodice," and "The Equipoise Waist," made by George Frost and Company of Boston. The latter is described as "A Corset, a Waist, and a Corset Cover Combined: The Corset Substitute Long Looked For" (*Godey's*, August 1890). An ad in *The Delineator* in August 1891 read: "Doctors recommend Reast's Patent Invigorator Corsets, for ladies, maids, boys, girls, and children." Reast's patents included a contraption of shoulder braces and straps in a children's version but a still smartly small-waisted, sharply curved, laced corset in a womanly style.

The corset, so long a part of fashionable dress, was, however, too firmly entrenched for the notion of bodily freedom to progress very far as yet. In *The Ladies' Home Journal* in January 1890, corsets were even used as sales incentives: subscriptions for the *Mme Demorest's Monthly Fashion Journal* were to be sold at fifty cents per year, and 500,000 corsets were to be given away as prizes in the six-month campaign.

The short-lived fashion for Empire dress styles in 1893, featuring waistlines anywhere from just below the bust to a position about two inches above the natural waistline, occasioned the production of special corsets. "Empire short stays . . . admirably adapted for wear with the short-waisted Empire Styles now so fashionable, as well as with tea-gowns, Greek Gowns, Wrappers, Lounging Robes, and other loosely-fitted garments. . . . Buttons are arranged at appropriate intervals along the lower part of the Short Stay for the attachment of the Empire Petticoat" (*The Delineator,* July 1893).

Corsets of every type and degree of lacing were advertised in the nineties—some of the reform style, but many more of fashionable shape. Throughout the decade, dressier corsets were still made in colored silks, and black corsets were specifically advertised in 1891 in very tight-laced formal styles, suitable for evening dress. In 1898 *The Ladies' Home Journal* featured a full back cover advertisement by the R. and G. Corset Company of New York showing a fully curved and shaped corset with parallel stays that severely reduced the lower rib cage and flared sharply above and below, with a rather low top having slight cups for the breasts and with hooks down the front over a distended belly. In the same issue the Cresco, another tightly laced corset made by the Michigan Corset Company of Jackson, Michigan, was advertised along with the following information: "It cannot break at the waist. Disconnected in front at waist line and with hip lacing." Such a style allowed even tighter lacing than usual. Another support garment is advertised as giving "Improved Breast Support, Made with skirt and hose supporter attachments. All deficiency of development supplied." This reform-style garment was offered by "Mrs. C. D. Newell, 1017 LeMoyne St., Chicago."

By the end of the eighties the petticoat too had already changed drastically, becoming softer, shorter, and lighter in weight:

> The fashionable petticoat is the one which fits well. It may be of silk, cambric, nainsook, or lawn, but must be shapely in cut, must not tend to make the waist look larger, must draw the fullness well to the back and must not interfere with the walking of the wearer. . . . Heavy embroidered flounces are no longer liked.

. . . .

White cambric is used for this petticoat, which reaches just a little below the knee, and has for its finish a deep frill of point d'esprit lace. The front fits almost as closely as a sheath skirt, the fullness being drawn to the back by means of a casing that extends from each side across the back about midway of the skirt. It has an opening in the centre of the back formed by buttonholes, and out of which come broad, pink ribbons that draw the fullness as it should be, and are then tied in a pretty way in the back. (*Ladies' Home Journal*, March 1891)

When the narrow skirts of 1890 and 1891 gave way in 1893 to the nostalgia-inspired wider styles, there was a change in petticoats to match: "The fashionable flaring effect is produced by wearing . . . skirts over an Empire Petticoat that is gored to flare well at the bottom, and made with a deep, full flounce that falls over narrow, gathered ruffles to further increase the flare" (*The Delineator,* May 1893). A pattern for the above, #6100, is offered for l s., or 25 cents, in the magazine. "The box-plaited Elizabethan petticoat performs the same service as the farthingale used in the days of 'England's Eliza.' A skirt that is made without stiffening will stand out stylishly over this petticoat, which flares considerably near the bottom" (*The Delineator,* July 1893).

The chemise, as worn underneath the corset, had not entirely disappeared:

When chemises are worn, those with a round or pompadour neck outline and having no sleeves, are chosen. A very narrow frill of lace, with feather-stitching holding it in place is the decoration liked. However, a great many women no longer wear chemise [*sic*] but instead choose the small silk vests that fit the figure so closely, keep one warm, and extend quite a distance below the waist. They may be gotten in all colors, but a distinct preference is shown for black. (*Ladies' Home Journal,* March 1891)

Lingerie is by no means as ornate as it was a few years since. The finest French lingerie is handmade and trimmed with small neat scallops and narrow Valenciennes lace, with perhaps groups of pin tucks alternating with insertion. For inexpensive underclothing, very fine torchon or Medici lace is proper. . . . They are usually sold in sets, consisting of the nightgown, chemise, and drawers. . . . Union undergarments of silk or wool are often substituted . . . (*Godey's,* February 1896)

This trend to "combinations," or "Union suits," is marked.

WRAPS

Sleeves of dresses and suits from 1890 to 1892 were fairly narrow, and though they were puffed high at the tip of the shoulder, they fit well into a coat sleeve designed in the same manner. Sleeves of jackets, especially, began to have a very pronounced high puff at the shoulder by 1890, rising vertically from the arm. Short coats and jackets were very popular during the first two years of the decade. They were fitted over the hips, often embroidered or otherwise surface-decorated, and many were fur-trimmed. The standing, flaring Valois collar was a favorite shape, made either of fur or of embroidered cloth with a fur band inside. Fur jackets retained their popularity from the previous decade; in January 1890 *The Ladies' Home Journal* claimed that "For slender young ladies nothing is prettier for mid-winter wear than a plain, elegantly fitted sealskin cuirass with Valois collar of the same."

In the same issue an enormous variety of other kinds of wraps is described. In long coats, the "Huguenot" style was considered most elegant, with sleeves falling to the floor and with shaggy fur or fluffy feather trim. Long cloaks of black or shot velvet, plush, or *velour du nord* are also advertised, and a "high Medici collar" is featured in the descriptions. Fur trims described were "brown, black, and 'Isabelle' bear, silver, blue and black fox, black martin, and lynx." In this period before the overlarge sleeves, the long coat reigned, and the more closely fitted the better. In this so-called "close-rig" style, the "Princess redingote" appears as a long fitted shape, some with fur sleeves and trim of close-cropped fur such as "castor, beaver, seal, astrakhan, and chinchilla." According to *The Ladies' Home Journal* of November 1890, "The natural gray curly astrakhan is new this season and is very effective in trimming jackets of light cloth, which almost invariably have a toque and muff to match." The Russian collar, a high-standing shape folded double with deep front points, is often shown in astrakhan. Capes and coats were of all lengths, with a long, plain circular cloak surmounted by a wrist-length cape seemingly the most popular form. Later in the decade the expanding sleeve rendered narrow coats and jackets unstylish and unworkable, and capes superseded them in popularity.

Throughout the decade, wraps were available from numerous catalog sources: Stern Brothers, Chas. A. Stevens and Brothers, B. Altman, The National Cloak Company, Montgomery Ward, Sears and Roebuck, and Marshall Field, to name only a very few. Department stores had wide selections as well. It is likely that few women had to make winter wraps for their families in the nineties.

We are Manufacturors of Ladies' Misses' and children's Cloaks and Wraps of all kinds, and by selling direct to you save you the jobber's and retailer's profits amounting to about one-third the cost of a garment. We cut and make every cloak to order, thus insuring a perfect-fitting and beautifully-finished garment. We pay all express charges at our own expense. . . . Our new Fall and Winter catalogue should be in the hands of every lady who admires beautiful and stylish garments. . . . We will mail it to you together with a 48-inch linen tape measure, new measurement diagram (which insures perfect-fitting garments), and more than forty samples of the cloths and plushes from which we make the garments . . . (*Ladies' Home Journal*, October 1890)

In the matter of style, the *Journal* was adamant: "The collar must be high, and a coat without a high collar is almost as dowdy-looking as the one which does not have its sleeves raised on the shoulder" (November 1892).

The "waterproof," a cape or cloak of some impervious material (often rubber coated), evidently did not present a perfect solution, for in a column written for the *Journal* in February 1890, one writer said, "I never buy a waterproof. A good one costs too much and a cheap one is an abomination. I substitute a plain ulster. I can wear this all year around by using a chamois skin jacket in the coldest weather."

The shawl, the standby of the well-dressed woman for over a century, had fallen on hard times by the 1890s. The *Janesville Weekly Gazette* noted on March 13, 1895, that "In Paris the Cashmere shawl, so expensive and so highly valued as an article of wearing apparel in our grandmother's day, is utilized as a piano cover. How the mighty have fallen."

As noted, the enlarged sleeve, beginning in 1893, forced both long and short fitted coats out of fashion, and a woman had either to forgo the popular new sleeves and wear an out-of-date coat, to wear a cape, or to buy one of the new jackets with large sleeves. Manufacturers did make such jackets for a short time, but the style was not long-lasting, mostly because jacket sleeves, no matter how large, were difficult to wear over the huge sleeves of dresses; the armscye required to support the large jacket sleeve was too small. Wool walking suits were made with the very large sleeves for a few years, but overjackets and coats faded out of popularity in favor of wide capes after about 1893.

REFORM DRESS

All accounts agree that the bicycle was the most influential element in the reform dress movement in the decade of the nineties. Dress reformers by this date had not been concentrating on a bloomer style so much as on the reduction of corset restrictions. Day dress was already lenient enough to satisfy most reformers, but with the advent of the popularity of "the wheel," the bloomer again became a matter of polarized opinion—and not all of its critics were men. The 1896 April issue of *Godey's* is called the "bicycle number" and is almost completely devoted to that subject, including many stories as well as advertisements. Bicycle stories were solicited in the form of a competition, and those published mostly stressed that riding a "wheel" did not interfere with being a "true woman." Numerous arguments concerning dress are included with the fiction, with most of the authors addressing the issues but being too conservative to support a bloomer style.

THE COSTUME OF THE FUTURE:

... hampered by all generations, verily since Eve first essayed dressmaking in the garden of Eden, by clothes that sadly restricted anything like freedom of action, the locomotion of women has been always passive and dependent ...

The world is a new and another sphere under the bicyclist's observation ... were the gift given us to look a bit into the future, what should we probably find the middle-of-the-twentieth-century girl wearing on her wheel, bloomers, very short tunics, or trouserettes and similar abominations in the sight of grace and femininity? . . . In time may petticoats triumph over the women who fail to recognize that bloomers are too great a sacrifice for our sex ever to make, and that in skirts only can they maintain at once in the eyes of men their womanliness and their independence.

. . . .

CYCLING COSTUME:

The advanced women advocate bloomers, whose greatest crime is, perhaps, the utter lack of beauty; while in favor with some women, they do not seem to take with the society belle, who prefers skirts; when properly cut, the skirt is graceful and feminine, and need not impede the movements of the wearer. The regulation costume for the conservative woman is a skirt, either pleated or sufficiently full to be comfortable, with either a jaunty silk-lined Eton, a short reefer, open-fronted coat, or a Norfolk waist confined by a leather belt. The jacket or Eton is preferable, because in warm weather it is readily removed, the shirt-waist beneath looking neat and comfortable.

. . . .

THE COSTUME OF THE FUTURE:

We are told that the bloomer girl is going to outstrip her sisters because of her unconventional attire. At the State University at Berkeley, California, the young women students have decided to don the bloomer costume, which they declare best adapted for a school dress.

On October 3, 1894, the *Janesville Weekly Gazette* had already conceded the contest: "Today women in trousers riding a bicycle cause little or no comment, while three years ago a woman in ordinary street costume on a bicycle was hissed and booed at in the city streets."

Mourning Dress

With the reduction of formal restrictions in other kinds of dress, it might be expected that mourning dress would have lost its importance by the nineties. This does not seem to have been the case, however. Although there is no way to measure the degree of compliance there might have been with the manuals of etiquette, their written regulations were more stringent than ever before. Perhaps deep mourning was a kind of fashion that, like large sleeves, had its apogee on the very eve of its dismissal.

Widow's, which is the deepest of all mourning, consists of a plain gown of Henrietta cloth or bombazine, with crape upon it or not. . . . A tiny Marie Stuart cap, made of footing and net, is pinned on the head in the house . . . the length of the veil differs, of course, according to one's height, but the real widow's veil should reach to the edge of the skirt, back and front, and be finished by a hem a quarter of a yard wide. This is worn so that the whole figure is shrouded for three months; after that it is thrown back, and at the end of another three months, a single veil, reaching to the waist, is worn. This may be worn for six months, and crape then be laid aside.

My dear woman, feathers are not mourning. Jet, even if it be dull, is not mourning. Lace is not mourning, and except the ribbon used to tie your bonnet, ribbon, as a decoration, is certainly not permissible when mourning is worn. All these things are allowable with black, which is assumed for from one to three months, but their use when one is wearing crape is in extremely bad taste. (*Ladies' Home Journal,* August 1891)

Mourning dresses of Henrietta cloth were pictured and described in the B. Altman catalog for winter 1892–93. One such suit had a band of crepe near the hem, bordered on each edge with a tiny pleated frill of the dress goods. The basque bodice had crepe at front and in a small yoke in back and a crepe collar and cuffs. Prices were listed as, "for Quality 1, $38.00, and for Quality 2, $40.00."

ACCESSORIES

In July 1891 *The Ladies' Home Journal* remarked that "The fashionable brooch, for the lace pin has disappeared from among us, is the round one of twisted gold, with an enameled heart just in the centre." The heart was prominently featured in all jewelry during the nineties, but many other things were represented as well: a "golf-brooch" was mentioned in *Godey's* in April 1896 as being a miniature replica of a golf stick and ball, and chain-and-padlock bracelets were popular love tokens, as were cupids, bows and arrows, etc. An engagement ring, according to the current etiquette, could be of any stone, though diamonds were preferred. Earrings were small and close; any drops were very slender and small.

The watch chain, so very important in earlier years, was used less in the nineties, with the watch instead pinned to the bosom; the fashion was for "elegant small watches on the corsage" with a fancy watchpin for security. The advent of cycling brought about an entirely new way of wearing the watch—on the wrist, so that it could be consulted without a resultant accident to the cyclist. Wristwatches are increasingly featured in ads after mid-decade.

A dislike of the sun-darkened complexion, which was thought to indicate a coarse upbringing, made the parasol still a necessary accessory in the nineties. *The Ladies' Home Journal* in May 1890 claimed that "these dainty toys" were "made for the protection of beauty against its greatest enemy except time."

For morning or street use the fashionable girl carries her [parasol] en tout cas [in a complete case] of silk serge, in black or some dark shade, or in color to match the material or trimmings of her tailor-made gown or favorite walking costume, and these have handles of natural wood, elaborately carved, or of highly polished wood without ornamentation; if her gown is of India silk, a parasol of the same silk is in good taste; and if plaid is used in the construction of her costume, a parasol of plaid to match is appropriate . . . checkerboard plaids of black and white . . . are good for utility parasols, as they can be carried with almost any toilette.

With afternoon toilettes, and for watering place use, our elegante carries a dainty affair made of silk gauze or some thin material, and no lining to speak of, decorated with ruffles or shirrings, tiny puffs or rich fringes.

The fan was almost equally a subject for attention in the nineties.

> Fans are of moderate size, and, except for very ordinary use, are of lisse, or lace, or a combination of both. The Watteau fans might pass for heirlooms, they are so similar to those carried by our grandmothers; of lace in antique patterns with inserted medallions hand-painted in Watteau effects and colors. . . . There are some new varieties in Japanese fans with odd shapes and eccentric folds; those in black and gold or black and silver are most approved. (*Ladies' Home Journal*, August 1890)

Godey's said in February 1896 that "The Japanese black-and-gold fans are suitable for any occasion."

Gloves, too, were important in this decade, as usual, and were governed by etiquette as to type and occasion. The "sack" glove, one without a placket opening or buttons, had been in use for some years by 1890 and was appropriate with tailor-suits and morning dress during this decade, though a short one-button kid glove with prominent stitching was more fashionable. Colors were sometimes allowed, though not glaring contrasts, and the natural-tan leather glove was still favored for daytime. Nothing but the long white kid glove, of varying button lengths, was considered proper for dinner or evening dress.

Neck wear of many kinds was featured in fashion in the nineties. The feather boa of this period was short and tied with ribbons, loosely, just around the neck. It was most generally of white or black, though occasionally colored to match evening dresses, and made of clipped chicken feathers. The fichu was restyled and shaped somewhat like the old pelerine:

> The fichu renders important service in the economy of dress, and freshens up a half-worn toilette amazingly. The fichu, however, worn ungracefully is anything but attractive! To be pretty it must be fashioned of some soft, silky material, never in anything stiff or heavy. The nicest ones are filmy chiffon, or mousseline de soie, edged with frills of lace or pleatings of the material; they are crossed over the bust, and, when the ends are long, passed about the waist and tied behind; when short, the ends may be tucked away beneath the belt. (*Godey's,* February 1896)

HEADGEAR

Soft, short bangs and a very small topknot with more or less loose, short hair around the temples and cheeks, depending mostly on a woman's age, marked the hairstyles of the early nineties. The hair was usually knotted very high on the crown, especially for fashionable dress, but is often seen in photographs worn in a bun at the nape. This more relaxed style was worn by deliberately unfashionable young girls and older matrons, and most often without the bangs. Bangs, while popular throughout the nineties, were more controlled than in the past decade.

> While you let your hair show a little, do not put your bonnet far back; the shapes of the season are not suited to being placed in that way. And then remember too that the "bang" is no longer a heavy "mop," but should be a softly curled fringe that comes like a halo about one's face, not overshadowing the eyes or hiding the forehead, only shading and softening the entire face. The frizzy bang is essentially bad form. (*Ladies' Home Journal,* July 1890)

> The bolero, or Spanish hat, is shown in felt, and is becoming to young girls; in shape it is a conical crown, and then from it comes a broad brim which rolls up in turban fashion. Bonnets are always fashionable and a lady always feels herself well-dressed when she has one on. Velvet flowers are used upon them almost entirely to the exclusion of everything else.... Worn well off the face, the bang shows just enough to soften. (*Ladies' Home Journal,* October 1890)

By 1896 the bang was a thing of the past, and the growing-out hair was flattened down from a central part into waves along the temples: "Nine women out of ten look horribly homely with their hair plastered down and parted, and with the portion back of the ears bunched out like the wool of a Kafir chief . . . while the bang has been abused and overdone, it is more generally becoming than the now accepted mode of coiffure, where simplicity reigns supreme" (*Godey's,* February 1896).

It is very difficult to tell the 1890s bonnet from the hat, for bonnets no longer had back curtains, and some had substantial brims, like those of hats, at front and sides. In the first year or so of the decade, narrow, high shapes in dark colors predominated, with crushed satin and ostrich tips the preferred trim. A youthful, jaunty, sailor straw hat appears to have been a favorite all through the decade for sporty summer dress. A moderately wide-brimmed hat style in 1893 was typically decorated with crushed fabric and a pair of either flowers or feather ornaments fastened at the center front of the brim and sticking stiffly up like antennae at either side.

By mid-decade hats were quite substantial: they perched level on the head, somewhat to the front, and most of them were trimmed lavishly with crushed ribbon, velvet and cotton flowers, leaves, and feathers. Because of their perched appearance and the look of fluffed material at the back, these hats were still sometimes called "settin' hens." The toque shape, quite round and fitted low on the forehead, was a popular matronly style, and there were many styles of brimmed felts trimmed only with dyed and curled ostrich tips.

FOOTWEAR

Women's fashionable shoes and boots in the nineties had progressively more pointed toes. The favored dressy walking boot at mid-decade laced to above the ankle and had rather high, curved heels and pointed toes. The "Pingree Shoe," advertised in 1896 in *Godey's* at three dollars a pair, had about an inch-and-a-half, sharply incurved heel and a very long, needle-pointed toe and a soft tongue and broad laces. Black was no longer the only, or even the favored, color in shoes and boots; shades of champagne, bronze, and brown were advertised. Dress boots were often buttoned; both boot and glove buttoners—actually silver or steel hooks with ornate handles—were familiar dressing table ornaments. For dress, fancy low-cut shoes came in many styles, most with very high, curved heels. "Swedish kid shoes, and sandals with embroidery in silk, jet, or metal beads, are worn for house shoes; also the Queen Anne shoe, with long instep and large buckle of silver or brilliants. . . . Although black shoes and stockings are in good taste with almost any costume, still it must be confessed that a dainty foot dressing to match the gown does give a chic air to any get-up" (*Ladies' Home Journal,* May 1890).

Fashions for Men

The ordinary man of the nineties wore nothing but mass-produced clothing. Suits, separates, and overcoats were all available in standardized styles and sizes from many outlets, including mail order, and were relatively inexpensive. Zeigler's, of Janesville, Wisconsin, advertised in the *Janesville Weekly Gazette* in January 1894 a single-breasted sack suit, a business suit in sack or cutaway, and a double-breasted sack coat, each for seven dollars, and "Dress Suits, Sacks & Cutaway in Corkscrew, clays & Cheviots" for fifteen dollars.

The ideal male figure of the nineties presented a typically narrow silhouette, the small, short coats of the eighties becoming even more markedly skimpy during this decade. The sleeves were narrow and short enough to cause shirt cuffs to "pop" out about an inch. The sack coat, which was still the most universally worn style, was made very short, narrow of sleeve, close fitting, and with extremely narrow lapels and was rounded at the bottom fronts. To add to the skimpy effect, it was the custom to button the coat all the way to the top, especially the dressier versions. All other styles of coat were made to fit equally snugly, even the morning coat and the frock coat. The informal custom of wearing light pants with dark jackets persisted, but the three-pieced black wool sack suit was unquestionably the most common mode of dress. This suit was by the 1890s made in expensive as well as cheaper materials and became even more the business suit of choice. The sack jackets of the nineties, especially the dressier ones, were often fully lined. And while there were some cheap suits made in stripes or plaids and some light tweeds, black was still the universal choice in ordinary men's wear for this decade.

Trousers, too, were made narrower and fitted the leg in a close tubular style. Dress trousers lost all tendency to flare at the hem and became just a bit shorter, so as not to break unbecomingly at the shoe top. Most photographs of ordinary men, no matter what the occasion, show narrow-legged, black wool trousers without creases.

While dress shirts in advertisements are featured in colored stripes on white, white shirts seem to prevail in the photographs. Shirts were made trim and close to the body with a high armscye and narrow sleeves, to fit under the stylish jackets. Shirt collars were uniformly small and stiff, usually made on a band, and had small points. A multitude of manufacturers were still making the separate collars, some of linen or cotton and some of paper, which were intended to be fastened to neckbands by buttonholes and studs. Cuffs were starched to boardlike stiffness and, as noted, showed considerably below the coat sleeves. Photographs of men at work usually show either a plain, light-colored work shirt, most likely of blue chambray, or an ordinary white shirt, without its collar, with the sleeves rolled or pushed to the elbows. A vest is almost always worn over the work shirt, usually an old black one, and there is often also a long narrow necktie. Plaid cotton or flannel shirts of cotton or wool were advertised as cold-weather work shirts, and sweaters appear in many photographs of working men, ranging from the jersey through a V-necked military pullover to the cardigan-style coat sweater. Most photographs of farmers and other workers show retired dress clothing—black pants, vests, and even sack coats—used for work. The most common 1890s addition to the working man's wardrobe was the bib overall, which was meant to be worn over the ordinary clothing.

A black bow tie was commonly worn, even sometimes with working dress, and long narrow ties of black or patterned silk were often worn with suits, tied in a simple slipknot and with the ends left hanging.

As before, hats were made in every form, and the stiffened bowlers and derby styles gained so much in popularity during this decade that they occasionally even show up in a work-place photograph. A soft felt slouch hat in gray or black seems to have been most common and is even seen on men sitting behind the plow. Stocking caps, billed caps, and soft caps were plentiful. And as before, in photographs the hat is almost always in place, even when the coat and necktie have been laid aside because of the heat. Under the hats can be seen very short haircuts, almost shaved up the sides, and clipped necks. A center part was usual, and the hair was oiled. A generous walrus-style mustache appears with some frequency in the photographs.

Children's Styles

Information about and illustrations of children's styles were abundant in women's magazines in the nineties.

There are few changes in the fashion of garments for little folks. American mothers have very conservative taste in this regard, and generally prefer plain English styles to the elaborate French ones . . .

Tiny tots, of two to three years, are covered to the feet; for a girl of eight the frocks should reach only a few inches below the knee, and should increase in length with advancing years until at age twelve they should reach the ankle . . .

Little Spanish jackets of velvet of a darker or contrasting shade, are very pretty with high-pointed sleeves reaching to elbow, over a full undersleeve . . . these jackets are trimmed . . . with the tiniest possible pearl or cut-steel buttons . . .

Some plain cashmere frocks have high-necked waists shirred to form a yoke, and full bishop sleeves shirred at the wrist . . .

Gingham dresses are made with English yokes [smocked] or Hamburg embroidery and full bishop sleeves, gathered to a cuff of the same; these are corded with white around the yoke, the armholes, and the bottom of the waist.

The Nassau is the popular suit for small boys for ordinary wear, having jacket with square front, braided, or frogged, with black, and a simulated vest which is buttoned in at side seams and can be exchanged for a shirt-waist if desirable; this is worn with breeches or kilts, according to the age or size. Often the kilt is of plaid and the jacket of plain cloth.

Little "middies" suits of blue flannel with long trousers and sailor-jacket and cap, are still shown. Highland suits are in favor again, along with everything Scotch; these are very complete, with kilt of tartan, plain jacket, and the tartan crossing over the shoulder and fastened by a large cairngorm, and the pouch or spoon dangling in front.

"Lord Fauntleroy" suits are still worn, and nothing can be prettier with blouse and sash of washable silk, and large cuffs of vandyked Russian or Irish-point lace. . . . Windsor ties, in all the different plaids, are used for small boys. . . . The tuxedo dress suit for boys differs from the Eton regulation dress in that there is a short sacque coat instead of the jacket. (*Ladies' Home Journal,* May 1891)

The little woman of today is very sensibly dressed. Her hat shades her eyes, without being very weighty; her gown fits her prettily, and yet is not of a fabric so expensive that she cannot enjoy herself in it, and her coat is at once picturesque, and gives the needed amount of warmth. (*Ladies' Home Journal,* August 1891)

Such complete information as this was not found in every issue of the women's magazines, but there were illustrated children's clothing catalogs, and the newest readymades were present in all the stores. Fashions for children did change throughout the nineties, though not as readily as those for adults, the sleeve changes happening a bit later for little girls than for women, for example.

Black stockings were preferred in the nineties for both boys and girls, and both wore ankle-high black shoes for everyday, though the favored dress shoe for little girls was the black patent-leather "Mary Jane," with its rounded toe and single strap.

Dress hats even for very little children often echoed adult types, but both little boys and girls wore the wide, flat, sailor hats of dark straw with long ribbons, and little boys wore English school caps for everyday. Girls' hats are very grown-up in style but simpler in trim, though often surprisingly large and full of ribbon bows.

Summary

Women's fashions in the nineties changed greatly—from the upright, narrow cut of the late eighties to the flowing, full-busted and wide-bottomed look of 1900. Sleeves in this decade were especially expressive; they began with the extremely tight, short-wristed styles of the first year or two; then moved to gradually larger upper-arm puffs that blossomed rapidly from 1892 to 1896 into the largest sleeves yet seen in our period; and then collapsed into several kinds of full or partially full sleeves at the end of the century, often with additions that emphasized shoulder fullness. These extreme sleeve styles were not restricted to elaborate dress; they were also featured on inexpensive shirtwaists and wrappers. Even with all the variety, nineties fashions are easily identified as different from those of earlier decades.

For men, the trend was toward minimizing, with the narrowest cut, smallest jacket and hat, and trimmest silhouette possible. Even the hair was shaved close and high on the head, with the crown smoothed flat, during the height of the nineties mode.

Deciding on and acquiring clothing was entirely different in the 1890s than it had been in 1840. All of the rules had changed. No longer was there one basic cut, one ideal of good looks, or even just a single source of ideas. The ladies' magazines for the most part reached the end of their cycle of influence by the turn of the century; Paris became merely the wonderland of the wealthy, and no longer the dictatress of fashion for the multitude. The "New Woman" took action and made certain that her dress allowed her to participate more fully in all aspects of life. This trend ensured that women had more physical freedom and that the new styles of clothing were accessible to the millions, since it became possible to dress in separates and simpler clothing for appropriate occasions and, thus, economize in buying.

For men, who had long had the advantage of mass-produced clothing as well as access to the finer products of the tailoring trade, the nineties was merely a culmination of the trend toward the democratization of clothes.

None of this mass production stops the progress of high fashion; instead it allows a "proper" but economical parallel style to be fully socially acceptable for the first time, one that may be followed for daytime by rich and poor alike, thus contributing to the actuality of a national norm.

PHOTOGRAPHS
1890

1889–91

*Courtesy of the National Museum of
American History (C85.280.63)*

THE OCCASION, OR any other documentation, for this solemn group portrait is regrettably lost to us, but from the disparity in age and the earnestness of expression, it was apparently one of great importance to the sitters. This photograph, because of the amount of late-eighties detail of much of the costume, is debatably a late example from that decade, yet the upward-standing sleeve puff of the one dark silk bodice moves the apparent date of the portrait into the nineties. The upward sleeve puff was not in general use until 1891. The two capote bonnets, with their extreme narrowness and height, are late 1880s styles, and none of the women's hair is done with the softened puffs at the temples so popular by 1890. Many photographs taken in the first two years of this decade reflect surviving 1880s styles.

Standing at far left, the young lady wears a very tight-sleeved late-eighties style with a deep V corsage outlined by ruching or lace and a finely "wrinkled" short apron drape, which indicates the presence of some bustle padding. The woman seated at left in the checked dress, which is probably of black and white, has the easier straight sleeve, long-waisted torso, and side skirt pleats that show a date very close to 1890. It is worn over the swelling corset form of the late eighties and fitted with several darts at each side. The narrow, straight collar is finished at the neck with a small white frill. Tiny, closely spaced buttons close the front. Her capote bonnet has dark ribbon puffs rising vertically from a narrow rolled brim to an extreme height. She wears small drop earrings.

The other seated woman wears a dress made with a dark contrasting silk bodice and a printed silk skirt with a fold of trim near the hem that matches the bodice. The dark silk of the bodice reveals groups of small shoulder tucks released at the yoke line. There is a bit of fashionable fullness at the point of the shoulder, over the narrow, somewhat shortened sleeves. A fine lace frill finishes the cuff edge. The polka-dot printed silk skirt is made with a "Swiss waist"—that is, boned to a point at top and bottom—and the skirt is set on with fine gathers. A neat, rather pointed black boot shows at the hem, and her frou-frou bonnet of black net sets off the outfit.

Less distinguishable in detail is the light costume of the woman standing at right, but it can be seen to have a short, pointed basque bodice and almost no shoulder ease, and the skirt is set into the waistband at one side and drawn low across to the opposite side, a style used from 1888 through 1890. A soft white scarf of lace or silk is loosely tied around the high-collared bodice front.

The men all wear narrow sack coats over white shirts with identical small, folded-point collars and narrow trousers. The trousers of the young man seated at left are finely striped and apparently light-weight, and those on the gentleman seated at right are of wool tweed. The man standing at right wears a handsome suit with pinstriped black trousers and a cutaway sack. Two of the men wear white vests, either of linen or silk. One wears a bow tie and another a light-colored patterned tie. While the gentleman seated at center wears ankle-high tied shoes, the other visible men's shoes are pull-on, squared-toed, short boots.

1890

Courtesy of the California Historical Society
(File 65, FN-28402)

POSING AT THE annual "Ironmongers Picnic, 1890," a better-dressed gathering of ladies and gentlemen would be hard to find, proving that the working man and his family had the knowledge and the means to maintain a genteel and fashionable appearance.

Silhouetted at top center, under the little flag, are three figures that represent most clearly the common understanding of fashion. The central woman, who has two (champagne?) bottles in her hands, wears the pointiest little bonnet, the smartest bits of puffs at the tops of her narrow sleeves, an extremely narrow skirt, and a chatelaine bag clipped to her waist by a silver chain. These elements are all present in the very earliest 1890s fashion plates. Seated at her feet are two

women with equally up-to-date bonnets of a different shape, sporting the balanced, vertical feather trimming seen in the latest plates. One at least wears the same up-tufted sleeve points as the central figure.

Women's wrap styles in the image are varied. The long coat and hip-length jacket commonly featured in catalog and fashion plates are seen in plenty here; at least two are of seal or plush, and one has smart fur trim. Fur neck pieces are worn by some of the older women.

The gentlemen display enough variety in hat and suit styles to satisfy doubt as to their fashion sense, and one at least wears an overcoat in the newly popular short length.

JOSEPHINE BEASLEY POSED for this graceful, full-length portrait for Savannah photographer J. W. Wilson in an elegant and fashionable gown. According to the census records, Josephine Beasley was a domestic who worked in Savannah, and her husband, Abram, was, like his father before him, a butler. The evidence of this photograph supports the claim that servants, working people, and lower-middle-class families did know how to dress well and made the effort in spite of modest circumstances.

Both the sleeve cut of her dress and the divided overskirt style date this photograph at almost precisely 1890. The sleeve is still set out at the shoulder tip, and there is no ease at all, let alone puff, at the top, as there would be by 1891. While poorer women certainly wore their good dresses for a year or two, it seems likely that only a very new dress would inspire a full-length portrait.

The two-piece dress is made of heavy dark silk and has divided skirt fronts and a tablier underskirt of stitched-down pleats. It is smoothly fitted over the proper corset. The bodice and skirt fronts are trimmed with black braid and jet passementerie, and a small gold watch hangs at the bosom from one of the small jet buttons. Knitted silk mitts and a large black silk parasol with a curled bone handle complete the costume in perfect taste.

Mrs. Beasley wears her hair parted simply in the center and has not cut her short bangs in the manner typical of most of the nineties, though the soft fullness above the temples is quite up-to-date.

*Courtesy of the Association for the Study of Afro-American
Life and History, King-Tisdell Cottage*

THE EARLY BRACKET date for this photograph of Georgia Knox Horton, a "beloved" teacher at the West Broad Street School for black children in Savannah, Georgia, is determined by the elongated waist, so popular in 1890, and the presence of a hip-draped skirt and a falling back panel, details that do not persist long into the nineties. The sleeve type is very similar to those of nineties fashion plates, but these are set into a narrower shoulder than is usually seen before 1892.

Her careful corseting perfectly sets off the long-waisted, smoothly fitted bodice of cut velvet. The cut velvet is done in a pattern of squares in a color to set off the dress of heavy silk, which is of some moderately dark color, possibly deep brown, red, or green. The narrow sleeves are elegantly puffed and raised at the shoulders on a narrow shoulder line that went out of style in the late eighties but was revived when sleeves began to enlarge at the top. The tailored basque skirts of the bodice hang in points over a rather plain skirt that swells fashionably at the hips and displays the still-popular asymmetrically draped, "wrinkled" lap. A panel of the velvet hangs at the back, with one long edge showing down the left hip, where it apparently buttons.

GLASS-PLATE NEGATIVE, 1891–92

*Courtesy of the State Historical Society of Wisconsin
(WHi [V22/D] 1333)*

When this group of friends dropped by his studio in Black River Falls, Wisconsin, popular photographer Charles Van Schaick posed them in their attractive outdoor wear. Everyone in this small town knew "Charlie" and evidently humored his hobby of recording everything he wanted with his camera. This portrait may well be one of the impromptu ones he so often proposed. In this case, the overheated studio seems to have been a hardship, as a fan was needed to cool the sitters in their warm clothing.

It is the peculiar, upstanding puffs of the sleeves at the very top of the shoulders that pinpoint this date; this clothing was made to be worn in the winter of 1891, since by 1892 the most fashionable upper sleeves had some horizontal fullness and were not so vertical in their line.

The woman seated at left wears a close-fitting coat of tattersall-checked wool that shows several popular features of the day: a very high collar, high sleeve puffs, and the dagged black velvet and gilt braid trim on collar and cuffs. The large buttons down the double-breasted front show gilt ornaments on a dull steel ground, a newly popular style of button. The perky little "turk's cap" just reveals the short bangs, and it leaves room for a large hair ribbon at the back of the neck. The skirt of the wool dress or suit is of striped (probably gray and white) wool flannel, a common everyday winter choice. She wears a warm, knitted mitten on one hand.

The child is dressed in a cloak of small plaid. It has a full-length cape with the important tiny shoulder puffs. The cape is attached at the neck seam to the long-sleeved and close-fitting undercoat, which may be a short jacket. The coat front is unbuttoned to show the plaid woolen dress and the end of the silk moiré ribbon that serves as a sash. The colors used in the cloak are quite possibly deep-red on red-brown and cream, with the dress most likely in red plaid. A thick knitted bonnet with a rolled brim and three large yarn pom-poms is tied snugly under the chin. The child's straight, long hair is cut in extremely short bangs over the forehead.

The woman at back wears a simple high-collared, dark wool coat, probably full length. The side view gives us a good look at the manner of parting the hair to form short fluffy curls and bangs at the forehead, while the back hair is knotted tightly low on the crown. Both women wear tiny drop earrings.

GLASS-PLATE NEGATIVE, CA. 1891

Courtesy of the State Historical Society of Wisconsin
(WHi [V22/D] 1301)

POSING FOR A wedding portrait seems to be almost a part of the ceremony for this Black River Falls couple. The date is determined by the high point and lack of fullness in the upper sleeve of the bride's dress, which, even though a very cheap costume, would have had fashionable sleeves within a season of their introduction.

Plain working folk, these two have made an economical preparation for their wedding day. The bride has chosen to wear an inexpensive, certainly readymade, dress of black or navy-blue with white braid trim, probably just purchased. At the neck, she has added a drooping white silk ribbon neck bow and fastened it with a bar pin. The dress still shows heavy creasing, possibly still from the dry goods store. A length of plain veiling that looks like cheesecloth (the raw edges are visible) has been thrown over her head and shoulders, as has the trailing wreath of wax orange blossoms over the crown, both possibly provided by the photographer for the occasion.

The groom is splendid in his morning suit, a long black coat and striped trousers, with a properly stiff white shirtfront and narrow knotted tie. His walrus mustache is set off by a small chinwhisker below his lower lip, and his hair is cropped very short and parted to one side. Only his scuffed and wrinkled boots, and perhaps his heavy working man's hands, testify to his situation in life. It is quite possible that he was one of the lumberjacks who lived in the area.

GLASS-PLATE NEGATIVE, 1891–93

Courtesy of the State Historical Society of Wisconsin
(WHi [V2] 1154)

CHARLES VAN SCHAICK took this photograph of his wife on an outing near Black River Falls. Because of the narrow upper-sleeve fullness, still held close to the arm, and the asymmetrical closing of the bodice, the earliest date for this photograph is 1891. Some speculation is necessary in dating this image: if, as seems likely, the costume is a cotton twill or duck "camp suit," it would surely have been worn for several years; if it is simply a walking dress, it would not have been worn for camping until it was at least a year old. In either case, an extended bracket date is necessary.

Mrs. Van Schaick appears as chief cook and pot-washer for at least one tent and is dressed in what passes for camp clothing for women. Probably made of khaki cotton twill, the suit has a skirt with enough flare for walking and a narrow flounce to hold it away from the feet. The jacket, however, is as closely fitted as for any other day dress and requires a corset underneath. It is buttoned down with tiresome small buttons and has full-length sleeves with the fashionable standing puff at the shoulder. We cannot see her feet, but high-laced shoes or hiking boots were worn with such outdoor clothing.

IN A RELAXED pose against a lush canyon wall, obviously enjoying some kind of outing, these men and boys are all dressed more or less in everyday clothing, though some are in more casual attire than others; soft sweaters and shirt-jackets are worn by several of the men. Coat sweaters show up for the first time in 1890s photographs of men's leisure wear.

Remarkable in this photo are the examples of the cap, ranging from the large, heavy tweed "Irish"-style cap so often found in men's hat advertisements to a soft, crushed version at left to a very wide and flat soft crown at upper center to a forage cap at upper left. The two derby styles both accompany white shirts; two other gentlemen wear soft felts. One man, near the center, wears a hard felt bowler shape with narrow brim, but it is in a surprisingly light color.

GLASS-PLATE NEGATIVE, 1892–95

Courtesy of the State Historical Society of Wisconsin
(WHi [V2] 1154)

THIS BLACK RIVER FALLS early spring-cleaning scene, taken by Charles Van Schaick, has traditionally been thought to present the back of a house; however, it is more likely the façade of a summer kitchen, a lean-to that was added on like a shed at the back of many small-town houses. Such a room provided a safe storage place for wash tubs and equipment, as well as serving as a frozen-food locker during the winter months and as a place to cook and can without heating up the house in summer. The sleeves of the wrapper date this photograph; such extreme, vertical puffs are first seen in fashion plates in late 1891. Wrapper sleeves closely followed the dictates of fashion.

The young woman, said to be Mrs. Van Schaick, wears a good wrapper, cut in Mother Hubbard style, with fullness gathered all around into a straight yoke and with extremely smart high-puffed, full-length narrow sleeves that she has pushed up to her elbows. The dress has a small, pointed self-collar, and is worn belted in.

Her visitor is bundled up in a dark wool everyday blanket shawl with striped borders crossing in plaids at the corners and with fringe all around, and her skirt can be seen to be one of the side-draped models with the low back bustle drape of 1889–90. Both young women wear their hair in short bangs, with the knot of hair high at the top of the head.

The baby, warmly dressed and sitting on a folded blanket in his highchair, appears to be wearing soft leather bootees or moccasins. His bonnet and sweater are knitted, and he wears an ankle-length dress, probably of white wool flannel.

1892–94

Courtesy of the Museum of American Textile History
(P 1918.1)

THIS PHOTOGRAPH WAS taken in a studio somewhere in the Merrimack River Valley, where the
textile mills were still active through the nineties and where many women found employment.
Mill girls in the 1890s were still having their pictures taken in full working dress, complete with
tools. It is evident from both written records and
remaining photographs that girls in the weaving
room generally dressed quite well for work, wearing good clothing, though not their best, with
protective aprons and sometimes sleeves.

It is the puffed, short oversleeves and narrow
shoulder line that date this dress. The fullness of
this sleeve is very modest, indicating that the
dress was made and worn early in the dated
bracket, though it is true that somewhat outdated
clothing was often worn in the workplace.

This excellent image shows a young woman
in a pretty, dark silk print with small puffed
oversleeves over narrow, long sleeves covered by
(probably) knitted protective sleeves tacked in
place. She even wears a dressy, large black silk
bow at the neck, and a gold watch chain hangs
beside the small, closely spaced buttons. A full-
length apron protects the silk dress. Except for
the apron and sleeve covers, she is dressed as she
would be for any occasion, even to the corset
underneath. In her leather tool belt, she carries
a reed-hook, and in her hands she holds two
shuttles and a bobbin.

June 30, 1891

Courtesy of the San Francisco Public Library (MC)

A YOUNG SAN FRANCISCO girl, with the last name of Meussdorfer, poses here for a portrait on her fourteenth birthday.

The sleeves and collar of this fashionable dark silk dress are quite up-to-date for 1891, and the young lady's face is framed by a grown-up pompadour hairstyle and a sheer girlish hat of horsehair and straw braid. The narrow hat strings hang untied under the brim. The dress is apparently of sheer silk, woven in a striped pattern, and is so dark as to make us believe that it is black; an uncharacteristically dark pointed collar of lace is worn with it, and the combination brings to mind mourning dress. The extremely fashionable puffs of the bishop sleeves, the rosette-trimmed bodice, and the silk flounces testify to the quality of the costume. Neat black boots with moderately pointed toes show to the ankles, and the dress comes to the boot tops.

GLASS-PLATE NEGATIVE, CA. 1892

*Courtesy of the State Historical Society of Wisconsin
(WHi [V24] 1695)*

CHARLES VAN SCHAICK, as the self-appointed chronicler of his town, took this photograph, probably just before Easter 1892, of a Black River Falls milliner and her family. The little clapboard building, with its curtained windows, may well have served as both home and shop to this young milliner, and on this warm spring day it is a charming showcase for her wares. Even her houseplants are getting an airing.

The date is based on the fashionable 1892-style sleeves of the riding dress shown on the woman on horseback: they have modest fullness, rise high at the shoulder, and the puff ends well above the elbow. The trim wool suit worn by the young milliner is made with the narrow shoulder and vertical sleeve puffs brand-new in late 1890, and it has a short fitted bodice. The skirt is cut short enough for walking, and low-heeled black ankle boots show beneath the hem.

Behind her against the wall is a board covered with black fabric, probably velvet, on which she displays the pretty new silk, velvet, and cotton flowers with which she will trim bonnets this year. Above the board hangs a leghorn straw bonnet and a few white ribbons and bows. But it is the little tree branch with its surprising fruit of fancy bonnets that catches the eye; here the artiste has placed her most delectable creations to tempt the ladies. Besides the wide-brimmed styles piled with flowers and bows, there are one or two of the tiny bonnets with pointed brims and vertical trimming which are so popular.

At the front of the stoop, her little boy pushes a toy wheelbarrow full of hat trimmings; this is another little display contrived by the milliner, as assuredly the trimmings were not commonly used as toys. The child wears a strange little hat composed of a round skullcap under a board and pom-pom and a double-breasted plaid coat. A silk scarf is tied at his throat, and he wears high boots and black stockings. Not quite so warmly dressed is the older sister, who sits on the porch in her dark wool dress and pinafore apron rocking her doll.

Street photographs done by "Charlie" Van Schaick are plentiful still in Black River Falls, and we know that the livery stable is just down the street from this shop, nearly next door. The young girl on horseback may just be riding by, or may be related to the family. Her midcalf-length, black riding dress is in good fashion, of wool, and has a very deep flounce with pleats concentrated at the back. Riding boots show in the sidesaddle posture. A wide-brimmed straw hat seems an unlikely style for riding, but it is held firmly on the head by ties under the chin.

THE VERY PICTURE of working men of the nineties, these gents pose in their coat sweaters and derbies at a table, with a rumpled paper "tablecloth," making believe that they are sharing an after-work libation at a tavern. Despite the suggestive whiskey bottle, one holds a beer stein and one a water tumbler, probably props provided by the photographer.

Nineties men are typified by such short, plastered-down haircuts and this style of mustache. Their coat sweaters and narrow-brimmed hats are further identifying factors. These men are nearly twins in their appearance and dress and may in fact be brothers; little distinguishes them other than that one parts his slicked-down hair in the center, the other at one side, and there is perhaps a slight difference in the mustache shape. Both wear plain dark work shirts, though only one wears a tie, and narrow-legged, worn woolen trousers. The boots are similar, but those on the left are apparently of a dark buckskin. The one sweater worn open shows a double-breasted, rounded-front vest underneath.

DECEMBER 17, 1892

Courtesy of the California State Library (21.208)

WHILE USEFUL MAINLY as a record of men's everyday cap and hat styles in the nineties, this group picture of the employees of the San Francisco Stove Works also offers some other information about work clothing. The date is chalked on the board at the men's feet.

An interesting style of work shirt is seen on the two men at lower left: of soft material, either of wool or of cotton chambray, these shirts have narrow tucks running down the fronts. They are probably, like so many work shirts, in shades of gray or blue.

The group is unique in that only two men are wearing vests, usually such an indispensable wardrobe item. The man second from right in the bottom row wears a plaid vest that may be a sweater vest. Many, but not all, of the men wear braces, and one wears a bibbed overall. At upper left, one man wears a dark woolen shirt with a "plastron" type of bib front buttoned in place and a narrow band collar.

At center front a well-dressed man, probably the owner, wears good striped trousers and a matched sack and vest, a large silk necktie under his small turn-down collar, and a good felt bowler.

THIS YOUNG COUPLE, photographed on the dusty plains "At Rosedale Ranch, 1892," near Bakersfield, California, seem to be fairly recent settlers; their small, plain house must be about a year old, judging from the row of young trees across the front.

The optimism expressed by these small trees, the neat house and outbuildings, and the attitudes of the people in such a bleak setting make a powerful statement about human spirit. The young mother poses in her Sunday best. Complete with full corset and hat, she is but little out of date. Her wool "best" dress is of a style fashionable about two years before the date of this photograph, having straight overskirt fronts, tablier underskirt, and strongly contrasting velvet trim. At a guess, the velvet is probably of a deep burgundy color, or perhaps dark brown, and the wool may be a light cream. The felt hat certainly matches the velvet trim, and upon closer view, ostrich tips may trim the hat. She is only pretending, of course, to be working; while she undoubtedly does do the hoeing, as well as

caring for the house, the child, the trees and flowers, the vegetable garden, and any stock, her dress for such chores would be quite different from what she is wearing. In the hot, dry climate of Bakersfield, a real option for such work would have been the loose freedom of the Mother Hubbard.

The little boy is as well dressed as any city child in his white middy, short dark pants, and broad sailor hat. Father, who is also merely posing with his horses, may actually have been plowing the fields before pulling the team up for the photograph. In good Western style, he wears either denims or wool trousers tucked into his high pull-on boots, and his white shirt and black wool vest, like work clothing for farmers anywhere in the nation, are retired dress clothing. He wears a neckerchief, and his large felt hat, also quite Western in style, shades him from the sun. Rows of growing crops and outbuildings in the background are an important and intentional part of this picture, as much so as the team of horses and the plow.

IN THIS PHOTOGRAPH we find a vision of the "ideal life" in California in the nineties: a snug clapboard ranch house with a flower garden and fruit trees, boys and horses, and even a calf and a dog. Probably some of the men are employees; the presence of the calf indicates that the farm supports a herd of milk cows, and many hands were probably required to keep the work going. Immediate confirmation of the date is to be found in the leg-o'-mutton sleeves; these are the large but still somewhat drooping styles worn just before the shoulder line became stiffly horizontal in 1895–96.

The family members pictured are beautifully dressed. The ladies are typical of women all over the country in their large-sleeved styles and corsets. The young woman near the center wears a striped cotton shirtwaist that is very up-to-date for 1895, with the crisp cotton sleeves made very full and only slightly tapered to the cuff, and with her black wool skirt she wears a snug leather belt. On the far right, the older woman wears a very similar outfit, with the more drooping sleeves of 1893, their cuffs hanging well over the hand. Both women wear small ribbon ties at the neck, but each in a different manner.

The two young women between them wear the outdated sleeves of the past year, with smaller puffs at the top, one in the contrasting style so much featured in 1892 fashion plates. Their hair is identically done, with short bangs and crown hair pulled to the back. The youngest girl in the short skirt is wearing high-topped laced boots and black stockings and a youthful style of puffing in the contrast material across the yoke.

The young boy holding the horses is wearing only his suspendered woolen trousers and dark shirt, but he carries his soft black felt hat. Next to him, we see dark bibbed overalls, tucked into tall boots, and a cloth cap. The littlest fellow wears his bibbed coverall suit over a long-sleeved white shirt, and the man holding him wears a light-plaid shirt and light trousers, probably khaki.

1893–96

Courtesy of the Connecticut Historical Society (882)

AT THE CHAPIL PLANE works, in Hartford, Connecticut, the workers wear their good shirtwaists at their jobs, despite the rough appearance of the shop and the menial tasks to be done. Not even protected by sleeve guards, these waists could probably be worn for only one day, two at most, before they had to be either washed by hand or in the manual washing machine and then starched, dampened, and ironed. It says something about the desire to appear feminine and well-groomed in the nineties that these women persisted in wearing them under such circumstances. Overwhelming evidence proves that only a properly cut alternative blouse would have been appealing, and even a dark fabric shirtwaist made in this style would have to be laundered in much the same manner, if not as frequently. Further testimony to the importance placed on appearance is the fact that one, at least, if not all, of the young women is definitely corseted.

1893–96

Courtesy of the California Historical Society (21.210)

THE ONLY MEANS of arriving at a date for this photograph taken outside of Max Mueller's blacksmith shop in Sacramento is to note the sleeve style worn by the girl; such sleeves cannot date before 1893, and by 1897 they would not have been worn.

Everything in this photograph is evocative of the life of a California community in the nineties—the blacksmith shop with its windmill and water tank in back, the wagon and cart waiting in front, and even the posters on the shed, one advertising a local tailor who makes suits to order for $12.50 and another pushing chocolates and cocoas.

The girl wears a bloused black silk, or more likely cotton sateen, waist with leg-o'-mutton sleeves, and over her midcalf-length skirt she wears a lace-edged apron, as if she had just come from the kitchen to call the men to lunch. Her dark stockings are not black but either brown or red, and her flat-heeled everyday shoes are al-

most like slippers. Her hair is pulled straight back and is probably worn in a long fall or braid and tied at the nape with ribbons.

The oldest gentleman wears black wool trousers, a short vest, and a dark wool shirt. His flat-crowned black felt hat has a modest brim. And since the shoes he wears are not adequate for wear around the forge, he is either a semi-retired owner or an old handyman.

The other men wear conspicuously thick-soled boots or clogs, no doubt insurance against stepping on live coals or nails while working at the forge. The central figure wears a short vest over a sweater, with a white undershirt or shirt front showing at the neck, and somewhat loose denim trousers that probably cover his ordinary woolen ones. He wears a flat cap. The man at right wears overalls over his white shirt and ordinary pants and a rather long, loose sack coat of ancient vintage. A cloth cap protects his hair.

THE MEMBERS OF this Wilmette, Illinois, grade school class are likely from fairly affluent families, as Wilmette was at this time a wealthy suburb of Chicago. However, there is little appreciable difference, to modern eyes, in the dress of these children and the dress of less-advantaged boys and girls seen in other photographs.

The sleeves' shape and fullness are the main telling characteristics of fashion in the nineties. In both the fashion plate and the photograph, young girls' dresses show sleeve changes occurring only slightly later than women's, while bodice and skirt styling retains certain juvenile characteristics. The dresses worn by these students reflect the full, grown-up range of sleeve variations that were featured on almost every contemporary girlish dress style.

The young lady at center front in the light skirt and tunic, with arms akimbo, has the most extravagantly large sleeves, and they are thickly pleated into the very high armscye in mid-decade fashion. The lower sleeves are very tight and rise well up the arm into the droop of the full upper sleeve. Only the sleeves of the light-colored costume at upper left (on the girl with the hat) approach these for size. The other girls wear a range of more conservative sleeves, from the simple raised puffs and very slightly enlarged upper arm to a smaller "gigot" puff; but all of their sleeves are tight on the lower arm. Two of the dresses have shoulder ruffles set into the seam for accent.

Bodice shapes vary, from the tailored bretelle fashion on the tall girl in the front row to yoked styles to puffed, gathered, and even plain fronts. The skirts are uniformly gathered. In one case only, at upper left, the waistline appears long and is finished with a soft fold around the hips, which is due to the presence of a wide ribbon sash. All of the dresses have high band collars, and all actual waistlines are at the normal waist.

Many of the girls wear knitted tam-o'-shanter caps, and the girl at upper left wears an astonishingly up-to-date hat with twin symmetrically placed vertical trimmings, identical to women's styles of 1893; these are not usually worn by girls, and this one may have been borrowed from an older relative for the occasion. One seated girl wears a more girlish small hat with an upturned brim. Two of the girls, probably sisters, wear identical elbow-length capes of patterned wool, and the seated little girl in the small hat wears a handsomely detailed elbow cape of tweed, which is possibly the shoulder cape of a cloak.

Most of the boys wear double-breasted wool English jackets, white shirts, and matching knee-length straight trousers. All wear neckties. One smaller boy near the center has wide white or at least light-colored revers turned back over his black double-breasted jacket. While one boy is hatless, all the others—except the lad at upper right, who wears a very grown-up black fedora—wear wool caps.

All the children wear black stockings, probably held up by garter belts, and black high-topped ankle boots. The girls' are mostly buttoned at the sides, and the boys' are laced into hooks at the ankles and tied.

ENTITLED SIMPLY "Mexican Family, Mora Valley, New Mexico," this photograph shows an extended family that is probably representative of the area's poorer ranchers. There are few characteristics in the clothing worn that would make it possible to pinpoint the date here, so it is fortunate that the photographer dated the image. More than most, this photograph gives the common, bottom line of dress throughout the decade.

Both of the women cover their heads in an ethnic manner common to their heritage, but their dresses differ very little from what every farm wife in the country might have worn throughout the decade for everyday; they are, in fact, made in the same manner as working dresses of the previous decade, a style that prevailed, with minor changes, through the nineties. The obvious difference here is that these women are not corseted. Also, it is possible that these dresses are the best, if not the only ones, these women have.

The younger woman's dress is clearly visible. It is made with a fitted front-fastening bodice and has plain, somewhat loose sleeves set high on the shoulder. The full skirt is gathered all around, hangs nearly to the ground, and is apparently covered in front by a long, full, gathered apron. The older woman has a dark calico dress or shirt-waist with white-trimmed frills at the cuffs, and she wears a full, long apron or separate skirt of faint (probably faded) checks. The skirts of both dresses are apparently very full.

The men dress in the same style trousers and shirts that any farmer or rancher would wear in the field, one with a single-breasted dark vest buttoned down and a white shirt and a wide-brimmed felt hat, while the other wears a light-colored vest buttoned over his shirt. A wide-brimmed felt hat is turned up sharply over this man's face. Even the youngster wears a dark vest over his long-sleeved shirt and dungarees, and his black felt hat is turned back like the men's. The baby is nicely dressed, with a fitted frock and leather shoes.

THIS YOUNG COUPLE, Effie and Alonzo Kinder, farmed rented property on Maple Ridge, about five miles northwest of the small southern Wisconsin town of Boscobel. While never well-to-do, Effie is known to have kept herself and her family well-dressed and presentable, to which this portrait bears witness.

The good-looking walking dress she wears for this portrait is of black wool, and it has the latest huge, pleated sleeves with fancy pointed shoulder yokes of black velvet lying out along the tops. The high velvet collar is set off by a bar pin. Her basque bodice buttons snugly over the stylish corset, and the skirt is gored in the accepted trumpet shape. Effie's severe hairstyle is a combination of the no-nonsense approach of a busy young mother and a nostalgic fondness for the tiny crimped bangs of her girlhood. (A portrait of her as a child appears in chapter 5's 1880s photographs.)

Alonzo wears what is probably his wedding suit: a sack coat and matching vest over striped black trousers. His tie, worn with a black shirt, is a wide, soft bow of light silk. A gold watch chain loops at the lower vest front, where the coat curves away.

Their sons, Howard and Anson Jerome, born in 1890 and 1892, respectively, wear plaid cotton shirts with frills down the fronts and around the wide collars and white ribbon bow ties. Their trousers are short, and their black stockings show over well-polished ankle boots.

1895

Courtesy of the Valentine Museum (72.23.3)

GERTRUDE BUCKNER GRADUATED from nursing school in 1895, and this is her graduation photograph, taken at the Foster Studio in Richmond, Virginia.

So thin as not to need a corset at all, Miss Buckner still wears one under this stiffly starched two-piece uniform, which consists of a white shirtwaist, with a stiff standing collar, tucked into a Swiss-waisted starched skirt. The fact that sleeve styles are reflected in such uniforms, when their care is so much more time-consuming than plain sleeves, is most interesting.

Gertrude does not wear bangs, but instead wears her curly hair parted in the center and neatly brushed back from her temples, with soft fullness at either side under the prim nurse's cap.

1895

Courtesy of the Atlanta History Center (4209)

THIS PHOTOGRAPH WAS used as an illustration for an article on bicycling that was printed in the *Atlanta Constitution* on August 25, 1895. Along with all the other periodicals read by women in the nineties, this newspaper paid a great deal of attention at mid-decade to the changing trend in women's sportswear, which was sparked by the bicycle mania.

This young Atlanta girl still wears the very long skirts soon to be displaced by what American women called "bicycling attire," mainly somewhat shorter, fuller skirts, sometimes with trousers hidden underneath, but often with the much maligned full-blown bloomer pants legs bravely showing under the shortened skirts.

There is nothing to distinguish this woolen dress with its leg-o'-mutton sleeves from any walking dress of 1893–95. The shoulders of the bodice are already widening from the extremely narrow cut, and the sleeves are slightly stiffened in their folds. The boned waist is finished with a rosette at each side at the waistband, and the skirt is plain and gored. The dress is apparently worn over the usual tight corset. Well before the end of the decade, however, corset styles especially designed for cyclists were offered; these new corsets had the hips cut high, and the stays cut well below the arm, where they might otherwise chafe.

1895–98

*Courtesy of the National Archives,
Signal Corps Collection (111-SC-89608)*

A LOG RANCH house is the background for this photograph, labeled "Group at Wilkins, New Mexico," of settlers with their children and a Native American woman, possibly a domestic servant. The very large sleeves and pronounced shoulder flounces at right set the bracket dates for the photograph at the middle of the decade.

In spite of their obviously remote location, the everyday clothing of the women in this picture is no different from that of women anywhere else in the country. The dress worn by the woman at center is the oldest, dating from about 1891–92, however all the dresses appear much washed and faded and quite old and worn. All of the garments are of cotton wash fabric and are mainly house-dress styles. Some were probably purchased and some obviously homemade. On the woman standing just left of center, in the same spotted dark print as the central dress (from the same bolt of material), is a housedress, made probably in 1892, showing the small leg-o'-mutton-style sleeve and the easy, gathered bodice used throughout the decade for working dress. The woman at right wears a light cotton housedress similar to those available through mail-order catalogs and somewhat in an 1893 fashion, featuring gathered shoulder bretelles and full, drooping sleeves. It is notable that all three of these women are corseted. Each woman no doubt owned better clothing in more up-to-date styles.

The Native American woman, seated in the folding chair, wears moccasins and has a hand-woven blanket on one shoulder that drapes over the chair back. It is impossible to tell from the shoulder of her garment whether the bodice matches the worn calico skirt, which has a deep flounce and a contrasting band at the hem.

The little fellow at left is dressed in a frock of calico, which he wears over black stockings and ankle shoes. His flat-topped cap has wide military braid around the crown. The barefooted smaller boy who leans against the Indian woman is quite differently dressed in a short smock over short cotton trousers.

The men's attire is unremarkable, having the same unironed cotton shirts, denim or wool trousers, vests, suspenders, and felt hats found all over the country. Or maybe that is remarkable.

GLASS-PLATE NEGATIVE, 1895–1900

*Courtesy of the State Historical Society of Wisconsin
(WHi [X3] 41553)*

THE EYE OF Gerhart Gesel was taken by any number of picturesque situations in Alma, Wisconsin, and he quite obviously took pleasure in posing these quaintly dressed little girls to suit his fancy. The girls' dresses have the very full bishop sleeve not seen before about 1895 but which lasted throughout the decade in children's wear.

Both children wear pinafore aprons over their rather dark dresses, the pinafores differing only in material and in the amount of fabric in the gathered sleeve cap. Such garments fastened down the back and came to the hems of the dresses.

The sunbonnets are also made alike, except that the dark one has a longer skirt, and shows where the strings pull it together and tie in back. Black stockings and flat-heeled ankle-high shoes, with their side-buttoned scallops, complete the everyday attire of these young friends or sisters.

The summer edition of the Butterick pattern catalog in 1899 featured many garments similar to those worn by these girls, including apron styles identical to that on the girl at left plus separate sleeve patterns for a "Girl's Bishop Dress Sleeve," like those of both dresses.

1895–97

Courtesy of the Valentine Museum (X60.7.1)

BABY ALICE BLAIR poses contentedly for Heustis Cook with her nurse, Pinkie. The young nurse wears a smart black dress with enormous (and datable) leg-o'-mutton sleeves under a puffy fichu of white lawn and (probably) Valenciennes lace. She wears a lace-trimmed white cap on her center-parted hair, and its white ribbon loops fall behind her ears at either side. The fichu and cap are meant to define her position as nursemaid.

The baby's dress is probably of nainsook, the finest white cotton weave, and is made with a waistband, into which the long skirt is gathered. The sleeves are very full and long and are gathered into narrow cuffs with Valenciennes lace frills. Wide shoulder ruffles are edged with matching lace. The white undershirt sleeves may be seen underneath.

MAY 14, 1896

Courtesy of the Library of Congress
(7467 LC-US262 34430)

SOMEWHERE IN KENTUCKY or Tennessee, a crowd gathers at the railroad station to send the "First Regiment, D.C.V.," off to camp to serve in the Spanish-American War. It is a well-dressed throng for the most part, and fine hats are especially noticeable: most of the men's are bowlers or derbies; most of the women's are sailor hats with straight brims and are generally piled with flowers and ribbons.

The back and side views of women's skirts clearly show the gored fullness, now concentrated at the back, and the smooth sweep of the skirt front. The set of the bodice back may also be seen in detail at right, under the parasol, where the shirtwaist sleeves are thickly pleated into the high shoulder line; the back is smooth and tight, and the skirt is supported with a rounded hip pad.

Several boys in knicker suits are in evidence: the one at left in a small jockey cap, the one in the foreground in a dark felt, and the more central one in a small soft cap. The children all wear black stockings. The little black boy at right wears knickers and black stockings, too, and his many-pocketed long jacket appears to be of canvas or linen.

Glass-Plate Negative, July 26, 1896

Courtesy of the Museum of New Mexico (77440)

June 30, 1894: Went to Miss Brown's this morning to "try on" my new dresses she is making for me. A very pretty white dotted swiss and pink chambray.
—Martha Farnsworth, *Plainswoman: The Diary of Martha Farnsworth*

THIS CHARMING PORTRAIT is important, in spite of the severe damage to the plate, because of its included date. The inscription on this photograph of a young New Mexico woman pretending to read a letter from a beau reads: "He says he loves me but I don't believe it. July 26–'96." The dresses here show the all-important sleeve treatment for both women's and girls' dresses in 1896. The shoulder flounce of the young woman's dress is a special detail that became popular after mid-decade, especially for summer dresses.

Most prominently visible is the dress of the child at right, which is of a light-colored, probably cream, challis or soft cotton with small dots and made with a broad bertha collar bound with satin and a fine lace frill that lies horizontally out over the tops of the leg-o'-mutton sleeves. A frill of the wide lace edges the neckline, and there are small buttons down the bodice front. A ribbon belt is finished at front in a rosette. The younger girl's dress is of the same fabric, but much more plainly made, having a sailor collar and a plain waist, but it does have the same sleeve treatment.

Only the wide, ruffled bertha collar and the belt around the slim waist are clearly seen in the young lady's white summer dress, but she wears a small gold heart on a gold chain at her neck, and her petticoat is edged deeply with white lace. A fine frill is used at the wrist.

GLASS-PLATE NEGATIVE, SEPTEMBER 1896

Courtesy of the State Historical Society of Wisconsin
(WHi [V2] 89)

ALWAYS THE HISTORIAN, Charles Van Schaick photographed this Norwegian couple in La Crosse, a northern Wisconsin city, as they walked toward him down the street. The two, probably recent settlers, have most likely come to attend the Interstate Fair, which is advertised on the banner hung over the street. The actual date for this photograph has been extrapolated from the September days enumerated on this banner; the only year in the nineties when Sunday fell on September 17, given that state fairs in Wisconsin traditionally end on a Sunday, is 1896.

The walking suit worn by this woman is not terribly out of style, and she will no doubt meet many women wearing similar outfits to the fair. The bodice is made with revers that open over a snowy white shirtfront, and the sleeves have the drooping shape of 1893, rather than the stiff, supported horizontal of 1896; there are deep gathers, not pleats, in the top. Still, the entire costume has an "old-country" flavor not in its cut and fashion but in how it is worn. For one thing, she wears the mannish hat in an uncompromising manner, without any trimming whatsoever, which, in the New World, certainly marks its wearer as "different."

One other feature sure to have been noticed by townswomen is that this strong young "foreign" woman wears no corset. Her apron, while it would probably not be worn by many American women at fair time on the downtown streets, is not so unusual that by itself it would draw attention to her. The woman seems to be staunchly unaware of any undue attention, if she has indeed attracted any. Her confident stride is at least the match of her husband's, who is left a bit in her lea.

The shirt he wears is not white; rather, it seems to be of a light-colored soft fabric, probably blue, and is buttoned to the neck. His wide suspenders show, and he is remarkable for wearing neither a tie nor a vest. His hat, however, is a derby shape with a somewhat relaxed brim, no different from what might be seen on any farmer.

GLASS-PLATE NEGATIVE, CA. 1896

*Courtesy of the State Historical Society of Wisconsin
(WHi [V22/D] 1438)*

THE DATE OF this portrait of a handsome elderly couple, probably taken to celebrate some special occasion, perhaps a wedding anniversary, is indicated by the breadth of the sleeve puffs of the lady's suit and the horizontal nature of the decorated shoulder panels, both very new in 1896. The plain background framing them has the appearance of the back of a theater set and does not appear to be a part of photographer Charles Van Schaick's studio, though the photograph is from his collection.

The woman wears the hairstyle newly favored, with no bangs, short waved hair at front, a central part, and a knot of hair so close to the top of the crown that the decorative comb tucked in front of it appears to have been driven into the skull. The collar and sleeve edges of the heavy black silk dress are finished with seed-shaped jet beads and outlined in frills of sheer black lace. A ribbon sash ties at one side of the waist, and a wide matching bow finishes the back of the high collar. The bodice front is softly gathered, and a fine gold watch chain is doubled back and forth at the puffed front. A bar pin is fastened at the throat, and one white violet decorates her corsage.

In his neat black sack suit and stiff shirt cuffs, the walrus-whiskered old gentleman is fully as spruce and trim as she. Small folded-down collar points frame the large knot of a wide black silk tie.

CALIFORNIAN NELLIE REED MAYON poses for this portrait in her new tweed suit, made in the latest style for 1896, with the sleeves the largest possible size. These enormous sleeves are taken into the extremely narrow shoulders with large, bulky pleats, stiffly inner-lined, which add to the wide horizontal effect. Most tailors had widened the bodice shoulder line by this date in order to better support the heavy sleeves. The lapels of the suit reach all the way to the shoulder seams, also a typical treatment in 1896 fashion plates. This extreme style did not last more than two seasons, 1895 and 1896, in the fashion plates.

In the neckline, Nellie wears a jabot of lace fastened with a gold brooch. Other important fashion notes for mid-decade are the extra-large buttons, of mother-of-pearl, and the crimped hair parted in the center, the most popular substitute for bangs.

The front breadth of Nellie's suit skirt is cut in an A shape, the side gores are set on with the straight edge to the bias of the front, and a deep gusset will typically have been set into straight lengths at the back, probably box-pleated at center back, for fullness and flare. Such skirts were lined and stiffened for about twelve or fourteen inches at the hem and hem-saver braid, often made in a stiff brush style, was inserted at the very edge to protect and stiffen the skirt bottoms.

GLASS-PLATE NEGATIVE, 1896–98

Courtesy of the State Historical Society of Wisconsin
(WHi [V22] 1332)

THIS CEREMONIAL PORTRAIT was taken at Charles Van Schaick's studio in Black River Falls. The woman's plain black alpaca dress is adorned with one of the small pointed shoulder capes in fashion after 1896; it is made of heavy silk and finished with a broad bertha collar of black lace and has a wide black lace frill around the outside, lying in proper horizontal style across the shoulders.

It is the gentleman's plaid suit, striped shirt, and patterned tie that catch the eye here. Surely this is a mail-order marvel; the loose sleeves and the too-long jacket can be blamed on not having had the option of trying on the garments. Seen in full motion, with the large black felt on his head, he must have been an awesome sight to his friends and neighbors.

1896–98

Courtesy of the Library of Congress
(7467 LC-US262 26365)

"Refugees on the Levee" is the title scrawled below this undated photograph. Since no location is given for the photograph, it is impossible to date this flood. Evidence of a protracted stay at this uncomfortable site is all around, from the pots and pans to the blankets on their makeshift racks. Surely worry and patience have never been more sadly and clearly shown. The impact of this photograph is so strong that it takes an effort to concentrate on the clothing, but there are details that make this an important fashion document as well. Precise dating is a problem, of course, as it is evident that all the clothing is old and that much was probably handed down to begin with. The latest details to be seen are the leg-o'-mutton-sleeve styles worn by two of the women, which are very full, with the breadth of 1895 sleeves.

The women's headgear is notable—the real marvel being that they wear hats at all—for while some of the younger women wear hats of reasonably fashionable shape, none has any trimming whatsoever. Two of the older women wear variations of the age-old turban worn by slave women when first brought to this country.

The women are not corseted, and they wear everyday wash dresses. The plainest of these, worn by the central figure, is of plaid cotton, and what is probably the top of a housedress is visible. The woman seated below her wears a plaid shirtwaist with a broad matching bertha collar piped in white, with full (probably bishop) sleeves pushed up to the elbow. The standing woman at the rear wears a hip-length cape with a braid-trimmed shoulder capelet and a so-called "Spanish" hat of black straw. All of the women wear aprons, in either checked gingham or calico prints.

The seated man in the foreground wears a torn and ragged sack coat over jeans and worn boots. His hat appears to be a leather skull cap. The children wear dark cotton clothing much washed and worn. The child on the chair has a little dark bonnet with ribbon rosettes, and a straw sailor is worn by the child on the crate. The children are not barefoot; they wear shoes that appear to be the right size. They are not wearing obviously ill-fitting clothing, even though, surely very poor, they are possibly all wearing hand-me-downs.

1896–1900

Courtesy of the State Historical Society of Wisconsin
(WHi [X3] 27247)

MARJORIE BISH was photographed here, while doing her laundry chores, by her grandfather, A. A. Bish of Chippewa Falls, Wisconsin. Marjorie's doll sits in her chemise at right, waiting for dry clothing. Marjorie's dress is reasonably datable, as it has the very full elbow-length sleeves and frilled shoulder flounces that were such a favorite late-nineties fashion for little girls.

The entire front of her lace-trimmed petticoat is showing, as someone has pinned up the skirt of her dress in a fold and fastened it at the back to keep it dry. The dress is of striped cotton, and the bodice is made crosswise, the sleeves and skirt lengthwise, of the fabric. Little flat-soled black patent gaiters are worn with black stockings.

September 1897

Courtesy of the University of Washington Libraries (LaR 2049)

THIS PHOTOGRAPH is from a series taken by Seattle photographer Frank La Roche entitled "Actresses bound for the Klondike at Happy Camp."

The party is said to be traveling via Dyea-Skagway, a route north from Seattle. In an 1898 set of LaRoche's photographic views, a similar party (perhaps the same one) is said to have been contracted to perform for two seasons in a Dawson City theater. Seattle was a provision and embarkation point during the Alaskan gold rush days.

Modern speculation is that these ladies, besides being actresses, were also prostitutes, though it is true that many "respectable" women were attracted to the Klondike gold fields for the purpose of making their fortunes in other, less scandalous, ways. According to advertisements, there were rare chances in Dawson for women of "courage and respectability." Dancers and actresses were of course in demand, but cooks were wanted too. Dressmakers received twenty-five dollars for making plain dresses and fifty dollars for silk costumes. Opportunities were said to be limitless for the staunch and hardy.

The costumes of this set of adventurers certainly proclaim them to be of the hardy variety and of a type not much deterred by ideas of "proper" dress. Good health, plus sturdy boots and walking sticks, were necessities for their trek, which was to take them eighteen days, by foot, from Juneau to Dawson. The wearing of men's clothing was far from common, though the men's trousers, braces, boots, and headgear cannot disguise the fact that these are all quite feminine creatures: there are curvaceous, tight-laced corsets under the plain jerseys of several of the girls, and only two of them wear anything like masculine-looking attire with their trousers. The one in the background actually wears a ladylike hiking costume, consisting of a black wool short skirt and a dark plaid shirtwaist with leg-o'-mutton sleeves.

1897

Courtesy of the State Historical Society of Wisconsin
(WHi [X3] 43893)

ANNIE SIEVERS SCHILDHAUER, a Madison-area artist, pursued the hobby of photography in the nineties, taking many artistic shots of her own home and of her friends and their homes. In the summer of 1897 she took this outdoor portrait of the F. D. Eyerley family in the front yard of their West Johnson Street house. (Note the front wheel and handlebars of a bicycle behind the couple.) The sleeve style is right on for the 1897 date, tight into the upper arm and with a ball-shaped puff.

Mrs. Eyerley wears her hair skinned back as much as possible from a center part; not only was this probably the coolest way to wear it, but it was also a quite acceptable style for everyday. She and her little girl wear white cotton dresses, hers with the ball-puffed upper sleeve, the popular bertha collar, a full flounced skirt, and a snug belt over her corseted figure. The little girl wears juvenile versions of the bertha and long sleeves, but her dress is gathered full into a high yoke and made with tucks and lace around the bottom edge.

Mr. Eyerley wears the standard black sack suit and white shirt with a white summer bow tie.

1897

Courtesy of Deborah Fontana Cooney

A. G. McClellan . . . was reported in 1890 to have established an independent position in Charleston. He had graduated from Howard Medical College in the eighties, after having been a midshipman at Annapolis one year, and set up his practice in Charleston about 1884. In 1897 he founded the Charleston Training School for Colored Nurses, which still exists.

—George B. Tindall, *South Carolina Negroes, 1877–1900*

THIS STUDIO PORTRAIT is of the 1897 graduating class of nurses from Dr. McClellan's school in Charleston, South Carolina. They have reason to appear proud, in their starched white uniforms with their fashionable sleeves, as education for nursing was not widely available for blacks, and it required a firm basis of general education to even apply for it. The training of African American nurses was initiated in the nineties in order to have nurses who would be willing to serve the black population, which was increasingly able by this time to afford to go to hospitals for their illnesses, and even to give birth, though many institutions would not accept them as patients.

These young women studied obstetrical nursing "under L. Hughes Brown, a graduate of the Women's Medical College of Philadelphia, and wife of a colored Presbyterian minister," according to Tindall. Mrs. Brown is no doubt the young woman seated at right foreground, while Dr. McClellan sits at left.

Mrs. Brown wears a tailor-suit that appears to be of medium-weight fabric and may be of wool. Her bodice shows the tendency at the end of the decade toward a full, slightly drooping waistfront, with jacket fronts attached at the armholes and side seams. The sleeves are fitted at the lower arm but are of a modified full shape above and are accented with broad shoulder flounces exaggerating the width. A very snug, high collar matches those on the nurses' crisp uniforms. A small white straw sailor hat perches squarely on her narrow coiffure.

The variations among the white uniforms as to style cover the gamut of sleeve options for the late nineties. The favored style seems to be the extremely high, round puff on a restricted tight lower sleeve, which reached the height of its popularity in 1898.

THESE YOUNG PEOPLE, wearing the ribbons representing their individual honors, constitute the graduating class of the "College for Colored Youths" in Savannah, Georgia. Dating is helped here by the fact that three of the young men wear uniforms, which probably means that they will be going into military service directly after graduation; the Spanish-American War did not end until July 26, 1898. The "officer's" collars of the girls' shirtwaists are another good dating tool.

All of the women wear shirtwaists, and all have extremely high collars and modestly shaped sleeves. The young woman at right front wears her light-colored woolen skirt with a shirtwaist of dark cotton sateen or dull silk. The shirtwaist worn by the woman standing behind her is more elaborate, made of floral printed silk with ruching at the yoke line. The other shirtwaists are all of striped white cotton, a most popular and practical type. The plain, tailored skirt is now made in such a manner that it is close around the knees and let out either with pleats or gores from that point to the hem. The girls wear several versions of this new style; the large-checked wool tweed at left front is an especially smart model. Their hair is worn very simply in the late-century manner, brushed back on the head without a part.

The sack jacket is in general use by the young men, worn with a matching vest but usually not with matching trousers. Neckties, as usual, are a matter of taste; two of the uniformed young men wear white silk and one a small black bow tie.

GLASS-PLATE NEGATIVE, 1897–1900

Courtesy of the State Historical Society of Wisconsin
(WHi [V22/D] 1398)

IT APPEARS THAT after stepping off a lumber raft moored at Black River Falls, these men either came or were hailed into Charles Van Schaick's studio for this impromptu portrait. They wear rough denims and flannel shirts, none of which have seen a laundry for some time. All three of the plaid shirts are alike, which indicates that the company store may have sold them to the men. The man standing at left has a straight-cut woolen jacket of common style, probably of navy-blue, buttoned with metal buttons. Three wear soft felt hats, all individually shaped from long use, and the fourth wears a dark wool cap. These men do not wear their cleats; rather, they wear plain, rather thin-soled boots.

1897–1900

Courtesy of the Association for the Study of Afro-American
Life and History, King-Tisdell Cottage

UNFORTUNATELY THERE IS no documentation for this handsome family portrait, but it can be dated close to the end of the decade based in particular on the narrowness of the sleeves, the high collars, and the slim skirts worn by the women. Everything, in fact, about this family's appearance is actually datable to this period, from their corseted figures and smart hairstyles to their dressy shirtwaists. Each of the waists is made with the extremely high, boned "officer's" collar just introduced, and all are of fine and expensive materials. The sleeves of the younger girls' waists are gently puffed just at the top, and the armscye is cut to come just to the point of the shoulder, a wider placement than earlier in the decade. The mother's sleeves are made in the dolman style, a really new fashion, thus setting the stripes in a smart diagonal pattern at the shoulder. A silk scarf brought around the neck and puffed at one side adds a distinctive touch, and the plain woolen skirt is held by a belt at her trim corseted waist.

The girl at right wears a one-piece dress of printed silk with a prettily defined high shoulder yoke. The dark collar effect is probably made by a wide black velvet ribbon tied in the back. She wears a plain leather belt. Her sister is probably wearing a colored silk ribbon in the same manner, over her white shirtwaist. The girls wear their hair simply parted in the center and slightly puffed, in accordance with the latest style, and the mother's hair is brushed back from a center part.

The distinguished-looking father wears the usual sack suit with extremely narrow trouser legs and worn old shoes. His silk scarf neck cloth is tied in a small puff at his white shirtfront. The rather large, light-colored felt hat has a smooth, undented crown and a slightly rolled brim. His cane, obviously not carried merely for show, rests at hand.

Glass-Plate Negative, 1897–1903

Courtesy of the State Historical Society of Wisconsin (WHi [X22/D] 1392)

This pair of young lumberjacks has come into Black River Falls still in their working gear, complete with spiked boots. The area around the Black River was totally lumbered off during the nineties, and lumber rafts came down the river from more northern lumbering areas as well. The lumber industry was the lifeblood of this small town. Not only were crews a common sight, but many lumber barons retired there.

Except for their one-sided down-brushed hairstyles, which show up in portraits at the very end of the decade, the men in this portrait cannot really be dated. What is known is that Charles Van Schaick did his "workingmen" series mostly between 1897 and 1903.

These young men are dressed fairly typically for any outdoorsmen at the time, except for the spiked shoes. The outfits consist of warm flannel shirts, either of cotton or wool, woolen trousers and/or wool long-johns under denim pants, wool socks, and felt hats. The warm woolen jackets are distinctive and were probably, like all of the clothing, mail ordered. In some camps, clothing was stocked and sold to the "jacks" by the company store.

WE KNOW LITTLE about this photograph except that the subject is a member of the prominent De Young family and that it was taken somewhere in California, probably in San Francisco. The distinctive small ball puff at the top of the sleeve is the clue for dating this photograph close to 1898, and the tiny top-knot of the hairstyle is confirmation.

This traveling costume of lightweight dark wool has a bloused front formed of horizontal tucks and a gored skirt. The jacket she carries is made with the leg-o'-mutton sleeve, a style now out of date but which would fit easily over the smaller puffs of the suit sleeves.

THIS APPEALING PHOTOGRAPH by T. G. Mernin shows an elderly woman standing outside a substantial ranch house at "the Harvey Ranch in Hollinger Canyon, near Las Vegas, New Mexico."

The dress she wears appears to be of new material, almost certainly a bright, cheerful calico, and was probably made by the lady herself. The sleeves are in the very latest fashion for 1898, having had a round puff added over the narrow sleeve, with the tight underportion carried well up the arm and pushing the puff to ball shape. The curved yoke is edged with self-ruffles at edge and neck, according to the latest notion. The dress is very well fitted and worn over a good corset. In short, this woman has gone to some pains to look her best. Probably fresh from her kitchen, she protects the skirt of her new dress by wearing a generous apron made from an older dress.

This dress, so inexpensively yet so carefully made, is testimony to the desire and ability of even the most isolated women to have the newest and prettiest clothing possible. It is apparent that neither isolation, hardship, nor age can seriously inhibit this seemingly frivolous necessity, which in fact did so much to mitigate difficult conditions for American women.

1898–1901

Courtesy of the State Historical Society of Wisconsin
(WHi [B451] 50)

THE PHOTOGRAPHER Hermann C. Benke recorded in this photograph the proprietress and employees in front of a Manitowoc, Wisconsin, millinery shop. The most fashionable detail always defines the earliest estimated date, and here the small ball puffs of the sleeves on the dressiest costumes were at their height of popularity in 1898. The bishop sleeves worn by the younger girls are of late-nineties shape as well, with their extremest width being near the wrist.

Variations in style among these women and girls are demarcations mainly of age. The central figure, in her magnificent hat, is assumed to be the proprietress. Her smart walking suit has the high collar and ball-puffed long sleeves expected of afternoon dress at this date, and the smoothly flared skirt is full length.

At extreme left, one mature woman employee poses in a tea apron, carrying a featherduster. Her well-made dark wool dress is almost floor length and is modest but fashionable. It has a surplice bodice edged in dark silk ruching, showing a white insert at the neck and a black ribbon band collar.

The sleeves are quite dressy, having a double sleeve cap ruffle, with edges trimmed in the dark silk, over tight lower sleeves.

The two girls next to her are younger and are dressed in the popular everyday skirt-and-shirt-waist style, with short skirts. The late-style large bishop sleeve, with its broad cuff, is noticeable, as are the popular high collars. Snug leather belts cinch their waists. One of the girls wears a rather long plaid ribbon around her neck, tied in a knot and left hanging. Her well-polished walking boots are very high and have modestly high heels. Both of these girls wear their hair drawn to the back, either in a long braid or a fall, and fastened at the back of the neck, probably with ribbons.

The girl at the right of the doorway wears a black dress with doubled ball puffs at the upper arms and a flaring ribbon bow at the neck. Her skirt is also short, ending at shoe-top level. With her is another girl in a bishop-sleeved shirtwaist; her high collar is finished with a dark polka-dot neck ribbon. Both girls wear their parted hair waved at the temples and rather flat on top.

GLASS-PLATE NEGATIVE, 1898–1903

*Courtesy of the State Historical Society of Wisconsin
(WHi [X24] 1914)*

THIS OLD GENTLEMAN and his caregiver were photographed in this bare, sparsely furnished upper room, evidently a sickroom. The "nurse" may be a member of his family, as she wears a cheap cotton wrapper probably not worn far from home.

While not really a "fashion," this cheap cotton readymade has some attributes that help in dating the photograph. It is full at front, with the fullness held in by the self-belt, and hangs narrowly from waist to floor in late-nineties style. The presence of the deep flounce at the hem and the wide neck ruffle are typical of wrapper styles at around the turn of the century. This wrapper is certainly one of those offered in the ready-to-wear catalogs

of the late nineties. It is cheaply made; the deep ruff at the neck is cut on the selvage, rather than more extravagantly on the bias. The moderately easy sleeves are set-in sharply and gathered at the top, and sleeves and cuffs hang fairly loosely on the arm.

The old man, who appears to be weak and ill, wears an old, worn pair of tweed, narrow-legged trousers with a dark plaid shirt and his accustomed long, narrow black necktie. An old black sack coat protects his dignity, and woolen socks keep his swollen feet warm.

GLASS-PLATE NEGATIVE, 1898–1903

Courtesy of the State Historical Society of Wisconsin
(WHi [V22] 1402)

CHARLES VAN SCHAICK's workingmen series may all have been done free of charge; the cigars so often present may even have been bribes (Charlie himself did not smoke or drink).

This pair may have been painting a storefront on the street near the studio and been hailed in on their lunch hour. Their clothing is not remarkable in the least, though it must have intrigued Charlie, and it does show some unexpected details.

The young fellow on the right has been working in his long-johns with a pair of paint-spattered, faded overalls to cover them. He wears a small neckerchief, and his cloth hat with its stitched, rolled brim is like a sailor's hat. His companion wears more typical clothing: a high-waisted old pair of black wool pants, held by a set of leather braces buttoned to the waistband, over a striped cotton shirt. His similar soft cloth hat is worn with its brim turned toward the face.

1899

Courtesy of the Southern Oregon Historical Society
(877)

THIS DETAIL IS from a photograph of the Whetstone family taken in front of the family home in Jackson County in southern Oregon. Pictured are Lavinia Whetstone Walters and husband John Walters with their three sons, Clyde, Marion, and Raymond. In the Jackson County census report of 1900, Lavinia and John are listed as the parents of four children, the youngest being one year old; Lavinia's obvious pregnancy dates this photograph some time in 1899, when she was carrying the fourth child.

The unusually plain form of Mother Hubbard worn by the pregnant woman is a key to the use of such dresses throughout their period of popularity; the style of sleeve and shoulder cut changed along with current fashion and were modified as need demanded. The bodice shoulder breadth of this dress is not narrow, as it would have been about 1893; rather, it shows the greater width that came about in 1896 when the weight of fabric in the sleeve demanded it. It is likely that this dress has served for more than one, and possibly for all, of the pregnancies of this young mother, which would mean that it was made about 1895 or 1896. It does not have the extreme sleeve width of that period, but that makes sense; what pregnant woman would put such elaborate details on an everyday maternity dress, which had to be washed and ironed so frequently? Still, the gigot sleeves are definitely of the nineties and have the long, snug forearm of fashion. The body fullness has not been created with gathers and a yoke but more in the style of 1890s daydresses, with soft pleats from the neck opening. This is a gown that could be worn in very early pregnancy with a belt, when it would not be an obvious maternity style. Lavinia almost certainly made this dress for herself, rather than purchasing one of the cheap but obvious Mother Hubbard dresses. Such ingenuity was necessary both for economy and "decency," even this late in the century. It is quite surprising that Lavinia consented to having her photograph taken in her "condition."

The two older boys, who seem to have been growing too fast for their pants legs, wear the one-piece bibbed coverall that only recently had become universal play clothing. Of denim or other sturdy cottons, this coverall could be worn over any type of shirt. The oldest boy wears a long-sleeved colored shirtwaist, buttoned to the neck, with a wide, rounded collar edged with white. The middle boy wears a plain-collared shirt that may have been made to match his coverall. The littlest child wears with his short pants a loose, full shirt with a broad collar with white trim and long front ruffles, probably blue. The children all have neat, short haircuts, and all are barefooted.

Mr. Walker wears the expected white shirt, and though he has left off his stiff collar and necktie, the shirt is fastened at the neck front with a stud. He wears his everyday black wool trousers and single-breasted, collarless vest. With his short, side-parted haircut and thick mustache, he is a typical turn-of-the-century young man.

1899–1900

Courtesy of the Library of Congress

(7467 LC-US262 26366)

THIS EXPRESSIVE DOUBLE portrait is entitled "An old-time Charleston 'Mommer' and her charge." Except for a slight compromise to the dictates of fashion in the style of her everyday dress, this woman is still dressed in the old, traditional manner. The cotton bandanna headcloth and the crossed fichu are familiar as slave/servant wear, though both have changed in fabric and pattern. The dress she wears is of a new, small floral print. The sleeves and wide cuffs tell the story; they are of the modest bishop shape worn by women doing housework throughout the nineties, with their tops eased and puffed into a shoulder seam just at shoulder point. The skirt is not gathered much, and the bodice closes down the front. Small gold "ear-bobs" are worn.

The little girl wears the end-of-the-century yoked dress, fully gathered to a high yoke, not belted, and finished with bertha collar and deep frilled sleeve caps. The sleeves are bishop style, with rather open frills, and the edges are trimmed with rickrack. A baby-style, close bonnet, probably crocheted, is worn over the golden hair, with its ribbons tying under the chin; the bonnet has a typically top-of-the-crown, centered rosette decoration.

GLASS-PLATE NEGATIVE, 1899–1903

*Courtesy of the State Historical Society of Wisconsin
(WHi [V22/D] 1394)*

YET ANOTHER PAIR of Charles Van Schaick's workingmen, these young telephone linesmen must have been stringing the first line in Black River Falls, which was in place by 1903, when Charlie hailed them into the studio. Their gear is as much a historical record as their clothing: the coil of wire, the leather harness and spikes, and the test phone. The brush hatchet indicates the rough territory covered by the team, and their clothing is rugged yet light so that they can do this strenuous job more easily.

The thick, heavy sweater on the man at right has a shawl collar and is probably a pullover. It is worn layered over a shirt and lighter sweater and covered with denim coveralls of an unusual stripe and with many handy pockets. The other man's outfit appears to consist of trousers and a jacket of heavy, twill-weave cotton, probably a brown or olive-green color; the jacket is made in sack style and the trousers are full enough to be worn over other pants and/or long-johns. The high boots are laced with hooks for quick changes. Both men wear neckties, probably for warmth, and both wear soft woolen caps that pull down firmly on the head so as not to blow off in the wind.

Glass-Plate Negative, 1899–1900

Courtesy of the State Historical Society of Wisconsin (WHi [SV2] 2500)

This Charles Van Schaick photograph illustrates not only the photographer's own sense of fun but the trust and friendship felt for him by the entire community of Black River Falls. These clowning young women are definitely "acting up for Charlie," probably at his suggestion, and in the process providing a look at some of the handicaps presented by proper dress in the nineties.

All of these girls wear the most relaxed and flexible outfits possible—the shirtwaist and skirt—yet they are, when fully dressed, very far from being really comfortable, especially in hot weather. In order to have this kind of freedom of the legs, not only was it necessary to remove stockings and garters, but yards of skirt and petticoat material had to be moved out of the way.

Most of these skirts are of cotton, some in print and some in stripes, though two or three are of black wool. The one that is pulled up between the legs and rolled under at the thighs appears to be black and finished with a narrow ruffle of the polka-dotted waist material. The shirtwaist worn by the woman at extreme left has been pulled out of the skirt at the front, giving view of the extreme front fullness of the shirt that is normally belted in so neatly. The backs of shirtwaists are never this full, but at their most relaxed are cut straight; more frequently, they are fitted closely and held to the figure by ties from the side seams.

THESE THREE WOMEN pose at the front of their home in Las Vegas, New Mexico, for photographer T. G. Mernin. Theirs is the most typical attire for the entire nineties, and only small details help us to place them at the end of the decade.

The most important of these is the ever-present capelet or shoulder trimming, which takes various shapes in the three costumes but which is similar in proportion. Those on the blouse at left take the form of large epaulettes, while those on the other waist are more like continuations of the three-tiered bertha collar. At the center, the oversleeves of the black wool dress are capped with an inverted tulip-shaped flounce of black silk. Sleeves on women's waists and dresses at the end of the century run the gamut of styles,

from very full bishop sleeves, full or elbow length, to small leg-o'-mutton shapes to very long tight sleeves with ball caps, but all tend to have this shoulder trim.

Another detail underlining the 1900 date is the overpuffed front of the striped cotton blouse at left. This puff droops below the waistline and indicates the beginning of the famous "mono-bosom" style of the first few years of the new century.

Most women's shirtwaists and dresses of this date have very high, tight collars, like the white one shown on the older woman, but both young girls show modified ring-collars, probably a hot-weather alternative for the young.

A LITTLE FELLOW in typical late-nineties suspenders and sailor hat is caught here peeping through a crack in a barn door. His full white shirt has been pulled almost entirely out of his pants, but he still wears his fancy straw sailor hat with its jaunty black ribbon. The long-legged little trousers with their matching braces are of a dark wool, probably navy-blue, and a black silk "sailor" tie no doubt graces the shirt collar.

Glossary

❧

ALPACA: A thin, but sturdy, cloth made of cotton and alpaca wool and with a hard, shiny surface.

AMERICAN COSTUME: One term for women's dress as adopted by the National Dress Reform Association in the 1850s; made in current style but cut short over trousers. Also called "American Dress," "bloomer," "reform dress," "Turkish costume."

ARMSCYE: Circular opening into which set-in sleeve is sewn to garment.

ARTISTIC DRESS: Women's garments designed to imitate the flowing gowns depicted in paintings by pre-Raphaelite masters; supposedly in a "natural" style, of naturally dyed fabrics and colors and fitted to be worn without corseting. A late 1870s and 1880s fad originating in England.

BALYEUSE: *(Fr.)* Set of stiffened ruffles set inside the hem of a trained skirt; popular in late 1870s and 1880s.

BARÈGE: *(Fr.)* Sheer gauzelike plain weave for dresses or veils, with fine silk warp and worsted filling. Warp may also be of cotton or other fibers.

BASQUE: *(Fr.)* Fitted bodice or jacket with short, hip-length flared skirt; reminiscent of uniform jackets of Basque soldiers.

BASQUINE: *(Fr.)* An outer wrap of basque form popular in 1850s.

BAVOLET: *(Fr.)* Gathered back neck curtain of bonnet.

BERTHA, BERTHE: *(Fr.)* A deep fall of lace or silk, usually gathered, of equal depth all around and set on with the top edge at the shoulderline. *Secondary:* In the 1840s often used to mean either a pelerine or a chemisette.

BISHOP SLEEVE: Long-sleeve cut full and gathered into cuff and either full or plain at top.

BLONDE: A fine silk lace, usually natural cream in color but also made in black.

BLOOMER: Usual term for costume consisting of trousers beneath a shortened skirt. Mistakenly named for Amelia Bloomer, who wore the costume for some years as a dress reform statement. *Secondary:* Term transferred to gathered, knee-length underdrawers or gym suits toward end of ninteenth century.

BODICE: Upper portion of garment, usually made to fit body.

BOLERO: A "Spanish jacket," or short, sleeveless jacket, usually with curved, open fronts and braid or other trim.

Bosom: *f:* Front part of garment covering the breast. *m:* Separate starched shirt front with collar. *See also* Shirtee.

Botas: A Spanish-Mexican legging wrapped around the lower leg, leaving a vertical flap.

Bretelles: *(Fr.)* Bodice trim consisting of bands of fabric tapered from greatest width at shoulder to nothing at waist and generally meeting at waist center front and back. May be either gathered or plain. Attached to bodice at straight inner edge.

Broché: *(Fr.)* Material woven in figures with a patterning weft used only for the figures. Sometimes erroneously applied by nineteenth-century fashion writers to include embroidery when referring to shawls.

Brodérie d'Anglaise: *(Fr.)* Literally "English embroidery," refers to white-on-white work, distinguished by having patterns of small holes outlined in buttonhole stitch.

Brogans: Heavy ankle-high work shoes with thick soles and heels and front lacing.

Busk: A one- to three-inch-wide flat strip of wood or whalebone slipped into a long pocket at corset front in the 1840s that prevented the wearer from bending the body forward naturally.

Bustle: Support for upper-back portion of skirt; enlarged at rear and worn fastened around the waist or incorporated as understructure into skirt back.

Calico: Plain woven cotton cloth with figured pattern printed in colors. Name derives from "Calcutta," indicating the East Indian origin of such fabrics.

Cadet style: A fashion in women's dress where the dress front was buttoned at the top button and at the lower torso, leaving an open oval over a white chemisette.

Capote: *(Fr.)* Bonnet with stiff projecting brim framing the face, soft gathered fabric crown, and ribbons tied at one side.

Cartridge pleats: Measured (gauged) pleats formed by taking two or more rows of running stitches directly in line near the top edge of a fold, then pulling them up together to form small rounded pleats. Stroking between each pleat with the blunt end of a needle straightened the folds and gave the characteristic "cartridge belt" appearance. Also called "gaugeing" or "stroked gathers."

Casaque: *(Fr.)* Long, fitted bodice cut in one with no waistline seam, divided overskirt, and vertical seams.

Challis: *(Fr.)* Beginning in 1832, a soft, plain weave, plain or printed, of silk and worsted, woven in Norwich, England.

Chemise: *(Fr.)* Loose short-sleeved cotton or linen undergarment of about knee length worn under corset. Referred to as "shimmy" in nineteenth-century personal accounts.

Chemisette: *(Fr.)* Plain or ornamental white sleeveless underbodice covering neck, shoulders, and breast and worn to show above dress neckline. Called variously "bertha" or "berthe," "gimp" or "guimpe," "spencer," or "underhandkerchief."

Chip: Thin strips of wood used like straw and woven into ladies' hats and bonnets.

Cloth: Nineteenth-century English term for plain-woven woolen material; from a medieval English worsted fabric made six yards long and two yards wide.

CLOUD: Loosely crocheted or knitted scarf of soft, feathery yarns; worn wrapped around head and shoulders.

COATSLEEVE: A style of sleeve derived from those of men's coats and used for women's dresses, 1860s–70s. It is cut in two pieces, both curved at the elbow, with the narrower piece at the underarm.

COMBINATION: A single undergarment resembling a chemise or corset cover and drawers joined at waist. Also called "union suit."

CONDÉ: *(Fr.)* In 1860s refers to a sleeve shape, "sleeves à la condé," long and close to the arm and made with an elbow; a modification of the coatsleeve, cut in two pieces, an underarm and an overarm, both angled at the elbow.

CORSAGE: *(Fr.)* Front of dress bodice, especially neckline.

CORSET: Garment made to support, shape, and constrict the upper body. Also called "stays."

CORSET COVER: Short fitted garment of cotton or silk, designed to be worn over a corset to soften the lines of the bodice.

COUCHED: Fastened to a surface with overcast stitches, usually done over fine braid or cord. Finished work called "couching."

CRAPE, CRÈPE: *(Fr.)* Plain woven fabric with a crinkled or grained surface effect.

CRAVAT: *m:* A folded neck scarf tucked into the neckline; worn especially with morning coat.

CRIN: *(Fr.)* Horsehair.

CRINOLINE: *(Fr.)* Generic term for stiff, full petticoats (later hoops); taken from early 1850s petticoats stiffened with horsehair. By mid-1850s applied to all hoop-shaped skirt supports, including those of whalebone, cane, or steel.

CUIR: *(Fr.)* Leather, but extended to mean leather-colored.

CUIRASSE: *(Fr.)* Literally, that part of a suit of armor that fitted snugly over the torso and hips. In fashion, an 1870s dress style fitted in the same manner.

DELAINE: *(Fr.)* "Of wool." Used in nineteenth century to define a particular lightweight, fine-woven wool fabric often used for children's clothing.

DITTOES: *m:* In 1840s–50s, a suit of clothes of one fabric and color.

DOLMAN: A wrap popular in the late 1870s through 1880s; made to fit snugly above the bustle in back and fall over it. Cut narrowly from shoulders to elbows, the wrap had either vestigial sleeves or mere arm slits at about waist level.

DRAWERS: *f:* The most common late-nineteenth-century term for the white cotton pantalettes of earlier years. *m:* Long underwear.

DRAWN: Gathered over an inserted filament of cord, wire, or reed; a bonnet so constructed is "a drawn bonnet."

ENGAGEANT: *(Fr.)* Literally "engaging" or "attractive," but in the late 1840s through the 1850s refers specifically to undersleeves of white cotton attached beneath dress sleeves.

EPAULETTES: *(Fr.) f:* In 1840s through 1850s refers to applied oversleeve caps set into armscye, usually adding visual width. *m:* Shoulder tabs of braid and fringe used on officers' uniforms.

FALLFRONT: Rectangular dropped panel at front of trouser that buttoned at side fronts. Term for trouser with such an opening.

FASCINATOR: Scarf knitted or crocheted of soft, loose yarns and worn over head and shoulders. Probably a late term for the "cloud."

FICHU: *(Fr.) f:* Traditional term for the neckerchief worn by eighteenth-century women and in the nineteenth century mostly by slaves and servants. It was formed of a fine white linen or cotton square folded diagonally and carried around the neck, with the narrow ends tucked into the belt at waistfront. *Secondary:* In the late nineteenth century a shoulder wrap of sheer fabric crossed in front and with ends crossed in back and tied or brought around to tie at waistfront. *Secondary:* In 1890s a sheer shoulder-capelet with long ends that crossed at waistfront and tied in back.

FILET: *(Fr.)* Net lace having square mesh.

FINDINGS: Jewelry fittings: clasps, rings, etc.

FLATLINING: Lining cut and sewn as one with garment piece, as opposed to having been separately constructed and inserted.

FROGS: Decorative arrangements of braid formed to use as garment closures. One side is worked with a loop, the other with a knot.

FROCK: *f:* One-piece dress. *m:* Term for long overshirt used as a smock for work. Also a child's loose dress.

FROCK COAT: *m:* Coat made with waist seam and skirt with squared front bottom corners.

GABRIELLE: *(Fr.)* A dress style made with long gores and no waist seam; popular in the 1860s.

GAITER: Women's and girls' ankle-high boot, usually of cloth with glazed leather toes and heels. *Secondary:* In the 1890s, a separate cloth covering for foot and ankle worn over shoe or boot.

GANT DE SUEDE, GANT DE SWEDE: *(Fr.)* Moderately long gloves with deep flared "gauntlet" cuffs, especially worn in 1860s.

GARIBALDI: A shirt named for Italian patriot Giuseppe Garibaldi, whose men wore red wool shirts with long, full sleeves in the 1850s as part of their uniform. Worn by women and children in the 1860s in red or black wool and also in white cotton.

GAUGEING: Cartridge pleating.

GIGOT SLEEVE: *(Fr.)* The leg-o'-mutton-shaped sleeve.

GIMP, GUIMPE: *(Fr.)* In the 1840s and 1850s, a chemisette worn with a low-necked dress. *Secondary:* A fine cord couched onto a garment for trimming.

GINGHAM: Yarn-dyed washable cotton fabric woven in solids, checks, stripes, or plaids, but best known in checks.

GIPSY BONNET: Rather flat, open bonnet style with a short brim with ends coming to points at or below chin level but tying under back hair; ribbon "strings" tied under the chin. Popular from the 1840s through the 1850s.

GODET: *(Fr.)* Fabric gore inset at hem for extra flare and tapered to a point at upper extremity.

GUSSET: Triangular, diamond-shaped, tapered, or otherwise specially shaped piece of fabric inserted at stress point in garment seam for additional strength and ease.

HABIT FRONT: A style of women's dress where the neckline is open very deeply and worn over a white chemisette.

HEMSAVER: A tough braid, sometimes with a brush edge, of wool and/or horsehair; later merely a rolled band of velveteen, attached at edge of skirt to save wear on hem. Used especially in 1840s and in 1890s.

HENRIETTA CLOTH: A fine twill-weave, lightweight, lustrous material woven of fine Saxony wool weft on a spun silk warp; a substitute for cashmere. Most often used in black for mourning dress.

HOOPS: Generic term for dome-shaped framework worn under a full skirt, ca. 1853–69.

IMPERATRICE: *(Fr.)* In 1850s and 1860s refers to the Empress Eugénie of France and her styles (i.e., hair worn "à l'imperatrice").

INDIGO: A vegetable dye producing blue colors; the blue color derived from this dye.

INGÉNUE: *(Fr.)* Youthful; a youthful style.

INSERTION: A band of either lace or embroidery meant to be inserted between two sections of plain fabric.

JACONET: *(Fr.)* The sheerest cotton muslin dress fabric, very cheaply made and heavily sized or glazed; often used for book binding.

JOSIE: Short, loose, front-closing overblouse of wash material worn for work or leisure.

JUPE: *(Fr.)* Skirt.

JUPON: *(Fr.)* Underskirt.

LEG-O'-MUTTON SLEEVE: Sleeve with very large, puffed top and tight lower arm. *See also* Gigot sleeve.

LISSE: A fine, sheer plain-weave silk crepe.

MITT, MITTEN: A fingerless glove knitted, netted, or crocheted of dark thread and worn for dress.

MOTHER HUBBARD: A loose, full-length cotton dress, gathered and hanging free from a yoke. First worn in 1880s.

MUFFIN HAT: *m:* A round plush hat with tall flat crown and narrow upturned brim; worn for country wear by men of working class in the 1840s–50s.

MULL: Soft, thin plain-weave cotton summer fabric, often woven with a heavier stripe and usually overprinted in colors. Generally bleached or dyed in pastel tones.

MUSLIN: Soft cotton fabric of loose plain weave; usually sheer in the nineteenth century.

NANKEEN: Firm, close-woven glazed cotton, of a yellowish-tan color, with no size or bleach, used for linings or facings.

NET: Openwork fabric in mesh of various sizes; originally made by hand with a netting tool and later machine made. *See also* Reseau.

PAGODA SLEEVES: Open, flared sleeve style of the 1850s; thought to resemble Chinese sleeves.

PALETÔT: *(Fr.)* Short, loose coat worn by women and boys in the 1860s; style derived from men's yachting jacket.

PANTALOONS: Men's and boys' full-length trousers.

PAMELA HAT: A low-crowned, straight-brimmed straw hat for girls and young women, from late 1850s through 1860s, usually having a short veil gathered and hanging from brim.

PAMELA SLEEVE: In 1860s a sheer bishop sleeve tied around with ribbons in several places to form puffs.

PANNIER: Beginning in late 1860s, a nostalgic term used in fashion literature for support made of steel or cane worn under raised, draped skirts. Term derived from one applied to hip panniers of the Elizabethan period, a jocular reference to donkey carrying-baskets. *See also* Bustle.

PANTALETTES: *(Fr.)* Term for underdrawers made long and narrow on the leg. Sometimes called "drawers" or even "trowsers." Alternatively, the tucked, ruffled, embroidered, and/or lace-trimmed edgings used on such cotton drawers.

PARAPLUIE: *(Fr.)* An umbrella for rain.

PARASOL: *(Fr.)* An umbrella for sun.

PARDESSUS: *(Fr.)* Woman's long overcoat with sleeves.

PASSEMENTERIE: *(Fr.)* Applied trimming, especially braids, beads, cord, gimp, or a mixture.

PELERINE: *(Fr.)* Literally a "pilgrim" collar: a cape-collar, usually near elbow length, with or without long ends at front; either made to match a dress or of sheer white fabric or of lace. Sometimes referred to as a "bertha" in 1840s.

PHRYGIAN BONNET: Pointed cap, usually fitting over the ears.

PIPING: An enclosed cord incorporated into a seam.

PLEAT, PLAIT: Interchangeable terms for treatment of fabric wherein folds are taken into a seam.

POINT LACE: Lace made with a needle.

POLONAISE: *(Fr.)* A long overbodice, at least knee-length, fitted to the body without a waist seam and worn over a long skirt. Supposedly designed to resemble an eighteenth-century Polish uniform coat.

PRINCESS, PRINCESSE: A dress style introduced by the House of Worth in about 1875 for the Princess Alexandra and constructed with shoulder-to-hem seams and no waist seam.

PRUNELLA: Strong, smooth warp-faced fabric of worsted warp and cotton filling, usually dyed purple and often used for women's gaiters in 1840s and 1850s.

PUFFING: An insertion of a puffed strip of cloth formed by drawing up running stitches along both long edges.

QUAKER: A very deep-brimmed, reinforced straw or fabric bonnet; made commercially of mixed dark and light straw in a fine weave.

REFORM DRESS: Dress intended to release wearer from tight corseting, inhibiting skirt lengths, and other fashionable foibles. The actual design usually left to individuals, but always consisting of a more or less normal dress cut off at below-knee length and worn over trousers. Persisted as an aspect of the National Dress Reform Association through the 1890s.

REP: Silk fabric with closely spaced narrow ribs running in the direction of the filling.

REPOUSSÉ: *(Fr.)* A silversmith's term, meaning hammered out from the inside, over a hollowed form, to create a raised surface pattern.

RESEAU: *(Fr.)* Handmade net ground, usually a background for lace elements.

RESERVES: Areas of dyed cloth reserved from the dye bath by treatment with a resist.

RESIST: Coating treatment that prevents areas of cloth from taking up a dye color.

REVERS: *(Fr.)* Literally, reverse, but in fashion refers to the turn-back of lapels.

ROUNDABOUT: Snug, fitted jacket worn by boys in 1840s through 1860s; buttoned at front and cut off at or slightly below the waist.

ROUND SKIRT: Skirt without a train.

ROUND WAIST: Waist seam made level all around the figure.

RUCHE: *(Fr.)* To draw up on threads, especially to draw up a narrow strip of fabric on a center line of stitching or cording.

SACK, SACQUE: *(Fr.)* A loose, unlined, semifitted jacket with long sleeves. French term usually used in women's fashion notes. *m:* "Sack" spelling preferred.

SELVAGE: Finished edge of woven fabric.

SHAWL: Flat wrap of any shape, worn folded or draped around the body.

SHAWL COLLAR: Rolled collar without notches.

SHIMMY: *See* Chemise.

SHIRRING: A method of puffing fabric. To shirr fabric is to draw up running stitches in several parallel rows.

SHIRTEE: *m:* A separate starched shirtfront. *See also* Bosom.

SLIDE: Jewelry finding made to slip over both ends of a chain, locking in place wherever desired to alter length of loop.

SLOP(s): Work clothing, specifically loose outer garments of wash fabrics. Originally a cheap readymade clothing, as for slaves.

SMOCK: *m:* A loose, washable garment of cotton, linen, or wool; in appearance, like a long shirt with long sleeves, designed to be worn over other clothing for work. Not commonly seen after the 1860s.

SMOCKING: A technique involving the stitching of small pleats of fabric together with embroidery floss in alternate rows to form a pattern.

SNOOD: An openwork pouch, either netted or crocheted, to hold the long back hair. Popular in the 1860s.

SOUTÀCHE: *(Fr.)* A fine braid used to create couched designs on the surface of a garment, particularly in the 1860s.

SPENCER: Until the 1830s an extremely short, long-sleeved jacket, just below the bust in length; after 1840s often applied to the chemisette.

SPRING SKIRT: A commercially made hoop formed of covered wires.

STAYS: *See* Corset.

STRAIGHTS: A pair of shoes made of identical shapes, so as to be worn on either foot.

STROKED GATHERS: *See* Cartridge pleats.

SURPLICE NECKLINE: A V neckline formed by crossing the side fronts of the bodice to overlap at the waistfront and taking them into the waistline seam.

SWISS WAIST: A wide belt, usually black, with points both above and below the waist in front, where it was sometimes laced. Popular with skirts and waists in the 1860s and again in the 1890s.

TABLIER: *(Fr.)* "Apron," but in fashion an apron-shaped decorative front skirt panel.

TACKING: A type of loose stitching used to join two layers of fabric, using long stitches on the reverse and very short invisible stitches on the face of the fabric.

TAMBOUR: *(Fr.)* Embroidery frame; embroidery made on such a frame, by hand or machine, and consisting of chain stitches.

TATTING: A kind of lace made by hand with a small shuttle; most often consisting of circular elements.

TIPS: In reference to hats and bonnets, curled ostrich feather tips.

TOILET, TOILETTE: *(Fr.)* Term employed when meaning full costume.

TOURNIERE, TOURNURE: *(Fr.)* See Bustle; Pannier.

TROUSERS, TROWSERS: Full-length pants. Secondary spelling is called "English" and is usually used when referring to small boys' trousers or little girls' pantalettes.

TUCKS: Parallel pleats, usually small, stitched down entire length.

TURKISH COSTUME: *See* Bloomers.

TWILIGHT: A soft head-and-shoulder wrap; probably an alternate term for "cloud" or "fascinator."

UNION SUIT: *See* Combination.

VALENCIENNES: *(Fr.)* A handmade bobbin lace characteristic of the Valenciennes area in France; recognizable by its diamond-shaped reseau and the row of little holes outlining each motif.

VALOIS COLLAR: *(Fr.)* A popular collar shape of the 1890s, rising from a V neck and wired to stand in square points at either side of the face and very high in back. Named for a famous royal family of France, 1328–1589, and obviously taken from an existing portrait. Used mostly for coats and wraps, especially fur.

VISITE: *(Fr.)* Lightweight cape of silk or of lace lined with silk.

WARP PRINT: Material woven with a plain weft through a colorfully printed warp, producing a blurred and attractive effect.

WHITEWORK: *See* Broderie d'Anglaise.

WIDEAWAKE HAT: *m:* A stiff black felt hat with deep crown and stiff, rather wide brim; especially popular for men and boys in the 1850s.

WORKED: Term used to describe hand-embroidered articles.

YOKE: Fitted shoulder portion of bodice, cut short above the bosom, into which lower portion of bodice or gown is usually gathered or pleated.

ZOUAVE JACKET: *(Fr.)* Short, loose jacket without a back seam, with sleeves either long or below elbow and fronts rounded off and fastened at the neck only. Usually trimmed with military braid and closed with a frog. Worn by an elite band of French cavalry in the late 1850s, then by a band of American cavalry, and then by women and little boys in the 1860s.

Photograph Sources

❧

I GRATEFULLY ACKNOWLEDGE the following institutions and individuals for granting permission to publish their photographs.

Museum of American Textile History
800 Masachusetts Ave.
North Andover, MA 01845

Association for the Study of Afro-American Life and History
King-Tisdell Cottage
710 West Victory Dr.
Savannah, GA 31405-1728

Atlanta History Center
130 West Paces Ferry Rd., NW
Atlanta, GA 30305-1366

The Bancroft Library
University of California, Berkeley
Berkeley, CA 94720

The Bronx Museum of the Arts
1040 Grand Concourse
Bronx, NY 10456-3999

California Historical Society
678 Mission St.
San Francisco, CA 94105

The California State Library
California Section P
Box 942837
Sacramento, CA 94235

The Charleston Museum
360 Meeting St.
Charleston, SC 29403

Chicago Historical Society
Clark St. at North Avenue
Chicago, IL 60614

Circus World Museum
Robert L. Parkinson Library and Research Center
426 Water St.
Baraboo, WI 53913-2597

The Connecticut Historical Society
1 Elizabeth St.
Hartford, CT 06105

Deborah Fontana Cooney
205 E. Indian Spring Dr.
Silver Spring, MD 20901

Joseph Covais
P.O. Box 848
Middlebury, VT 05753

The Essex Institute
Peabody and Essex Museum
East India Square
Salem, MA 01970

Nancy Marshall Fischer
4N003 Wild Rose Rd.
St. Charles, IL 60174

Fort Pulaski
National Park Service
P.O. Box 30757
Savannah, GA 31410-0757

Georgia Historical Society
501 Whitaker St.
Savannah, GA 31499

Joy McGee Heitmann
Preservation Photography
4513 Pell St.
Raleigh, NC 27609

The Huntington Library
1151 Oxford Rd.
San Marino, CA 91108

International Museum of Photography
George Eastman House
900 East Ave.
Rochester, NY 14607-2298

Matt Isenburg
1 Dayhill Rd.
P.O. Box 189
Hadlyme, CT 06439

Kern County Museum
3801 Chester Ave.
Bakersfield, CA 93301

Mrs. Chester Kinder
900 Schultz Place
Monona, WI 53716

Kings County Museum
Public Works Department
Parks and Facilities
1400 W. Lacey Blvd.
Hanford, CA 93230

The Library of Congress
Photograph Archives
Washington, DC 20540

Juliette Gordon Low Girl Scout National Center
142 Bull St.
Savannah, GA 31401

National Archives
Still Picture Branch
8601 Adelphi Rd.
College Park, MD 20740

National Museum of American History
Division of Photographic History
The Smithsonian Institution
Washington, DC 20560

The Neville Public Museum
210 Museum Place
Green Bay, WI 54303-3767

Museum of New Mexico
Box 2087
Santa Fe, NM 87504-2087

University of North Carolina at Chapel Hill
Southern History Collection
Wilson Library 24-A
Chapel Hill, NC 27514

Historic Northampton
46 Bridge St.
Northampton, MA 01060

The Oakland Museum
History Department
1000 Oak St.
Oakland, CA 94607

Oberlin College Archives
420 Mudd Center
Oberlin College
Oberlin, OH 44074-1532

Old Dartmouth Historical Society
Whaling Museum
18 Johnny Cake Hill
New Bedford, MA 02740

Oshkosh Public Museum
Algoma Blvd.
Oshkosh, WI 54901

Gail Putnam
Box 141 Fish Hatchery Rd.
Remsen, NY 13438

Nancy E. Rexford
9 Gould St.
Danvers, MA 01923

Rock County Historical Society
PO Box 896
10 S. High St.
Janesville, WI 53547-0896

San Francisco Public Library
Civic Center
San Francisco, CA 94102

Roger Schranz
109 Carillon Dr.
Madison, WI 53705

Southern Oregon Historical Society
Library
106 N. Central Ave.
Medford, OR 97501-5926

The Valentine Museum
1015 East Clay St.
Richmond, VA 23219

Villa Louis Historic Site
PO Box 65
Prairie du Chien, WI 53821

University of Washington Libraries
Special Collections and Preservation, SM-25
Seattle, WA 98195

Wilmette Historical Museum
609 Ridge Rd.
Wilmette, IL 60091

The State Historical Society of Wisconsin
Visual and Sound Archives
816 State St.
Madison, WI 53706

Worcester Historical Museum
30 Elm St.
Worcester, MA 01609

Bibliography

∾

Annotated Listing of Personal Accounts

Georgia

Atlanta Historical Society
Barry, Carry. Diary. 1864–86. Child in Atlanta during Civil War.

Illinois

Chicago Historical Society
Blakely, Sara. Diary. 1852–54. Member of concert troupe touring Midwest cities and towns.
Boyden, Emily. Diary. 1828–93. Chicago author.
Boyden, Helen. Journal. 1889. Records travels west from Chicago.
Briggs, Emma. Diary. 1863–72. Records teaching experiences in Wisconsin.
Glessner, Frances. Diary. 1879–81. From small Ohio town, becomes the wife of prominent Chicago business leader; records family, household, social life.
Hariford, Jenny. Diary. 1888. Thirteen-year-old in Aurora, Illinois.
Kane, Laura. Diary. 1879–84. Records family, social life on farm near Waukegan, Illinois.
Ketcham, Rebecca. Diary. 1853. Pioneer on the Oregon Trail.
Pullman, Emily Minton. Diaries and papers. 1830–1913. From prominent Chicago family.
Wight, Henrietta Calmes. Diary. 1855. Records visiting cousins in Ohio.
Newberry Library, Chicago
Everett, Mary Holywell. Papers. 1830–1916. One of the first female surgeons in United States.
Gookin, Elizabeth. Diary. 1864–95. Records daily life in Joliet and Chicago.
Gookin, Mary. Diary. 1879–82. Daughter of Elizabeth; records social life in Chicago.
Rich, Albina. Diary. 1853–54. Runs farm by herself; records daily life.
University of Illinois, Chicago Circle Women's Center
Addams, Jane. Papers. 1868–78. Social reformer; Hull House records.
Chicago Exchange for Women's Work. 1880–85. Records of outlets for hand-made articles by needy women.

Iowa

State Historical Society of Iowa
Gillespie, Miss [no first name given]. Diary. 1881. Manchester, Iowa. Fifteen- or sixteen-year-old girl; sketches of clothing made at home.

LOUISIANA

Historic New Orleans Collection

Bateman, Mary. 1856. Records life on an antebellum plantation.

Dymond Family Papers. 1860s. Northern family buys plantations after Civil War.

Natchitoches Records. 1845–65. Household records of plantations run by free people of color.

Robb, James. Papers. 1858–60. Letters between mother and daughter.

Walton, Sarah. Papers. 1860s. Prominent family in Vicksburg during the Civil War.

MASSACHUSETTS

Historic Northampton

French, Frances Trefethan. Diaries and letters. Young middle-class wife and mother.

Schlesinger Library, Cambridge

Robinson, Harriet Hansen. Scrapbook and letters. 1850–89. Millworker.

Browne, Sarah Ellen. Letters. 1850–60.

OHIO

Western Reserve Historical Society, Cleveland

Leggett, Mariella Wells. 1848–76. Wife of Cleveland businessman and Civil War general; records family, social life in Cleveland and Zanesville, Ohio.

Lewis, Charlotte. Diary. 1870–91. Seamstress; records daily life while husband employed as farmhand in Hudson, Ohio.

VIRGINIA

Richmond Historical Society

Maury, Betty Herndon. Diary. 1861–63. Southern women's Civil War activities.

WASHINGTON, D.C.

American Museum of History

Copp Family Collection. 1754–1885.

Kulp Collection Account Books. 1755–1904. Mt. Joy Daybook, 1863–64; Treadwell Accountbook, 1861–65; Fuller Accountbook, 1856–62; Kent Records, 1879–83; Ramsey Family Papers, 1749–1924; Textile Mills Collection, 1856–1909.

Library of Congress

Ames, Harriet Ann Moore. 1840–42. Reminiscences written in 1893.

Grimké, Sarah. Letters. 1844–50. To sister, Angelina Grimké Weld.

Harrison, Constance. Diary 1867. Author of *Bar Harbor Days*.

Jones, George. 1846. Letter written while visiting Kentucky.

Oliphant, Catherine. 1864. Certificate for services as Civil War nurse.

Roedel, Josephine Forney. 1863. Records travels from the South during the Civil War.

WISCONSIN

The State Historical Society of Wisconsin, Madison

Bailey, Louise. 1898–1900. Whitewater Normal School student.

Baird, Elizabeth. [In Henry Baird Papers]. 1798–1937. Records frontier life in Green Bay.

Bartow, Helen. 1851, 1854, 1856. Records domestic, social, local events in Waukesha.

Blaine, Anita McCormick. [In McCormick Papers.] Diaries. 1875–1929. Records household and charity work.

Bliss, Ida. 1867–88. Records school and social life.

Chynoweth, Edna. 1860s. Records student life.

Fairchild, Sarah. [In Lucius Fairchild Papers.] 1826–1923. Records lives of women in Madison and Superior.

Fishburn, Mrs. M. P. 1840s. Records move from Ohio to Iowa.

Franzisha, Mathilde. 1840–84. Records emigration from Germany and settlement in Wisconsin.

Gattiker, Anna. 1848–79. Records student days at University of Wisconsin, 1875–79.

Gattiker, Emma. 1848–79. Swiss immigrant.

Greenman, Caroline. 1847–54. Records daily life and work of a single girl in Massachusetts.

Gunnison, Martha. 1879. Housewife in Waupun.

Isham, Ruth. Letters. 1880–84, 1897–1900. Schoolteacher in Argentina.

Jones, Nellie Kedzie. 1881–. Pioneer educator in college home economics.

Kelly, Jane Bewell. 1866–98. Records life in a religious rural community.

McCormick, Nettie Fowler. [In McCormick Papers.] 1875–1929. Records daily life, business, philanthropy.

McKinnon. 1852. Records journey from Scotland to Otsego.

Marston, Annie Gorham. [In James Gorham Papers.] 1870–85. Records life on a farm and social events in Madison.

Merrill, Maria. 1890–99. Records life on a farm in Sechlerville.

Quiner, Emilie. 1861–63. Civil War nurse in Memphis.

Rock County Historical Society, Janesville

Menzies, Jesse Campbell. 1877–78. Records daily life of farm family outside Janesville.

Pratt, Sarah. 1845. Young schoolteacher in rural Rock County; records sewing for herself and others.

Pritchard, Miss. 1882. Sixteen-year-old daughter of Judge Amos Pritchard.

Tallman, Cornelia Augusta. 1860. Unmarried daughter of lawyer and developer; records daily life, interest in fashion.

Tallman, Mrs. E. D. 1869–79. Sister-in-law of Cornelia; records family pharmaceutical business and family and social life.

MICROFILM SOURCES

Guide to American Women's Diaries. 1789–1915. New England diaries.

American Antiquarian Society (New Canaan, Connecticut), 1983: Susan Forbes. Diary. 1824–1910.

Plantation Diaries (Louisiana State University, Baton Rouge): Mrs. Issac Hilliard, 1849–50; Julia Bond, 1859–61.

Collections and Resource Centers

The Warshaw Collection. The National Museum of American History. Washington, D.C.

Schlesinger Library on the History of Women in America: The Manuscript Inventory and the Catalogs of the Manuscripts, Books and Pictures. Radcliffe College, Cambridge, Mass.

Published Sources

Abbott, Edith. *Women in Industry.* New York: D. Appleton, 1909.

Addams, Jane. *Twenty Years at Hull House.* New York: Signet, 1960.

Adickes, Sandra. "Mind among the Spindles: An Examination of Some Journals, Newspapers and Memoirs of the Lowell Female Operatives." *Women's Studies* 1, 3 (1973): 279–87.

Allport, Gordon. *The Use of Personal Documents in Psychological Science.* New York: The Social Science Research Council, 1942.

Ames, Kenneth. "The Stuff of Everyday Life: American Decorative Arts and Household Furnishings." *Material Culture: A Research Guide.* Ed. Thomas Schlereth. Lawrence: Univ. of Kansas Press, 1985.

Anderson, John Q., ed. *Brokenburn: Journal of Kate Stone, 1861–1868.* Baton Rouge: Univ. of Louisiana Press, 1955.

Andrews, Eliza. *Wartime Journal of a Georgia Child.* New York: D. Appleton, 1908.

Andrews, W. R. *The American Code of Manners.* New York: Andrews, 1880.

Arksey, Laura, ed. *American Diaries.* Detroit: Gale Research, 1983.

Arnold, Janet. *Patterns of Fashion.* Vols. 1 and 2. New York: Drama Books Specialists, 1978–80.

Arpad, Susan, ed. *Sam Curd's Diary: The Diary of a True Woman.* Athens: Ohio Univ. Press, 1984.

Banner, Lois. *American Beauty.* New York: Alfred A. Knopf, 1983.

Barnhart, Jacqueline. *The Fair but Frail: Prostitution in San Francisco, 1849–1900.* Reno: Univ. of Nevada Press, 1986.

Baxandall, Rosalyn, Linda Gordon, and Susan Reverby, eds. *America's Working Women.* New York: Random House, 1976.

Beecher, Catherine. *A Treatise on Domestic Economy, for the Use of Young Ladies at Home and at School.* New York: Harper and Bros., 1849.

Beecher, Catherine, and Harriet Beecher Stowe. *The American Woman's Home.* New York: Harper and Bros., 1869.

Bell, Quentin. *On Human Finery.* Rev. ed. New York: Shocken Books, 1978.

Bernard, Richard. "The Female School Teacher in Massachusetts." *Journal of Social History* 10 (1977).

Bibliography in the History of American Women. Bronxville, N.Y.: Sarah Lawrence College, n.d.

Billington, Ray Allen, ed. *The Journal of Charlotte L. Forten: A Free Negro in the Slave Era.* New York: Dryden Press, 1953.

Bird, Lucy Isabella. *The Englishwoman in America.* 1856. Toronto: Univ. of Toronto Press, 1966.

Bloomer, D. C. *Life and Writings of Amelia Bloomer.* Boston: Arena Publishing Co., 1895.

Blum, Stella, ed. *Fashions and Costumes from Godey's Ladies Book.* New York: Dover Publications, 1985.

———. *Victorian Fashions and Costumes from Harper's Bazaar: 1867–1898.* New York: Dover Publications, 1974.

Blumer, Herbert. "Fashion: From Class Differentiation to Collective Selection." *Sociological Quarterly* 10 (1969): 275–91.

Bradfield, Nancy. *Costume in Detail: Women's Dress 1730–1930.* Boston: Plays, Inc., 1968.

Brandon, Ruth. *A Capitalist Romance: Singer and the Sewing Machine.* New York: J. P. Lippincott Co., 1977.

Brinker, Marie Mathilde. *Backwards from Ninety: The Autobiography of Marie Mathilde Brinker, 1848–1940.* Privately printed, 1938.

Brown, Jean. *Household Workers.* Chicago: Chicago Science Research Association, 1940.

Brownlee, Eliot, and Mary Brownlee. *Women in the American Economy.* New Haven: Yale Univ. Press, 1976.

Bull, Thomas. *Hints to Mothers, for the Management of Health during the Period of Pregnancy, and in the Lying-In Room.* London: Longman, Brown, Green, and Longman's, 1851.

Burleigh, Celia. "The Relation of Woman to Her Dress." *First Woman's Congress of the Association for the Advancement of Women.* New York: Mrs. Wm. Ballard, 1874.

Burnap, George. *The Sphere and Duties of Woman.* Pittsburgh: John Murray, 1848.

Bushman, Claudia L. *A Good Poor Man's Wife.* Hanover, N.H.: Univ. Press of New England, 1981.

Calasibetta, Charlotte, ed. *Fairchild's Dictionary of Fashion.* New York: Fairchild Publications, Inc., 1988.

Clark, Clifford Edward, Jr. *The American Family Home, 1800–1960.* Chapel Hill: Univ. of North Carolina Press, 1986.

Cole, George. *A Complete Dictionary of Dry Goods.* Chicago: J. B. Herring Publishing Co., 1894.

Colt, Miriam Davis. *Went to Kansas.* Watertown, Iowa: L. Ingalls and Co., 1862.

Connor, Seymour V., and Jimmy M. Skaggs. *Broadcloth and Britches, The Santa Fe Trade.* College Station: Texas A&M Univ. Press, 1977.

Coons, Mattie Mails. *Pioneer Days in Kansas.* Manhattan, Kans.: N.p., 1939.

Cooper, Zachary. *Black Settlers in Rural Wisconsin.* Madison: The State Historical Society of Wisconsin, 1977.

Culley, Margo, ed. *A Day at a Time.* New York: The Feminist Press at CUNY, 1985.

Cummins, Maria. *Mabel Vaughan.* N.p., 1857.

Danky, James, Christine Rongone, Beverly Youtz, Maxine Fleckner, and Christine Schelshorn, eds. *Women's History Resources at the State Historical Society of Wisconsin.* Madison: State Historical Society of Wisconsin, 1980.

Davies, Phillip G. *Welsh in Wisconsin.* Madison: The State Historical Society of Wisconsin, 1982.

Devere, Louis. *The Handbook of Practical Cutting on the Centre Point System.* 1866. Lopez Island, Wash.: R. L. Shep Publishers, 1986.

Draper, Mabel Hobson. *Through the Long Trail.* New York: Rinehart and Co., 1946.

Dublin, Thomas. *Farm to Factory, Women's Letters 1830–1860.* New York: Columbia Univ. Press, 1981.

———. *Women at Work.* New York: Columbia Univ. Press, 1979.

Dudden, Faye. *Serving Women: Household Service in Nineteenth-Century America.* Middletown, Conn.: Wesleyan Univ. Press, 1983.

Eisler, Benita, ed. *The Lowell Offering: Writings by New England Mill Women.* New York: J. B. Lippincott Co., 1977.

Faragher, J., and Christine Stansell. "Women and their Families on the Overland Trail, 1842–1867." *Feminist Studies* 2, no. 213 (1975): 150–66.

Fischer, Chistaine. *Let Them Speak for Themselves: Women in the American West, 1849–1900.* New York: E. P. Dutton, 1978.

Foner, Philip. *The Factory Girls*. Chicago: Univ. of Illinois Press, 1977.

Foote, Shelly. "Bloomers." *Dress* 5 (1980): 1–12.

Forty, Adrian. *Objects of Desire*. New York: Pantheon Press, 1986.

Freeman, Samuel. *The Emigrants Handbook: Guide to Wisconsin*. Milwaukee: Sentinel and Gazette Power Press Print, 1851.

Fuller, Margaret. *Woman in the 19th Century*. New York: Greenley and McGrath, 1845.

Gernsheim, Alison. *Victorian and Edwardian Fashion: A Photographic Survey*. New York: Dover Publications, 1963.

Gitelman, Howard. *Workingmen of Waltham, Mobility in American Urban Industrial Developement, 1830–1890*. Baltimore: Johns Hopkins Univ. Press, 1974.

Gluck, Sherna. *From Parlor to Prison: Five American Suffragists Talk about Their Lives*. New York: Vintage Books, 1976.

Gottschalk, Louis. *The Use of Personal Documents in History, Anthropology and Sociology*. Washington, D.C.: Social Science Research Council, 1945.

Goude, Erwin G. *California Gold Camps*. Berkeley: Univ. of California Press, 1975.

Hale, Frederick. *Danes in Wisconsin*. Madison: The State Historical Society of Wisconsin, 1981.

———. *Swedes in Wisconsin*. Madison: The State Historical Society of Wisconsin, 1983.

———. *Swiss in Wisconsin*. Madison: The State Historical Society of Wisconsin, 1984.

Hale, Sarah Josepha. *Manners: or, Happy Homes and Good Society*. New York: Arno Press, 1872.

———. *Sketches of All Distinguished Women from the Creation to AD 1868*. New York: Harper and Bros., 1874.

Harkness, Marjory. *Lucy Blake's Tamworth*. Tamworth, N.H.: Tamworth Historical Society, 1959.

Harper, Ida Husted. *The Life and Work of Susan B. Anthony*. Indianapolis: The Hollenbeck Press, 1898.

Hecklinger, Charles. *Dress and Cloak Cutter: Women's Costumes 1877–1882*. Rev. ed. Lopez Island, Wash.: R. L. Shep Publishers, 1986.

Helvenston, Sally. "Popular Advice for the Well-Dressed Woman in the 19th Century." *Dress* 5 (1980): 31–47.

Hempsten, Elizabeth. *Read This Only to Yourself: The Private Writings of Midwestern Women, 1880–1910*. Bloomington: Indiana Univ. Press, 1983.

Hill, Joseph A. *Women in Gainful Occupations: 1870–1920*. U.S. Bureau of the Census Monographs 9. Washington, D.C.: Government Printing Office, 1929.

Holsti, Ole. *Content Analysis for the Social Sciences and Humanities*. Reading, Mass.: Addison-Wesley, 1969.

Holt, Hamilton, ed. *The Life of Undistinguished Americans as Told by Themselves*. New York: J. Pott and Co., 1906.

Holzueter, John. *Norwegians in Wisconsin*. Madison: The State Historical Society of Wisconsin, 1977.

Hoover, Ethel. "Retail Prices after 1850." *Studies in Income and Wealth*. Report of the National Bureau of Economic Research. Vol. 30. Princeton: Princeton Univ. Press, 1960.

Isely, Else. *Sunbonnet Days*. Caldwell, Idaho: Caxton Printers, 1935.

Jeffrey, Julie Roy. *Frontier Women: The Trans-Mississippi West: 1840–1880*. New

York: Hill and Wang, 1979.

Jensen, Joan, and Sue Davidson, eds. *A Needle, A Bobbin, A Strike: Women Needleworkers in America.* Philadelphia: Temple Univ. Press, 1984.

Josephson, Hannah. *The Golden Thread: New England Mill Girls and Magnates.* New York: Russell and Russell, 1966.

June, Jennie. *Talks on Women's Topics.* Boston: Lee and Shepherd, 1864.

Katznelson, Ira, and Ariste R. Zolberg, eds. *Working Class Formation: Nineteenth Century Patterns in Western Europe and the United States.* Princeton: Princeton Univ. Press, 1986.

Kemble, Frances. *Journal of a Resident on a Georgia Plantation.* New York: Alfred A. Knopf, 1961.

Kidwell, Claudia Brush. *Cutting a Perfect Fit.* Washington, D.C.: Smithsonian Institution Press, 1979.

Kidwell, Claudia Brush, and Margaret Christman. *Suiting Everyone: The Democratization of American Clothing.* Washington, D.C.: Smithsonian Institution Press, 1974.

Kidwell, Claudia Brush, and Valerie Steele, eds. *Men and Women: Dressing the Part.* Washington, D.C.: Smithsonian Institution Press, 1989.

Kinsey, Sally. "A More Reasonable Way to Dress." *The Art That Is Life: The Arts and Crafts Movement in America, 1875–1920.* Ed. Wendy Kaplan. Boston: Museum of Fine Arts, 1986.

Knight, Peter. *The Plain People of Boston, 1830–1860: A Study in City Growth.* New York: Oxford Univ. Press, 1971.

Knipping, Mark. *Finns in Wisconsin.* Madison: The State Historical Society of Wisconsin, 1977.

Larcom, Lucy. *A New England Girlhood.* Boston: Houghton Mifflin, 1889.

Larsen, Carol, and Violet Frazel. "Dressing Geneva." *Geneva, Illinois: A History of Its Times and Places.* Geneva, Ill.: Geneva Public Library District, 1977.

Lauer, Robert, and Jeanette Lauer. *The Meaning of Fashion in American Society.* Englewood Cliffs, N.J.: Prentice-Hall, 1981.

Lebergott, Stanley. *Labor Force and Employment 1800–1900.* Vol. 3 of *Studies in Income and Wealth.* Report of the National Bureau of Economic Research. Princeton: Princeton Univ. Press, 1960.

Lerner, Gerda L. *The Woman in American History.* Reading, Mass.: Addison-Wesley, 1971.

———, ed. *The Female Experience: An American Documentary.* New York: Oxford Univ. Press, 1992.

Leslie, Mrs. Frank. *A Social Mirage.* New York: F. Tennyson Neely, 1899.

Levitt, Sarah. *Victorians Unbuttoned.* London: George Allen and Unwin, 1986.

Lowenberg, Bert, and Ruth Bogin, ed. *Black Women in 19th Century America: Their Words, Thoughts, Feelings.* University Park: Pennsylvania State Univ. Press, 1976.

Luchetti, Cathy, and Carol Olwell. *Women of the West.* St. George, Utah: Antelope Island Press, 1980.

Massey, Mary Elizabeth. *Bonnet Brigades.* New York: Alfred A. Knopf, 1967.

Matthews, William. *American Diaries: Annotated Bibliography.* Los Angeles: Univ. of California Press, 1945.

———. *American Diaries in Manuscript.* Athens: Univ. of Georgia Press, 1974.

Meier, Peg, ed. *Bring Warm Clothes: Letters and Photos from Minnesota's Past.* Minneapolis: Minneapolis Star and Tribune Co., 1981.

Melder, Keith. "Woman's High Calling: The Teaching Profession in America 1830-60." *American Studies* 13 (1972): 19–32.

Meyer, Annie Nathan. *Woman's Work in America*. New York: Henry Holt, 1891.

Mott, Frank Luther. *A History of American Magazines 1850–65*. Cambridge: Harvard Univ. Press, 1938.

Mowatt, Anna Cora. *Fashion, or Life in New York*. New York: French, 1849.

Myers, Sandra. *Ho! for California: Women's Overland Diaries from the Huntington Library*. San Marino, Calif.: Huntington Library, 1980.

Napheys, George H. *The Physical Life of Woman: Advice to the Maiden, Wife, and Mother*. Philadelphia: George Maclean, 1872.

Nelson, D. L., ed. and trans. *The Diary of Elizabeth Koren 1853–55*. Northfield, Minn.: Norwegian American Historical Association, 1955.

Palmer, Joel. *Journal of Travels over the Rocky Mountains to the Mouth of the Columbia River; Made during the Years 1845 and 1846: Containing a List of Necessary Outfits for Emigrants*. Vol. 30: *Early Western Travels*. Cleveland: Arthur H. Clark Co., 1905.

Paoletti, Jo Barraclough. "The Role of Choice in the Democratization of Fashion: A Case Study, 1875–1885." *Dress* 5 (1980): 47–56.

Penny, Virginia. *The Employments of Women: A Cyclopaedia of Women's Work*. Boston: Walker, 1863.

Petterson, Lucille, ed. and trans. "Ephraim Is My Home Now: Letters of Anna and Anders Petterson, 1884–9." *Wisconsin Magazine of History* 69–70 (1986).

Pope, Jesse E. *The Clothing Industry in New York*. Columbia: Univ. of Missouri Press, 1905.

Pullan, Marion. *Beadle's Guide to Dressmaking and Millinery*. New York: Beadles, 1860.

Rexford, Nancy. *Women's Shoes, 1795–1930*. New York: Holmes and Meier Publishers, Inc., forthcoming.

Riley, Glenda. *Frontierswoman: The Iowa Experience*. Ames: Iowa State Univ. Press, 1985.

Roach, Mary Ellen, and Kathleen Musa. *New Perspectives on the History of Western Dress*. N.p.: Nutriguides, Inc., 1980.

Robertson, Constance Noyes. *Oneida Community: An Autobiography*. Syracuse Univ. Press, 1970.

Robinson, Harriet. *Loom and Spindle*. 1845. Kailua, Hawaii: Press Pacifica, 1976.

Rodoff, Theodore. *Pioneering in the Wisconsin Lead Region*. Wisconsin Historical Collections Vol. 15. Madison: The State Historical Society of Wisconsin, 1900.

Ross, Ishbel. *Crusades and Crinolines—The Life and Times of Ellen Curtis Demorest and Wm. Jennings Demorest*. New York: Harper and Row, 1963.

Sandler, Marten, W. *The Way We Lived*. Boston: Little, Brown, 1977.

Sandoz, Mari. *Old Jules*. Boston: Little, Brown, 1935.

Schlissel, Lillian. *Women's Diaries of the Westward Journey*. New York: Schocken Books, 1982.

Sedgwick, Catherine. *Means and Ends*. New York: Harper, 1842.

Segale, Sister Blandina. *At the End of the Oregon Trail*. Columbus, Ohio: The Columbia Press, 1915.

Selden, Bernice. *The Mill Girls*. New York: Atheneum, 1983.

Seller, Maxine. *Immigrant Women*. Philadelphia: Temple Univ. Press, 1981.

Severa, Joan, and Merrill Horswill. "Costume as Material Culture." *Dress* 15 (1989): 50–64.

Sklar, Kathryn. *Catherine Beecher: A Study in American Domesticity*. New Haven: Yale Univ. Press, 1973.

Sochen, June. *Herstory*. New York: Alfred Publishing, 1974.

Spring, Agnes Wright. *A Bloomer Girl on Pike's Peak, 1858*. Ed. Julia Holmes. Denver: Western History Department, Denver Public Library, 1949.

Springer, Marlene, and Haskell Springer, eds. *Plains Woman: The Diary of Martha Farnsworth, 1882–1922*. Bloomington: Indiana Univ. Press, 1986.

Spruil, Julia Cherry. *Women's Life and Work in the Southern Colonies*. Chapel Hill: Univ. of North Carolina Press, 1938.

Stephens, Ann Sophia. *Fashion and Famine*. New York: Brew and Bros., 1854.

Sterne, Madeline. *We the Women: Career Firsts of the 19th Century*. New York: Schulte Publishing Co., 1963.

Stevens, Frances. *Usages of the Best Society*. New York: A. L. Burt, 1884.

Stewart, Elinor. *Letters of a Woman Homesteader*. New York: University of New York Press, 1961.

Stratton, J. L. *Pioneer Women*. New York: Simon and Schuster, 1981.

Sutherland, Daniel. *Americans and Their Servants: Domestic Service in the United States from 1800–1920*. Baton Rouge: Louisiana State Univ. Press, 1981.

Swint, Henry. *The Northern Teacher in the South 1862–72*. Nashville: Vanderbilt Univ. Press, 1941.

Taft, Robert. *Photography and the American Scene*. New York: McMillan Co., 1938.

Tandberg, Gerilyn. "Field Hand Clothing in Louisiana and Mississippi during the Ante-Bellum Period." *Dress* 5 (1980): 89–104.

Tracy, Stephen. *The Mother and Her Offspring*. New York: Harper and Bros., 1853.

Trautman, Pat. "Personal Clothiers: A Demographic Study of Dressmakers, Seamstresses and Tailors." *Dress* 5 (1979): 74–95.

U.S. Bureau of the Census. *Statistics of Women at Work*. Washington, D.C.: Government Printing Office, 1907.

Veblen, Thorstein. *The Theory of the Leisure Class*. New York: McMillan and Co., 1889.

Walsh, Margaret. "The Democratization of Fashion: The Emergence of the Women's Dress Pattern Industry." *The Journal of American History* 66 (1979): 299–313.

Ware, Caroline. *The Early New England Cotton Manufactures: Study in Industrial Beginnings*. New York: Russell and Russell, 1966.

Ware, Norman. *The Industrial Worker, 1840–1860*. Chicago: Quadrangle, 1964.

Webb, Allie, ed. *Mistress of Evergreen Plantation: Rachael O'Connor's Legacy of Letters, 1823–1845*. Albany: State Univ. of New York Press, 1983.

White, Philip, ed. "An Irish Immigrant Housewife on the New York Frontier." *New York History* 48 (April 1967): 182–88.

Wilkins, Mary Freeman. *A New England Nun and Other Stories*. Ridgewood, N.J.: The Gregg Press, 1891.

Willet, Mabel. *The Employment of Women in the Clothing Trade*. 1902. New York: AMS Press, 1968.

Wilson, W. Emerson. *Plantation Life at Rose Hill*. Wilmington, Del.: Wilmington Historical Society, 1976.

Wingate, Isabel, ed. *Fairchild's Dictionary of Textiles*. New York: Fairchild Publications Inc., 1979.

Wood, Ann. "The War within a War: Women Nurses in the Union Army." *Civil War History* 18 (September 1972): 197–212.

Wood, James. *Magazines in the United States*. New York: The Ronald Press, 1971.

Woodward, C. Vann. *Mary Chestnut's Civil War Diary*. New Haven: Yale Univ. Press, 1981.

Worthing, Ruth Shaw. "Lawe Family Letters." *Wisconsin Magazine of History* 17 (1988): 16, 17.

Wright, Carroll. *The Working Girls of Boston*. 1889. New York: *New York Times*, 1969.

Young, Agnes. *The Recurring Cycles of Fashion*. New York: Harper and Bros., 1937.

Zeitlin, Richard. *Germans in Wisconsin*. Madison: The State Historical Society of Wisconsin, 1977.

UNPUBLISHED SOURCES

Brew, Margaret. "American Clothing Consumption, 1879–1909." Ph.D. diss. University of Chicago, 1945.

Brown-Larimore, Karen. "The Changing Line of the Corset." M.F.A. thesis, University of Wisconsin-Madison, 1984.

Brush, Claudia. "Sarah Josepha Hale and Woman's Role 1840 to 1849." History Department, Pennsylvania State University, 1964. Copy in author's possession.

Helvenston, Sally. "Feminine Response to a Frontier Environment as Reflected in the Clothing of Kansas Women: 1854–1895." Ph.D. diss. Kansas State University, 1985.

Hooper, Susan. "Rural Dress in Southwestern Missouri between 1860 and 1880." Master's thesis. Iowa State University, 1976.

Labbe, Dolores Egger. "Women in Early 19th Century." Ph.D. diss. University of Delaware, 1975.

Lambert, Margaret. "Women's Costume in Northwest America during the 1890's with a Time-Lag Study of Fashion Diffusion." Master's thesis. University of Washington, 1971.

Larson, Joyce. "Clothing of Pioneer Women of Dakota Territory 1861–1889." Master's thesis. South Dakota State University, 1978.

Love, Deanna. "Dress of American Woman Pioneer in the Westward Movement from 1836–1889." Master's thesis. University of Maryland, 1969.

McMartin, Barbara. "Dress of the Oregon Trail Emigrants: 1843–1855." Master's thesis. Iowa State University, 1977.

Ordonez, Margaret. "A Frontier Reflected in Costume: Tallahassee, Leon County, Florida 1824–1861." Ph.D. diss., Florida State University, 1978.

Contemporary Periodicals, Catalogs, and Newspapers

B. Altman & Co. catalogs
American Ladies Magazine (1828–36)
La Belle Assemblé
Dakota Republican (Vermillion, N.D.)
The Delineator
Demorest's Monthly Magazine
Demorest's Portfolio of Fashion Semi-Annual
Demorest's Quarterly Mirror of Fashion
Demorest's What to Wear (semiannual)
Ehrich's Fashion Quarterly
Ehrich's Manual of Shopping
Ehrich's Purchaser's Guide

Godey's Lady's Book (Magazine)
Graham's Magazine
Handbook of the Toilette (1841)
Harper's New Monthly Magazine
Janesville (Wisc.) *City Times*
Janesville (Wisc.) *Daily Recorder*
Janesville (Wisc.) *Gazette* (various editions)
Jordan Marsh catalogs
The Ladies' Home Journal and Practical Housekeeper
Leslies' Illustrated Newsletter
Marshall Field catalogs
Montgomery & Ward catalogs
The National Cloak Company catalogs
Oakland (Calif.) *Daily Evening Tribune*
Peterson's Ladies National Magazine
The Prairie Farmer (Lawrence, Kans.)
The Rock County Recorder (Janesville, Wisc.)
Sears & Roebuck catalogs
Stern Bros. catalogs
Chas. A. Stevens & Bros. catalogs
The Sybil: A Review of Taste, Errors, and Fashions of Society
R. H. White & Co. Catalog, Custom Tailoring, Materials and Shoes
Wisconsin Tribune (Dodgeville)
The Young Englishwoman

Index

1860s, 211–12
1880s, *416–17*
1890s, 473–74
boys', *262,* 389–90, 432, *490–91*
girls', *286, 420–21, 489, 499*
dolls', *288–89*
men's
1840s, 11, 20, 22, *30–31, 57*
1850s, 106, *136–37, 138–39, 170*
1860s, 210
1870s, 314, *356*
1880s, 388, *410–11,* 436–37, *442–43*
1890s, 472, *510, 525, 526, 532–33*
women's
1850s, 86
1860s, *206–7,* 232, *240–41, 245, 274–75*
1870s, 294, 300, *311–13, 332–33, 349–50*
1880s, 378, *385–86, 394–95*
in California, *410–11, 414–15, 432–33*
in Kingston, *448–49*
in Oregon, *416–17*
in Richmond, *436–37*
Schuetzenverein members', *434–35*
1890s, *470–71, 494, 510, 512–13, 517*
See also Berets; Bonnets; Bowler hats; Brighton hats;
Caps; Derby hats; Fedora hats; Flats (hats);
Gainsborough hats; Homburg hats; Muffin hats;
Panama hats; Plug hats; Pork-pie hats; Princess
feather hats; Sailor hats; Slouch hats; Sombreros;
Spanish hats; Straw hats; Sun hats; Top hats; Toques;
Velasquez hats; Wideawake hats; Work hats
Hawes, Alice, *173*
Hawes, Josiah Johnson, 35, 43
Hawes, Nancy Southworth, *34–35,* 43, *173*
Headgear
girls', 389
men's, 106, 210, *493*
women's
1840s, 10–11, 32, *40–41*
1850s, 101–2
1860s, 205–7
1870s, 311–13
1880s, 385–87
1890s, 470–71
See also Bandannas; Bonnets; Caps; Hats;
Hoods; Pith helmets; Turbans; Veils
Health resorts, 205. *See also* Our Home on the
Hill (Dansville)
Health stays, 205
Helmets, *422, 423*
Helvenston, Sally
on Everett, 190
Kansas Farmer quoted by, 375
Prairie Farmer quoted by, 192, 295
on Toothaker, 193
on western life, 88, 298–99
Hem-savers, 8, *515*
Hesler, Alexander, 153
Hesler's Metropolitan Gallery, 153
Hill, Emily, *276–77*
Hill (military commander), 187
Hip extenders. *See* Panniers

Hispanics, *452–53. See also* Mexicans
Historic Northampton, 131
Historical costume, 300
Hodgdon, Elizabeth, 6
Holbein hats, 385
Homburg hats, 388, *410–11*
Home crafts, 14, 186
Home sewing
1840s, 9, 11, *48*
1850s, 86, 90–92, 100
1860s, 186, 187, 208, 209
1870s, 293–97
1880s, 373–74, 378
1890s, 455
Hoods, 11, *42*
Hoops
1850s, 97–98, 109, *150, 153, 172, 176–77*
work dresses over, 95
wraps and, 104
1860s, 200–202, *224–25,* 242, *253, 260–61,
272–73, 276–77, 286*
in Chicago, 193
in mills, 263
oval, 194, 201
in California, *270–71*
skirt-and-waist outfits over, 197
in South, 186
in Wisconsin, *240–41*
wraps and, 204
1870s, *332–33, 340–41*
Hops, *346–47*
Horse handlers, 131
Horsehair, 17, 97, *377–78,* 489
Horton, Georgia Knox, *480–81*
Hosiery. *See* Stockings
Hough, Mary Oakley, *42*
Housedresses. *See* Work dresses
Household workers. *See* Domestic workers; Nursemaids;
Servant women
Howard Medical College, 522
Hoyle's (firm), 204
Hubbard, Hattie, *245*
Hudson and Reed (firm), 86
Hudson, Mary, 299
Huguenot coats, 465
Huit, Alice Warner, *325*
Human body
as artifact, xviii
compression of, 16
display of, 454
freedom of, 462
posture of, 15
slenderness of, 395
Hurd, F. Wilson, 249
Hyde, Mrs., 192
"Hygeian Corset," 383

Idealized woman concept. *See* "True womanhood" ideal
Illinois, *176–77*
Illinois State Historical Library, 354
Imitation cashmere shawls, *350,* 385
Immigrants, 297–98

DRESSED FOR THE PHOTOGRAPHER

was composed in Linotype-Hell Adobe Minion
using Aldus PageMaker 5.0 for Windows
at The Kent State University Press;
printed by sheet-fed offset
on 70-pound Enamel Matte stock,
Smyth sewn with 88-point binder's board
in ICG Kennett book cloth,
and wrapped with duskjackets printed in
three colors on 100-pound enamel stock
by Thomson-Shore, Inc.;
designed by Diana Gordy;

THE KENT STATE UNIVERSITY PRESS
KENT, OHIO 44242